Merriam-Webster's
Pocket
Atlas

Compliments of
Educational Talent Search II
Morehead State University

```
D1622561
```

Merriam-Webster, Incorporated
Springfield, Massachusetts

A GENUINE MERRIAM-WEBSTER

The name *Webster* alone is no guarantee of excellence. It is used by a number of publishers and may serve mainly to mislead an unwary buyer.

Merriam-Webster™ is the name you should look for when you consider the purchase of dictionaries and other fine reference books. It carries the reputation of a company that has been publishing since 1831 and is your assurance of quality and authority.

Copyright © 2000 by Encyclopædia Britannica, Inc.

ISBN 0-87779-515-0

All rights reserved. No part of this book covered by the copyrights hereon may be reproduced or copied in any form or by any means—graphic, electronic, or mechanical, including photocopying, taping, or information storage and retrieval systems—without written permission of the publisher.

Printed and bound in the United States of America

345678NFWP0403020100

Contents

Preface

Merriam-Webster's Pocket Atlas provides basic information about nearly 200 countries of the world. A full page is provided for each country with information including a color map showing both populated places and major natural features; a locator map; a fact box containing information on the country's official name, head of government, official language, monetary unit, population, per capita GNP, and principal exports; a color representation of the country's flag and interesting information about it; and a graph showing ethnic, religious, language, or age composition of the country's population. Additional information is provided in tables showing country capitals and membership in international organizations; communications; longest rivers; tallest mountains; and largest lakes. Finally, a country by country listing shows many of the largest cities with their coordinates.

As advances in transport and communication have brought distant corners of the globe closer to home, a convenient atlas has become an indispensable reference tool. This colorful pocket-size book was created by the Cartography Department of Encyclopædia Britannica in association with the editors of Merriam-Webster, and is designed to help readers visualize the changing world in which we live in a handy affordable format.

Abbreviations

Ala.	Alabama	Nat'l	National
Ark.	Arkansas	N.C.	North Carolina
Arm.	Armenia	NE	northeast,
Azer.	Azerbaijan		northeastern
Belg.	Belgium	N.H.	New Hampshire
Calif.	California	N.J.	New Jersey
C.A.R.	Central African	N.P.	National Park
	Republic	NW	northwest,
CFA	African Financial		northwestern
	Community	N.Y.	New York
	(Communaute	N.Z.	New Zealand
	Financiere	Okla.	Oklahoma
	Africaine)	Penin.	Peninsula
C.I.S.	Commonwealth	Penn.	Pennsylvania
	of Independent	Pk.	Peak
	States	Port.	Portugal
Conn.	Connecticut	Pt.	Point
D.C.	District of	Rep.	Republic
	Columbia	R.I.	Rhode Island
Del.	Delaware	S	south, southern
Dem.	Democratic	S.A.R.	Special
Den.	Denmark		Administrative
E.	east, eastern		Region
Fla.	Florida	S.C.	South Carolina
Fr.	France	SE	southeast,
ft.	foot (feet)		southeastern
GNP	gross national	St.	Saint
	product	SW	southwest,
I.	Island		southwestern
Ill.	Illinois	Switz.	Switzerland
Ind.	Indiana	Tenn.	Tennessee
Indon.	Indonesia	Turkmen.	Turkmenistan
Is.	Islands	U.A.E.	United Arab
km	kilometer(s)		Emirates
La.	Louisiana	U.K.	United Kingdom
Mass.	Massachusetts	U.S.	United States
Md.	Maryland	U.S.S.R.	Union of Soviet
mi	mile(s)		Socialist
Mich.	Michigan		Republics
Minn.	Minnesota	Va.	Virginia
Miss.	Mississippi	Vt.	Vermont
Mt.	Mount	W	west, western
Mtn.	Mountain	Wash.	Washington
Mts.	Mountains	Wis.	Wisconsin
N	north, northern	W.Va.	West Virginia

Guide to Map Projections

Technically, the earth is not round but is flattened at the poles and takes a shape most accurately described as an ellipsoid. The deviation from a perfect sphere is relatively minor, and although the distinction is of critical importance in surveying and geodesy, for most purposes it can be assumed that the earth is spherical.

A globe is the only true means of representing the surface of the earth and maintaining accurate relationships of location, direction, and distance, but it is often more desirable to have a flat map for reference. However, in order for a round globe to be portrayed as a flat map, various parts of the globe's surface must stretch or shrink, thereby altering the geometric qualities associated with it. To control this distortion, a systematic transformation of the sphere's surface must be made. The transformation and resultant new surface is usually derived mathematically and is referred to as the map projection.

An infinite number of map projections can be conceived, but the only ones which are effective are those projections which ensure that the spatial relationships between true (known) locations on the three-dimensional sphere are preserved on the two-dimensional flat map.

The four basic spatial properties of location are area, angle, distance, and direction. No map projection can preserve all four of these basic properties simultaneously. In fact, every map will possess some level of distortion in one or more of these dimensions. The map surface can be developed such that individual properties are preserved to a certain extent, or that certain combinations of properties are preserved to some extent, but every projection is, in some way, a compromise and must distort some properties in order to portray others accurately.

Choosing a Map Projection

The question of which map projection is best might be better stated as which map projection is most appropriate for the intended purpose of the map. For example, navigation demands correct direction, while road atlases will be concerned with preserving distance. Another important consideration is the extent and area of the region to be mapped. Some common guidelines include the use of cylindrical projections for low latitudes, conic projections for middle latitudes, and azimuthal projections for polar views. World maps are rather special cases and are commonly shown on a class of projection that may be neither equal-area nor conformal, referred to as compromise projections, typically on an oval grid.

Common Map Projections

Name	Class	Attribute	Common Uses
Mercator	Cylindrical	Conformal	Best suited for navigation uses, but often used inappropriately for world maps.
Sinusoidal	(Pseudo-)	Equal-area	Used occasionally for world maps cylindrical and in combination with Mollweide to derive other projections.
Mollweide	(Pseudo-)	Equal-area	Used for world maps, especially cylindrical for showing thematic content.
Lambert Conformal Conic	Conic	Conformal	Used extensively for mapping areas of extensive east-west extent in the mid-latitudes (such as the U.S.).
Albers Equal-area	Conic	Equal-area	Similar to Lambert Conformal Conic in use.
Polyconic	Polyconic	Neither Equal-area nor Conformal	Used by U.S. Geological Survey in mapping topographic quadrangles and was used for early coastal charts and some military mapping.
Bonne	(Pseudo-)	Equal-Area	Frequently used in atlases for conic showing continents.
Gnomonic	Azimuthal	Equal-Area	Used most frequently in navigation.
Stereographic	Azimuthal	Conformal	Most often used for topographic maps of polar regions and for navigation.
Orthographic	Azimuthal	Neither Equal-area nor conformal	Most popular use is for pictorial views of earth, especially as seen from space.

Map Legend

Cities and towns

Ottawa ⊛   National Capital

Edinburgh ◉   Second level
political capital

São Paulo •   City symbol

Boundaries

▬▬   International

▬ ▬   Disputed

– – –   Defacto

······   Line of control

———   Political subdivisions

Other Features

SERENGETI
NATIONAL PARK ■   National park

Mount Everest
29,028 ft. ▲   Mountain Peak

⌣◯   Dam

∿∿   Falls

∿∿   Rapids

———   River

– – –   Intermittent river

———   Canal

•—•—•   Aqueduct

∿∿∿   Reef

viii

Official name: Islamic State of Afghanistan.
Head of government: Prime Minister.
Official languages: Pashto; Dari (Persian).
Monetary unit: afghani.
Area: 251,825 sq mi (652,225 sq km).
Population (1996): 22,664,000.
GNP per capita (1988): U.S.$220.
Principal exports (1992): dried fruits and nuts 51.3%; carpets and rugs 13.1%
to (1994): Belgium-Luxembourg 3.8%; Pakistan 3.7%; Germany 3.6%.

Ethnic Composition

Ḥazāra 19% — Other 18%
Tadzhik 25% — Pashtun 38%

The government that flies this flag controls only a few northern provinces, but internationally the flag is recognized for Afghanistan. Adopted on Dec. 3, 1992, it contains a coat of arms in gold emphasizing traditional Muslim values. The more reactionary Muslim forces known as the Taleban fly white flags in the rest of the country.

Official name: Republic of Albania.
Head of government: Prime Minister.
Official language: Albanian.
Monetary unit: lek.
Area: 11,100 sq mi (28,748 sq km).
Population (1996): 3,249,000.
GNP per capita (1994): U.S.$360.
Principal exports (1994): manufactured
  goods 45.3%; mineral fuels 26.7%;
  food, beverages, live animals, and
  tobacco 14.3% *to:* Italy 52.1%; United
  States 11.1%; Greece 10.4%; states of
  the former Yugoslavia 6.0%.

Religious Affiliation

Roman
Catholic
10%

Muslim
70%

Albanian
Orthodox
20%

On Nov. 28, 1443, the flag was first raised by Skanderbeg, the
national hero. After independence from Turkish rule was proclaimed on Nov. 28, 1912, the flag was flown by various
regimes, each of which identified itself by adding a symbol
above the double-headed eagle. The current flag, which features only the eagle, was adopted on May 22, 1993.

Map

PORTUGAL SPAIN — Murcia
Sevilla · Málaga · MEDITERRANEAN SEA
ATLANTIC OCEAN
Tangier
Algiers · Bejaïa · Skikda · Annaba · Tunis
Mostaganem · Medéa · Constantine · Süsah
Oran · Sétif · Batna · Tébessa
Sidi Bel Abbés · Tiaret · Djelfa · Djebel Chélia · Süsah
Tlemcen · Saïda · Biskra · 2,38 m · Safáqis
Rabat · El-Oued
Casablanca · Fés
Safi · Khouribga · Tooggourt · TUNISIA
Marrakech · Mt. Aïssa · Ghardaïa · Ouargla
7,337 ft · MAGHREB · NAFÜSAH PLATEAU
MOROCCO · Béchar · GREAT WESTERN ERG · HAMADAH EL HAMRA
Beni Abbes · GREAT EASTERN ERG
WESTERN SAHARA (Occupied by Morocco) · TADEMAÏT PLATEAU · LIBYA
Tindouf · Adrar · In-Salah
ERG IGUIDI · Wadi Saoura
ERG CHECH · H A H A G A R
Wadi Djaret · TASSILI NATIONAL PARK
MAURITANIA · Tropic of Cancer
Tahat Peak 9,571 ft · TASSILI PLATEAU
Tamanghasset · HAGGAR MTS.
ADRAR DES IFORAS
MALI · NIGER
©2000, Encyclopædia Britannica, Inc.

ALGERIA

Scale 1: 33,443,000

0 — 150 — 300 mi
0 — 200 — 400 km

Ethnic Composition

Arab 80%
Berber 20%

Official name: Democratic and Popular Republic of Algeria.
Head of government: Prime Minister.
Official language: Arabic.
Monetary unit: Algerian dinar.
Area: 11,100 sq mi (28,748 sq km).
Population (1996): 28,566,000.
GNP per capita (1994): U.S.$1,690.
Principal exports (1994): crude petroleum 45.7%; natural gas 31.2%; refined petroleum 18.8% *to:* Italy 17.9%; U.S. 16.5%; France 15.4%; The Netherlands 10.3%; Spain 7.6%.

In the early 19th century, during the French conquest of North Africa, Algerian resistance fighters led by Emir Abdelkader supposedly raised the current flag. Its colors and symbols are associated with Islam and the Arab dynasties of the region. The flag was raised over an independent Algeria on July 2, 1962.

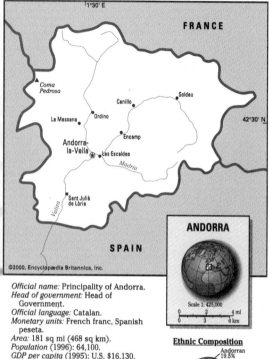

1°30' E

FRANCE

▲ *Coma Pedrosa*

Canillo • Soldeu •

La Massana • Ordino •

42°30' N

Encamp •

Andorra-la-Vella ⊛ • Les Escaldes

Madriu

Valira

Sant Julià de Lòria •

SPAIN

©2000, Encyclopædia Britannica, Inc.

ANDORRA

Scale 1: 425,000

0 — 2 — 4 mi
0 — 3 — 6 km

Official name: Principality of Andorra.
Head of government: Head of Government.
Official language: Catalan.
Monetary units: French franc, Spanish peseta.
Area: 181 sq mi (468 sq km).
Population (1996): 64,100.
GDP per capita (1995): U.S. $16,130.
Principal exports (1995): transport equipment 26.4%; textiles and wearing apparel 21.5%; electrical machinery 8.7% *to:* France 47.8%; Spain 47.0%.

Ethnic Composition

Andorran 19.5%
Spanish 46.4%
Portuguese 10.8%
Other 23.3%

The flag may date to 1866, but the first legal authority for it is unknown. The design was standardized in July 1993. Possible sources for its colors are the flags of neighboring Spain (red-yellow-red) and France (blue-white-red). The coat of arms incorporates both French and Spanish elements dating to the 13th century or earlier.

Ethnic Composition

Other 28%
Ovimbundu 37.2%
Kongo 13.2%
Mbundu 21.6%

Official name: Republic of Angola.
Head of government: President.
Official language: Portuguese.
Monetary unit: kwanza .
Area: 481,354 sq mi (1,246,700 sq km).
Population (1996): 11,904,000.
GNP per capita (1989): U.S. $620.
Principal exports (1994): mineral fuels
96.0%; diamonds 3.2% *to* (1991):
United States 56.6%; Germany 5.6%;
Brazil 4.9%; The Netherlands 4.2%;
United Kingdom 3.4%; Belgium-
Luxembourg 3.3%.

After Portugal withdrew from Angola on Nov. 11, 1975, the
flag of the leading rebel group gained recognition. Inspired by
designs of the Viet Cong and the former Soviet Union, it
includes a star for internationalism and progress, a cogwheel
for industrial workers, and a machete for agricultural workers. The black stripe is for the African people.

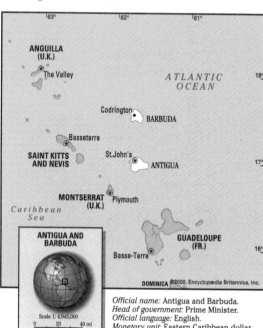

Scale 1: 4,945,000

0   20   40 mi
0   30   60 km

Religious Affiliation

Other 15.5%
Roman Catholic 10.8%
Protestant 73.7%

Official name: Antigua and Barbuda.
Head of government: Prime Minister.
Official language: English.
Monetary unit: Eastern Caribbean dollar.
Area: 170.5 sq mi (441.6 sq km).
Population (1996): 64,400.
GNP per capita (1994): U.S.$6,970.
Principal exports (1992): reexports [significantly, petroleum products reexported to neighbouring islands] 78.0%, domestic exports 22.0% *to* (1989): United States 41.0%; United Kingdom 19.0%; Germany 19.0%.

When "associated statehood" was granted by Britain on Feb. 27, 1967, the flag was introduced, and it remained after independence (Nov. 1, 1981). Red is for the dynamism of the people, the V-shape is for victory, and the sun is for the climate. Black is for the majority population and the soil, blue is for the sea, and white is for the beaches.

©2000, Encyclopædia Britannica, Inc.

ARGENTINA

Scale 1: 57,746,000

0   250   500 mi
0   400   800 km

Official name: Argentine Republic.
Head of government: President.
Official language: Spanish.
Monetary unit: peso.
Area: 1,073,518 sq mi (2,780,400 sq km).
Population (1996): 34,995,000.
GNP per capita (1994): U.S.$8,060.
Principal exports (1994): food products
and live animals 35.2%; manufactured
products 12.5%; machinery and
transport equipment 11.2% *to:* Brazil
23.1%; U.S. 11.0%; The Netherlands
7.5%; Chile 6.3%; Italy 4.1%.

Ethnic Composition

European
85%

Mestizo and
Amerindian
15%

The uniforms worn by Argentines when the British attacked
Buenos Aires (1806) and the blue ribbons worn by patriots in
1810 may have been the origin of the celeste-white-celeste
flag hoisted on Feb. 12,1812. The flag's golden "sun of May"
was added on Feb. 25,1818, to commemorate the yielding of the
Spanish viceroy in 1810.

Official name: Republic of Armenia.
Head of government: Prime Minister.
Official language: Armenian.
Monetary unit: dram.
Area: 11,500 sq mi (29,800 sq km).
Population (1996): 3,765,000.
GNP per capita (1994): U.S.$670.
Principal exports (1994): jewelry 34.4%;
   machinery and equipment 16.8%;
   mineral products 8.3%; textiles and
   textile products 7.1% *to:* Russia 44.3%;
   Turkmenistan 20.9%; Belgium 9.9%;
   Iran 7.7%; Germany 3.4%.

Ethnic Composition

Azerbaijani 2.6%
Other 4.1%
Armenian 93.3%

In 1885 an Armenian priest proposed adopting the "rainbow flag given to the Armenians when Noah's Ark came to rest on Mt. Ararat." On Aug. 1, 1918, a flag was sanctioned with stripes of red (possibly symbolizing blood), blue (for homeland), and orange (for courage and work). Replaced during Soviet rule, it was readopted on Aug. 24, 1990.

©2000, Encyclopædia Britannica, Inc.

AUSTRALIA

Scale 1: 70,500,000

| 0 | 300 | 600 mi |
| 0 | 400 | 800 km |

Age Breakdown

60 and over 15.9%

15–59 62.8%

Under 15 21.3%

Official name: Commonwealth of Australia.
Head of government: Prime Minister.
Official language: English.
Monetary unit: Australian dollar.
Area: 2,966,200 sq mi (7,682,300 sq km).
Population (1996): 18,287,000.
GNP per capita (1994): U.S.$17,980.
Principal exports (1994): mineral fuels and lubricants 14.4%; crude materials excluding fuels 13.7%; food and live animals 13.2% *to:* Japan 23.5%; U.S. 8.1%; New Zealand 7.2%.

After Australian confederation was achieved on Jan. 1, 1901, the flag was chosen in a competition. Like the blue flags of British colonies, it displays the Union Jack in the canton. Also shown are the Southern Cross and a "Commonwealth Star." The design became official on May 22, 1909, and it was recognized as the national flag on Feb. 14, 1954.

Official name: Republic of Austria.
Head of government: Chancellor.
Official language: German.
Monetary unit: Austrian Schilling.
Area: 32,378 sq mi (83,858 sq km).
Population (1996): 8,102,000.
GNP per capita (1994): U.S.$24,950.
Principal exports (1994): machinery and
transport equipment 39.0%; chemical
products 9.2%; paper and paper
products 5.8%; iron and steel 5.3%
to: Germany 38.1%; Italy 8.1%;
Switzerland 6.4%; France 4.5%.

Religious Affiliation

Roman Catholic 78%
Lutheran 4.8%
Other 8.6%
Nonreligious and atheist 8.6%

The colors of the Austrian coat of arms date from the seal of
Duke Frederick II in 1230. With the fall of the Austro-
Hungarian Empire in 1918, the new Austrian republic adopted
the red-white-red flag. The white is sometimes said to represent the Danube River. The imperial eagle, with one or two
heads, has been an Austrian symbol for centuries.

©2000, Encyclopædia Britannica, Inc.

AZERBAIJAN

Scale 1: 8,146,000

| | 40 | 80 mi |
| 0 | 60 | 120 km |

Ethnic Composition

Azerbaijani 82.7%
Other 6%
Armenian 5.6%
Russian 5.7%

Official name: Azerbaijani Republic.
Head of government: Prime Minister.
Official language: Azerbaijani.
Monetary unit: manat.
Area: 33,400 sq mi (86,600 sq km).
Population (1996): 7,570,200.
GNP per capita (1994): U.S.$500.
Principal exports (1994): petroleum
products 32.5%; metals 16.5%; cotton
15.5%; machinery and equipment
14.2%; food products 10.0% *to:* Iran
38.0%; Russia 22.0%; United Kingdom
9.7%; Ukraine 9.1%; Turkey 2.5%.

In the early 20th century anti-Russian nationalists exhorted the Azerbaijanis to "Turkify, Islamicize, and Europeanize," and the 1917 flag was associated with Turkey and Islam. In 1918 the crescent and star (also symbols of Turkic peoples) were introduced. Suppressed under Soviet rule, the flag was re-adopted on Feb. 5, 1991.

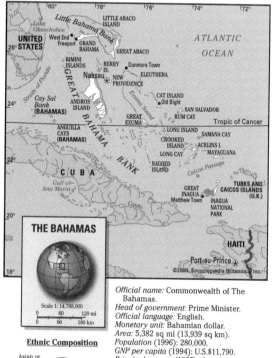

Official name: Commonwealth of The Bahamas.
Head of government: Prime Minister.
Official language: English.
Monetary unit: Bahamian dollar.
Area: 5,382 sq mi (13,939 sq km).
Population (1996): 280,000.
GNP per capita (1994): U.S.$11,790.
Principal exports (1995): domestic exports 52.6%, of which crayfish 31.9%; reexports 47.4%, of which machinery and transport equipment 26.1% *to:* U.S. 81.1%; EC 9.2%.

Ethnic Composition

Asian or Hispanic 3%
White 12%
Black 85%

The flag of The Bahamas was adopted on July 10, 1973, the date of independence from Britain. Several entries from a competition were combined to create the design. The two aquamarine stripes are for the surrounding waters, the gold stripe is for the sand and other rich land resources, and the black triangle is for the people and their strength.

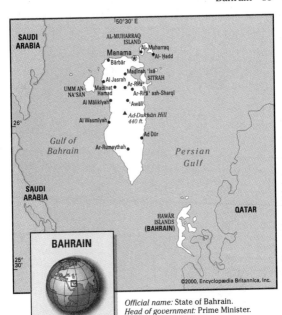

50°30' E

SAUDI ARABIA

AL-MUHARRAQ ISLAND

Al-Muharraq
Manama
Bārbār
Madīnah 'Īsā
Al Jasrah
Al Malikiyah
Ar-Rifā'
SITRAH
Ar-Rifā' ash-Sharqī
Madīnat Hamad
UMM AN-NA'SĀN
'Awālī
Al Wasmliyah
▲ Ad-Dukhān Hill 440 ft.
Ad Dūr
Ar-Rumaythah

Gulf of Bahrain

Persian Gulf

SAUDI ARABIA

QATAR

HAWĀR ISLANDS (BAHRAIN)

25° 30'

26°

©2000, Encyclopædia Britannica, Inc.

BAHRAIN

Scale 1: 1,454,000

0   6   12 mi
0   8   16 km

Religious Affiliation

Other 9.7%
Christian 8.5%
Sunni Muslim 24.5%
Shi'ite Muslim 57.3%

Official name: State of Bahrain.
Head of government: Prime Minister.
Official language: Arabic.
Monetary unit: Bahrain dinar.
Area: 268.0 sq mi (694.2 sq km).
Population (1996): 598,000.
GNP per capita (1994): U.S.$7,500.
Principal exports (1993): petroleum
   products 65.7%; basic manufactured
   goods 19.1% *to:* Saudi Arabia 15.8%;
   Japan 15.1%; South Korea 9.1%; United
   States 8.1%; not specified 5.5%.

Red was the color of the Kharijite Muslims of Bahrain about 1820, and white was chosen to show amity with the British. The flag was recognized in 1933 but was used long before. The current flag law was adopted on Aug. 19, 1972. Between the white and red there may be a straight or serrated line, but the latter is most common.

BANGLADESH

Scale 1: 11,181,000

0   50   100 mi
0   80   160 km

Religious Affiliation

Muslim 88.3%

Hindu 10.5%

Other 1.2%

Official name: People's Republic of Bangladesh.
Head of government: Prime Minister.
Official language: Bengali.
Monetary unit: Bangladesh taka.
Area: 56,977 sq mi (147,570 sq km).
Population (1996): 123,063,000.
GNP per capita (1994): U.S.$230.
Principal exports (1994): ready-made garments 56.6%; jute manufactures 10.4%; fish and prawns 10.1% *to* (1993): Western Europe 40.2%; United States 33.6%.

The flag is dark green to symbolize Islam, plant life, and the hope placed in Bengali youth. Its original design included a red disk and a silhouette of the country. On Jan. 13, 1972, the silhouette was removed and the disk shifted off-center. The disk is the "rising sun of a new country" colored by the blood of those who fought for independence.

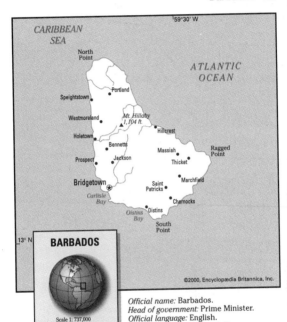

CARIBBEAN SEA

North Point

ATLANTIC OCEAN

Portland
Speightstown
Westmoreland
Mt. Hillaby 1,104 ft.
Holetown
Hillcrest
Bennetts
Jackson
Massiah
Ragged Point
Prospect
Thicket
Bridgetown
Marchfield
Saint Patricks
Curtisle Bay
Charnocks
Oistins Bay
Distins
South Point

159°30' W

13° N

©2000, Encyclopædia Britannica, Inc.

BARBADOS

Scale 1: 737,000

| 0 | 2 | 4 | 6 | 8 mi |
| 0 | | 6 | | 12 km |

Religious Affiliation

Roman Catholic 4.4%
Anglican 33%
Other 12.6%
Nonreligious 20.2%
Other Protestant 29.8%

Official name: Barbados.
Head of government: Prime Minister.
Official language: English.
Monetary unit: Barbados dollar.
Area: 166 sq mi (430 sq km).
Population (1996): 265,000.
GNP per capita (1994): U.S.$6,260.
Principal exports (1995): domestic exports 71.6%, of which chemicals 11.3%, sugar 11.0%; reexports 28.4% *to* (1993): United States 20.6%; United Kingdom 14.2%; Trinidad and Tobago 12.2%; Jamaica 9.0%; Canada 7.1%.

The flag was designed by Grantley Prescod, a Barbadian art teacher. Its stripes of blue-yellow-blue are for sea, sand, and sky. The black trident head was inspired by the colonial flag of Barbados, which featured a trident-wielding Poseidon, or Neptune, figure. The flag was first hoisted on Nov. 30, 1966, the date of independence from Britain.

BELARUS

Scale 1: 9,358,000

0   40   80 mi
0   60   120 km

Ethnic Composition

Other 5.6%
Ukrainian 3%
Russian 13.5%
Belarusian 77.9%

Official name: Republic of Belarus.
Head of government: President.
Official languages: Belarusian; Russian.
Monetary unit: rubel.
Area: 80,200 sq mi (207,600 sq km).
Population (1996): 10,442,000.
GNP per capita (1994): U.S.$2,160.
Principal exports (1995): Mainly trucks, diesel fuel, synthetic fibres, refrigerators, tires, potassium fertilizer, milk and milk products *to:* Commonwealth of Independent States (CIS) 88.9%; non-CIS countries 11.1%.

In 1951 the former Soviet republic created a striped flag in red (for communism) and green (for fields and forests), with the hammer, sickle, and star of communism. In 1991–95 an older design was used, but the Soviet-era flag was then altered and readopted without communist symbols. The vertical stripe is typical of embroidery on peasant clothing.

Map labels:

NORTH SEA · THE NETHERLANDS

Brugge-Zeebrugge Canal · Breda · Tilburg
Blankenberge · Kapellen · Turnhout · Eindhoven
Ostend · Zandvliet · KEMPENLAND · Weert
Nieuwpoort · Brugge · Antwerp · Peer · Bree
Torhout · Aalter · Sint-Niklaas · Geel · Tessenderlo
Staden · Ghent · Mechelen · Rupel · Demer · Genk · Maastricht
Roeselare · Aalst · Schaerbeek · Louvain · Hasselt · GERMANY
Ypres · Kortrijk · Brussels · Tienen · Riemst · Aachen
Mouscron · Enghien · Uccle · Ixelles · Waremme · Liège · Eupen
Lille · Ath · Braine-l'Alleud · Wanze · Seraing · Verviers
Tournai · Mons · La Louvière · Spy · Namur · CONDROZ · Spa · Botrange 2,277 ft.
Boussu · Charleroi · Dinant · Ciney · HAUTES FAGNES-EIFEL NATIONAL PARK
Thuin · Philippeville · Marche-en-Famenne
Lake Plate Taille · Couvin · Saint-Hubert
FRANCE · Bouillon · Bastogne
Florenville · LUXEMBOURG · Luxembourg
Arlon · Athus

Rivers/features: Schelde, Westerschelde, East Schelde, Ijzer, Scheldt, Sambre, Meuse, Lesse, Oise, Moselle, POLDERS, FLANDERS, ARDENNES

©2000, Encyclopædia Britannica, Inc.

BELGIUM

Scale 1: 4,176,000

| 0 | 20 | 40 mi |
| 0 | 30 | 60 km |

Official name: Kingdom of Belgium.
Head of government: Prime Minister.
Official languages: Dutch; French; German.
Monetary unit: Belgian franc.
Area: 11,787 sq mi (30,528 sq km).
Population (1996): 10,185,000.
GNP per capita (1994): U.S.$22,920.
Principal exports (1994): machinery and transport equipment 28.1%; chemicals 16.7%; food and live animals 9.1%; non-industrial [gem] diamonds 6.8% *to:* Germany 21.0%; France 19.0%.

Language Composition

Other 8%
Dutch 59%
French 33%

A gold shield and a black lion appeared in the seal of Count Philip of Flanders as early as 1162, and in 1787 cockades of black-yellow-red were used in a Brussels revolt against Austria. After a war for independence, the flag was recognized on Jan. 23, 1831. By 1838 the design, which was influenced by the French tricolor, became standard.

Official name: Belize.
Head of government: Prime Minister.
Official language: English.
Monetary unit: Belize dollar.
Area: 8,867 sq mi (22,965 sq km).
Population (1996): 219,000.
GNP per capita (1994): U.S.$2,550.
Principal exports (1994): domestic
   exports 83.5%, of which sugar 28.2%,
   garments 12.8%, orange and grapefruit
   concentrate 11.7%, bananas 10.4%;
   reexports 16.5% *to:* United States
   44.0%; United Kingdom 30.0%.

BELIZE

Scale 1: 5,244,000

| 0 | 20 | 40 mi |
| 0 | 30 | 60 km |

Ethnic Composition

Garifuna 6.7%
Other 8.9%
Mayan Indian 11%
Mestizo 43.6%
Creole 29.8%

The flag of Belize (former British Honduras) was based on the
flag of the nationalist People's United Party. Its coat of arms
shows a mahogany tree, a shield, and a Creole and a Mestizo.
The red stripes, symbolic of the United Democratic Party,
were added on independence day (Sept. 21, 1981), when the
flag was first officially hoisted.

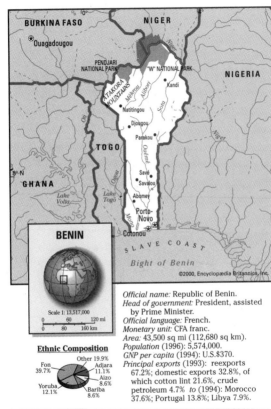

©2000, Encyclopædia Britannica, Inc.

BENIN

Scale 1: 13,517,000

0   60   120 mi

0   80   160 km

Ethnic Composition

Fon 39.7%

Other 19.9%

Adjara 11.1%

Aizo 8.6%

Bariba 8.6%

Yoruba 12.1%

Official name: Republic of Benin.
Head of government: President, assisted by Prime Minister.
Official language: French.
Monetary unit: CFA franc.
Area: 43,500 sq mi (112,680 sq km).
Population (1996): 5,574,000.
GNP per capita (1994): U.S.$370.
Principal exports (1993): reexports 67.2%; domestic exports 32.8%, of which cotton lint 21.6%, crude petroleum 4.7% *to* (1994): Morocco 37.6%; Portugal 13.8%; Libya 7.9%.

Adopted on Nov. 16, 1959, the flag of the former French colony used the Pan-African colors. Yellow was for the savannas in the north and green was for the palm groves in the south. Red stood for the blood of patriots. In 1975 a Marxist-oriented government replaced the flag, but after the demise of Communism it was restored on Aug. 1, 1990.

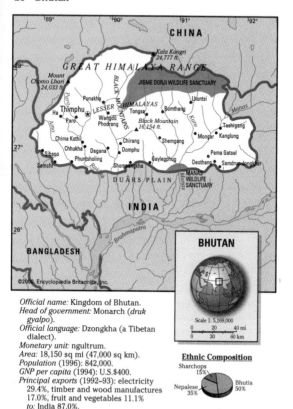

Official name: Kingdom of Bhutan.
Head of government: Monarch (*druk gyalpo*).
Official language: Dzongkha (a Tibetan dialect).
Monetary unit: ngultrum.
Area: 18,150 sq mi (47,000 sq km).
Population (1996): 842,000.
GNP per capita (1994): U.S.$400.
Principal exports (1992–93): electricity 29.4%, timber and wood manufactures 17.0%, fruit and vegetables 11.1% *to:* India 87.0%.

Ethnic Composition

Sharchops 15%
Bhutia 50%
Nepalese 35%

The flag of Bhutan ("Land of the Dragon") features a dragon grasping jewels; this represents natural wealth and perfection. The white color is for purity and loyalty, the gold is for regal power, and the orange-red is for Buddhist sects and religious commitment. The flag may have been introduced as recently as 1971.

©2000, Encyclopædia Britannica, Inc.

Official name: Republic of Bolivia.
Head of government: President.
Official languages: Spanish, Aymara, Quechua.
Monetary unit: boliviano.
Area: 424,164 sq mi (1,098,581 sq km).
Population (1996): 7,592,000.
GNP per capita (1994): U.S.$770.
Principal exports (1995): zinc 13.8%; gold 12.1%; soybeans 10.9%; natural gas 8.6%; tin 7.9%; jewelry articles 6.9%; silver 6.6% *to:* United States 23.3%; United Kingdom 15.1%; Peru 14.2%.

BOLIVIA

Scale 1: 23,517,000

| 0 | 100 | 200 mi |
| 0 | 100 | 200 | 300 km |

Ethnic Composition

White 14.5%
Other 12%
Mestizo 31.2%
Quechua 25.4%
Aymara 16.9%

A version of the flag was first adopted on July 25, 1826, but on Nov. 5, 1851, the order of the stripes was changed to red-yellow-green. The colors were often used by the Aymara and Quechua peoples; in addition, red is for the valor of the army, yellow for mineral resources, and green for the land. The current flag law dates from July 14, 1888.

BOSNIA AND HERZEGOVINA

Scale 1: 6,252,000

0   30   60 mi
0   40   80 km

Ethnic Composition

Muslim 49.2%

Serb 31.3%

Croat 17.3%

Other 2.2%

Official name: Republic of Bosnia and Herzegovina.
Head of government: 2 cochairmen assisted by the Council of Ministers.
Official language: Serbo-Croatian.
Monetary unit: Bosnian dinar.
Area: 19,741 sq mi (51,129 sq km).
Population (1996): 3,200,000.
GNP per capita (1992): U.S.$1,500.
Principal exports (1995) to: Italy 29%; Germany 23%; Croatia 13%; Slovenia 13%.

Upon independence from Yugoslavia on March 3, 1992, the Bosnian-led government chose a neutral flag in order to appease the Serb and Croat populations. The flag was adopted on May 4, 1992, and although civil war caused the administrative division of the country in 1995, the white flag is recognized internationally.

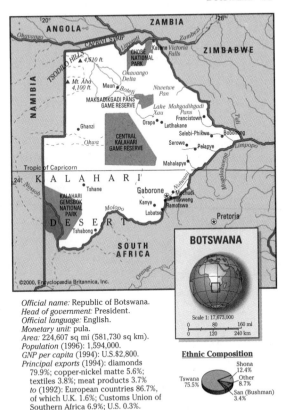

©2000, Encyclopædia Britannica, Inc.

BOTSWANA

Scale 1: 17,673,000

0 — 80 — 160 mi
0 — 120 — 240 km

Official name: Republic of Botswana.
Head of government: President.
Official language: English.
Monetary unit: pula.
Area: 224,607 sq mi (581,730 sq km).
Population (1996): 1,594,000.
GNP per capita (1994): U.S.$2,800.
Principal exports (1994): diamonds
79.9%; copper-nickel matte 5.6%;
textiles 3.8%; meat products 3.7%
to (1992): European countries 86.7%,
of which U.K. 1.6%; Customs Union
of Southern Africa 6.9%; U.S. 0.3%.

Ethnic Composition

Shona 12.4%
Other 8.7%
Tswana 75.5%
San (Bushman) 3.4%

Adopted in 1966, the flag was designed to contrast symboli-
cally with that of neighboring South Africa, where apartheid
was then in effect. The black and white stripes in Botswana's
flag are for racial cooperation and equality. The background
symbolizes water, a scarce resource in the expansive Kalahari
Desert.

BRAZIL

Scale 1: 69,689,000

| 0 | 300 | 600 mi |
| 0 | 400 | 800 km |

©2000, Encyclopædia Britannica, Inc.

Racial Composition

- White 54%
- Mulatto and Mestizo 39%
- Other 7%

Official name: Federative Republic of Brazil.
Head of government: President.
Official language: Portuguese.
Monetary unit: real.
Area: 3,300,171 sq mi (8,547,404 sq km).
Population (1996): 157,872,000.
GNP per capita (1994): U.S.$3,370.
Principal exports (1994): iron and steel fabricated products 9.5%, non-electrical machinery and apparatus 9.1% *to:* U.S. 20.6%; Argentina 9.5%; The Netherlands 7.1%; Japan 6.0%.

The original flag was introduced on Sept. 7, 1822, when Dom Pedro declared independence from Portugal. In 1889 the blue disk and the motto Ordem e Progresso ("Order and Progress") were added. The Brazilian states and territories are symbolized by the constellations of stars. Green is for the land, while yellow is for gold and other mineral wealth.

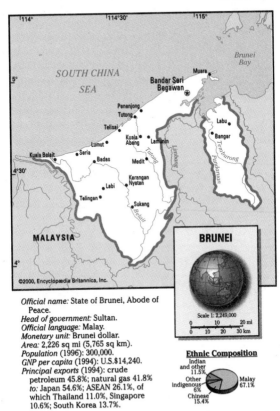

Official name: State of Brunei, Abode of Peace.
Head of government: Sultan.
Official language: Malay.
Monetary unit: Brunei dollar.
Area: 2,226 sq mi (5,765 sq km).
Population (1996): 300,000.
GNP per capita (1994): U.S.$14,240.
Principal exports (1994): crude petroleum 45.8%; natural gas 41.8% *to:* Japan 54.6%; ASEAN 26.1%, of which Thailand 11.0%, Singapore 10.6%; South Korea 13.7%.

BRUNEI

Scale 1: 2,249,000

| 0 | 10 | 20 mi |
| 0 | 10 | 20 | 30 km |

Ethnic Composition

Indian and other 11.5%
Other indigenous 6%
Chinese 15.4%
Malay 67.1%

When Brunei became a British protectorate in 1906, diagonal stripes were added to its yellow flag. The yellow stood for the sultan, while white and black were for his two chief ministers. Introduced in September 1959, the coat of arms has a parasol as a symbol of royalty and a crescent and inscription for the state religion, Islam.

Official name: Republic of Bulgaria.
Head of government: Prime Minister.
Official language: Bulgarian.
Monetary unit: lev.
Area: 42,855 sq mi (110,994 sq km).
Population (1996): 8,366,000.
GNP per capita (1994): U.S.$1,217.
Principal exports (1994): fuels, minerals, and metals 30.4%; chemicals and rubber 16.6%; food and beverages 14.8%; machinery and equipment 12.2% *to* (1994): C.I.S. 17.0%; Germany 8.4%; Italy 8.2%; Greece 6.9%.

©2000, Encyclopædia Britannica, Inc.

BULGARIA

Scale 1: 8,710,000

| 0 | 40 | 80 mi |
| 0 | 60 | 120 km |

Ethnic Composition

Bulgarian 85.7%

Turkish 9.4%

Other 4.9%

The flag was based on the Russian flag of 1699, but with green substituted for blue. Under communist rule, a red star and other symbols were added, but the old tricolor was reestablished on Nov. 27, 1990. The white is for peace, love, and freedom; green is for agriculture; and red is for the independence struggle and military courage.

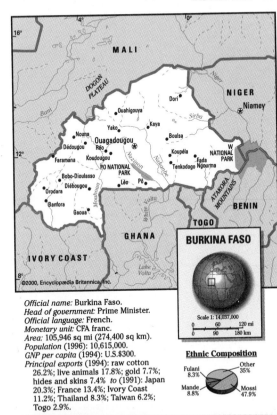

Official name: Burkina Faso.
Head of government: Prime Minister.
Official language: French.
Monetary unit: CFA franc.
Area: 105,946 sq mi (274,400 sq km).
Population (1996): 10,615,000.
GNP per capita (1994): U.S.$300.
Principal exports (1994): raw cotton
    26.2%; live animals 17.8%; gold 7.7%;
    hides and skins 7.4% *to* (1991): Japan
    20.3%; France 13.4%; Ivory Coast
    11.2%; Thailand 8.3%; Taiwan 6.2%;
    Togo 2.9%.

Ethnic Composition

Fulani 8.3%
Mande 8.8%
Mossi 47.9%
Other 35%

On Aug. 4, 1984, Upper Volta was renamed Burkina Faso by
the revolutionary government of Thomas Sankara, and the
current flag was adopted with Pan-African colors. The yellow
star symbolizes leadership and revolutionary principles. The
red stripe is said to stand for the revolutionary struggle,
while the green stripe represents hope and abundance.

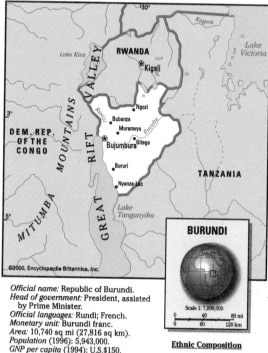

@2000, Encyclopædia Britannica, Inc.

BURUNDI

Scale 1: 7,899,000

0   40   80 mi

0   60   120 km

Official name: Republic of Burundi.
Head of government: President, assisted by Prime Minister.
Official languages: Rundi; French.
Monetary unit: Burundi franc.
Area: 10,740 sq mi (27,816 sq km).
Population (1996): 5,943,000.
GNP per capita (1994): U.S.$150.
Principal exports (1995): coffee 80.7%; tea 7.8%; cotton 1.6% *to:* Germany 21.6%; Belgium-Luxembourg 17.6%; France 10.9%; United States 6.7%; Rwanda 3.6%; United Kingdom 3.6%.

Ethnic Composition

Other 3.6%

Tutsi 13.6%

Hutu 82.8%

The flag became official on June 28, 1967. Its white saltire (diagonal cross) and central disk symbolize peace. The red color is for the independence struggle, and green is for hope. The stars correspond to the national motto, "Unity, Work, Progress." They also recall the Tutsi, Hutu, and Twa peoples and the pledge to God, king, and country.

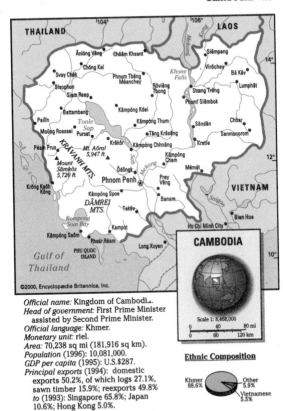

©2000, Encyclopædia Britannica, Inc.

Official name: Kingdom of Cambodia.
Head of government: First Prime Minister assisted by Second Prime Minister.
Official language: Khmer.
Monetary unit: riel.
Area: 70,238 sq mi (181,916 sq km).
Population (1996): 10,081,000.
GDP per capita (1995): U.S.$287.
Principal exports (1994): domestic exports 50.2%, of which logs 27.1%, sawn timber 15.9%; reexports 49.8% *to* (1993): Singapore 65.8%; Japan 10.6%; Hong Kong 5.0%.

CAMBODIA

Scale 1: 8,468,000

| 0 | 40 | 80 mi |
| 0 | 60 | 120 km |

Ethnic Composition

Khmer 88.6%
Other 5.9%
Vietnamese 5.5%

Artistic representations of the central ruined temple of Angkor Wat, a 12th-century temple complex, have appeared on Khmer flags since the 19th century. The current flag design dates to 1948. It was replaced in 1970 under the Khmer Republic and in 1976 under communist leadership, but it was again hoisted on June 29, 1993.

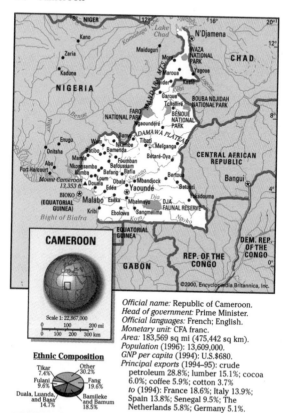

Official name: Republic of Cameroon.
Head of government: Prime Minister.
Official languages: French; English.
Monetary unit: CFA franc.
Area: 183,569 sq mi (475,442 sq km).
Population (1996): 13,609,000.
GNP per capita (1994): U.S.$680.
Principal exports (1994–95): crude
petroleum 28.8%; lumber 15.1%; cocoa
6.0%; coffee 5.9%; cotton 3.7%
to (1994): France 18.6%; Italy 13.9%;
Spain 13.8%; Senegal 9.5%; The
Netherlands 5.8%; Germany 5.1%.

Ethnic Composition

Tikar 7.4%
Fulani 9.6%
Duala, Luanda and Basa 14.7%
Bamileke and Bamum 18.5%
Fang 19.6%
Other 30.2%

The flag was officially hoisted on Oct. 29, 1957, prior to independence (Jan. 1, 1960). Green is for the vegetation of the
south, yellow for the savannas of the north, and red for union
and sovereignty. Two yellow stars were added (for the British
Cameroons) in 1961, but these were replaced in 1975 by a sin-
gle star symbolizing national unity.

CANADA

Scale 1: 75,618,000

0   300   600 mi

0   300   600   900 km

Ethnic Composition

French 22.8%

British 20.8%

German 3.4%

Multiple origin and other 53%

Official name: Canada.
Head of government: Prime Minister.
Official languages: English; French.
Monetary unit: Canadian dollar.
Area: 3,849,674 sq mi (9,970,610 sq km).
Population (1996): 29,784,000.
GNP per capita (1994): U.S.$19,570.
Principal exports (1993): machinery and
transport equipment 39.4%; mineral
fuels 10.5%; food 6.4%; lumber 5.0%;
newsprint 3.2%; wood pulp 2.5%.
to: U.S. 80.4%; Japan 4.5%; U.K. 1.4%;
China 1.2%; Germany 1.2%.

During Canada's first century of independence the Union Jack
was still flown, but with a Canadian coat of arms. The maple
leaf design, with the national colors, became official on Feb.
15, 1965. Since 1868 the maple leaf has been a national symbol, and in 1921 a red leaf in the coat of arms stood for
Canadian sacrifice during World War I.

©2000, Encyclopædia Britannica, Inc.

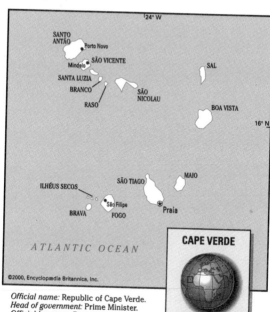

©2000, Encyclopædia Britannica, Inc.

Official name: Republic of Cape Verde.
Head of government: Prime Minister.
Official language: Portuguese.
Monetary unit: escudo.
Area: 1,557 sq mi (4,033 sq km).
Population (1996): 403,000.
GNP per capita (1994): U.S.$910.
Principal exports (1993): fish and fish
   preparations 62.6%; bananas 11.7%
   to: Portugal 48.8%; Angola 16.0%;
   The Netherlands 3.4%.

CAPE VERDE

Scale 1: 6,137,000

0   25   50 mi

0   25   50   75 km

Religious Affiliation

Roman
Catholic
93.2%

Protestant
and other
6.8%

After the elections of 1991, the flag was established with a
blue field bearing a ring of 10 yellow stars to symbolize the
10 main islands of Cape Verde. The stripes of white-red-white
suggest peace and national resolve. Red, white, and blue also
are a symbolic link to Portugal and the United States. The
new flag became official on Sept. 25, 1992.

Official name: Central African Republic.
Head of government: Prime Minister.
Official languages: French; Sango.
Monetary unit: CFA franc.
Area: 240,324 sq mi (622,436 sq km).
Population (1996): 3,274,000.
GNP per capita (1994): U.S.$370.
Principal exports (1995): diamonds
49.7%; coffee 15.7%; wood products
15.0%; cotton 12.1% *to* (1994):
Belgium-Luxembourg 61.4%; Spain
8.6%; France 5.7%; Iran 5.7%;
Italy 4.3%.

Scale 1: 21,022,000

0   100   200 mi
0   100   200   300 km

Religious Affiliation
Roman Catholic 25%
Traditional 24%
Muslim 15%
Protestant 25%
Other 11% (Christian majority)

Barthélemy Boganda designed the flag in 1958. It combines
French and Pan-African colors. The star is a guide for
progress and an emblem of unity. The blue stripe is for liberty, grandeur, and the sky; the white is for purity, equality, and
candor; the green and yellow are for forests and savannas;
and the red is for the blood of humankind.

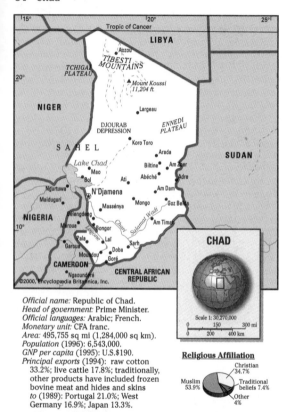

Official name: Republic of Chad.
Head of government: Prime Minister.
Official languages: Arabic; French.
Monetary unit: CFA franc.
Area: 495,755 sq mi (1,284,000 sq km).
Population (1996): 6,543,000.
GNP per capita (1995): U.S.$190.
Principal exports (1994): raw cotton
33.2%; live cattle 17.8%; traditionally,
other products have included frozen
bovine meat and hides and skins
to (1989): Portugal 21.0%; West
Germany 16.9%; Japan 13.3%.

CHAD

Scale 1: 30,270,000

0   150   300 mi
0   200   400 km

Religious Affiliation

Christian
34.7%

Muslim
53.9%

Traditional
beliefs 7.4%

Other
4%

In 1958 a tricolor of green-yellow-red (the Pan-African colors) was proposed, but that design was already used by the Mali-Senegal federation, another former French colony. Approved on Nov. 6, 1959, the current flag substitutes blue for the original green stripe. Blue is for hope and sky, yellow for the sun, and red for the unity of the nation.

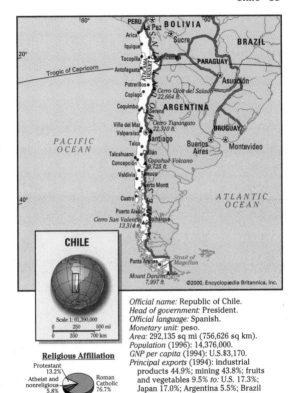

Official name: Republic of Chile.
Head of government: President.
Official language: Spanish.
Monetary unit: peso.
Area: 292,135 sq mi (756,626 sq km).
Population (1996): 14,376,000.
GNP per capita (1994): U.S.$3,170.
Principal exports (1994): industrial
    products 44.9%; mining 43.8%; fruits
    and vegetables 9.5% to: U.S. 17.3%;
    Japan 17.0%; Argentina 5.5%; Brazil
    5.2%; Germany 5.0%; Taiwan 4.6%;
    U.K. 4.5%; France 3.5%.

Religious Affiliation

Protestant
13.2%

Atheist and
nonreligious
5.8%

Other
4.3%

Roman
Catholic
76.7%

On Oct. 18, 1817, the flag was established for the new republic. The blue is for the sky, and the star is "a guide on the
path of progress and honor." The white is for the snow of the
Andes Mountains while the red recalls the blood of patriots.
In the 15th century the Araucanian Indians gave red-white-
blue sashes to their warriors.

Controlled by China; claimed by India

RUSSIA

KAZAKHSTAN

Astana

ALTAY SHAN

MONGOLIA

Tashkent
UZBEKISTAN
Dushanbe
TAJIKISTAN

Bishkek
KYRGYZSTAN

Ürümqi

TIAN SHAN

Victory Peak
24,400 ft.

Tarim

TAKLIMAKAN
DESERT

Lop
Nur

GOBI

QAIDAM BASIN

Koko
Nor

Xining

Lanzhou

KUNLUN SHAN

AFGHANISTAN

Kabul

Islamabad

PAKISTAN

PAMIRS

HIMALAYAS

PLATEAU
OF TIBET

Lhasa

WENCHUAN WOLONG
NATURE RESERVE

SICHUAN
BASIN

Tongtian

New Delhi

NEPAL

Mount Everest
29,028 ft.

Kathmandu

HIMALAYAS

Thimphu

BHUTAN

Yulongxue
Shan
18,355 ft.

Kunming

INDIA

INDIA

BANGLADESH

Red

Dhaka

MYANMAR

LAOS

Bay of
Bengal

THAILAND

CHINA

Scale 1: 49,053,000

| 0 | 200 | 400 mi |
| 0 | 300 | 600 km |

Age Breakdown

60 and over
8.6%

15–59
63.7%

under 15
27.7%

The flag was hoisted on Oct. 1, 1949. The red is for communism and the Han Chinese. The large star was originally for the Communist Party, and the smaller stars were for the proletariat, the peasants, the petty bourgeoisie, and the "patriotic capitalists." The large star was later said to stand for China, the smaller stars for minorities.

Official name: People's Republic of China.
Head of government: Premier.
Official language: Mandarin Chinese.
Monetary unit: yuan.
Area: 3,696,100 sq mi (9,572,900 sq km).
Population (1996): 1,218,700,000.
GNP per capita (1994): U.S.$530.
Principal exports (1994): products of textile industries, rubber and
metal products 19.2%; machinery and transport equipment 18.1%;
food and live animals 8.3%; chemicals and allied products 5.2%
to: Hong Kong 26.7%; Japan 17.8%; United States 17.7%; Germany
3.9%; South Korea 3.6%; Singapore 2.1%; United Kingdom 2.0%; The
Netherlands 1.9%; Taiwan 1.9%; Italy 1.3%; Russia 1.3%.

COLOMBIA

Scale 1: 26,728,000

0   100   200 mi
0 100 200 300 km

Racial Composition

White 20%

Mulatto 14%

Mestizo 58%

Other 8%

Official name: Republic of Colombia.
Head of government: President.
Official language: Spanish.
Monetary unit: peso.
Area: 440,762 sq mi (1,141,568 sq km).
Population (1996): 35,652,000.
GNP per capita (1994): U.S.$1,620.
Principal exports (1994): coffee 23.7%;
  forestry and fisheries products 14.8%;
  petroleum products 14.7%; textiles
  and apparel 9.5%; coal 6.6%; chemicals
  6.5% *to:* U.S. 36.5%; Germany 10.4%;
  Venezuela 6.3%; Japan 4.2%.

In the early 19th century "the Liberator" Simon Bolívar created a yellow-blue-red flag for New Granada (which included
Colombia, Venezuela, Panama, and Ecuador). The flag symbolized the yellow gold of the New World separated by the
blue ocean from the red of "bloody Spain." The present
Colombian flag was established on Nov. 26, 1861.

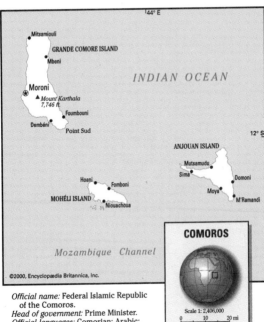

Mitsamiouli
GRANDE COMORE ISLAND
Mbeni
⊛ **Moroni**
▲ *Mount Karthala*
7,746 ft.
Foumbouni
Dembéni
Point Sud

INDIAN OCEAN

144° E

12° S

ANJOUAN ISLAND
Mutsamudu
Sima
Domoni
Moya
M'Ramandi

Hoani   Fomboni
MOHÉLI ISLAND
Niouachoua

Mozambique Channel

©2000, Encyclopædia Britannica, Inc.

Official name: Federal Islamic Republic of the Comoros.
Head of government: Prime Minister.
Official languages: Comorian; Arabic; French.
Monetary unit: franc.
Area: 719 sq mi (1,862 sq km).
Population (1996): 562,000.
GNP per capita (1994): U.S.$510.
Principal exports (1995): vanilla 54.8%; ylang-ylang 20.2%; cloves 3.2%. *to:* France 36.5%; United States 28.4%; Germany 8.0%.

COMOROS

Scale 1: 2,406,000

0   10   20 mi
0   15   30 km

Age Breakdown

15–59
47.5%
Under 15
48.5%
60 and over
4%

The flag was adopted on Oct. 3, 1996. Its green background and white crescent are symbols of Islam, and the Arabic words for Allah and Muhammad are inscribed in the corners. The four stars are for the islands of Njazidja (formerly Grande-Comore), Mwali (Mohéli), Nzwani (Anjouan), and Mayotte (a French territory that is claimed by Comoros).

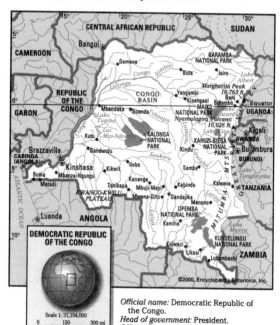

Official name: Democratic Republic of
the Congo.
Head of government: President.
Official language: French.
Monetary unit: zaïre.
Area: 905,354 sq mi (2,344,858 sq km).
Population (1996): 45,259,000.
GNP per capita (1991): U.S.$220.
Principal exports (1995): diamonds
17.2%; crude petroleum 11.4%; coffee
8.8%; copper 7.9% *to:* Belgium-
Luxembourg 36.3%; U.S. 16.9%; Italy
9.7%; Japan 5.0%; Germany 4.0%.

Ethnic Composition

Rwanda 10.3%
Mongo 13.5%
Kongo 16.1%
Luba 18%
Other 42.1%

In 1877 the flag of the Congo Free State was blue with a gold
star, for a shining light in the "Dark Continent." At independence (June 30, 1962) six stars were added for the existing six
provinces, but in 1971 the flag was replaced with a green flag
depicting an arm and a torch. The regime led by Laurent
Kabila restored the old flag on May 17, 1997.

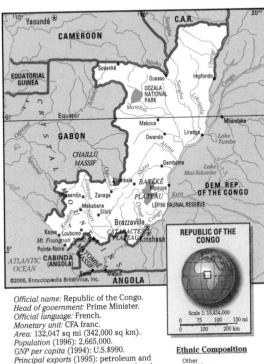

REPUBLIC OF THE CONGO

Scale 1: 15,434,000

| 0 | 75 | 100 | 150 mi |
| 0 | 100 | 200 km |

©2000, Encyclopædia Britannica, Inc.

Official name: Republic of the Congo.
Head of government: Prime Minister.
Official language: French.
Monetary unit: CFA franc.
Area: 132,047 sq mi (342,000 sq km).
Population (1996): 2,665,000.
GNP per capita (1994): U.S.$990.
Principal exports (1995): petroleum and petroleum products 84.6%; wood and wood products 8.4%; other 7.0% *to:* Italy 22.6%; U.S. 15.4%; The Netherlands 12.5%; France 9.2%; Spain 4.6%.

Ethnic Composition

Other 19.7%

Teke 17.3%

Mboshi 11.5%

Kongo 51.5%

First adopted on Sept. 15, 1959, the flag uses the Pan-African colors. Green was originally said to stand for Congo's agriculture and forests, and yellow for friendship and the nobility of the people, but the red was unexplained. Altered in 1969 by a Marxist government, the flag was restored to its initial form on June 10, 1991.

COSTA RICA

Scale 1: 5,424,000

0 — 25 — 50 mi
0 — 40 — 80 km

Ethnic Composition

White 87%
Mestizo 7%
Other 6%

Official name: Republic of Costa Rica.
Head of government: President.
Official language: Spanish.
Monetary unit: Costa Rican colón.
Area: 19,730 sq mi (51,100 sq km).
Population (1996): 3,400,000.
GNP per capita (1994): U.S.$2,380.
Principal exports (1993): bananas 29.6%;
coffee 10.4%; textiles, clothing, and
footwear 5.7%; fish and shrimp 4.7%;
ornamental plants, leaves, and flowers
4.6% *to:* United States 41.6%; Germany
8.9%; Italy 4.5%; Guatemala 4.5%.

The blue and white stripes originated in the flag colors of the
United Provinces of Central America (1823–40). On Sept. 29,
1848, the red stripe was added to symbolize sunlight, civiliza-
tion, and "true independence." The current design of the coat
of arms, which is included on government flags, was established in 1964.

CROATIA

Scale 1: 7,071,000

0	30	60 mi
0	30	60	90 km

Ethnic Composition

Croat 78.1%
Serb 12.1%
Other 9.8%

Official name: Republic of Croatia.
Head of government: Prime Minister.
Official language: Croatian.
Monetary unit: kuna.
Area: 21,359 sq mi (55,322 sq km).
Population (1996): 4,775,000.
GDP per capita (1994): U.S. $2,482.
Principal exports (1994): miscellaneous
   ready-made products 29.0%;
   machinery and transport equipment
   17.5%; chemical products 12.9%; food
   and live animals 9.3% *to* (1994):
   Germany 21.1%; Italy 20.3%.

During the European uprisings of 1848, Croatians designed a flag based on that of Russia. In April 1941 the fascistic Ustasa used this flag, adding the checkered shield of Croatia. A communist star soon replaced the shield, but the current flag was adopted on Dec. 22, 1990. Atop the shield is a "crown" inlaid with historic coats of arms.

Official name: Republic of Cuba.
Head of government: President.
Official language: Spanish.
Monetary unit: Cuban peso.
Area: 42,804 sq mi (110,861 sq km).
Population (1996): 11,117,000.
GNP per capita (1991): U.S.$1,580.
Principal exports (1992): sugar 63.4%;
  minerals and concentrates 10.6%; fish
  products 5.9%; raw tobacco and
  tobacco products 4.6% *to:* Russia
  22.1%; Canada 11.5%; China 8.9%; The
  Netherlands 7.1%; Spain 5.7%.

Religious Affiliation

Other 5.3%
Nonreligious 48.7%
Atheist 6.4%
Roman Catholic 39.6%

In the mid-19th century Cuban exiles designed the flag, which
was later carried into battle against Spanish forces. It was
adopted on May 20, 1902. The stripes were for the three military districts of Cuba and the purity of the patriotic cause.
The red triangle was for strength, constancy, and equality,
and the white star symbolized independence.

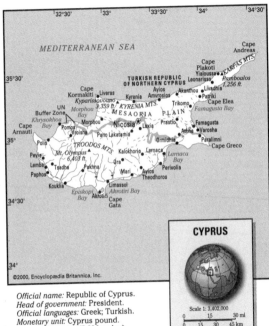

MEDITERRANEAN SEA

@2000, Encyclopædia Britannica, Inc.

Official name: Republic of Cyprus.
Head of government: President.
Official languages: Greek; Turkish.
Monetary unit: Cyprus pound.
Area: 2,276 sq mi (5,896 sq km).
Population (1996): 657,000.
GNP per capita (1994): U.S.$11,440.
Principal exports (1995): reexports
  50.0%; domestic exports 41.8%, of
  which clothing 8.0%, potatoes 7.8%;
  ships' stores 8.2% *to:* Russia 13.7%;
  U.K. 13.3%; Bulgaria 9.1%; Greece 6.0%.

CYPRUS

Scale 1: 3,402,000

0   15   30 mi

0   15   30   45 km

Age Breakdown

60 and over
14.9%

15–59
59.8%

Under 15
25.3%

On Aug. 7, 1960, the Republic of Cyprus was proclaimed with a national flag of a neutral design. It bears the island in silhouette and a green olive wreath, for peace. In 1974 there was a Turkish invasion of the island. A puppet government, which adopted a flag based on the Turkish model, was set up on the northern third of Cyprus.

©2000, Encyclopædia Britannica, Inc.

CZECH REPUBLIC

Scale 1: 6,810,000

| 0 | 20 | 40 mi |

| 0 | 40 | 60 km |

Official name: Česká Republika.
Head of government: Prime Minister.
Official language: Czech.
Monetary unit: koruna.
Area: 30,450 sq mi (78,864 sq km).
Population (1996): 10,315,842.
GNP per capita (1994): U.S.$3,198.
Principal exports (1995): manufactured
    goods 32.4%; machinery and transport
    equipment 26.3%; miscellaneous
    manufactured articles 12.6% *to:*
    Germany 31.8%; Slovakia 16.2%;
    Austria 6.5%; Italy 4.0%; Russia 3.5%.

Ethnic Composition

Czech 81.2%

Moravian 13.2%

Other 5.6%

When Czechs, Slovaks, and Ruthenians united to form
Czechoslovakia in 1918, a simple white-red bicolor flag was
chosen; in 1920 it incorporated a blue triangle at the hoist.
Czechoslovakia divided into Slovakia and the Czech Republic
in 1993, but the latter country readopted the Czechoslovak
flag as its own.

Official name: Kingdom of Denmark.
Head of government: Prime Minister.
Official language: Danish.
Monetary unit: Danish krone.
Area: 16,639 sq mi (43,094 sq km).
Population (1996): 5,244,000.
GNP per capita (1994): U.S.$28,110.
Principal exports (1994): nonelectrical
  and electrical machinery 24.2%, fresh
  or frozen swine meat 6.4%, furniture
  4.5%, pharmaceuticals 4.3%
  to: Germany 22.4%; Sweden 10.4%;
  United Kingdom 8.2%; Norway 6.5%.

DENMARK

Scale 1: 6,930,000

0 — 20 — 40 mi
0 — 30 — 60 km

Age Breakdown

Under 15
17.3%

15–59
62.9%

60 and over
19.8%

A traditional story claims that the Danish flag fell from
heaven on June 15, 1219, but the previously existing war flag
of the Holy Roman Empire was of a similar design, with its
red field symbolizing battle and its white cross suggesting
divine favor. In 1849 the state and military flag was altered
and adopted as a symbol of the Danish people.

Ethnic Composition

Arab 6%
Other 12.3%
Afar 20%
Somali 61.7%

Official name: Republic of Djibouti.
Head of government: President.
Official languages: Arabic; French.
Monetary unit: Djibouti franc.
Area: 8,950 sq mi (23,200 sq km).
Population (1996): 603,600.
GNP per capita (1993): U.S.$780.
Principal exports (1991): unspecified special transactions 71.7%; live animals [including camels] 15.5%; food and food products 12.8% *to:* Somalia 39.0%; Ethiopia 34.2%; Yemen 20.8%; Saudi Arabia 0.6%.

First raised by anti-French separatists, the flag was officially hoisted on June 27, 1977. The color of the Afar people, green, stands for prosperity. The color of the Issa people, light blue, symbolizes sea and sky, and recalls the flag of Somalia. The white triangle is for equality and peace; the red star is for unity and independence.

©2000, Encyclopædia Britannica, Inc.

DOMINICA

Scale 1: 852,000

0   3   6 mi
0   5   10 km

Religious Affiliation

Other 12.7%

Protestant 17.2%

Roman Catholic 70.1%

Official name: Commonwealth of Dominica.
Head of government: Prime Minister.
Official language: English.
Monetary unit: East Caribbean dollar.
Area: 285.3 sq mi (739.0 sq km).
Population (1996): 73,800.
GNP per capita (1994): U.S.$2,830.
Principal exports (1992): domestic exports 97.1%, of which bananas 55.7%, coconut-based laundry and toilet soaps 20.7% *to:* United Kingdom 47.6%; Caricom countries 27.9%.

The flag was hoisted on Nov. 3, 1978, at independence from Britain. Its background symbolizes forests; its central disk is red for socialism and bears a sisserou (a rare local bird). The stars are for the parishes of the island. The cross of yellow, white, and black is for the Carib, Caucasian, and African peoples and for fruit, water, and soil.

Official name: Dominican Republic.
Head of government: President.
Official language: Spanish.
Monetary unit: Dominican peso.
Area: 18,792 sq mi (48,671 sq km).
Population (1996): 7,502,000.
GNP per capita (1994): U.S.$1,320.
Principal exports (1995): ferronickel
30.1%; raw sugar 13.8%; raw coffee
10.9%; cacao 7.3%; gold 6.2% *to* (1994):
U.S. 52.3%; The Netherlands 12.9%;
Puerto Rico 6.3%; South Korea 5.8%;
Belgium 5.1%.

Ethnic Composition

Mixed 73%

White 16%

Black 11%

On Feb. 28, 1844, Spanish-speaking Dominican revolutionaries added a white cross to the simple blue-red flag of eastern Hispaniola, in order to emphasize their Christian heritage. On November 6 of that same year the new constitution established the flag, but with the colors at the fly end reversed so that the blue and red would alternate.

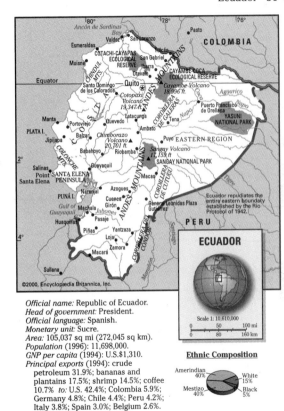

©2000, Encyclopædia Britannica, Inc.

ECUADOR

Scale 1: 10,610,000

| 0 | 50 | 100 mi |
| 0 | 80 | 160 km |

Official name: Republic of Ecuador.
Head of government: President.
Official language: Spanish.
Monetary unit: Sucre.
Area: 105,037 sq mi (272,045 sq km).
Population (1996): 11,698,000.
GNP per capita (1994): U.S.$1,310.
Principal exports (1994): crude
  petroleum 31.9%; bananas and
  plantains 17.5%; shrimp 14.5%; coffee
  10.7% *to:* U.S. 42.4%; Colombia 5.9%;
  Germany 4.8%; Chile 4.4%; Peru 4.2%;
  Italy 3.8%; Spain 3.0%; Belgium 2.6%.

Ethnic Composition

Amerindian 40%
White 15%
Black 5%
Mestizo 40%

Victorious against the Spanish on May 24, 1822, Antonio José de Sucre hoisted a yellow-blue-red flag. Other flags were later used, but on Sept. 26, 1860, the current flag design was adopted. The coat of arms is displayed on the flag when it is used abroad or for official purposes, to distinguish it from the flag of Colombia.

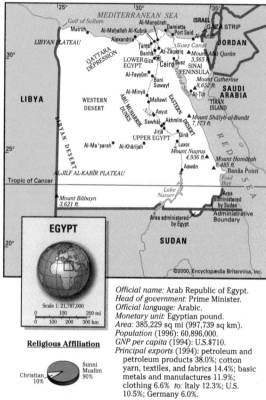

Official name: Arab Republic of Egypt.
Head of government: Prime Minister.
Official language: Arabic.
Monetary unit: Egyptian pound.
Area: 385,229 sq mi (997,739 sq km).
Population (1996): 60,896,000.
GNP per capita (1994): U.S.$710.
Principal exports (1994): petroleum and
   petroleum products 38.0%; cotton
   yarn, textiles, and fabrics 14.4%; basic
   metals and manufactures 11.9%;
   clothing 6.6% *to:* Italy 12.3%; U.S.
   10.5%; Germany 6.0%.

The 1952 revolt against British rule established the red-white-
black flag with a central gold eagle. Two stars replaced the
eagle in 1958, and in 1972 a federation with Syria and Libya
was formed, adding the hawk of Quraysh (instead the tribe of
Muhammad). On Oct. 9, 1984, the eagle of Saladin (a major
12th-century ruler) was substituted.

©2000, Encyclopædia Britannica, Inc.

EL SALVADOR

Scale 1: 3,810,000

0   25 mi
0   20   40 km

Age Breakdown

Under 15
38.7%

60 and over
7.4%

15–59
53.9%

Official name: Republic of El Salvador.
Head of government: President.
Official language: Spanish.
Monetary unit: colón.
Area: 8,124 sq mi (21,041 sq km).
Population (1996): 5,897,000.
GNP per capita (1994): U.S.$1,480.
Principal exports: coffee 32.5%; paper
and paper products 7.0%; clothing
4.6%; pharmaceuticals 4.2%; raw sugar
4.2% *to:* United States 22.6%;
Guatemala 21.9%; Germany 14.9%;
Costa Rica 8.9%; Honduras 6.9%.

In the early 19th century a blue-white-blue flag was designed
for the short-lived United Provinces of Central America, in
which El Salvador was a member. On Sept. 15, 1912, the flag
was reintroduced in El Salvador. The coat of arms in the center resembles that used by the former federation and
includes the national motto, "God, Union, Liberty."

Scale 1: 6,500,000

0   20   40 mi
0   30   60 km

©2000, Encyclopædia Britannica, Inc.

Ethnic Composition

Fang
82.9%

Bubi
9.6%

Other
7.5%

Official name: Republic of Equatorial
  Guinea.
Head of government: Prime Minister.
Official language: Spanish.
Monetary unit: CFA franc.
Area: 10,831 sq mi (28,051 sq km).
Population (1996): 406,000.
GNP per capita (1994): U.S.$470.
Principal exports (1994): petroleum
  products 50.5%; wood 35.6%; food
  products 4.6%, of which cocoa 4.3%
  to: Japan 14.7%; Spain 11.8%; Ivory
  Coast 10.7%; Nigeria 8.4%.

The flag was first hoisted at independence (Oct. 12, 1968). Its
coat of arms shows the silk-cotton tree, or god tree, which
recalls early Spanish influence in the area. The sea, which
links parts of the country, is reflected in the blue triangle.
The green is for vegetation, white is for peace, and red is for
the blood of martyrs in the liberation struggle.

Official name: State of Eritrea.
Head of government: President.
Official language: none.
Monetary unit: Ethiopian birr.
Area: 45,300 sq mi (117,400 sq km).
Population (1996): 3,627,000.
GNP per capita (1993): U.S.$115.
Principal exports (1995): raw materials 29.8%; food products 26.2%; manufactured goods 19.3%; beverages and tobacco 3.8%; machinery and transport equipment 3.8% *to:* Ethiopia 63.3%; Sudan 16.4%; Yemen 4.9%.

Language Composition

Semitic languages 81%
Cushitic languages 14%
Nilotic languages 5%

Officially hoisted at the proclamation of independence on May 24, 1993, the national flag was based on that of the Eritrean People's Liberation Front. The red triangle is for the blood of patriots, the green is for agriculture, and the blue is for maritime resources. Around a central branch is a circle of olive branches with 30 leaves.

©2000, Encyclopædia Britannica, Inc.

ESTONIA

Scale 1: 4,840,000

| 0 | 20 | 40 mi |
| 0 | 30 | 60 km |

Ethnic Composition

Estonian 63.9%
Russian 29%
Other 7.1%

Official name: Republic of Estonia.
Head of government: Prime Minister.
Official language: Estonian.
Monetary unit: kroon.
Area: 17,462 sq mi (45,227 sq km).
Population (1996): 1,475,000.
GNP per capita (1994): U.S.$2,820.
Principal exports (1995): food products
16.4%; textiles and clothing 16.1%;
wood, wood products, and paper
products 13.4%; nonelectrical and
electrical machinery 13.1% *to:* Finland
21.3%; Russia 17.7%; Sweden 10.7%.

In the late 19th century an Estonian students' association
adopted the blue-black-white flag. Blue was said to stand for
the sky, black for the soil, and white for aspirations to freedom and homeland. The flag was officially recognized on July
4, 1920. It was replaced under Soviet rule, and readopted on
Oct. 20, 1988.

Ethiopia **57**

Official name: Federal Democratic Republic of Ethiopia.
Head of government: Prime Minister.
Official language: none.
Monetary unit: birr.
Area: 437,794 sq mi (1,133,882 sq km).
Population (1996): 56,713,000.
GNP per capita (1994): U.S.$130.
Principal exports (1992): coffee 67.1%, hides 16.8%, petroleum products 3.8% *to* (1993): Germany 19.7%; Japan 19.0%; Djibouti 12.1%; Saudi Arabia 9.9%; U.S. 9.1%; Italy 7.6%.

ETHIOPIA

Scale 1: 25,422,000

| 0 | 100 | 200 mi |
| 0 | 200 | 400 km |

Language Composition

Oromo 31%

Other 39%

Amharic 30%

The flag is red (for sacrifice), green (for labor, development, and fertility), and yellow (for hope, justice, and equality). Tricolor pennants were used prior to the official flag of Oct. 6, 1897, and a tricolor was flown by antigovernment forces in 1991. On Feb. 6, 1996, the disk (for peace) and star (for unity and the future) were added.

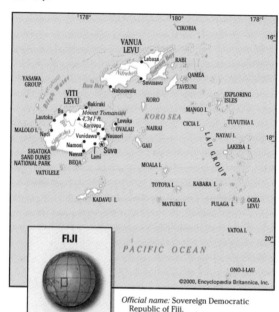

CIKOBIA

VANUA
LEVU

Labasa • RABI

Ndreketi QAMEA

Savusavu • TAVEUNI
Nabouwalu •

Buca Bay

KORO EXPLORING
ISLES

YASAWA
GROUP

MANGO I.

KORO SEA

CICIA I. TUVUTHA I.

Rakiraki NAIRAI

VITI
LEVU

Ba • LEVUKA NAYAU I.

Lautoka *Mount Tomaniivi*
4,341 ft. OVALAU LAKEBA I.

Korovou •

MALOLO I. Nadi Vunidawa • Nausori GAU LAU GROUP

Namosi • ⊛ Suva

Navua • Lami

SIGATOKA BEQA MOALA I.

SAND DUNES
NATIONAL PARK

VATULELE KABARA I.

TOTOYA I. OGEA
LEVU

KADAVU I. MATUKU I. FULAGA I.

VATOA I.

PACIFIC OCEAN

ONO-I-LAU

©2000, Encyclopædia Britannica, Inc.

FIJI

Scale 1: 8,153,000

0   40   80 mi
0   60   120 km

Ethnic Composition

Indian
43.5%

Fijian
50.7%   Other
5.8%

Official name: Sovereign Democratic
Republic of Fiji.
Head of government: Prime Minister.
Official language: English.
Monetary unit: Fiji dollar.
Area: 7,055 sq mi (18,272 sq km).
Population (1996): 802,000.
GNP per capita (1994): U.S.$2,320.
Principal exports (1995): sugar 36.1%;
clothing 24.2%; fish 8.3%; gold 7.8%;
timber 6.9%; molasses 2.8%; coconut
oil 0.5% *to:* Australia 26.0%; United
Kingdom 22.9%; United States 13.0%.

The national flag, introduced on Oct. 10, 1970, is a modified
version of Fiji's colonial flag. It includes the Union Jack on a
light blue field. The shield has the red cross of St. George on
a white background, below a yellow lion, which holds a cocoa
pod. Local symbols (sugar cane, coconuts, bananas, and the
Fiji dove) are also shown.

Official name: Republic of Finland.
Head of government: Prime Minister.
Official languages: Finnish; Swedish.
Monetary unit: markka.
Area: 130,559 sq mi (338,145 sq km).
Population (1996): 5,132,000.
GNP per capita (1994): U.S.$18,850.
Principal exports (1995): metal products
   and machinery 39.1%; paper, paper
   products, and publishing 27.4%;
   chemicals and chemical products 9.3%
   to: Germany 13.4%; United Kingdom
   10.4%; Sweden 10.1%.

FINLAND

Scale 1 : 18,656,000

| 0 | 25 | 50 | 150 mi |

| 0 | 120 | 240 km |

Religious Affiliation

Nonreligious 12%

Other 2.1%

Evangelical Lutheran 85.9%

In 1862, while Finland was under Russian control, a flag was proposed that would have a white background for the snows of Finland and blue for its lakes. The blue was in the form of a "Nordic cross" similar to those used by other Scandinavian countries. The flag was officially adopted by the newly independent country on May 29, 1918.

FRANCE

Scale 1: 18,620,000

| 0 | 80 | 160 mi |
| 0 | 80 | 160 | 240 km |

Religious Affiliation

Roman Catholic 76.4%

Other 23.6%

Official name: French Republic.
Head of government: Prime Minister.
Official language: French.
Monetary unit: franc.
Area: 210,026 sq mi (543,965 sq km).
Population (1996): 58,392,000.
GNP per capita (1994): U.S.$22,760.
Principal exports (1995): machinery and
  transport equipment 42.6%; chemical
  products 8.4%; plastics 3.2%;
  to: Germany 17.7%; Italy 9.5%;
  Belgium-Luxembourg 8.6%; U.K. 7.6%;
  U.S. 7.4%; Spain 6.2%.

From 1789 blue and red, the traditional colors of Paris, were
included in flags with Bourbon royal white. In 1794 the tricol-
or was made official. It embodied liberty, equality, fraternity,
democracy, secularism, and modernization, but there is no
symbolism attached to the individual colors. It has been the
sole national flag since March 5, 1848.

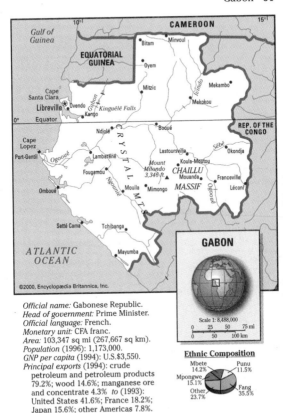

Official name: Gabonese Republic.
Head of government: Prime Minister.
Official language: French.
Monetary unit: CFA franc.
Area: 103,347 sq mi (267,667 sq km).
Population (1996): 1,173,000.
GNP per capita (1994): U.S.$3,550.
Principal exports (1994): crude
petroleum and petroleum products
79.2%; wood 14.6%; manganese ore
and concentrate 4.3% *to* (1993):
United States 41.6%; France 18.2%;
Japan 15.6%; other Americas 7.8%.

GABON

Scale 1: 8,488,000

Ethnic Composition

Mbete 14.2%
Punu 11.5%
Mpongwe 15.1%
Other 23.7%
Fang 35.5%

After proclaiming independence from France, Gabon adopted its national flag on Aug. 9, 1960. The central yellow stripe is for the Equator, which runs through the country. Green stands for the tropical forests that are one of Gabon's most important resources. Blue represents its extensive coast along the South Atlantic Ocean.

©2000, Encyclopædia Britannica, Inc.

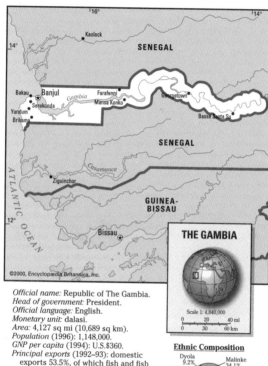

©2000, Encyclopædia Britannica, Inc.

THE GAMBIA

Scale 1: 4,840,000

| 0 | 20 | 40 mi |
| 0 | 30 | 60 km |

Official name: Republic of The Gambia.
Head of government: President.
Official language: English.
Monetary unit: dalasi.
Area: 4,127 sq mi (10,689 sq km).
Population (1996): 1,148,000.
GNP per capita (1994): U.S.$360.
Principal exports (1992–93): domestic
exports 53.5%, of which fish and fish
preparations 4.4%; reexports 46.5%
to (1993): Belgium-Luxembourg 50.9%;
Japan 22.0%; Guinea 5.7%; United
Kingdom 5.0%; Hong Kong 2.5%.

Ethnic Composition

Dyola 9.2%
Malinke 34.1%
Wolof 12.6%
Fulani 16.2%
Other 27.9%

The Gambia achieved independence from Britain on Feb. 18, 1965, under the current flag. The center stripe is blue to symbolize the Gambia River. The red stripe is for the sun and the equator. The green stripe is for agricultural produce (peanuts, grains, and citrus fruits), while the white stripes are said to stand for peace and unity.

Official name: Republic of Georgia.
Head of government: President.
Official language: Georgian.
Monetary unit: lari.
Area: 26,831 sq mi (69,493 sq km).
Population (1996): 5,360,625.
GNP per capita (1993): U.S.$560.
Principal exports (1994): food products
30.0%; ferrous metals 29.7%; textiles
7.0%; chemicals 5.0% *to:* Russia 46.0%;
Turkey 17.6%; Turkmenistan 8.8%;
Kazakstan 6.5%; Azerbaijan 5.8%.

Ethnic Composition

Georgian 70.1%
Other 15.5%
Armenian 8.1%
Russian 6.3%

According to tradition, Queen Tamara (1184–1213) and other
rulers used white, black, and cherry red for their flags. The
current flag was first hoisted on March 25, 1917. It was
replaced under Soviet rule, but readopted on Nov. 14, 1990.
Cherry red is the national color, black stands for past
tragedies, and white is for hope.

Official name: Federal Republic of Germany.
Head of government: Chancellor.
Official language: German.
Monetary unit: Deutsche Mark.
Area: 137,830 sq mi (356,978 sq km).
Population (1996): 81,891,000.
GNP per capita (1994): U.S.$25,580.
Principal exports (1995): machinery and transport equipment 49.6%; chemicals and chemical products 13.5%;
to: France 11.6%; U.K. 8.0%; Italy 7.5%; U.S. 7.5%; The Netherlands 7.3%.

GERMANY

Scale 1: 15,019,000

| 0 | 40 | 80 | 120 mi |

| 0 | 60 | 120 | 180 km |

Age Breakdown

60 and over 20.7%
15–59 63%
Under 15 16.3%

In the early 19th century German nationalists displayed black, gold, and red on their uniforms and tricolor flags. The current flag was used officially from 1848 to 1852 and re-adopted by West Germany on May 9, 1949. East Germany flew a similar flag but only the flag of West Germany was maintained upon reunification in 1990.

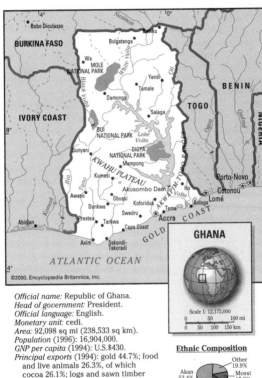

©2000, Encyclopædia Britannica, Inc.

Official name: Republic of Ghana.
Head of government: President.
Official language: English.
Monetary unit: cedi.
Area: 92,098 sq mi (238,533 sq km).
Population (1996): 16,904,000.
GNP per capita (1994): U.S.$430.
Principal exports (1994): gold 44.7%; food
and live animals 26.3%, of which
cocoa 26.1%; logs and sawn timber
13.5%; electricity 4.6%; diamonds 1.7%
to: United Kingdom 15.5%; Italy 7.9%;
Japan 6.7%; United States 6.6%.

GHANA

Scale 1: 12,173,000

0   50   100 mi
0   50   100   150 km

Ethnic Composition

Akan 52.4%
Ewe 11.9%
Mossi 15.8%
Other 19.9%

On March 6, 1957, independence from Britain was granted
and a flag, based on the red-white-green tricolor of a nationalist organization, was hoisted. A black "lodestar of African
freedom" was added and the white stripe was changed to yellow, symbolizing wealth. Green is for forests and farms, red
for the independence struggle.

GREECE

Scale 1: 11,646,000

0 ___ 50 ___ 100 mi
0 ___ 80 ___ 160 km

Age Breakdown

Under 15
17.4%

15–59
61.3%

60 and over
21.3%

Official name: Hellenic Republic.
Head of government: Prime Minister.
Official language: Greek.
Monetary unit: drachma.
Area: 50,949 sq mi (131,957 sq km).
Population (1996): 10,493,000.
GNP per capita (1994): U.S.$7,710.
Principal exports (1994): food, beverages,
and tobacco 28.9%, of which olives
and olive oil 3.7%, tobacco 2.3%;
textiles 23.8%; petroleum products
11.6% *to:* Germany 25.9%; U.S. 17.2%;
Italy 11.3%; France 6.6%; U.K. 6.4%.

In March 1822, during the revolt against Ottoman rule, the
first Greek national flags were adopted; the most recent revi-
sion to the flag was made on Dec. 22, 1978. The colors symbolize Greek Orthodoxy while the cross stands for "the wis-
dom of God, freedom and country." The stripes are for the
battle cry for independence: "Freedom or Death."

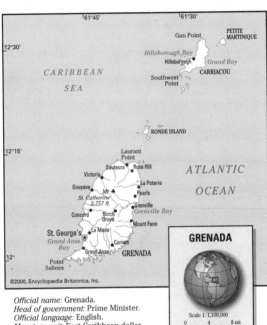

CARIBBEAN SEA

ATLANTIC OCEAN

PETITE MARTINIQUE

Gun Point
Hillsborough Bay
Hillsborough *Grand Bay*
Southwest Point CARRIACOU

RONDE ISLAND

Laurant Point
Sauteurs • Rose Hill
Victoria
Gouyave • La Poterie
Mt. St. Catherine
2,757 ft. • Pearls
Concord • Grenville
Birch *Grenville Bay*
Grove
St. George's • Mount Fann
Grand Anse Bay La Mode
Corinth
Grand Anse
Point Salines GRENADA

©2000, Encyclopædia Britannica, Inc.

12°30'
12°15'
12°
61°45'
61°30'

Official name: Grenada.
Head of government: Prime Minister.
Official language: English.
Monetary unit: East Caribbean dollar.
Area: 133 sq mi (344 sq km).
Population (1996): 97,900.
GNP per capita (1994): U.S.$2,620.
Principal exports (1995): domestic exports 89.4%, of which fish 15.7%, cocoa beans 15.3%, nutmeg 14.4%, bananas 8.8%, clothing 6.0%; reexports 10.6% *to (1994):* United States 28%; Venezuela 14%; United Kingdom 14%.

GRENADA

Scale 1: 1,100,000

0   6   12 km
0   8 mi

Religious Affiliation

Roman Catholic 53.1%

Protestant 38.1%

Other 8.8%

Grenada's flag was officially hoisted on Feb. 3, 1974. Its background is green for vegetation and yellow for the sun, and its red border is symbolic of harmony and unity. The seven stars are for the original administrative subdivisions of Grenada. Nutmeg, a crop for which the "Isle of Spice" is internationally known, is represented as well.

Official name: Republic of Guatemala.
Head of government: President.
Official language: Spanish.
Monetary unit: quetzal.
Area: 42,042 sq mi (108,889 sq km).
Population (1996): 10,928,000.
GNP per capita (1994): U.S.$1,190.
Principal exports (1995): coffee 27.9%;
 sugar 12.3%; bananas 7.2%; vegetable
 seeds 3.2%; legumes 3.0% *to:* United
 States 31.0%; El Salvador 13.9%;
 Honduras 6.4%; Germany 5.8%; Costa
 Rica 5.2%; Nicaragua 3.7%.

Language Composition

Mayan
languages
35%

Spanish
64.7%

Garifuna
0.3%

The flag was introduced in 1871. It has blue and white stripes
(colors of the former United Provinces of Central America)
and a coat of arms with the quetzal (the national bird), a
scroll, a wreath, and crossed rifles and sabres. Different
artistic variations have been used but on Sept. 12, 1968, the
present pattern was established.

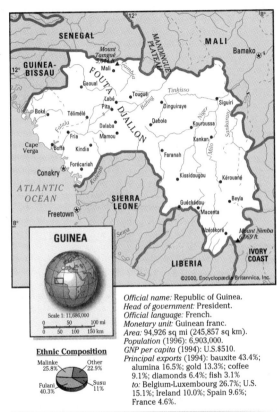

SENEGAL
MALI
Bamako
GUINEA-BISSAU
Mount Tamgué 5,044 ft.
FOUTA DJALLON
MANDINGUE PLATEAU
Gaoual
Tinkisso
Labé
Touguè
Mali
Pita
Dinguiraye
Siguiri
Boké
Télimélé
Dalaba
Dabola
Kouroussa
Niger
Fria
Mamou
Kankan
Boffa
Kindia
Faranah
Milo
Cape Verga
Forécariah
Kissidougou
Kérouané
Beyla
Conakry
ATLANTIC OCEAN
SIERRA LEONE
Guéckédou
Macenta
Freetown
Nzérékoré
Mount Nimba 6,069 ft.
LIBERIA
IVORY COAST

©2000, Encyclopædia Britannica, Inc.

GUINEA

Scale 1: 11,686,000

0   50   100 mi
0   50 100 150 km

Ethnic Composition

Malinke 25.8%
Other 22.9%
Fulani 40.3%
Susu 11%

Official name: Republic of Guinea.
Head of government: President.
Official language: French.
Monetary unit: Guinean franc.
Area: 94,926 sq mi (245,857 sq km).
Population (1996): 6,903,000.
GNP per capita (1994): U.S.$510.
Principal exports (1994): bauxite 43.4%;
  alumina 16.5%; gold 13.3%; coffee
  9.1%; diamonds 6.4%; fish 3.1%
  to: Belgium-Luxembourg 26.7%; U.S.
  15.1%; Ireland 10.0%; Spain 9.6%;
  France 4.6%.

The flag was adopted on Nov. 12, 1958, one month after independence from France. Its simple design was influenced by the French tricolor. The red is said to be a symbol of sacrifice and labor, while the yellow is for mineral wealth, the tropical sun, and justice. Green symbolizes agricultural wealth and the solidarity of the people.

Official name: Republic of Guinea-Bissau.
Head of government: Prime Minister.
Official language: Portuguese.
Monetary unit: Guinea-Bissau peso.
Area: 13,948 sq mi (36,125 sq km).
Population (1996): 1,096,000.
GNP per capita (1994): U.S.$240.
Principal exports (1991): cashews 57.7%;
   frozen fish, including shrimp 10.8%;
   lumber 5.9% *to:* India 40.3%; Spain
   37.7%; Portugal 5.2%; Italy 3.9%;
   Thailand 3.9%; Côte d'Ivoire
   3.9%; Japan 2.6%.

GUINEA-BISSAU

Scale 1: 4,928,000

0   15   35   45 mi

0   30   60 km

Ethnic Composition

Balante 27.2%
Fulani 22.9%
Pepel 10%
Other 17.1%
Mandyako 10.6%
Malinke 12.2%

The flag has been used since the declaration of independence
from Portugal on Sept. 24, 1973. The black star on the red
stripe was for African Party leadership, the people, and their
will to live in dignity, freedom, and peace. Yellow was for the
harvest and other rewards of work, and green was for the
nation's vast jungles and agricultural lands.

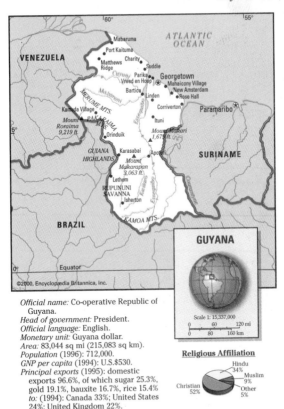

Official name: Co-operative Republic of
Guyana.
Head of government: President.
Official language: English.
Monetary unit: Guyana dollar.
Area: 83,044 sq mi (215,083 sq km).
Population (1996): 712,000.
GNP per capita (1994): U.S.$530.
Principal exports (1995): domestic
exports 96.6%, of which sugar 25.3%,
gold 19.1%, bauxite 16.7%, rice 15.4%
to: (1994): Canada 33%; United States
24%; United Kingdom 22%.

GUYANA

Scale 1: 15,337,000

| 0 | 60 | 120 mi |
| 0 | 80 | 160 km |

Religious Affiliation

Hindu
34%

Muslim
9%

Christian
52%

Other
5%

Upon independence from Britain on May 26, 1966, the flag
was first hoisted. The green stands for jungles and fields,
white suggests the rivers which are the basis for the Indian
word guiana ("land of waters"), red is for zeal and sacrifice in
nation-building, and black is for perseverance. The flag is
nicknamed "The Golden Arrowhead."

CUBA
ATLANTIC OCEAN
Windward Passage
TORTUGA
Port-de-Paix Saint-Louis du Nord
Môle Saint-Nicolas Jean Rabel Limbé Cap Haïtien Fort Liberté
Trou du Nord
Ouanaminthe
Golfe de la Gonâve
Gonaïves CENTRAL PLATEAU Saint-Michel de l'Atalaye
Desdunes
Petite Rivière de l'Artibonite NOIRES MTS. Hinche
ÎLE DE LA GONÂVE
Saint-Marc Thomassique
Verrettes Artibonite
Mirebalais Péligre Reservoir
Lake Saumâtre Lascahobas
Jérémie GRANDE CAYEMITE Roseaux Port-au-Prince
Anse-d'Hainault
MASSIF DE LA HOTTE Miragoâne Léogâne Pétionville
Macaya Peak MACAYA PEAK Petit Goâve Grand Goâve
7,698 ft. NATIONAL PARK
Jamaica Channel
Les Cayes Jacmel Mount La Selle 8,793 ft.
Gravois Point ÎLE À VACHE
DOMINICAN REPUBLIC
CARIBBEAN SEA
©2000, Encyclopædia Britannica, Inc.

HAITI

Scale 1: 4,550,000

0   20   40 mi
0   30   60 km

Official name: Republic of Haiti.
Head of government: Prime Minister.
Official languages: Haitian Creole;
French.
Monetary unit: gourde.
Area: 10,695 sq mi (27,700 sq km).
Population (1996): 6,732,000.
GNP per capita (1994): U.S.$220.
Principal exports (1993–94): local
manufactures 68.5%; coffee 9.0%;
handicrafts 7.4%; essential oils 4.9%;
sisal and twine 2.7% *to* (1994): United
States 71%; France 7%; Germany 6%.

Religious Affiliation

Protestant 15.8%
Other 3.9%
Roman Catholic 80.3%

After the French Revolution of 1789 Haiti underwent a slave revolt, but the French tricolor continued in use until 1803. The new blue-red flag represented the black and mulatto populations only. A black-red flag was used by various dictators, including François "Papa Doc" Duvalier and his son, but on Feb. 25, 1986, the old flag was reestablished.

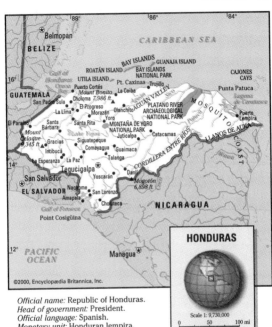

©2000, Encyclopædia Britannica, Inc.

Official name: Republic of Honduras.
Head of government: President.
Official language: Spanish.
Monetary unit: Honduran lempira.
Area: 43,277 sq mi (112,088 sq km).
Population (1996): 5,666,000.
GNP per capita (1994): U.S.$580.
Principal exports (1994): coffee 21.3%;
   bananas 18.6%; shrimp and lobsters
   17.0%; frozen meats 4.6%; melons
   2.9%; pineapples 2.4% *to:* United
   States 54.0%; Germany 7.2%; Belgium
   5.0%; United Kingdom 4.6%.

HONDURAS

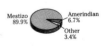

Scale 1: 9,730,000

| 0 | 50 | 100 mi |
| 0 | 80 | 160 km |

Ethnic Composition

Mestizo 89.9%   Amerindian 6.7%   Other 3.4%

Since Feb. 16, 1866, the Honduran flag has retained the blue-white-blue design of the flag of the former United Provinces of Central America, but with five central stars symbolizing the states of Honduras, El Salvador, Nicaragua, Costa Rica, and Guatemala. The flag design has often been associated with Central American reunification attempts.

Official name: Republic of Hungary.
Head of government: Prime Minister.
Official language: Hungarian.
Monetary unit: forint.
Area: 35,919 sq mi (93,030 sq km).
Population (1996): 10,201,000.
GNP per capita (1994): U.S.$3,840.
Principal exports (1995): intermediate
industrial goods 39.4%; industrial
consumer goods 24.9%; food and live
animals 22.0%; machinery and trans-
port equipment 11.3% *to:* Germany
28.6%; Austria 10.1%; Italy 8.5%.

Religious Affiliation

Protestant 25.1%
Other 7.1%
Roman Catholic 67.8%

The colors of the Hungarian flag were mentioned in a 1608
coronation ceremony, but they may have been used since the
13th century. The tricolor was adopted on Oct. 12, 1957, after
the abortive revolution of 1956. The white is said to symbolize Hungary's rivers, the green its mountains, and the red the
blood shed in its many battles.

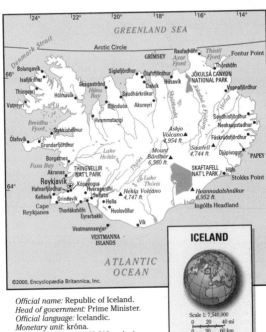

©2000, Encyclopædia Britannica, Inc.

Official name: Republic of Iceland.
Head of government: Prime Minister.
Official language: Icelandic.
Monetary unit: króna.
Area: 39,699 sq mi (102,819 sq km).
Population (1996): 270,000.
GNP per capita (1995): U.S.$25,680.
Principal exports (1995): marine products 71.9%, of which frozen fish 30.9%; aluminum 10.6%; ferrosilicon 2.8% *to:* United Kingdom 19.3%; Germany 13.7%; United States 12.3%; Japan 11.3%; Denmark 7.8%; France 6.8%.

ICELAND

Scale 1: 7,540,000

| 0 | 20 | 40 mi |
| 0 | 30 | 60 km |

Age Breakdown

Under 15
24.6%

15–59
60.4%

60 and over
15%

Approval for an Icelandic flag was given by the king of Denmark on June 19, 1915; it became a national flag on Dec. 1, 1918, when the separate kingdom of Iceland was proclaimed. The flag was retained upon the creation of a republic on June 17, 1944. The design has a typical "Scandinavian cross".

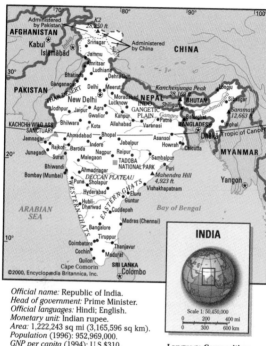

Official name: Republic of India.
Head of government: Prime Minister.
Official languages: Hindi; English.
Monetary unit: Indian rupee.
Area: 1,222,243 sq mi (3,165,596 sq km).
Population (1996): 952,969,000.
GNP per capita (1994): U.S.$310.
Principal exports (1994): cut and
polished diamonds and jewelry 17.1%;
machinery, transport equipment,
metal products, iron and steel, and
electronic components 13.2% *to:* U.S.
19.1%; Japan 7.7%; Germany 6.6%.

Language Composition

Other 38%
Telugu 8%
Bengali 7.6%
Marathi 7.4%
Hindi 39%

Earlier versions of the flag were used from the 1920s, but the
current flag was hoisted officially on July 22, 1947. The
orange was said to stand for courage and sacrifice, white for
peace and truth, and green for faith and chivalry. The blue
wheel is a chakra, associated with Emperor Asoka's attempts
to unite India in the 3rd century BC.

Official name: Republic of Indonesia.
Head of government: President.
Official language: Bahasa Indonesia.
Monetary unit: Indonesian rupiah.
Area: 741,052 sq mi (1,919,317 sq km).
Population (1996): 198,189,000.
GNP per capita (1994): U.S.$880.
Principal exports (1995): crude
  petroleum 11.3%; natural gas 8.9%;
  plywood 7.6%; garments 7.5%;
  preparation rubber 4.8% *to:* Japan
  27.1%; U.S. 13.9%; Singapore 8.3%;
  Hong Kong 3.6%.

Language Composition

Indonesian
(Malay)
12.1%

Javanese
39.4%

Sundanese
15.8%

Other
32.7%

Indonesia's red and white flag was associated with the
Majapahit empire which existed from the 13th to the 16th
century. It was adopted on Aug. 17, 1945, and it remained
after Indonesia won its independence from The Netherlands
in 1949. Red is for courage and white for honesty. The flag is
identical, except in dimensions, to the flag of Monaco.

IRAN

Scale 1 : 25,935,000

0   100   200 mi

0   100   200   300 km

Ethnic Composition

Other 28.5%

Azerbaijani 16.8%

Persian 45.6%

Kurd 9.1%

Official name: Islamic Republic of Iran.
Head of government: President.
Official language: Farsi (Persian).
Monetary unit: rial.
Area: 636,293 sq mi (1,648,000 sq km).
Population (1996): 62,231,000.
GNP per capita (1994): U.S.$2,680.
Principal exports (1994): petroleum and
  natural gas 76.6%; carpets 8.8%; fresh
  and dried fruit 3.0%; iron and steel
  1.5%. *to (1994):* Japan 13.0%; South
  Korea 6.0%; France 5.0%; Italy 5.0%;
  The Netherlands 5.0%; Greece 4.0%.

The tricolor flag was recognized in 1906 but altered after the
revolution of 1979. Along the central stripe are the Arabic
words Allahu akbar ("God is great"), repeated 22 times. The
coat of arms can be read as a rendition of the word Allah, as
a globe, or as two crescents. The green is for Islam, white is
for peace, and red is for valor.

Ethnic Composition

Arab 77.1%   Kurd 19%   Other 3.9%

Official name: Republic of Iraq.
Head of government: President.
Official language: Arabic.
Monetary unit: Iraqi dinar.
Area: 167,975 sq mi (435,052 sq km).
Population (1996): 21,422,000.
GNP per capita (1993): U.S.$1,250.
Principal exports (1994): mostly crude petroleum and petroleum products *to* (1993): Jordan 86.0%; Turkey 7.0%; Greece 5.0%.

Adopted on July 30, 1963, the Iraqi flag is based on the liberation flag first flown in Egypt in 1952. The stars express a desire to unite with Egypt and Syria. Red is for the willingness to shed blood, green is for Arab lands, black is for past suffering, and white is for purity. On Jan. 14, 1991, the Arabic inscription "God is Great" was added.

©2000, Encyclopædia Britannica, Inc.

Official name: Ireland.
Head of government: Prime Minister.
Official languages: Irish; English.
Monetary unit: Irish pound.
Area: 27,137 sq mi (70,285 sq km).
Population (1996): 3,599,000.
GNP per capita (1994): U.S.$13,630.
Principal exports (1994): machinery and
  transport equipment 30.1%; chemical
  products 20.8%; food 18.6%;
  manufactured goods 5.5% *to:* U.K.
  24.4%; Germany 14.1%; France 9.2%;
  U.S. 8.4%.

IRELAND

Scale 1: 6,725,000

0   25   50 mi
0   40   80 km

Age Breakdown

Under 15
26.7%

15–59
58.1%

60 and over
15.2%

In the 19th century various tricolor flags and ribbons became
symbolic of Irish opposition to British rule. Many of them
included the colors green (for the Catholics), orange (for the
Protestants), and white (for the peace between the two
groups). The tricolor in its modern form was recognized by
the constitution on Dec. 29, 1937.

ISRAEL

Scale 1: 6,301,000

| 0 | 25 | 50 mi |
| 0 | 40 | 80 km |

Official name: State of Israel.
Head of government: Prime Minister.
Official languages: Hebrew; Arabic.
Monetary unit: New (Israeli) sheqel.
Area: 7,846 sq mi (20,320 sq km).
Population (1996): 5,481,000.
GNP per capita (1994): U.S.$14,410.
Principal exports (1995): machinery and
transport equipment 28.3%; diamonds
25.8%; chemicals 12.4%; textiles and
leather apparel 5.4% *to:* U.S. 30.1%;
Japan 6.9%; U.K. 6.1%; Germany 5.5%;
Belgium 5.4%; Hong Kong 5.1%.

Religious Affiliation

Jewish
81%

Muslim
14.5%

Other
4.5%

Symbolic of the traditional *tallit,* or Jewish prayer shawl, and
including the Star of David, the flag was used from the late
19th century. It was raised when Israel proclaimed independence on May 14, 1948, and the banner was legally recognized on Nov. 12, 1948. A dark blue was also substituted for
the traditional lighter shade of blue.

ITALY

Scale 1: 18,825,000

| 0 | 50 | 100 | 150 mi |
| 0 | 100 | | 200 km |

Age Breakdown

Under 15
16.4%

15–59
63%

60 and over
20.6%

©2000, Encyclopædia Britannica, Inc.

Official name: Italian Republic.
Head of government: Prime Minister.
Official language: Italian.
Monetary unit: lira.
Area: 116,324 sq mi (301,277 sq km).
Population (1996): 57,500,000.
GNP per capita (1994): U.S.$19,270.
Principal exports (1994): machinery and
transport equipment 41.1%; chemicals
10.1%; textiles 8.4%; wearing apparel
7.7%; metal and processed metal 6.7%
to: Germany 19.0%; France 13.1%; U.S.
7.8%; U.K. 6.5%.

The first Italian national flag was adopted on Feb. 25, 1797, by
the Cispadane Republic. Its stripes were vertically positioned
on May 11, 1798, and thereafter it was honored by all Italian
nationalists. The design was guaranteed by a decree (March
23, 1848) of King Charles Albert of Sardinia, ordering troops
to carry the flag into battle.

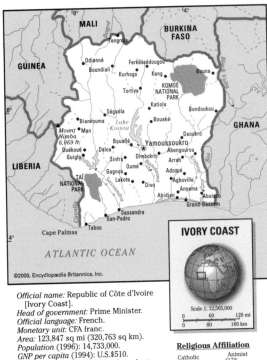

Official name: Republic of Côte d'Ivoire [Ivory Coast].
Head of government: Prime Minister.
Official language: French.
Monetary unit: CFA franc.
Area: 123,847 sq mi (320,763 sq km).
Population (1996): 14,733,000.
GNP per capita (1994): U.S.$510.
Principal exports (1994): food products 50.4%, of which cocoa beans and products 32.3%; wood and wood products 13.9%; petroleum products 9.6% *to:* France 16.1%; Germany 9.8%.

Religious Affiliation

Catholic 20.8%
Animist 17%
Atheist 13.4%
Other 10.1%
Muslim 38.7%

Adopted on Aug. 7, 1959, the flag of the former French colony has three stripes corresponding to the national motto (Unity, Discipline, Labor). The orange is for growth, the white is for peace emerging from purity and unity, and the green is for hope and the future. Unofficially the green is for forests and the orange is for savannas.

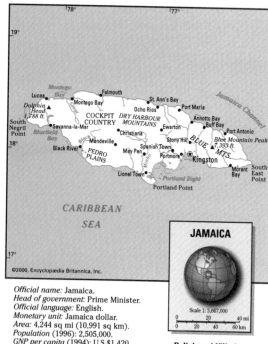

Official name: Jamaica.
Head of government: Prime Minister.
Official language: English.
Monetary unit: Jamaica dollar.
Area: 4,244 sq mi (10,991 sq km).
Population (1996): 2,505,000.
GNP per capita (1994): U.S.$1,420.
Principal exports (1995): alumina 44.2%;
raw sugar 6.7%; bauxite 5.0%; bananas
3.4%; coffee 2.0%; rum 1.6% *to (1994):*
United States 43.9%; United Kingdom
11.4%; Canada 9.5%; Norway 5.9%;
France 4.3%; Ghana 3.2%.

JAMAICA

Scale 1: 3,667,000

Religious Affiliation

Nonreligious 17%
Other 17%
Roman Catholic 5%
Rastafarian 5%
Protestant 56%

The flag was designed prior to independence from Britain
(Aug. 6, 1962). The black color stood for hardships faced by
the nation, green for agriculture and hope, and yellow for the
natural wealth of Jamaica. This was summed up in the
phrase, "Hardships there are, but the land is green and the
sun shineth."

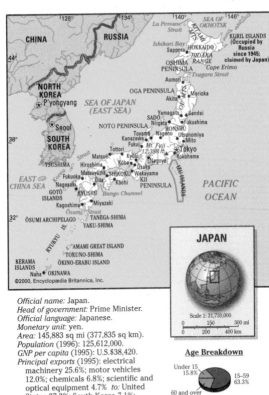

JAPAN

Scale 1: 31,730,000

| 0 | 150 | 300 mi |

| 0 | 200 | 400 km |

Official name: Japan.
Head of government: Prime Minister.
Official language: Japanese.
Monetary unit: yen.
Area: 145,883 sq mi (377,835 sq km).
Population (1996): 125,612,000.
GNP per capita (1995): U.S.$38,420.
Principal exports (1995): electrical
machinery 25.6%; motor vehicles
12.0%; chemicals 6.8%; scientific and
optical equipment 4.7% *to:* United
States 27.3%; South Korea 7.1%;
Taiwan 6.5%; Hong Kong 6.3%.

Age Breakdown

Under 15
15.8%

15–59
63.3%

60 and over
20.9%

The flag features a red sun on a cool white background.
Traditionally, the sun goddess founded Japan in the 7th century BC and gave birth to its first emperor, Jimmu. Even today
the emperor is known as the "Son of the Sun" and the popular
name for the country is "Land of the Rising Sun." The current
flag design was adopted on Aug. 5, 1854.

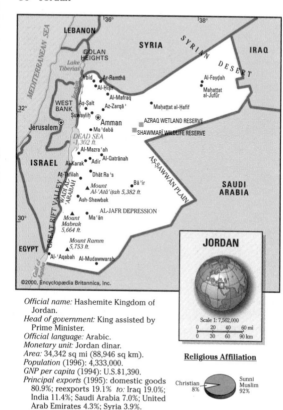

Official name: Hashemite Kingdom of Jordan.
Head of government: King assisted by Prime Minister.
Official language: Arabic.
Monetary unit: Jordan dinar.
Area: 34,342 sq mi (88,946 sq km).
Population (1996): 4,333,000.
GNP per capita (1994): U.S.$1,390.
Principal exports (1995): domestic goods 80.9%; reexports 19.1% *to:* Iraq 19.0%; India 11.4%; Saudi Arabia 7.0%; United Arab Emirates 4.3%; Syria 3.9%.

JORDAN

Scale 1: 7,562,000

0 20 40 60 mi
0 30 60 90 km

Religious Affiliation

Christian 8%

Sunni Muslim 92%

In 1917 Husayn ibn Ali raised the Arab Revolt flag. With the addition of a white seven-pointed star, this flag was adopted by Transjordan on April 16, 1928, and retained upon the independence of Jordan on March 22, 1946. White is for purity, black for struggle and suffering, red for bloodshed, and green for Arab lands.

Official name: Republic of Kazakstan.
Head of government: President assisted by Prime Minister.
Official language: Kazak.
Monetary unit: tenge.
Area: 1,052,100 sq mi (2,724,900 sq km).
Population (1996): 16,677,000.
GNP per capita (1994): U.S.$1,110.
Principal exports (1995): mainly energy-related commodities; base metals, ferrous metals, and chrome ores; chemical products *to:* Russia 64.1%; China 7.4%; Ukraine 6.8%; Italy 3.1%.

Ethnic Composition

Russian 34.8%
Other 14.3%
Kazak 46%
Ukrainian 4.9%

The flag was adopted in June 1992. Light blue is a traditional color of the nomads of Central Asia; it symbolizes peace and well-being. The golden sun and eagle represent freedom and the high ideals of the Kazaks. Along the edge is a band of traditional Kazak ornamentation; the band was originally in red but is now in golden yellow.

KENYA

Scale 1: 17,833,000

0   50   100   150 mi
0   100   200 km

Ethnic Composition

Kamba 9.8%
Kalenjin 9.8%
Luo 10.6%
Luhya 12.4%
Kikuyu 17.7%
Other 39.7%

Official name: Republic of Kenya.
Head of government: President.
Official languages: Swahili; English.
Monetary unit: Kenya shilling.
Area: 224,961 sq mi (582,646 sq km).
Population (1996): 29,137,000.
GNP per capita (1994): U.S.$260.
Principal exports (1994): tea 20.3%;
coffee 15.7%; fruits and vegetables
8.6%; petroleum products 4.4%;
cement 2.0%; hides and skins 2.0%;
to: Uganda 12.7%; United Kingdom
11.6%; Tanzania 10.6%; Germany 7.8%.

Upon independence from Britain (Dec. 12, 1963), the Kenyan
flag became official. It was based on the flag of the Kenya
African National Union. Black is for the people, red for
humanity and the struggle for freedom, green for the fertile
land, and white for unity and peace. The shield and spears
are traditional weapons of the Masai people.

Map

20°   180°   160°

HAWAIIAN IS.
(U.S.)

PACIFIC
OCEAN

MARSHALL
ISLANDS

TARAWA ⊛ Bairiki   KIRITIMATI

0°   Equator   LINE ISLANDS

BANABA   GILBERT IS.

PHOENIX ISLANDS

TUVALU   **KIRIBATI**

Fongafale ⊛   **TOKELAU**
       (N.Z.)   **COOK IS.**

SOLOMON
IS.   **SAMOA**   **AMERICAN**   **(N.Z.)**
         SAMOA
   WALLIS AND   ⊛ **(U.S.)**
VANUATU   **FUTUNA (FR.)**   Apia ⊛

FIJI   **TONGA**

20°   ⊛ Suva

        Nuku'alofa ⊛

©2000, Encyclopædia Britannica, Inc.

KIRIBATI

Scale 1: 66,436,000

0   300   600 mi
0   400   800 km

Official name: Republic of Kiribati.
Head of government: President.
Official language: English.
Monetary unit: Australian Dollar.
Area: 313 sq mi (811 sq km).
Population (1996): 81,800.
GNP per capita (1994): U.S.$730.
Principal exports (1992): domestic
   exports 86.7%, of which copra 66.8%,
   fish and fish preparations 11.3%;
   reexports 13.3% *to:* United States
   28.8%; Germany 20.3%; Sweden 6.8%;
   Denmark 1.7%; Italy 1.7%.

Age Breakdown

Under 15
40.3%

15–59
54%

60 and over
5.7%

Great Britain acquired the Gilbert and Ellice Islands in the
19th century. In 1975 the Gilbert Islands separated from the
Ellice Islands to form Kiribati, and a new flag was adopted
based on the coat of arms granted to the islands in 1937. It
has waves of white and blue, for the Pacific Ocean, as well as
a yellow sun and a local frigate bird.

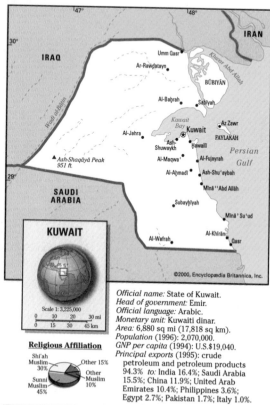

Official name: State of Kuwait.
Head of government: Emir.
Official language: Arabic.
Monetary unit: Kuwaiti dinar.
Area: 6,880 sq mi (17,818 sq km).
Population (1996): 2,070,000.
GNP per capita (1994): U.S.$19,040.
Principal exports (1995): crude
petroleum and petroleum products
94.3% to: India 16.4%; Saudi Arabia
15.5%; China 11.9%; United Arab
Emirates 10.4%; Philippines 3.6%;
Egypt 2.7%; Pakistan 1.7%; Italy 1.0%.

Religious Affiliation

Shi'ah Muslim 30%
Sunni Muslim 45%
Other 15%
Other Muslim 10%

The red flag of Kuwait, in use since World War I, was replaced
by the current flag on Oct. 24, 1961, shortly after independence from Britain. The symbolism is from a poem written
over six centuries ago. The green stands for Arab lands, black
is for battles, white is for the purity of the fighters, and red is
for the blood on their swords.

Official name: Kyrgyz Republic.
Head of government: President assisted by Prime Minister.
Official languages: Kyrgyz; Russian.
Monetary unit: som.
Area: 76,600 sq mi (198,500 sq km).
Population (1996): 4,521,000.
GNP per capita (1994): U.S.$610.
Principal exports (1995): food products 20.2%; light industrial products 20.1%; metals 17.7%; machinery 10.8% *to:* Russia 25.6%; Uzbekistan 17.1%; China 16.8%; Kazakhstan 16.3%.

KYRGYZSTAN

Scale 1: 13,484,000

| 0 | 60 | 120 mi |
| 0 | 80 | 160 km |

Ethnic Composition

Uzbek 12.9%
Other 13.2%
Kyrgyz 52.4%
Russian 21.5%

The Kyrgyz flag replaced a Soviet-era design on March 3, 1992. The red recalls the flag of the national hero Mansas the Noble. The central yellow sun has 40 rays, corresponding to the followers of Mansas and the tribes he united. On the sun is the stylized view of the roof of a yurt, a traditional nomadic home that is now seldom used.

Official name: Lao People's Democratic
Republic.
Head of government: Prime Minister.
Official language: Lao.
Monetary unit: kip.
Area: 91,429 sq mi (236,800 sq km).
Population (1996): 5,023,000.
GNP per capita (1994): U.S.$320.
Principal exports (1995): wood products
25.4%; garments 22.0%; electricity
6.9%; coffee 6.1% *to:* Thailand 40.9%;
Vietnam 25.2%; France 6.8%; United
States 3.2%; Russia 3.2%.

Ethnic Composition

Lao-Lum
67%

Lao-Theung
16.5%

Other
8.7%

Lao-Tai
7.8%

The Lao flag was first used by anticolonialist forces from the
mid-20th century. The white disk honored the Japanese who
had supported the Lao independence movement, but it also
symbolized a bright future. Red was said to stand for the
blood of patriots and blue was for the promise of future prosperity. The flag was adopted on Dec. 2, 1975.

© 2000, Encyclopædia Britannica, Inc.

LATVIA

Scale 1: 6,640,000

0   25   50 mi

0   40   80 km

Ethnic Composition

Latvian 54.8%

Russian 32.8%

Other 8.4%

Belarusian 4%

Official name: Republic of Latvia.
Head of government: Prime Minister.
Official language: Latvian.
Monetary unit: lats.
Area: 24,945 sq mi (64,610 sq km).
Population (1996): 2,516,843.
GNP per capita (1994): U.S.$2,290.
Principal exports (1994): textiles 13.4%;
   food and agricultural products 10.3%;
   forestry products 9.5%; transport
   equipment 6.2% *to:* Russia 28.1%;
   Germany 10.5%; United Kingdom 9.7%;
   Sweden 6.9%; Ukraine 5.9%.

The basic flag design was used by a militia unit in 1279,
according to a 14th century source. Popularized in the 19th
century among anti-Russian nationalists, the flag flew in 1918
and was legally adopted on Jan. 20, 1923. Under Soviet control the flag was suppressed, but it was again legalized in
1988 and flown officially from Feb. 27, 1990.

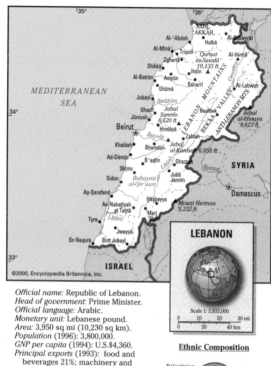

Official name: Republic of Lebanon.
Head of government: Prime Minister.
Official language: Arabic.
Monetary unit: Lebanese pound.
Area: 3,950 sq mi (10,230 sq km).
Population (1996): 3,800,000.
GNP per capita (1994): U.S.$4,360.
Principal exports (1993): food and
  beverages 21%; machinery and
  appliances 18%; textiles 17%; metal
  products 10% to: Saudi Arabia 7.7%;
  Switzerland 6.7%; U.A.E. 6.2%.

LEBANON

Scale 1: 2,833,000

0   10   20   30 mi
0   20   40 km

Ethnic Composition

Palestinian 12%

Other 8%

Lebanese 80%

On Sept. 1, 1920, French-administered Lebanon adopted a flag based on the French tricolor. The current red-white flag was established by the constitution of 1943, which divided power among the Muslim and Christian sects. On the central stripe is a cedar tree, which is a biblical symbol for holiness, peace, and eternity.

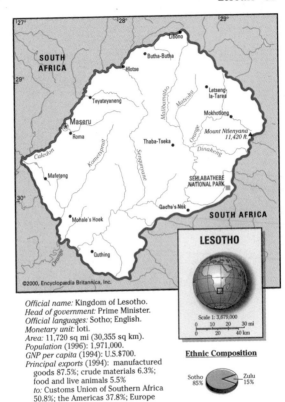

Official name: Kingdom of Lesotho.
Head of government: Prime Minister.
Official languages: Sotho; English.
Monetary unit: loti.
Area: 11,720 sq mi (30,355 sq km).
Population (1996): 1,971,000.
GNP per capita (1994): U.S.$700.
Principal exports (1994): manufactured
  goods 87.5%; crude materials 6.3%;
  food and live animals 5.5%
to: Customs Union of Southern Africa
  50.8%; the Americas 37.8%; Europe
  10.5%; Asia 0.3%.

Ethnic Composition

Sotho 85% Zulu 15%

The flag was hoisted on Jan. 20, 1987, after the military over-
threw the government of prime minister Leabua Jonathan.
It contains a white triangle (for peace) on which are an
animal-skin shield and traditional weapons used in battles
to preserve Sotho independence. The green triangle is for
prosperity, and the blue stripe is for rain.

LIBERIA

Scale 1: 10,783,000

0 — 100 mi
0 — 80 — 160 km

Religious Affiliation

Traditional beliefs and other 18.5%
Muslim 13.8%
Christian 67.7%

Official name: Republic of Liberia.
Head of government: President assisted by Council of State.
Official language: English.
Monetary unit: Liberian dollar.
Area: 38,250 sq mi (99,067 sq km).
Population (1996): 2,110,000.
GNP per capita (1992): U.S.$354.
Principal exports (1988): iron ore 55.1%; rubber 28.0%; logs and timber 8.4%; diamonds 2.1%; gold 1.8% *to* (1995): Belgium-Luxembourg 55.6%; Ukraine 12.1%; Greece 6.4%; Singapore 5.7%.

In the 19th century land was purchased on the African coast by the American Colonization Society, in order to return freed slaves to Africa. On April 9, 1827, a flag based on that of the United States was adopted, featuring a white cross. On Aug. 24, 1847, after independence, the cross was replaced by a star and the number of stripes was reduced.

©2000, Encyclopædia Britannica, Inc.

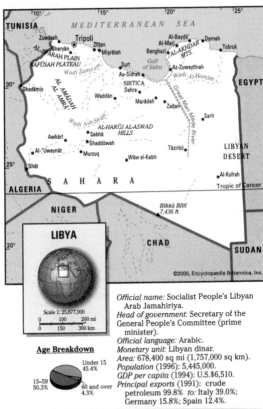

Official name: Socialist People's Libyan Arab Jamahiriya.
Head of government: Secretary of the General People's Committee (prime minister).
Official language: Arabic.
Monetary unit: Libyan dinar.
Area: 678,400 sq mi (1,757,000 sq km).
Population (1996): 5,445,000.
GDP per capita (1994): U.S.$6,510.
Principal exports (1991): crude petroleum 99.8% *to:* Italy 39.0%; Germany 15.8%; Spain 12.4%.

Age Breakdown

Under 15 45.4%
15–59 50.3%
60 and over 4.3%

After the coup d'état of 1969, Muammar al-Qaddafi adopted a flag based on the Egyptian flag. When the Egyptian president Anwar el-Sadat made peace with Israel, however, Qaddafi broke diplomatic relations and replaced the flag. In November 1977 he established a plain green banner, symbolizing promises of agricultural wealth.

Official name: Principality of
  Liechtenstein.
Head of government: Prime Minister.
Official language: German.
Monetary unit: Swiss franc.
Area: 61.8 sq mi (160.0 sq km).
Population (1996): 31,400.
GNP per capita (1991): U.S.$33,510.
Principal exports (1994): machinery
  and transport equipment 47.2%;
  metal products 16.3% *to:*
  EEC countries 39.6%;
  Switzerland 14.0%.

Religious Affiliation

Other 13.1%
Roman Catholic 80%
Protestant 6.9%

The blue-red flag was given official status in October 1921. At
the 1936 Olympics it was learned that this same flag was used
by Haiti; thus, in 1937 a yellow crown was added, which symbolizes the unity of the people and their prince. Blue stands
for the sky, red for the evening fires in homes. The flag was
last modified on Sept. 18, 1982.

LATVIA

BALTIC
SEA

Mažeikiai • Naujoji Akmenė
Skuodas • Joniškis • Biržai • Pandėlys
Palanga • Plungė • Telšiai • Kuršėnai • Pasvalys • Rokiškis
Šiauliai •
Klaipėda • Gargždai ŽEMAIČIAI Kelmė Radviliškis Panevėžys
Neringa • Priekulė UPLAND Šilalė Raseiniai Jonava LITHUANIAN
• Šilutė • Raseiniai • Anykščiai NATIONAL PARK
Tauragė • Jurbarkas • LITHUANIAN LOWLAND Širvintos • Mount
Pagėgiai • Vilkija • Nevėžis • Nepaišiai
Vilkija • 948 ft.
RUSSIA • MIDDLE LITHUANIAN
Neman Kaunas • Širvintos • BALTIC HIGHLANDS
Vilkaviškis • Kazlų • Trakai • Vilnius
• Rūda • Mount
ŠUVINTAS Alytus • Šalčininkai • Juozapinė
NATURE RESERVE • 957 ft.
Lazdijai •
POLAND Druskininkai • Varėna •
ČEPKELIAI
NATURE RESERVE BELARUS

©2000, Encyclopædia Britannica, Inc.

LITHUANIA

Scale 1: 7,165,000

0   30   60 mi
0 40 80 km

Ethnic Composition

Russian
8.4%
Lithuanian Polish
81.3% 7%
Other
3.3%

Official name: Republic of Lithuania.
Head of government: Prime Minister.
Official language: Lithuanian.
Monetary unit: litas.
Area: 25,213 sq mi (65,301 sq km).
Population (1996): 3,707,000.
GNP per capita (1994): U.S.$1,350.
Principal exports (1995): textiles 14.7%;
chemicals 12.2%; mineral products
11.9%; machinery 10.8%; base metals
8.7%; live animals 8.4% *to:* Russia
20.4%; Belarus 10.8%; Ukraine 7.5%;
Latvia 7.1%; Estonia 2.2%.

The tricolor flag of Lithuania was adopted on Aug. 1, 1922. It
was long suppressed under Soviet rule until its reestablish-
ment on March 20, 1989. The yellow color suggests ripening
wheat and freedom from want. Green is for hope and the
forests of the nation, while red stands for love of country,
sovereignty, and valor in defense of liberty.

Official name: Grand Duchy of Luxembourg.
Head of government: Prime Minister.
Official language: none.
Monetary unit: Luxembourg franc.
Area: 999 sq mi (2,586 sq km).
Population (1996): 415,000.
GNP per capita (1994): U.S.$39,850.
Principal exports (1994): metal products, machinery, and transport equipment 55.0%; plastic materials and rubber manufactures 13.7% *to:* Germany 28.2%; France 18.9%; Belgium 13.8%.

LUXEMBOURG

Scale 1: 1,177,000

| 0 | | 12 mi |
| 0 | 8 | 16 km |

Ethnic Composition

Other 15.7%
Luxemburger 67.4%
Portuguese 12.1%
Italian 4.8%

In the 19th century the national colors, from the coat of arms of the dukes of Luxembourg, came to be used in a tricolor of red-white-blue, coincidentally the same as the flag of The Netherlands. To distinguish it from the Dutch flag, the proportions were altered and the shade of blue was made lighter. It was recognized by law on Aug. 16, 1972.

Official name: Republic of Macedonia
Head of government: Prime Minister.
Official language: Macedonian.
Monetary unit: denar.
Area: 9,928 sq mi (25,713 sq km).
Population (1996): 1,968,000.
GNP per capita (1994): U.S.$853.
Principal exports (1994): manufactured products 37.7%; machinery and transport equipment 12.3%; food products 10.1%; raw materials 7.1% *to:* Bulgaria 22.1%; Germany 13.4%; Italy 11.6%; former U.S.S.R. 7.0%.

MACEDONIA

Scale 1: 4,190,000

| 0 | 20 | 40 mi |
| 0 | 30 | 60 km |

Ethnic Composition

Albanian 23.1%
Other 10.5%
Macedonian 66.4%

A "starburst" flag replaced the communist banner on Aug. 11, 1992. The starburst was a symbol of Alexander the Great and his father, Philip of Macedon, but its use by Macedonia was opposed by Greece. Thus on Oct. 6, 1995, the similar "golden sun" flag was chosen instead. The gold and red colors originated in an early Macedonian coat of arms.

©2000, Encyclopædia Britannica, Inc.

MADAGASCAR

Scale 1: 25,920,000

0   100   200 mi
0 150 300 km

Official name: Republic of Madagascar.
Head of government: Prime Minister.
Official languages: none.
Monetary unit: Malagasy franc.
Area: 226,658 sq mi (587,041 sq km).
Population (1996): 13,671,000.
GNP per capita (1994): U.S.$230.
Principal exports (1994): coffee 18.0%;
vanilla 16.7%; shrimp 13.2%; cotton
fabrics 2.9%; cloves and clove oil 2.6%
to (1992): France 26.6%; U.S. 15.5%;
Germany 9.9%; Japan 8.6%; Belgium-
Luxembourg 3.3%; Italy 3.1%.

Religious Affiliation

Roman
Catholic
26%

Protestant
22.8%

Traditional
beliefs
47%

Other
4.2%

The Madagascar flag was adopted on Oct. 16, 1958, by the newly
proclaimed Malagasy Republic, formerly a French colony. The
flag combines the traditional Malagasy colors of white and red
with a stripe of green. The white and red are said to stand for
purity and sovereignty, while the green represents the coastal
regions and symbolizes hope.

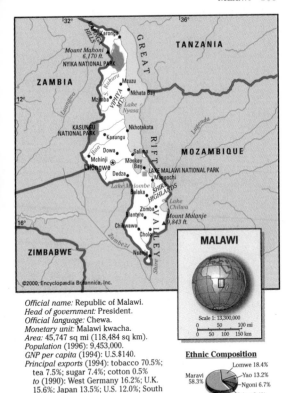

Official name: Republic of Malawi.
Head of government: President.
Official language: Chewa.
Monetary unit: Malawi kwacha.
Area: 45,747 sq mi (118,484 sq km).
Population (1996): 9,453,000.
GNP per capita (1994): U.S.$140.
Principal exports (1994): tobacco 70.5%;
  tea 7.5%; sugar 7.4%; cotton 0.5%
  to (1990): West Germany 16.2%; U.K.
  15.6%; Japan 13.5%; U.S. 12.0%; South
  Africa 7.2%.

MALAWI

Scale 1: 13,300,000

0   50   100 mi
0   50   100   150 km

Ethnic Composition

Lomwe 18.4%
Yao 13.2%
Maravi 58.3%
Ngoni 6.7%
Other 3.4%

The flag of the Malawi Congress Party was striped black for the African people, red for the blood of martyrs, and green for the vegetation and climate. The country's name means "flaming waters," referring to the setting sun on Lake Malawi. With independence on July 6, 1964, a new flag was created by adding the sun symbol to the party flag.

Official name: Malaysia.
Head of government: Prime Minister.
Official language: Malay.
Monetary unit: ringgit, or Malaysian
dollar.
Area: 127,584 sq mi (330,442 sq km).
Population (1996): 20,359,000.
GNP per capita (1994): U.S.$3,520.
Principal exports (1994): machinery and
transport equipment 53.5%; basic
manufactures 9.1%; inedible crude
materials 7.5% *to:* U.S. 21.2%;
Singapore 20.7%; Japan 11.9%.

MALAYSIA

Scale 1: 32,013,000

0   150   300 mi
0   200   400 km

Ethnic Composition

Malay
and other
indigenous
59.9%

Chinese
29.9%

Indian
and other
10.2%

The flag hoisted on May 26, 1950, had 11 stripes, a crescent,
and an 11-pointed star. The number of stripes and star points
was increased to 14 on Sept. 16, 1963. Yellow is a royal color
in Malaysia while red, white, and blue indicate connections
with the Commonwealth. The crescent is a reminder that the
population is mainly Muslim.

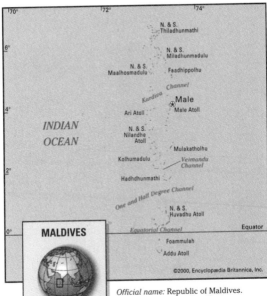

70° | 72° | 74°

N. & S.
Thiladhunmathi

N. & S.
Miladhunmadulu

N. & S.
Maalhosmadulu   Faadhippolhu

Kardiva Channel

⊛ Male
Male Atoll

Ari Atoll

**INDIAN
OCEAN**

N. & S.
Nilandhe
Atoll

Mulakatholhu

Kolhumadulu   *Veimandu
Channel*

Hadhdhunmathi

One and Half Degree Channel

N. & S.
Huvadhu Atoll

Equatorial Channel   Equator

Foammulah

Addu Atoll

©2000, Encyclopædia Britannica, Inc.

MALDIVES

Scale 1: 14,001,000

0   60   120 mi
0   80   180 km

Age Breakdown

60 and over
4.9%   Under 15
46.5%

15–59
48.6%

Official name: Republic of Maldives.
Head of government: President.
Official language: Divehi.
Monetary unit: Maldivian rufiyaa.
Area: 115 sq mi (298 sq km).
Population (1996): 266,000.
GNP per capita (1994): U.S.$900.
Principal exports (1993): canned tuna
26.9%; frozen skipjack tuna 21.4%;
apparel and clothing 15.9%; fish meal
3.4% *to:* Sri Lanka 30.3%; United
Kingdom 24.5%; Thailand 13.9%;
United States 11.3%; Germany 5.9%.

Maldivian ships long used a plain red ensign like those flown
by Arabian and African nations. While a British protectorate
in the early 20th century, the Maldives adopted a flag which
was only slightly altered upon independence (July 26, 1965).
The green panel and white crescent are symbolic of Islam,
progress, prosperity, and peace.

MALI

Scale 1: 26,608,000

0   100   200 mi

0   200   400 km

Official name: Republic of Mali.
Head of government: Prime Minister.
Official language: French.
Monetary unit: CFA franc.
Area: 482,077 sq mi (1,248,574 sq km).
Population (1996): 9,204,000.
GNP per capita (1994): U.S.$250.
Principal exports (1994): raw cotton and
   cotton products 47.8%; live animals
   29.2%; gold 15.7% *to:* Norway 28.8%;
   Thailand 18.3%; Brazil 13.7%; Ireland
   9.6%; Belgium-Luxembourg 5.8%;
   China 2.2%; France 1.9%; Tunisia 1.4%.

Language Composition

Voltaic
languages
18.8%

Fulani and
Tukulor 14%

Mande
languages
51%

Tamashek
(Tuareg) 7.3%

Other 8.9%

Designed for the Mali-Senegal union of 1959, the flag originally
included a human figure, the Kanaga, in its center. In 1960
Senegal and Mali divided. Muslims in Mali objected to the
Kanaga, and on March 1, 1961, the figure was dropped. Green,
yellow, and red are the Pan-African colors and are used by
many former French territories.

©2000, Encyclopædia Britannica, Inc.

MALTA

Scale 1: 572,700

0   2   4 mi
0   3   6 km

Age Breakdown

Under 15 22%

15–59 62.6%

60 and over 15.4%

Official name: Malta .
Head of government: Prime Minister.
Official languages: Maltese; English.
Monetary unit: Maltese lira.
Area: 122 sq mi (316 sq km).
Population (1996): 372,000.
GNP per capita (1992): U.S.$7,210.
Principal exports (1995): machinery and
    transport equipment 63.0%; manu-
    factured and semimanufactured goods
    26.7%; reexports 6.9% *to* (1994): Italy
    37.5%; Germany 14.2%; France 9.9%;
    U.S. 7.6%; U.K. 7.4%; Libya 3.6%.

The Maltese flag was supposedly based on an 11th-century
coat of arms, and a red flag with a white cross was used by
the Knights of Malta from the Middle Ages. The current flag
dates from independence within the Commonwealth (Sept.
21, 1964). The George Cross was granted by the British for
the heroic defense of the island in World War II.

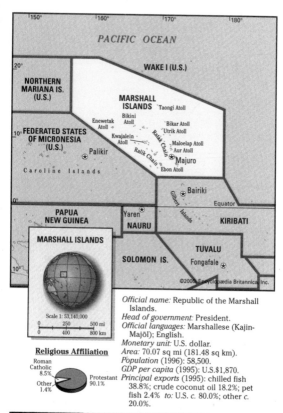

Official name: Republic of the Marshall Islands.

Head of government: President.

Official languages: Marshallese (Kajin-Majōl); English.

Monetary unit: U.S. dollar.

Area: 70.07 sq mi (181.48 sq km).

Population (1996): 58,500.

GDP per capita (1995): U.S.$1,870.

Principal exports (1995): chilled fish 38.8%; crude coconut oil 18.2%; pet fish 2.4% *to:* U.S. *c.* 80.0%; other *c.* 20.0%.

Religious Affiliation

Roman Catholic 8.5%

Other 1.4%

Protestant 90.1%

MARSHALL ISLANDS

Scale 1: 53,140,000

0   250   500 mi

0   400   800 km

©2000 Encyclopædia Britannica, Inc.

The island nation hoisted its flag on May 1, 1979. The blue stands for the ocean. The white is for brightness while the orange is for bravery and wealth. The two stripes joined symbolize the Equator, and they increase in width to show growth and vitality. The rays of the star are for the municipalities; its four long rays recall a Christian cross.

Official name: Islamic Republic of
Mauritania.
Head of government: President.
Official language: Arabic.
Monetary unit: ouguiya.
Area: 398,000 sq mi (1,030,700 sq km).
Population (1996): 2,333,000.
GNP per capita (1994): U.S.$480.
Principal exports (1994): fish 52.6%, of
which cephalopods 35.5%; iron ore
41.5%; gold 5.2% *to:* Japan 27.8%; Italy
14.9%; France 13.6%; Spain 11.4%;
Ivory Coast 6.3%.

Scale 1: 26,914,000

| 0 | 100 | 200 mi |

| 0 | 200 | 400 km |

Age Breakdown

Under 15
43.1%

15–59
51.7%

60 and over
5.2%

In 1958 Mauritania was granted autonomous status within the
French Community. The current flag replaced the French tricolor on April 1, 1959, and no changes were made to the
design at independence (Nov. 28, 1960). The green background of the flag and its star and crescent are traditional
Muslim symbols that have been in use for centuries.

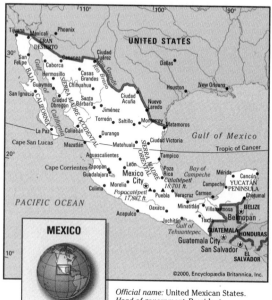

©2000, Encyclopædia Britannica, Inc.

MEXICO

Scale 1: 41,548,000

| 0 | 200 | 400 km |
| 0 | 300 | 600 km |

Ethnic Composition

Mestizo 60%
Amerindian 30%
Caucasian 9%
Other 1%

Official name: United Mexican States.
Head of government: President.
Official language: Spanish.
Monetary unit: Mexican peso.
Area: 756,066 sq mi (1,958,201 sq km).
Population (1996): 92,711,000.
GNP per capita (1994): U.S.$4,010.
Principal exports (1995): manufacturing goods 83.7%; crude petroleum 9.3%; agricultural goods 5.0% *to:* U.S. 83.6%; Canada 2.5%; Japan 1.2%; Spain 1.0%; Brazil 1.0%; Switzerland 0.8%; Germany 0.6%; U.K. 0.6%; Chile 0.6%.

The green-white-red tricolor was officially established in 1821. Green is for independence, white for Roman Catholicism, and red for union. The emblem depicts the scene supposedly witnessed by the Aztecs in 1325: an eagle with a snake in its beak standing upon a cactus growing out of rocks in the water. The flag was modified on Sept. 17, 1968.

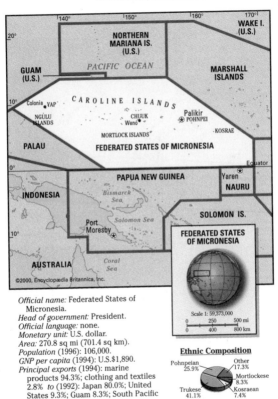

Official name: Federated States of Micronesia.
Head of government: President.
Official language: none.
Monetary unit: U.S. dollar.
Area: 270.8 sq mi (701.4 sq km).
Population (1996): 106,000.
GNP per capita (1994): U.S.$1,890.
Principal exports (1994): marine products 94.3%; clothing and textiles 2.8% *to* (1992): Japan 80.0%; United States 9.3%; Guam 8.3%; South Pacific Region 2.4%.

Scale 1: 59,373,000

Ethnic Composition

Pohnpeian 25.9%
Other 17.3%
Mortlockese 8.3%
Kosraean 7.4%
Trukese 41.1%

On Nov. 30, 1978, the flag of the former United States trust territory was approved by an interim congress. Based on the symbolism of the territory, the flag has stars for the four states of Micronesia. After sovereignty was granted in 1986, a dark blue background (for the Pacific Ocean) was substituted for the original "United Nations blue."

MOLDOVA

Scale 1: 5,251,000

0   20   40 mi

0   30   60 km

Ethnic Composition

Moldovan 64.5%
Ukrainian 13.8%
Russian 13%
Gagauz 3.5%
Other 5.2%

Official name: Republic of Moldova.
Head of government: Prime Minister.
Official language: Romanian.
Monetary unit: Moldovan leu.
Area: 13,011 sq mi (33,700 sq km).
Population (1996): 4,372,000.
GNP per capita (1994): U.S.$870.
Principal exports (1993): food 41.8%;
   machinery 19.6%; light industrial
   products 8.5%; metals 4.6% *to* (1994):
   Russia 69.9%; Ukraine 16.7%; Belarus
   5.7%; Azerbaijan 3.1%.

By 1989, Moldovans protested against communist rule, and
the traditional tricolor of blue-yellow-red, which had flown
briefly in 1917–18, became a popular symbol. It replaced the
communist flag in May 1990 and remained after independence
in 1991. The shield has an eagle on whose breast are an
aurochs head, a crescent, a star, and a flower.

Official name: Mongolia.
Head of government: Prime Minister.
Official language: Khalkha Mongolian.
Monetary unit: tugrik.
Area: 604,800 sq mi (1,566,500 sq km).
Population (1996): 2,334,000.
GNP per capita (1994): U.S.$340.
Principal exports (1995): copper
concentrate 54.9%; cashmere products
8.7%; gold ore 5.6%; fluorite
concentrate 3.4% *to:* Japan 18.7%;
Kazakstan 15.2%; China 14.3%;
Switzerland 13.2%; Russia 13.1%.

Ethnic Composition

Khalkha
Mongol
78.8%

Other
15.3%

Kazak
5.9%

In 1945, the flag symbolizing communism (red) and Mongol
nationalism (blue) was established. Near the hoist is a *soyon-
ba,* a grouping of philosophical symbols (flame, sun, moon,
yin-yang, triangles, and bars). Yellow traditionally stood for
Lamaist Buddhism. On Jan. 12, 1992, a five-pointed star (for
Communism) was removed from the flag.

MOROCCO

Scale 1: 19,664,000

| 0 | 100 | 200 mi |
| 0 | 150 | 300 km |

Official name: Kingdom of Morocco.
Head of government: King assisted by
Prime Minister.
Official language: Arabic.
Monetary unit: Moroccan dirham.
Area: 177,117 sq mi (458,730 sq km).
Population (1996): 26,736,000.
GNP per capita (1994): U.S.$1,150.
Principal exports (1994): food 28.0%;
consumer goods 25.9%; minerals
11.0% *to:* France 31.7%; Spain 9.3%;
Japan 6.6%; Italy 5.7%; Germany 4.3%;
U.K. 3.9%; U.S. 3.5%.

Ethnic Composition

Arab
70%

Berber
30%

After Morocco was subjected to the rule of France and Spain
in the 20th century, the plain red flag, which had been displayed on its ships, was modified on Nov. 17, 1915. To its center was added the ancient pentagram known as the "Seal of
Solomon." The flag continued in use even after the French
granted independence in 1956.

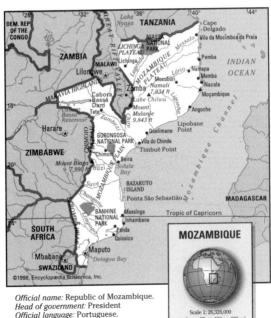

Official name: Republic of Mozambique.
Head of government: President
Official language: Portuguese.
Monetary unit: metical.
Area: 313,661 sq mi (812,379 sq km).
Population (1996): 17,878,000.
GNP per capita (1994): U.S.$80.
Principal exports (1994): shrimp 42.3%;
cotton 12.6%; petroleum 9.2%; sugar
7.4%; cashew nuts 2.2% *to:* Spain
22.4%; South Africa 14.8%; Japan
13.1%; Portugal 9.9%; United States
9.5%.

Language Composition

Other 36.1%
Makua 27.8%
Tsonga 12.4%
Sena 7.8%
Lomwe 7.8%
Shona 6.5%

In the early 1960s, anti-Portuguese groups adopted flags of
green (for forests), black (for the majority population), white
(for rivers and the ocean), gold (for peace and mineral
wealth), and red (for the blood of liberation). The current flag
was readopted in 1983; on its star are a book, a hoe, and an
assault rifle.

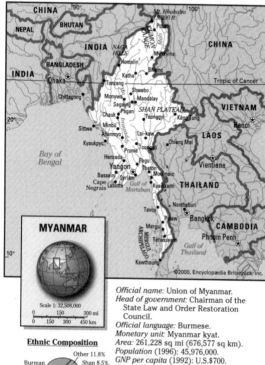

©2000, Encyclopædia Britannica, Inc.

Official name: Union of Myanmar.
Head of government: Chairman of the
   State Law and Order Restoration
   Council.
Official language: Burmese.
Monetary unit: Myanmar kyat.
Area: 261,228 sq mi (676,577 sq km).
Population (1996): 45,976,000.
GNP per capita (1992): U.S.$700.
Principal exports (1993): inedible crude
   materials 36.8%; food, beverages, and
   tobacco 34.5% *to:* Singapore 19.4%;
   Thailand 17.4%; India 15.0%.

Ethnic Composition

Burman
69%

Other 11.8%

Shan 8.5%

Karen 6.2%

Rakhine 4.5%

The current flag design dates to Jan. 4, 1974. Its 14 stars, for
the states and divisions of Myanmar, form a circle around a
cogwheel, for industrial workers, and ears and leaves of rice,
symbolizing the peasantry. Blue is for truthfulness and
strength; red for bravery, unity, and determination; and white
for truth, purity, and steadfastness.

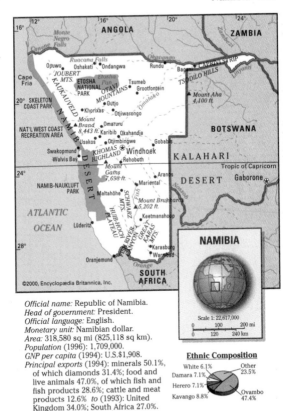

Official name: Republic of Namibia.
Head of government: President.
Official language: English.
Monetary unit: Namibian dollar.
Area: 318,580 sq mi (825,118 sq km).
Population (1996): 1,709,000.
GNP per capita (1994): U.S.$1,908.
Principal exports (1994): minerals 50.1%, of which diamonds 31.4%; food and live animals 47.0%, of which fish and fish products 28.6%; cattle and meat products 12.6% *to* (1993): United Kingdom 34.0%; South Africa 27.0%.

Ethnic Composition

White 6.1%
Damara 7.1%
Herero 7.1%
Kavango 8.8%
Ovambo 47.4%
Other 23.5%

The flag was adopted on Feb. 2, 1990, and hoisted on independence from South Africa, March 21, 1990. Its colors are those of the South West Africa People's Organization: blue (for sky and ocean), red (for heroism and determination), and green (for agriculture). The gold sun represents life and energy while the white stripes are for water resources.

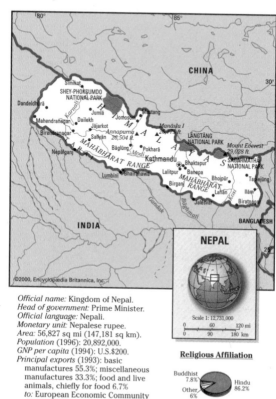

©2000, Encyclopædia Britannica, Inc.

NEPAL

Scale 1: 12,731,000

| 0 | 60 | 120 mi |
| 0 | 90 | 180 km |

Official name: Kingdom of Nepal.
Head of government: Prime Minister.
Official language: Nepali.
Monetary unit: Nepalese rupee.
Area: 56,827 sq mi (147,181 sq km).
Population (1996): 20,892,000.
GNP per capita (1994): U.S.$200.
Principal exports (1993): basic
  manufactures 55.3%; miscellaneous
  manufactures 33.3%; food and live
  animals, chiefly for food 6.7%
  to: European Economic Community
  47.7%; Americas 29.7%; India 13.3%.

Religious Affiliation

Buddhist 7.8%

Other 6%

Hindu 86.2%

Established on Dec. 16, 1962, Nepal's flag consists of two united pennant
shapes; it is the only non-rectangular national flag in the world. In the
upper segment is a moon with a crescent attached below; in the
bottom segment appears a stylized sun. The symbols are for different dynasties
and express a hope for the immortality of the nation. The crimson and
blue colors are common in Nepali art.

THE NETHERLANDS

Scale 1: 5,169,000

0   20   40 mi
0   30   60 km

Religious Affiliation

Roman Catholic 31%

Protestant 22%

Muslim 4%

Other 4%

No religion 39%

Official name: Kingdom of The Netherlands.
Head of government: Prime Minister.
Official language: Dutch.
Monetary unit: Netherlands guilder.
Area: 16,033 sq mi (41,526 sq km).
Population (1996): 15,589,000.
GNP per capita (1994): U.S.$21,970.
Principal exports (1994): machinery and transport equipment 23.5%; foodstuffs, beverages, and tobacco 18.8%; *to:* Germany 28.9%; Belgium-Luxembourg 13.4%; France 10.8%; U.K. 9.7%.

The history of the Dutch flag dates to the use of orange, white, and blue as the livery colors of William, Prince of Orange, and the use of the tricolor at sea in 1577. By 1660 the color red was substituted for orange. The flag was legalized by pro-French "patriots" on Feb. 14, 1796, and reaffirmed by royal decree on Feb. 19, 1937.

Official name: New Zealand.
Head of government: Prime Minister.
Official languages: English; Maori.
Monetary unit: New Zealand dollar.
Area: 104,454 sq mi (270,534 sq km).
Population (1996): 3,619,000.
GNP per capita (1994): U.S.$13,190.
Principal exports (1995): food and live
   animals 43.7%; basic manufactures
   26.0%; minerals, chemicals, and
   plastics 11.1%; metals and metal
   products 7.1% *to:* Australia 20.8%;
   Japan 16.3%; U.S. 10.4%; U.K. 6.2%.

NEW ZEALAND

Scale 1: 23,005,000

| 0 | 100 | 200 mi |
| 0 | 150 | 300 km |

Ethnic Composition

N.Z. Polynesian
(Maori) 9.6%
Other 8.5%
White
73.8%
Mixed race
4.5%
Other Polynesian
3.6%

The Maori of New Zealand accepted British control in 1840,
and a colonial flag was adopted on Jan. 15, 1867. It included
the Union Jack in the canton and the letters "NZ" at the fly
end. Later versions used the Southern Cross. Dominion status
was granted on Sept. 26, 1907, and independence on Nov. 25,
1947, but the flag was unchanged.

Official name: Republic of Nicaragua.
Head of government: President.
Official language: Spanish.
Monetary unit: córdoba oro.
Area: 50,893 sq mi (131,812 sq km).
Population (1996): 4,272,000.
GNP per capita (1994): U.S.$330.
Principal exports (1994): coffee 21.0%;
beef 18.0%; crustaceans 12.3%;
oilseeds 5.0%; raw sugar 4.5% *to:*
United States 42.9%; Germany 12.7%;
El Salvador 10.7%; Costa Rica 7.3%;
Honduras 3.6%.

NICARAGUA

Scale 1: 11,073,000

| 0 | 50 | 100 mi |
| 0 | 80 | 160 km |

Ethnic Composition

Mestizo 69%

White 17%

Black 9%

Amerindian 5%

On Aug. 21, 1823, a blue-white-blue flag was adopted by the
five member states of the United Provinces of Central
America, which included Nicaragua. From the mid-19th century various flag designs were used in Nicaragua, but the old
flag was readopted in 1908, with a modified coat of arms, and
reaffirmed by law on Aug. 27, 1971.

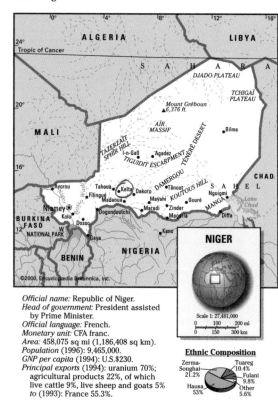

©2000, Encyclopædia Britannica, Inc.

Official name: Republic of Niger.
Head of government: President assisted by Prime Minister.
Official language: French.
Monetary unit: CFA franc.
Area: 458,075 sq mi (1,186,408 sq km).
Population (1996): 9,465,000.
GNP per capita (1994): U.S.$230.
Principal exports (1994): uranium 70%; agricultural products 22%, of which live cattle 9%, live sheep and goats 5% to (1993): France 55.3%.

NIGER

Scale 1: 27,481,000

| 0 | 100 | 200 mi |
| 0 | 150 | 300 km |

Ethnic Composition

Zerma-Songhai 21.2%
Tuareg 10.4%
Fulani 9.8%
Other 5.6%
Hausa 53%

The flag of Niger was chosen on Nov. 23, 1959. The white color is for purity, innocence, and civic spirit. The orange is for the Sahara Desert and the heroic efforts of citizens to live within it, while the orange central disk represents the sun. The green color stands for agriculture and hope; it is suggestive of the Niger River valley.

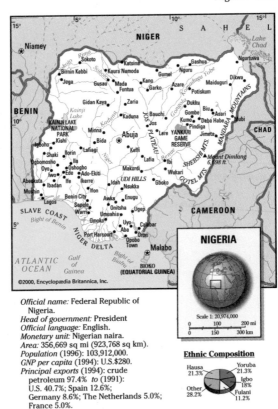

©2000, Encyclopædia Britannica, Inc.

Official name: Federal Republic of Nigeria.
Head of government: President
Official language: English.
Monetary unit: Nigerian naira.
Area: 356,669 sq mi (923,768 sq km).
Population (1996): 103,912,000.
GNP per capita (1994): U.S.$280.
Principal exports (1994): crude petroleum 97.4% *to* (1991):
U.S. 40.7%; Spain 12.6%;
Germany 8.6%; The Netherlands 5.0%;
France 5.0%.

NIGERIA

Scale 1: 20,974,000

0   100   200 mi
0   150   300 km

Ethnic Composition

Hausa 21.3%

Yoruba 21.3%

Igbo 18%

Fulani 11.2%

Other 28.2%

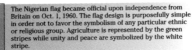

The Nigerian flag became official upon independence from Britain on Oct. 1, 1960. The flag design is purposefully simple in order not to favor the symbolism of any particular ethnic or religious group. Agriculture is represented by the green stripes while unity and peace are symbolized by the white stripe.

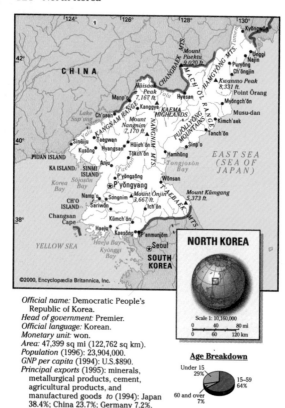

Official name: Democratic People's Republic of Korea.
Head of government: Premier.
Official language: Korean.
Monetary unit: won.
Area: 47,399 sq mi (122,762 sq km).
Population (1996): 23,904,000.
GNP per capita (1994): U.S.$890.
Principal exports (1995): minerals, metallurgical products, cement, agricultural products, and manufactured goods *to (1994):* Japan 38.4%; China 23.7%; Germany 7.2%.

NORTH KOREA

Scale 1: 10,160,000

| 0 | | 60 | | 80 mi |

| 0 | 60 | 120 km |

Age Breakdown

Under 15
29%

15–59
64%

60 and over
7%

The traditional Korean Taeguk flag (still used by South Korea) was official in North Korea until July 10, 1948, when the current flag was introduced. Its red stripe and star are for the country's commitment to communism, while blue is said to stand for a commitment to peace. The white stripes stand for purity, strength, and dignity.

©2000, Encyclopædia Britannica, Inc.

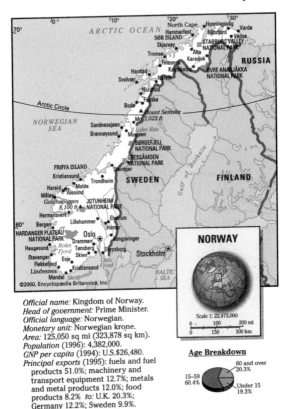

Official name: Kingdom of Norway.
Head of government: Prime Minister.
Official language: Norwegian.
Monetary unit: Norwegian krone.
Area: 125,050 sq mi (323,878 sq km).
Population (1996): 4,382,000.
GNP per capita (1994): U.S.$26,480.
Principal exports (1995): fuels and fuel
  products 51.0%; machinery and
  transport equipment 12.7%; metals
  and metal products 12.0%; food
  products 8.2% *to:* U.K. 20.3%;
  Germany 12.2%; Sweden 9.9%.

Age Breakdown

60 and over
20.3%

15–59
60.4%

Under 15
19.3%

The first distinctive Norwegian flag was created in 1814 while
the country was under Swedish rule. It was based on the red
Danish flag with its white cross. In 1821 the Norwegian parlia-
ment developed the current flag design. From 1844 to 1899,
six years before independence, the official flag included a
symbol of Swedish-Norwegian union.

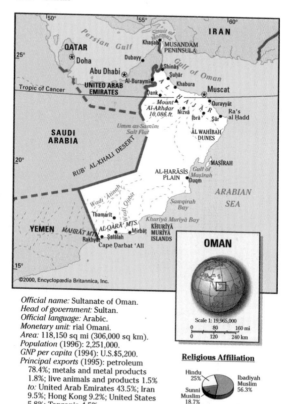

©2000, Encyclopædia Britannica, Inc.

Official name: Sultanate of Oman.
Head of government: Sultan.
Official language: Arabic.
Monetary unit: rial Omani.
Area: 118,150 sq mi (306,000 sq km).
Population (1996): 2,251,000.
GNP per capita (1994): U.S.$5,200.
Principal exports (1995): petroleum
78.4%; metals and metal products
1.8%; live animals and products 1.5%
to: United Arab Emirates 43.5%; Iran
9.5%; Hong Kong 9.2%; United States
5.8%; Tanzania 4.5%.

OMAN

Scale 1: 19,965,000

| 0 | 80 | 160 mi |
| 0 | 120 | 240 km |

Religious Affiliation

Hindu 25%

Ibadiyah Muslim 56.3%

Sunni Muslim 18.7%

The flag dates to Dec. 17, 1970, and it was altered on Nov. 18, 1995. The white is for peace and prosperity, red is for battles, and green is for the fertility of the land. Unofficially, white recalls the imamate, red the sultanate, and green Al-Jabal Al-Akhdar ("The Green Mountain"). The coat of arms has two swords, a dagger, and a belt.

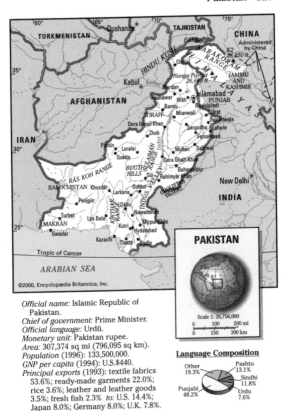

©2000, Encyclopædia Britannica, Inc.

PAKISTAN

Scale 1: 26,756,000

| 0 | 100 | 200 mi |
| 0 | 150 | 300 km |

Official name: Islamic Republic of Pakistan.
Chief of government: Prime Minister.
Official language: Urdū.
Monetary unit: Pakistan rupee.
Area: 307,374 sq mi (796,095 sq km).
Population (1996): 133,500,000.
GNP per capita (1994): U.S.$440.
Principal exports (1993): textile fabrics 53.6%; ready-made garments 22.0%; rice 3.6%; leather and leather goods 3.5%; fresh fish 2.3% *to:* U.S. 14.4%; Japan 8.0%; Germany 8.0%; U.K. 7.8%.

Language Composition

Other 19.3%
Pashto 13.1%
Sindhi 11.8%
Urdu 7.6%
Punjabi 48.2%

On Dec. 30, 1906, the All India Muslim League approved this typically Muslim flag, with its star and crescent. At independence (Aug. 14, 1947) a white stripe was added for minority religious groups. Also symbolized are prosperity and peace by the green and white colors, progress by the crescent, and knowledge and light by the star.

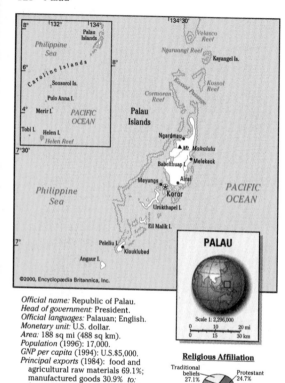

Official name: Republic of Palau.
Head of government: President.
Official languages: Palauan; English.
Monetary unit: U.S. dollar.
Area: 188 sq mi (488 sq km).
Population (1996): 17,000.
GNP per capita (1994): U.S.$5,000.
Principal exports (1984): food and
agricultural raw materials 69.1%;
manufactured goods 30.9% *to:*
Japan 58.8%; United States 8.0%.

Scale 1: 2,296,000

0   10   20 mi
0   15   30 km

Religious Affiliation

Traditional beliefs 27.1%

Protestant 24.7%

Roman Catholic 40.7%

Other 7.5%

Approved on Oct. 22, 1980, and hoisted on Jan. 1, 1981, the Palauan flag was left unaltered at independence in 1994. The golden disk represents the full moon, which is said on Palau to be propitious for fishing, planting, and other activities and gives the people "a feeling of warmth, tranquillity, peace, love, and domestic unity."

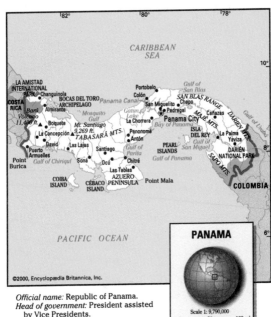

©2000, Encyclopædia Britannica, Inc.

Official name: Republic of Panama.
Head of government: President assisted
  by Vice Presidents.
Official language: Spanish.
Monetary unit: balboa.
Area: 29,157 sq mi (75,517 sq km).
Population (1996): 2,674,000.
GNP per capita (1994): U.S.$2,670.
Principal exports (1994): bananas 38.8%;
  shrimps 13.1%; clothing 3.9%; fish
  products 3.5%; raw sugar 3.2% *to:* U.S.
  37.6%; Germany 12.2%; Sweden 9.1%;
  Costa Rica 7.1%; Belgium 6.9%.

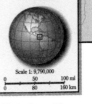

PANAMA

Scale 1: 9,790,000

| 0 | 50 | 100 mi |
| 0 | 80 | 160 km |

Ethnic Composition

Mestizo
64%

Black and
Mulatto 14%

White 10%

Amerindian 8%

Asian 4%

The Panamanian flag became official on July 4, 1904, after
independence from Colombia was won through the interven-
tion of the United States, which was determined to construct
the Panama Canal. The flag was influenced by the United
States, and its quartered design was said to symbolize the
power sharing of Panama's two main political parties.

Official name: Independent State of
   Papua New Guinea.
Head of government: Prime Minister.
Official language: English.
Monetary unit: Papua New Guinea kina.
Area: 178,704 sq mi (462,840 sq km).
Population (1996): 4,400,000.
GNP per capita (1994): U.S.$1,160.
Principal exports (1995): gold 24.7%;
   crude oil 24.3%; copper ore and
   concentrates 22.2%; timber 12.8%;
   coffee 6.3% *to* (1993): Australia 35.8%;
   Japan 21.4%; South Korea 10.0%.

Religious Affiliation

Protestant 63.8%
Roman Catholic 32.8%
Other 3.4%

The formerly German-, British-, and Australian-controlled territory officially recognized its flag on March 11, 1971, and flag
usage was extended to ships at independence (Sept. 16,
1975). The colors red and black are shown extensively in
local art and clothing. Featured emblems are a bird of par-
adise and the Southern Cross constellation.

©2000, Encyclopædia Britannica, Inc.

Scale 1: 26,523,000
0   100   200 mi
0   150   300 km

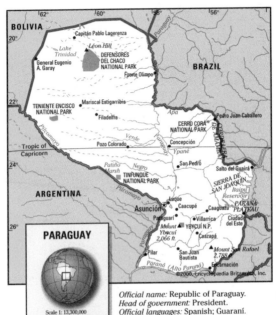

Official name: Republic of Paraguay.
Head of government: President.
Official languages: Spanish; Guaraní.
Monetary unit: Paraguayan Guaraní.
Area: 157,048 sq mi (406,752 sq km).
Population (1996): 4,964,000.
GNP per capita (1994): U.S.$1,570.
Principal exports (1995): cotton fibres
32.4%; soybean flour 24.1%; timber
7.5%; oilseed cakes 7.0%; vegetable oil
5.9%; processed meats 5.0% *to* (1995):
Brazil 45.8%; Germany 7.8%; Argentina
7.7%; U.S. 5.4%; Chile 5.2%.

Language Composition

Guarani 40.1%
Spanish 6.5%
Other 4.8%
Guarani/ Spanish 48.6%

Under the dictator José Gaspar Rodríguez de Francia
(1814–40) the French colors were adopted for the flag. The
coat of arms (a golden star surrounded by a wreath) is on the
obverse side, but the seal of the treasury (a lion, staff, and
liberty cap, with the motto "Peace and Justice") is on the
reverse; the flag is unique in this respect.

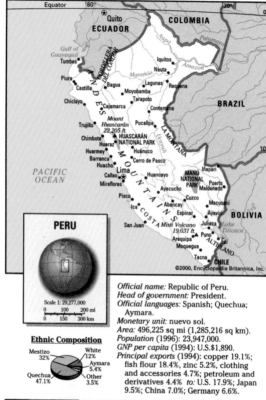

Official name: Republic of Peru.
Head of government: President.
Official languages: Spanish; Quechua;
Aymara.
Monetary unit: nuevo sol.
Area: 496,225 sq mi (1,285,216 sq km).
Population (1996): 23,947,000.
GNP per capita (1994): U.S.$1,890.
Principal exports (1994): copper 19.1%;
fish flour 18.4%; zinc 5.2%; clothing
and accessories 4.7%; petroleum and
derivatives 4.4% *to:* U.S. 17.9%; Japan
9.5%; China 7.0%; Germany 6.6%.

Ethnic Composition

Mestizo 32%
White 12%
Aymara 5.4%
Other 3.5%
Quechua 47.1%

Partisans in the early 19th century adopted a red-white-red
flag resembling that of Spain, but they soon made its stripes
vertical. In 1825 the current design was established. The
shield includes figures symbolic of national wealth—the vicu-
ña (a relative of the alpaca), a cinchona tree, and a cornu-
copia with gold and silver coins.

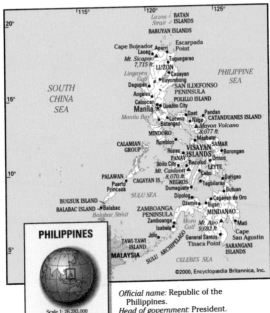

©2000, Encyclopædia Britannica, Inc.

PHILIPPINES

Scale 1: 26,283,000

| 0 | 100 | 200 mi |
| 0 | 150 | 300 km |

Language Composition

Tagalog 27.9%
Cebuano 24.3%
Ilocano 9.8%
Hiligaynon
Ilonggo 9.3%
Other 28.7%

Official name: Republic of the Philippines.
Head of government: President.
Official languages: Pilipino; English.
Monetary unit: Philippine peso.
Area: 115,860 sq mi (300,076 sq km).
Population (1996): 71,750,000.
GNP per capita (1994): U.S.$960.
Principal exports (1995): electronics 36.2%; garments 14.8%; coconut oil 4.6%; ignition wiring sets 2.5%; *to:* United States 35.3%; Japan 15.7%; Singapore 5.7%; United Kingdom 5.3.

In 1898, during the Spanish-American War, Filipinos established the basic flag in use today; it was officially adopted in 1936. The white triangle is for liberty. The golden sun and stars are for the three main areas of the Philippines: Luzon, the Visayan Islands, and Mindanao. The red color is for courage and the blue color is for sacrifice.

Official name: Republic of Poland.
Head of government: Prime Minister.
Official language: Polish.
Monetary unit: zloty.
Area: 120,727 sq mi (312,685 sq km).
Population (1996): 38,731,000.
GNP per capita (1994): U.S.$2,470.
Principal exports (1995): manufactured
goods 27.6%; machinery and transport
equipment 21.1%; miscellaneous
manufactured articles 20.9%; food
9.2% to: Germany 38.3%; The
Netherlands 5.6%; Russia 5.6%.

POLAND

Scale 1: 9,837,000

0   40   80 mi

0   60   120 km

Age Breakdown

Under 15
22.8%

15–59
61.4%

60 and over
15.8%

The colors of the Polish flag originated in its coat of arms, a
white eagle on a red shield, dating from 1295. The precise
symbolism of the colors is not known, however. Poland's
simple flag of white-red horizontal stripes was adopted on
Aug. 1, 1919. The flag was left unaltered under the Soviet-
allied communist regime (1944 to 1990).

PORTUGAL

Scale 1: 8,756,000

| 0 | 40 | 80 mi |
| 0 | 60 | 120 km |

Age Breakdown

Under 15
18.9%

15–59
61.8%

60 and over
19.3%

Official name: Portuguese Republic.
Head of government: Prime Minister.
Official language: Portuguese.
Monetary unit: escudo.
Area: 35,456 sq mi (91,831 sq km).
Population (1996): 9,927,000.
GNP per capita (1994): U.S.$9,370.
Principal exports (1994): textiles and
  wearing apparel 25.9%; machinery and
  transport equipment 21.2%; footwear
  8.7%; cork and wood products 6.2%
  to: Germany 18.7%; France 14.7%;
  Spain 14.4%; United Kingdom 11.7%.

The central shield includes five smaller shields for a victory
over the Moors in 1139, and a red border with gold castles.
Behind the shield is an armillary sphere (an astronomical
device) recalling world explorations and the kingdom of
Brazil. Red and green were used in many early Portuguese
flags. The current flag dates to June 30, 1911.

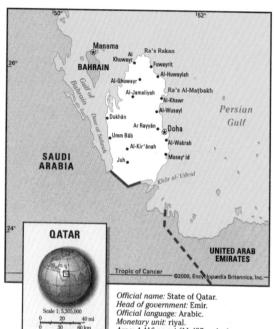

QATAR

Scale 1: 5,305,000

| 0 | 20 | 40 mi |
| 0 | 30 | 60 km |

Ethnic Composition

Arab 40%

Other (Pakistani, Indian, and Iranian) 60%

Official name: State of Qatar.
Head of government: Emir.
Official language: Arabic.
Monetary unit: riyal.
Area: 4,416 sq mi (11,437 sq km).
Population (1996): 590,000.
GNP per capita (1994): U.S.$14,540.
Principal exports (1994): mineral fuels and lubricants 81.2%; chemicals and chemical products 10.4%; manufactured goods 5.9% *to* (1989): Japan 54.4%; Thailand 5.0%; Singapore 4.0%; South Korea 3.6%; U.A.E. 3.4%.

The 1868 treaty between Great Britain and Qatar may have inspired the creation of the flag. Qataris chose mauve or maroon instead of red (a more typical color among Arab countries) perhaps to distinguish it from the flag used in Bahrain. Passages from the Quran, in Arabic script, have sometimes been added to the flag.

Official name: Romania.
Head of government: Prime Minister.
Official language: Romanian.
Monetary unit: Romanian leu.
Area: 92,043 sq mi (238,391 sq km).
Population (1996): 22,670,000.
GNP per capita (1994): U.S.$2,650.
Principal exports (1994): machinery
29.4%; textiles 18.8%; iron and steel
11.6%; mineral fuels 9.9%; chemicals
8.0% *to:* Germany 16.1%; Italy 12.9%;
France 5.1%; China 4.5%; Turkey 4.1%.

ROMANIA

Scale 1: 10,966,000

0   50   100 mi
0   80   160 km

Ethnic Composition

Romanian
89.4%

Hungarian
7.1%

Other
3.5%

In 1834 Walachia, an ancient region of Romania, chose a naval
ensign with stripes of red, blue, and yellow. The modern
Romanian tricolor was created in 1848 and flown for a brief
time. In 1867 Romania reestablished the vertical tricolor, and
with the fall of the 20th-century communist regime, it was
defined on Dec. 27, 1989.

RUSSIA

Scale 1: 55,746,000

0   300   600 mi

0   400   800 km

Ethnic Composition

Other 14.7%

Tatar 3.8%

Russian 81.5%

Tsar Peter the Great visited the Netherlands in order to modernize the Russian navy, and in 1699 he chose a Dutch-influenced flag for Russian ships. The flag soon became popular on land as well. After the Russian Revolution it was replaced by the communist red banner, but the tricolor again became official on Aug. 21, 1991.

Official name: Russian Federation.
Head of government: Prime Minister.
Official language: Russian.
Monetary unit: ruble.
Area: 6,592,800 sq mi (17,075,400 sq km).
Population (1996): 148,070,000.
GNP per capita (1994): U.S.$2,650.
Principal exports (1995): fuels and lubricants 39.9%; ferrous and
   nonferrous metals 28.8%; chemicals 9.4%; machinery and transport
   equipment 7.8%; forestry products 5.8%; food 3.4% *to:* Germany
   9.2%; United States 6.6%; Switzerland 5.4%; China 5.1%; Italy 5.0%;
   The Netherlands 4.8%.

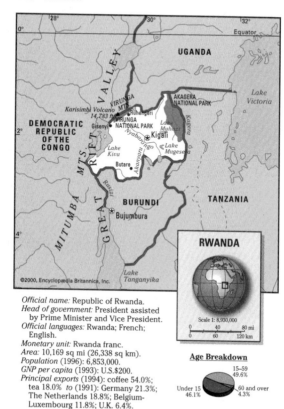

Official name: Republic of Rwanda.
Head of government: President assisted by Prime Minister and Vice President.
Official languages: Rwanda; French; English.
Monetary unit: Rwanda franc.
Area: 10,169 sq mi (26,338 sq km).
Population (1996): 6,853,000.
GNP per capita (1993): U.S.$200.
Principal exports (1994): coffee 54.0%; tea 18.0% *to* (1991): Germany 21.3%; The Netherlands 18.8%; Belgium-Luxembourg 11.8%; U.K. 6.4%.

RWANDA

Scale 1: 8,930,000

| 0 | 40 | 80 mi |
| 0 | 60 | 120 km |

Age Breakdown

- 15–59 49.6%
- Under 15 46.1%
- 60 and over 4.3%

On Jan. 28, 1961, the republic was proclaimed under a tricolor of red, yellow, and green—the Pan African colors. In Rwanda these symbolize the blood shed for liberation, peace and tranquility, and optimism. In 1961 a black "R" was added to distinguish the flag from that of Guinea and to stand for Rwanda, revolution, and referendum.

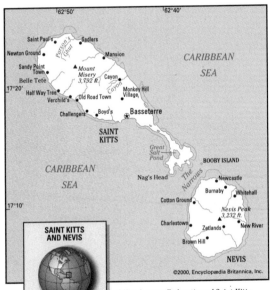

©2000, Encyclopædia Britannica, Inc.

SAINT KITTS AND NEVIS

Scale 1: 610,000

0 3 6 mi
0 4 8 km

Religious Affiliation

Protestant 76.4%

Other 12.9%

Roman Catholic 10.7%

Official name: Federation of Saint Kitts and Nevis.
Head of government: Prime Minister.
Official language: English.
Monetary unit: Eastern Caribbean dollar.
Area: 104.0 sq mi (269.4 sq km).
Population (1996): 39,400.
GNP per capita (1994): U.S.$4,760.
Principal exports (1994): electronic goods 38.0%; sugar 33.2%; miscellaneous manufactures 15.2%; *to:* United States 46.6%; U.K. 26.4%; Caricom countries 9.3%.

On Sept. 18, 1983, at the time of its independence from Britain, St. Kitts and Nevis hoisted the current flag. It has green (for fertility), red (for the struggle against slavery and colonialism), and black (for African heritage). The yellow flanking stripes are for sunshine, and the two stars, one for each island, are for hope and liberty.

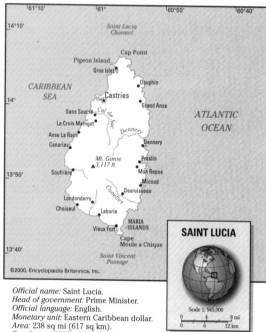

SAINT LUCIA

Scale 1: 945,000

| 0 | 4 | 8 mi |
| 0 | 6 | 12 km |

Official name: Saint Lucia.
Head of government: Prime Minister.
Official language: English.
Monetary unit: Eastern Caribbean dollar.
Area: 238 sq mi (617 sq km).
Population (1996): 144,000.
GNP per capita (1994): U.S.$3,450.
Principal exports (1993): food and live
animals 50.2%, of which bananas
47.7%; miscellaneous manufactures
24.8%; basic manufactures 9.0% *to:*
United Kingdom 49.6%; United States
27.0%; Dominica 7.7%; Germany 2.4%.

Ethnic Composition

Black 90.5%

Mixed 5.5%

Other 4%

The flag was hoisted on March 1, 1967, when the former
colony assumed a status of association with the United
Kingdom; it was slightly altered in 1979. The blue represents
Atlantic and Caribbean waters. The white and black colors
are for racial harmony, while the black triangle also represents volcanoes. The yellow triangle is for sunshine.

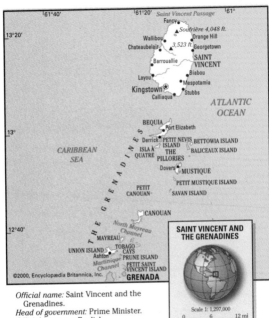

Official name: Saint Vincent and the Grenadines.
Head of government: Prime Minister.
Official language: English.
Monetary unit: Eastern Caribbean dollar.
Area: 150.3 sq mi (389.3 sq km).
Population (1996): 113,000.
GNP per capita (1994): U.S.$2,120.
Principal exports (1993): domestic exports 93.8%, of which bananas 47.4%, flour 18.7%; reexports 6.2% *to:* United Kingdom 40.7%; Saint Lucia 11.5%; Trinidad and Tobago 9.4%.

Ethnic Composition

Black 65.5%
Mulatto 19%
Other 6.5%
East Indian 5.5%
White 3.5%

At independence from Britain in 1979 a national flag was designed, but it was replaced by the current flag on Oct. 22, 1985. The three green diamonds are arranged in the form of a V. Green is for the rich vegetation and the vitality of the people, yellow is for sand and personal warmth, and blue is for sea and sky.

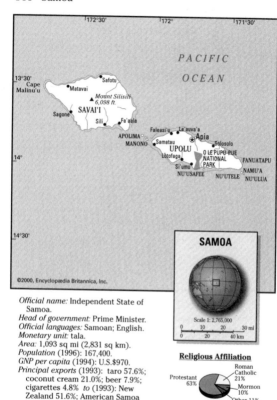

172°30' 172 171°30'

PACIFIC

OCEAN

13°30'
Cape
Malinu'u
• Safotu
• Matavai
▲ *Mount Silisili*
6,098 ft.
SAVAI'I
• Sagone
• Sili • Fa'aala
APOLIMA Faleasi'u • La'auva'a
MANONO Samatau • ⊛ **Apia** • Solosolo
14° **UPOLU** O LE PUPU-PUE
Lotofaga • NATIONAL FANUATAPU
PARK
Si'umu • NAMU'A
NU'USAFEE NU'UTELE NU'ULUA

14°30'

©2000, Encyclopædia Britannica, Inc.

SAMOA

Scale 1: 2,765,000
0   10   20   30 mi
0   20   40 km

Official name: Independent State of
Samoa.
Head of government: Prime Minister.
Official languages: Samoan; English.
Monetary unit: tala.
Area: 1,093 sq mi (2,831 sq km).
Population (1996): 167,400.
GNP per capita (1994): U.S.$970.
Principal exports (1993): taro 57.6%;
coconut cream 21.0%; beer 7.9%;
cigarettes 4.8% *to* (1993): New
Zealand 51.6%; American Samoa
17.4%; United States 12.6%.

Religious Affiliation

Roman
Catholic
21%
Protestant
63%
Mormon
10%
Other 11%

The first national flag of Samoa may date to 1873. Under
British administration, a version of the current flag was introduced on May 26, 1948. On Feb. 2, 1949, a fifth star was added
to the Southern Cross. White in the flag is said to stand for
purity, blue for freedom, and red for courage. The flag was
left unaltered upon independence in 1962.

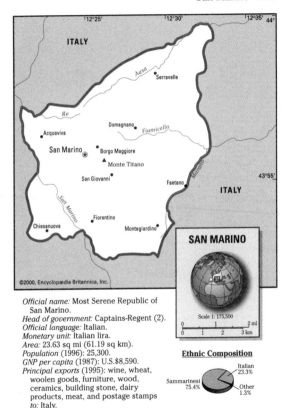

ITALY

Serravalle

Ausa

Re

Domagnano

Fiumicello

Acquaviva

San Marino ⊛ ● Borgo Maggiore

▲ Monte Titano

San Giovanni

Faetano

Marano

ITALY

Fiorentino

Chiesanuova

Montegiardino

©2000, Encyclopædia Britannica, Inc.

SAN MARINO

Scale 1: 175,500

0   1   2 mi

0   1   2   3 km

Official name: Most Serene Republic of San Marino.
Head of government: Captains-Regent (2).
Official language: Italian.
Monetary unit: Italian lira.
Area: 23.63 sq mi (61.19 sq km).
Population (1996): 25,300.
GNP per capita (1987): U.S.$8,590.
Principal exports (1995): wine, wheat, woolen goods, furniture, wood, ceramics, building stone, dairy products, meat, and postage stamps *to:* Italy.

Ethnic Composition

Italian 23.3%

Sammarinesi 75.4%

Other 1.3%

The colors of the flag, blue and white, were first used in the national cockade in 1797. The coat of arms in its present form was adopted on April 6, 1862, when the crown was added as a symbol of national sovereignty. Also in the coat of arms are three towers (Guaita, Cesta, and Montale) from the fortifications on Mount Titano.

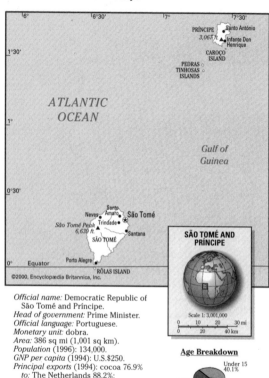

Official name: Democratic Republic of
São Tomé and Príncipe.
Head of government: Prime Minister.
Official language: Portuguese.
Monetary unit: dobra.
Area: 386 sq mi (1,001 sq km).
Population (1996): 134,000.
GNP per capita (1994): U.S.$250.
Principal exports (1994): cocoa 76.9%
    to: The Netherlands 88.2%;
    Portugal 0.6%.

Age Breakdown

Under 15
40.1%

15–59
53.1%

60 and over
6.8%

The national flag was adopted upon independence from
Portugal on July 12, 1975. Its colors are associated with Pan-
African independence. The red triangle stands for equality
and the nationalist movement. The stars are for the African
population living on the nation's two main islands. Green is
for vegetation and yellow is for the tropical sun.

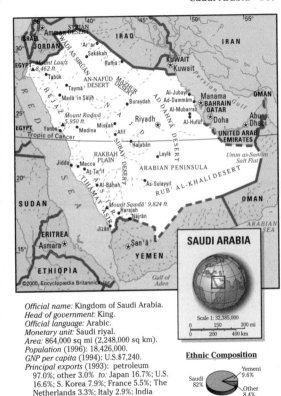

Official name: Kingdom of Saudi Arabia.
Head of government: King.
Official language: Arabic.
Monetary unit: Saudi riyal.
Area: 864,000 sq mi (2,248,000 sq km).
Population (1996): 18,426,000.
GNP per capita (1994): U.S.$7,240.
Principal exports (1993): petroleum
97.0%; other 3.0% *to:* Japan 16.7%; U.S.
16.6%; S. Korea 7.9%; France 5.5%; The
Netherlands 3.3%; Italy 2.9%; India
2.9%; U.K. 2.3%; Spain 2.2%.

SAUDI ARABIA

Scale 1: 32,385,000

| 0 | 150 | 300 mi |
| 0 | 200 | 400 km |

Ethnic Composition

Saudi 82%
Yemeni 9.6%
Other 8.4%

The Saudi flag, made official in 1932 but altered in 1968, originated in the military campaigns of Muhammad. The color green is associated with Fatima, the Prophet's daughter, and the Arabic inscription is translated as "There is no God but Allah and Muhammad is the Prophet of Allah." The saber symbolizes the militancy of the faith.

©2000, Encyclopædia Britannica, Inc.

SENEGAL

Scale 1: 14,627,000

| 0 | 60 | 120 mi |
| 0 | 80 | 160 km |

Official name: Republic of Senegal.
Head of government: Prime Minister.
Official language: French.
Monetary unit: CFA franc.
Area: 75,951 sq mi (196,712 sq km).
Population (1996): 8,532,000.
GNP per capita (1994): U.S.$610.
Principal exports (1994): fish and
  crustaceans 23.3%; peanut oil 11.1%;
  phosphates 8.7%; manufactured
  phosphate derivatives 5.4% *to:* France
  26.0%; Italy 8.5%; Mali 7.9%; Cameroon
  7.4%; Iran 3.6%; Spain 3.6%.

Ethnic Composition

Other 18.7%
Serer 14.9%
Peul 14.4%
Wolof 42.7%
Tukulor 9.3%
Joal

In a federation with French Sudan (now Mali) on April 4, 1959, Senegal used a flag with a human figure in the center. After the federation broke up in August 1960, Senegal substituted a green star for the central figure. Green is for hope and religion, yellow is for natural riches and labor, and red is for independence, life, and socialism.

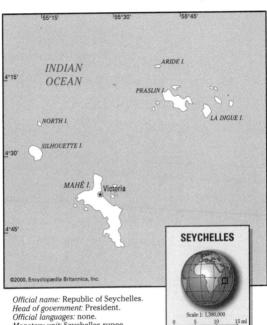

©2000, Encyclopædia Britannica, Inc.

Official name: Republic of Seychelles.
Head of government: President.
Official languages: none.
Monetary unit: Seychelles rupee.
Area: 176 sq mi (455 sq km).
Population (1996): 76,100.
GNP per capita (1994): U.S.$6,210.
Principal exports (1995): petroleum
products 47.2%; canned tuna 34.8%;
other fish 4.0%; frozen prawns 2.7%;
cinnamon bark 1.4% *to* (1995): China
15.0%; United Kingdom 12.4%;
Thailand 11.5%; India 3.5%.

SEYCHELLES

Scale 1: 1,380,000

0   5   10   15 mi
0   10   20 km

Age Breakdown

Under 15
31.2%

15–59
60.3%

60 and over
8.3%

The former British colony underwent a revolution in 1977.
The government was democratized in 1993, and on Jan. 8,
1996, a new flag was designed. The blue color is for sky and
sea, yellow is for the sun, red is for the people and their work
for unity and love, white is for social justice and harmony,
and green is for the land and natural environment.

Official name: Republic of Sierra Leone.
Head of government: President.
Official language: English.
Monetary unit: leone.
Area: 27,699 sq mi (71,740 sq km).
Population (1996): 4,617,000.
GNP per capita (1994): U.S.$150.
Principal exports (1994): mineral exports
90.0%, of which rutile and ilmenite
46.8%, diamonds 25.6%, bauxite 13.9%;
cocoa 2.5%; coffee 2.3% *to:* United
States 44.8%; United Kingdom 17.3%;
Belgium 16.8%; The Netherlands 4.1%.

Ethnic Composition

Other 25.3%
Limba 8.4%
Mende 34.6%
Temne 31.7%

Under British colonial control Sierre Leone was founded as a
home for freed slaves. With independence on April 27, 1961,
the flag was hoisted. Its stripes stand for agriculture and the
mountains (green); unity and justice (white); and the aspira-
tion to contribute to world peace, especially through the use
of the natural harbor at Freetown (blue).

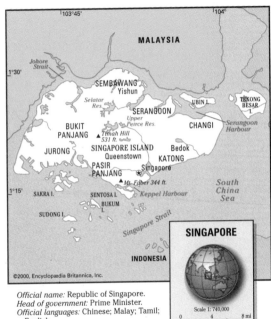

MALAYSIA

Johore Strait
1°30'
SEMBAWANG
Yishun
Selatar Res.
SERANGOON
UBIN I.
TEKONG BESAR I.
BUKIT PANJANG
Upper Peirce Res.
CHANGI
Serangoon Harbour
▲ Timah Hill 531 ft.
JURONG
SINGAPORE ISLAND
Queenstown
Bedok
KATONG
PASIR PANJANG
BUKUM
⋆ Singapore
South China Sea
1°15'
SAKRA I.
SENTOSA I.
BUKUM I.
▲ Mt. Faber 344 ft.
Keppel Harbour
SUDONG I.
Singapore Strait

INDONESIA

©2000, Encyclopædia Britannica, Inc.

Official name: Republic of Singapore.
Head of government: Prime Minister.
Official languages: Chinese; Malay; Tamil; English.
Monetary unit: Singapore dollar.
Area: 249.5 sq mi (646.1 sq km).
Population (1996): 3,045,000.
GNP per capita (1994): U.S.$23,360.
Principal exports (1995): office machines 24.5%; telecommunications apparatus 9.1%; petroleum products 6.7%; optical instruments 2.2% *to:* Malaysia 19.2%; U.S. 18.2%; Hong Kong 8.6%.

SINGAPORE

Scale 1: 740,000

0   4   8 mi
0   6   12 km

Ethnic Composition

Malay 14.2%
Chinese 77.4%
Indian 7.2%
Other 1.2%

On Dec. 3, 1959, the flag was acquired, and it was retained after separation from Malaysia on Aug. 9, 1965. The red and white stripes stand for universal brotherhood, equality, purity, and virtue. The crescent symbolizes the growth of a young country, while the five stars are for democracy, peace, progress, justice, and equality.

©2000, Encyclopædia Britannica, Inc.

SLOVAKIA

Scale 1: 6,249,000

0   30   60 mi
0   40   80 km

Official name: Slovak Republic.
Head of government: Prime Minister.
Official language: Slovak.
Monetary unit: Slovak koruna.
Area: 18,933 sq mi (49,036 sq km).
Population (1996): 5,372,000.
GNP per capita (1994): U.S.$2,200.
Principal exports (1994): semimanufactured products 39.4%; machinery and transport equipment 19.0%; manufactured goods 13.4%; chemical products 12.9% *to:* Czech Republic 37.4%; Germany 17.1%; former U.S.S.R. 6.1%.

Ethnic Composition

Slovak 85.7%

Hungarian 10.6%

Other 3.7%

In 1189 the kingdom of Hungary (including Slovakia) introduced a double-barred cross in its coat of arms; this symbol was altered in 1848-49 by Slovak nationalists. After a period of communist rule, the tricolor was made official in 1989. On Sept. 3, 1992, the shield was added to the white-blue-red flag to differentiate it from the flag of Russia.

©2000, Encyclopædia Britannica, Inc.

Official name: Republic of Slovenia.
Head of government: Prime Minister.
Official language: Slovene.
Monetary unit: Slovene tolar.
Area: 7,821 sq mi (20,256 sq km).
Population (1996): 1,958,746.
GNP per capita (1994): U.S.$7,161.
Principal exports (1994): machinery and
transport equipment 30.3%; basic
manufactures 24.0%; chemicals 10.3%;
food 4.0%, mineral fuels 1.1% *to:*
Germany 30.3%; Italy 13.5%; Croatia
10.1%; France 8.6%; Austria 5.5%.

SLOVENIA

Scale 1: 4,314,000

| 0 | 20 | 40 mi |

| 0 | 30 | 60 km |

Age Breakdown

60 and over
18.3%

15–59
63.9%

Under 15
17.8%

Under the current flag Slovenia proclaimed independence on
June 25, 1991, but it was opposed for a time by the Yugoslav
army. The flag is the same as that of Russia and Slovakia
except for the coat of arms. It depicts the peaks of Triglav
(the nation's highest mountain), the waves of the Adriatic
coast, and three stars on a blue background.

©2000, Encyclopædia Britannica, Inc.

Official name: Solomon Islands.
Head of government: Prime Minister.
Official language: English.
Monetary unit: Solomon Islands dollar.
Area: 10,954 sq mi (28,370 sq km).
Population (1996): 396,000.
GNP per capita (1994): U.S.$800.
Principal exports (1994): timber products
59.2%; fish products 21.2%; palm oil
products 9.5%; copra 4.2%; cacao
beans 2.7% *to:* Japan 41.1%; South
Korea 14.1%; United Kingdom 13.1%;
The Netherlands 8.5%; Thailand 4.5%.

SOLOMON ISLANDS

Scale 1: 26,575,000

| 0 | 100 | 200 mi |
| 0 | 150 | 300 km |

Age Breakdown

Under 15
43.7%

15–59
52%

60 and over
4.3%

The flag was introduced on Nov. 18, 1977, eight months
before independence from Britain. The yellow stripe stands
for the sun. The green triangle is for the trees and crops of
the fertile land, while the blue triangle symbolizes rivers,
rain, and the ocean. The five stars represented the original
five districts of the island.

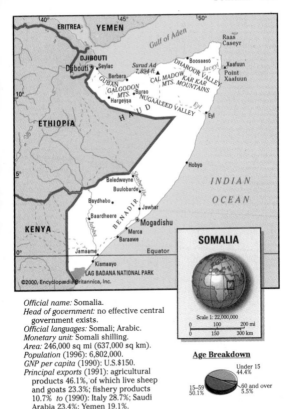

Official name: Somalia.
Head of government: no effective central
government exists.
Official languages: Somali; Arabic.
Monetary unit: Somali shilling.
Area: 246,000 sq mi (637,000 sq km).
Population (1996): 6,802,000.
GNP per capita (1990): U.S.$150.
Principal exports (1991): agricultural
products 46.1%, of which live sheep
and goats 23.3%; fishery products
10.7% *to* (1990): Italy 28.7%; Saudi
Arabia 23.4%; Yemen 19.1%.

Age Breakdown

Under 15
44.4%

15–59
50.1%

60 and over
5.5%

From the mid-19th century, areas in the Horn of Africa with
Somali populations were divided between Ethiopia, France,
Britain, and Italy. On Oct. 12, 1954, with the partial unification
of these areas, the flag was adopted with a white star,
each point referring to a Somali homeland. The colors were
influenced by the colors of the United Nations.

©2000, Encyclopædia Britannica, Inc.

SOUTH AFRICA

Scale 1: 29,306,000

| 0 | 100 | 200 mi |
| 0 | 150 | 300 km |

Official name: Republic of South Africa.
Head of government: President.
Official languages: Afrikaans; English;
  Ndebele; Pedi; Sotho; Swazi; Tsonga;
  Tswana; Venda; Xhosa; Zulu.
Monetary unit: rand.
Area: 470,693 sq mi (1,219,090 sq km).
Population (1996): 41,743,000.
GNP per capita (1994): U.S.$2,930.
Principal exports (1994): gold 25.5%; base
  metals and metal products 12.3%; gem
  diamonds 11.0%; food 9.1% *to:*
  Switzerland 6.7%; U.K. 6.6%; U.S. 4.9%.

Ethnic Composition

White 12.7%
Black 76.3%
Mixed race 8.5%
Asian 2.5%

With the decline of apartheid, the flag was hoisted on April 27, 1994, and confirmed in 1996. Its six colors collectively represent Zulus, English or Afrikaners, Muslims, supporters of the African National Congress, and other groups. The Y-symbol stands for "merging history and present political realities" into a united and prosperous future.

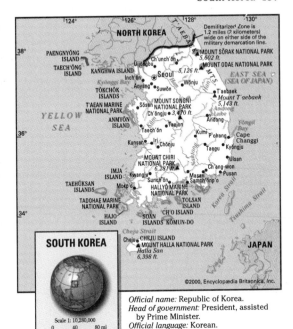

NORTH KOREA

Demilitarized Zone is 1.2 miles (2 kilometers) wide on either side of the military demarcation line.

MOUNT SŎRAK NATIONAL PARK *5,602 ft.*

MOUNT ODAE NATIONAL PARK

PAENGNYŎNG ISLAND

TAECH'ŎNG ISLAND

KANGHWA ISLAND

Ch'unch'ŏn

Ŭijŏngbu

5,126 ft.

EAST SEA (SEA OF JAPAN)

Inch'ŏn ● Seoul

Anyang ● Suwŏn

Wŏnju

Kyŏngan R.

TŎKCHŎK ISLANDS

Sŏsan

T'aebaek

Mount T'aebaek 5,143 ft.

T'AEAN MARINE NATIONAL PARK

MOUNT SONGNI NATIONAL PARK

Ch'ŏngju ▲ *3,470 ft.*

ANMYŎN ISLAND

Andong

Andong Lake

Taech'ŏn

Taejŏn

Yŏngil Bay

Kunsan

Iri

Chŏnju

Kumi

P'ohang

Cape Changgi

YELLOW SEA

Taegu

Kyŏngju

Ulsan

MOUNT CHIRI NATIONAL PARK *6,281 ft.*

Kwangju

Sunch'ŏn

Masan

Ch'ang-wŏn

Samch'ŏnp'o

Pusan

IMJA ISLAND

Kwangju

HALLYŎ MARINE NATIONAL PARK

TAEHŬKSAN ISLANDS

Mokp'o

TOLSAN ISLAND

Korea Strait

TADOHAE MARINE NATIONAL PARK

HAJO ISLAND

SOAN ISLANDS

CH'O ISLAND

KŎMUN-DO

Cheju Strait

Tsushima Strait

Cheju ▲ CHEJU ISLAND

MOUNT HALLA NATIONAL PARK

Halla San 6,398 ft.

JAPAN

©2000, Encyclopædia Britannica, Inc.

SOUTH KOREA

Scale 1: 10,280,000

| 0 | 40 | 80 mi |
| 0 | 60 | 120 km |

Age Breakdown

Under 15 23.2%

15–59 67.8%

60 and over 9%

Official name: Republic of Korea.
Head of government: President, assisted by Prime Minister.
Official language: Korean.
Monetary unit: won.
Area: 38,375 sq mi (99,392 sq km).
Population (1996): 45,232,000.
GNP per capita (1994): U.S.$8,220.
Principal exports (1995): machinery and transport equipment 52.5%; manufactured goods 22.0%; chemicals 7.2% *to:* United States 19.3%; Japan 13.6%; Hong Kong 8.5%; Singapore 5.3%.

The flag was adopted in August 1882. Its white background is for peace, while the central emblem represents yin-yang (Korean: *um-yang*), the duality of the universe. The black bars recall sun, moon, earth, heaven and other Confucian principles. Outlawed under Japanese rule, the flag was revived in 1945 and slightly modified in 1950 and 1984.

Official name: Kingdom of Spain.
Head of government: Prime Minister.
Official language: Castilian Spanish.
Monetary unit: peseta.
Area: 195,364 sq mi (505,990 sq km).
Population (1996): 39,270,000.
GNP per capita (1994): U.S.$13,280.
Principal exports (1995): transport
  equipment 20.3%; agricultural
  products 12.7%; machinery 8.3%
  to: France 20.5%; Germany 15.4%;
  Italy 11.5%; U.K. 8.0%.

SPAIN

Scale 1: 16,741,000

0   75   150 mi
0   100   200 km

Language Composition

Catalan 16.9%
Galician 6.4%
Other 2.3%
Spanish 74.4%

The colors of the flag have no official symbolic meaning.
Introduced in 1785 by King Charles III, the flag was changed
only under the Spanish Republic (1931–39). Under different
regimes, however, the coat of arms has been altered. The current design dates from Dec. 18, 1981, with the death of
Francisco Franco and the resurgence of democracy.

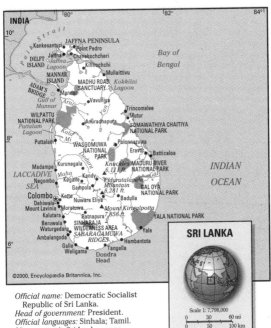

©2000, Encyclopædia Britannica, Inc.

Official name: Democratic Socialist
   Republic of Sri Lanka.
Head of government: President.
Official languages: Sinhala; Tamil.
Monetary unit: Sri Lanka rupee.
Area: 25,332 sq mi (65,610 sq km).
Population (1996): 18,318,000.
GNP per capita (1994): U.S.$640.
Principal exports (1994): clothing and
   accessories 46.2%; tea 13.0%; pearls
   7.0% *to:* U.S. 34.7%; U.K. 8.9%;
   Germany 6.9%; Belgium 5.9%; Japan
   5.1%; The Netherlands 3.5%.

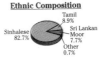

SRI LANKA

Scale 1: 7,798,000

0   30   60 mi
0   50   100 km

Ethnic Composition

Sinhalese
82.7%

Tamil
8.9%

Sri Lankan
Moor
7.7%

Other
0.7%

From the 5th century BC the Lion flag was a symbol of the
Sinhalese people. The flag was replaced by the Union Jack in
1815 but readopted upon independence in 1948. The stripes
of green (for Muslims) and orange (for Hindus) were added in
1951. In 1972 four leaves of the Bo tree were added as a symbol of Buddhism; the leaves were altered in 1978.

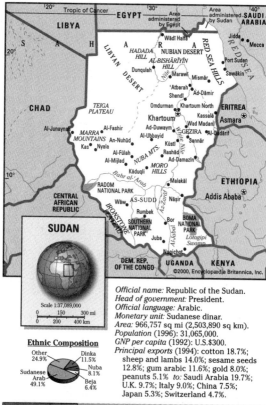

Official name: Republic of the Sudan.
Head of government: President.
Official language: Arabic.
Monetary unit: Sudanese dinar.
Area: 966,757 sq mi (2,503,890 sq km).
Population (1996): 31,065,000.
GNP per capita (1992): U.S.$300.
Principal exports (1994): cotton 18.7%;
  sheep and lambs 14.0%; sesame seeds
  12.8%; gum arabic 11.6%; gold 8.0%;
  peanuts 5.1% *to:* Saudi Arabia 19.7%;
  U.K. 9.7%; Italy 9.0%; China 7.5%;
  Japan 5.3%; Switzerland 4.7%.

Ethnic Composition

Other 24.9%
Dinka 11.5%
Nuba 8.1%
Beja 6.4%
Sudanese Arab 49.1%

The flag was first hoisted on May 20, 1970. It uses Pan-Arab colors. Black is for al-Mahdi (a leader in the 1800s) and the name of the country (sudan in Arabic means black); white recalls the revolutionary flag of 1924 and suggests peace and optimism; red is for patriotic martyrs, socialism, and progress; and green is for prosperity and Islam.

Official name: Republic of Suriname.
Head of government: President.
Official language: Dutch.
Monetary unit: Suriname guilder.
Area: 63,251 sq mi (163,820 sq km).
Population (1996): 436,000.
GNP per capita (1994): U.S.$870.
Principal exports (1994): alumina 63.6%;
    shrimp and fish 9.7%; rice 9.6%;
    aluminum 9.3%; petroleum 3.0%;
    bananas 2.9% to: Norway 32.6%; The
    Netherlands 26.9%; U.S. 13.1%; Japan
    6.6%; Brazil 6.3%; France 2.9%.

Ethnic Composition

Indo-Pakistani 33%
Suriname Creole 35%
Javanese 16%
Bush Negro 10%
Other 6%

Adopted on Nov. 21, 1975, four days before independence
from the Dutch, the flag of Suriname features green stripes for
jungles and agriculture, white for justice and freedom, and
red for the progressive spirit of a young nation. The yellow
star is symbolic of the unity of the country, its golden future,
and the people's spirit of sacrifice.

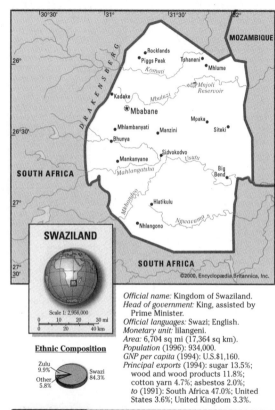

| 30°30' | 31° | 31°30' | 32° |

MOZAMBIQUE

Rocklands

Piggs Peak • Tshaneni • Mhlume

Komati

26°

Mbuluzi • *Mnjoli Reservoir*

Kadake •

✴ **Mbabane**

Mpaka •

Mhlambanyati • Manzini • Siteki

26°30'

Bhunya •

Sidvokodvo

Mankanyane • *Usutu*

Big Bend

Mahlangatsha

SOUTH AFRICA

27°

Hlatikulu •

Ngwavuma

Nhlangono •

SOUTH AFRICA

27°30'

©2000, Encyclopædia Britannica, Inc.

DRAKENSBERG

Mkhondvo

SWAZILAND

Scale 1: 2,956,000

0   10   20   30 mi

0   20   40 km

Ethnic Composition

Zulu 9.9%

Other 5.8%

Swazi 84.3%

Official name: Kingdom of Swaziland.
Head of government: King, assisted by
  Prime Minister.
Official languages: Swazi; English.
Monetary unit: lilangeni.
Area: 6,704 sq mi (17,364 sq km).
Population (1996): 934,000.
GNP per capita (1994): U.S.$1,160.
Principal exports (1994): sugar 13.5%;
  wood and wood products 11.8%;
  cotton yarn 4.7%; asbestos 2.0%;
  to (1991): South Africa 47.0%; United
  States 3.6%; United Kingdom 3.3%.

The flag dates to the creation of a military banner in 1941,
when Swazi troops were preparing for the Allied invasion of
Italy. On April 25, 1967, it was hoisted as the national flag.
The crimson stripe stands for past battles, yellow for mineral
wealth, and blue for peace. Featured are a Swazi war shield,
two spears, and a "fighting stick."

Official name: Kingdom of Sweden.
Head of government: Prime Minister.
Official language: Swedish.
Monetary unit: Swedish krona.
Area: 173,732 sq mi (449,964 sq km).
Population (1996): 8,858,000.
GNP per capita (1994): U.S.$23,630.
Principal exports (1995): machinery and transport equipment 45.6%; paper products 9.6%; chemicals 9.0%; wood and wood pulp 6.2%; iron and steel products 6.0% *to:* Germany 11.1%; U.K. 8.5%; Norway 6.8%; U.S. 6.7%.

Scale 1: 23,567,000

0   100   200 mi

0   100   200   300 km

Age Breakdown

60 and over 22.1%

15–59 59.1%

Under 15 18.8%

From the 14th century the coat of arms of Sweden had a blue field with three golden crowns, and the earlier Folkung dynasty used a shield of blue and white wavy stripes with a gold lion. The off-center "Scandinavian cross" was influenced by the flag of the rival kingdom of Denmark. The current flag law was adopted on July 1, 1906.

©2000, Encyclopædia Britannica, Inc.

SWITZERLAND

Scale 1: 5,214,000

| 0 | 20 | 40 mi |
| 0 | 30 | 60 km |

Language Composition

German 64%
French 19%
Other 9%
Italian 8%

Official name: Swiss Confederation.
Head of government: President.
Official languages: French; German; Italian.
Monetary unit: Swiss franc.
Area: 15,940 sq mi (41,285 sq km).
Population (1996): 7,087,000.
GNP per capita (1994): U.S.$37,180.
Principal exports (1995): machinery and electronics 29.8%; chemical products 25.6%; precision instruments, watches, and jewelry 16.2% *to:* Germany 24.5%; France 9.7%; U.S. 8.4%; Italy 7.8%.

The Swiss flag is ultimately based on the war flag of the Holy Roman Empire. Schwyz, one of the original three cantons of the Swiss Confederation, placed a narrow white cross in the corner of its flag in 1240. This was also used in 1339 at the Battle of Laupen. Following the 1848 constitution, the flag was recognized by the army, and it was established as the national flag on land on Dec. 12, 1889.

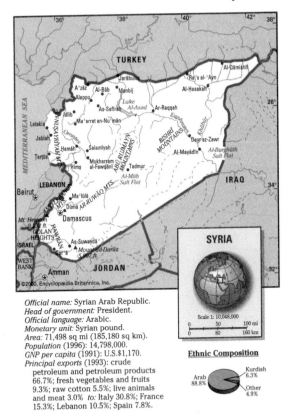

Official name: Syrian Arab Republic.
Head of government: President.
Official language: Arabic.
Monetary unit: Syrian pound.
Area: 71,498 sq mi (185,180 sq km).
Population (1996): 14,798,000.
GNP per capita (1991): U.S.$1,170.
Principal exports (1993): crude
   petroleum and petroleum products
   66.7%; fresh vegetables and fruits
   9.3%; raw cotton 5.5%; live animals
   and meat 3.0% *to:* Italy 30.8%; France
   15.3%; Lebanon 10.5%; Spain 7.8%.

Ethnic Composition

Arab
88.8%

Kurdish
6.3%

Other
4.9%

In 1918 the Arab Revolt flag flew over Syria, which joined
Egypt in the United Arab Republic in 1958 and based its new
flag on that of the Egyptian revolution of 1952; its stripes
were red-white-black, with two green stars for the constituent
states. In 1961 Syria broke from the union, but it readopted
the flag on March 29, 1980.

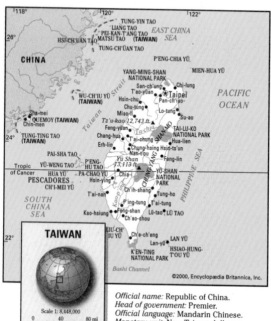

©2000, Encyclopædia Britannica, Inc.

Official name: Republic of China.
Head of government: Premier.
Official language: Mandarin Chinese.
Monetary unit: New Taiwan dollar.
Area: 13,969 sq mi (36,179 sq km).
Population (1996): 21,463,000.
GNP per capita (1995): U.S.$12,490.
Principal exports (1995): nonelectrical
machinery 21.7%; electrical machinery
21.5%; plastic articles 6.4%; synthetic
fibres 5.6% *to:* U.S. 24.9%; Hong Kong
22.4%; Japan 11.0%; Singapore 3.7%;
Germany 3.5%.

Religious Affiliation

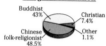

Buddhist 43%
Christian 7.4%
Chinese folk-religionist 48.5%
Other 1.1%

Under Chiang Kai-shek, a new Chinese national flag was
adopted on Oct. 28, 1928, and it was carried to Taiwan in
1949–50 when the Nationalists fled the mainland. The three
colors stand for the "Three Principles of the People" of the
Nationalist (Kuomintang) Party—nationalism, democracy, and
socialism.

Official name: Republic of Tajikistan.
Head of government: Prime Minister.
Official language: Tajik.
Monetary unit: Tajik ruble.
Area: 55,300 sq mi (143,100 sq km).
Population (1996): 5,945,000.
GNP per capita (1994): U.S.$350.
Principal exports (1993): base metals
  85.0%; textiles 14.3% to: Russia 42.0%;
  Uzbekistan 20.6%; Lithuania 12.4%;
  Kazakstan 9.2%; Ukraine 4.6%; Latvia
  3.1%.

Ethnic Composition

Tajik
63.8%

Uzbek
24%

Russian
6.5%

Other
5.7%

Following independence from the Soviet Union in 1991,
Tajikistan developed a new flag on Nov. 24, 1992. The green
stripe is for agriculture, while red is for sovereignty. White is
for the main crop—cotton. The central crown contains seven
stars representing unity among workers, peasants, intellectuals, and other social classes.

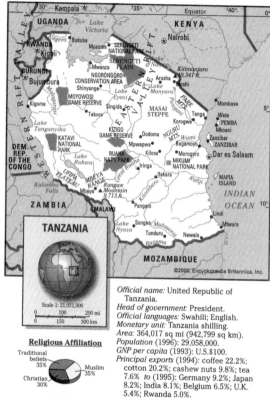

Official name: United Republic of Tanzania.
Head of government: President.
Official languages: Swahili; English.
Monetary unit: Tanzania shilling.
Area: 364,017 sq mi (942,799 sq km).
Population (1996): 29,058,000.
GNP per capita (1993): U.S.$100.
Principal exports (1994): coffee 22.2%; cotton 20.2%; cashew nuts 9.8%; tea 7.6% *to* (1995): Germany 9.2%; Japan 8.2%; India 8.1%; Belgium 6.5%; U.K. 5.4%; Rwanda 5.0%.

In April 1964 Tanganyika and Zanzibar united, and in July their flag traditions melded to create the current design. The black stripe is for the majority population, while green is for the rich agricultural resources of the land. Mineral wealth is reflected in the yellow fimbriations (narrow borders), while the Indian Ocean is symbolized by blue.

Official name: Kingdom of Thailand.
Head of government: Prime Minister.
Official language: Thai.
Monetary unit: Thai baht.
Area: 198,115 sq mi (513,115 sq km).
Population (1996): 60,003,000.
GNP per capita (1994): U.S.$2,210.
Principal exports (1994): electrical
  machinery 17.3%; nonelectrical
  machinery 12.7%; garments 9.4%;
  fresh prawns 6.0%; rubber products
  4.8%; precious jewelry 4.2% *to:* U.S.
  20.8%; Japan 16.9%; Singapore 13.5%.

Ethnic Composition

Chinese 12.1%
Malay 3.7%
Other 4.7%
Thai 79.5%

In the 17th century, the flag of Thailand was plain red, and Thai ships in 1855 displayed a flag with a central white elephant as a symbol of good fortune. The Thai king replaced the elephant with two white stripes in 1916 and added the blue stripe on Sept. 28, 1917. Red symbolizes the blood of patriots, white is for Buddhism, and blue is for royal guidance.

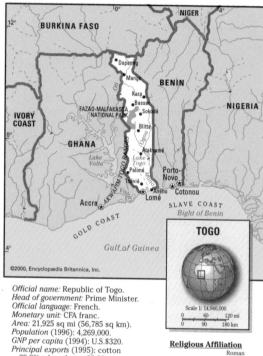

©2000, Encyclopædia Britannica, Inc.

TOGO

Scale 1: 14,946,000

0   60   120 mi

0   90   180 km

Official name: Republic of Togo.
Head of government: Prime Minister.
Official language: French.
Monetary unit: CFA franc.
Area: 21,925 sq mi (56,785 sq km).
Population (1996): 4,269,000.
GNP per capita (1994): U.S.$320.
Principal exports (1995): cotton
   29.8%, phosphates 23.8%,
   coffee 5.5%; reexports 26.7%
   to (1994): Canada 17.0%;
   Bolivia 7.6%;
   Indonesia 5.7%.

Religious Affiliation

Roman
Catholic
22%

Traditional
beliefs
59%

Muslim
12%

Protestant
7%

On April 27, 1960, Togo became independent from France
under the current flag. Its stripes correspond to the administrative regions and symbolize that the population depends on
the land for its sustenance (green) and its own labor for
development (yellow). The red is for love, fidelity, and charity, while the white star is for purity and unity.

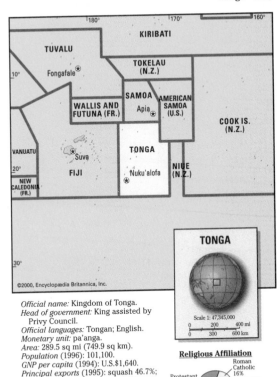

KIRIBATI

TUVALU

180°

TOKELAU
(N.Z.)

10°

Fongafale ⊛

SAMOA

WALLIS AND
FUTUNA (FR.)

Apia ⊛

AMERICAN
SAMOA
(U.S.)

170°

160°

COOK IS.
(N.Z.)

VANUATU

Suva ⊛

TONGA

20°

NEW
CALEDONIA
(FR.)

FIJI

Nuku'alofa
⊛

NIUE
(N.Z.)

30°

©2000, Encyclopædia Britannica, Inc.

TONGA

Scale 1: 47,345,000

0   200   400 mi
0   300   600 km

Official name: Kingdom of Tonga.
Head of government: King assisted by
Privy Council.
Official languages: Tongan; English.
Monetary unit: pa'anga.
Area: 289.5 sq mi (749.9 sq km).
Population (1996): 101,100.
GNP per capita (1994): U.S.$1,640.
Principal exports (1995): squash 46.7%;
fish 24.1%; vanilla beans 15.6%; root
crops 5.0%; coconut products 0.4%
to: Japan 49.2%; U.S. 26.7%; New
Zealand 8.4%; Australia 4.0%; Fiji 0.9%.

Religious Affiliation

Roman
Catholic
16%

Protestant
64.9%

Mormon
12.1%

Other
7%

The colors red and white were popular in the Pacific long
before the arrival of Europeans. The Tonga constitution (Nov.
4, 1875) established the flag, which was created by King
George Tupou I with the advice of a missionary. The cross
was chosen as a symbol of the widespread Christian religion,
and the color red was related to the blood of Jesus.

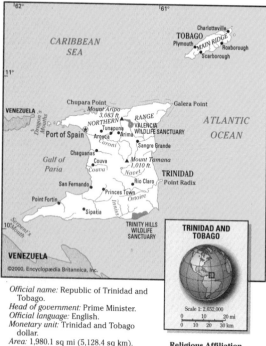

Official name: Republic of Trinidad and Tobago.
Head of government: Prime Minister.
Official language: English.
Monetary unit: Trinidad and Tobago dollar.
Area: 1,980.1 sq mi (5,128.4 sq km).
Population (1996): 1,262,000.
GNP per capita (1994): U.S.$3,740.
Principal exports (1994): refined petroleum 29.2%; crude petroleum 18.1%; urea 12.4% *to:* United States 46.4%; Jamaica 6.1%; Canada 3.8%.

Religious Affiliation

Hindu 23.7%
Other 11.3%
Muslim 5.9%
Roman Catholic 29.4%
Protestant 29.7%

Hoisted on independence day, Aug. 31, 1962, the flag symbolizes earth, water, and fire as well as past, present, and future. Black also is a symbol of unity, strength, and purpose. White recalls the equality and purity of the people and the sea that unites them. Red is for the sun, the vitality of the people and nation, friendliness, and courage.

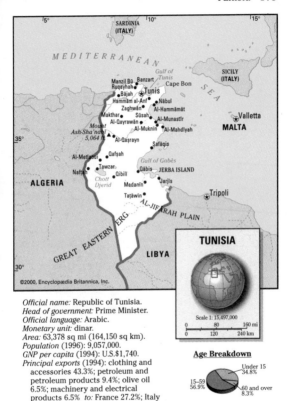

©2000, Encyclopædia Britannica, Inc.

TUNISIA

Scale 1: 15,497,000

| 0 | 80 | 160 mi |
| 0 | 120 | 240 km |

Official name: Republic of Tunisia.
Head of government: Prime Minister.
Official language: Arabic.
Monetary unit: dinar.
Area: 63,378 sq mi (164,150 sq km).
Population (1996): 9,057,000.
GNP per capita (1994): U.S.$1,740.
Principal exports (1994): clothing and accessories 43.3%; petroleum and petroleum products 9.4%; olive oil 6.5%; machinery and electrical products 6.5% *to:* France 27.2%; Italy 19.6%; Germany 15.5%; Belgium 6.5%.

Age Breakdown

Under 15
34.8%

15–59
56.9%

60 and over
8.3%

The Tunisian flag, established in 1835, contains the crescent and moon, a symbol used by the Ottoman Empire but dating from the ancient Egyptians and Phoenicians. More as a cultural than a religious symbol, the crescent and star came to be associated with Islam because of its widespread adoption in Muslim nations.

Official name: Republic of Turkey.
Head of government: Prime Minister.
Official language: Turkish.
Monetary unit: Turkish lira.
Area: 300,948 sq mi (779,452 sq km).
Population (1996): 62,650,000.
GNP per capita (1994): U.S.$2,450.
Principal exports (1995): textiles and
   clothing 26.1%; iron and steel 8.0%;
   edible fruits 5.7%; electrical and
   electronic machinery 4.6%
   to: Germany 23.3%; United States 7.0%;
   Italy 6.7%; Russia 5.7%; U.K. 5.3%.

TURKEY

Scale 1: 24,576,000

| 0 | 100 | 200 mi |
| 0 | 150 | 300 km |

Religious Affiliation

Sunni
Muslim
80%

Other
Muslim
20%

In June 1793 the flag was established for the navy, although
its star had eight points instead of the current five (since
about 1844). This design was reconfirmed in 1936 following
the revolution led by Ataturk. Various myths are associated
with the symbolism of the red color and the star and crescent, but none really explains their origins.

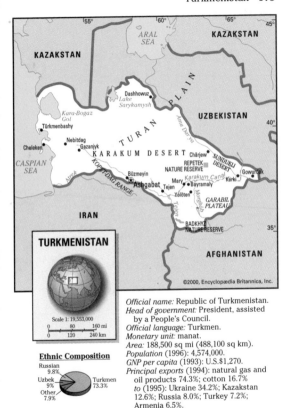

©2000, Encyclopædia Britannica, Inc.

TURKMENISTAN

Scale 1: 19,553,000

0   80   160 mi
0   120   240 km

Ethnic Composition

Russian 9.8%
Uzbek 9%
Other 7.9%
Turkmen 73.3%

Official name: Republic of Turkmenistan.
Head of government: President, assisted by a People's Council.
Official language: Turkmen.
Monetary unit: manat.
Area: 188,500 sq mi (488,100 sq km).
Population (1996): 4,574,000.
GNP per capita (1993): U.S.$1,270.
Principal exports (1994): natural gas and oil products 74.3%; cotton 16.7% *to (1995):* Ukraine 34.2%; Kazakstan 12.6%; Russia 8.0%; Turkey 7.2%; Armenia 6.5%.

The flag was introduced on Feb. 19, 1992. Its stripe contains intricate designs for five Turkmen tribes. Its green background is for Islam, and its crescent symbolizes faith in a bright future. The stars are for the human senses and the states of matter (liquid, solid, gas, crystal, and plasma). On Feb. 19, 1997, an olive wreath was added to the stripe.

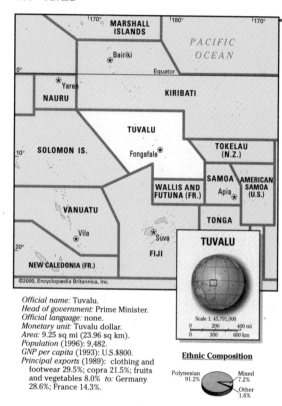

©2000, Encyclopædia Britannica, Inc.

Official name: Tuvalu.
Head of government: Prime Minister.
Official language: none.
Monetary unit: Tuvalu dollar.
Area: 9.25 sq mi (23.96 sq km).
Population (1996): 9,482.
GNP per capita (1993): U.S.$800.
Principal exports (1989): clothing and
footwear 29.5%; copra 21.5%; fruits
and vegetables 8.0% *to:* Germany
28.6%; France 14.3%.

TUVALU

Scale 1: 45,791,000

0   200   400 mi
0   300   600 km

Ethnic Composition

Polynesian 91.2%   Mixed 7.2%

Other 1.6%

On Oct. 1, 1978, three years after separating from the Gilbert
Islands, Tuvalu became independent under the current flag.
The stars represent the atolls and islands of the country. The
Union Jack recalls links with Britain and the Commonwealth.
Replaced by supporters of republicanism on Oct. 1, 1995, the
flag was reinstated on April 11, 1997.

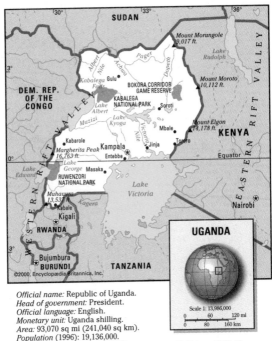

Official name: Republic of Uganda.
Head of government: President.
Official language: English.
Monetary unit: Uganda shilling.
Area: 93,070 sq mi (241,040 sq km).
Population (1996): 19,136,000.
GNP per capita (1994): U.S.$200.
Principal exports (1994): unroasted
coffee 76.0%; tea 1.7%; cotton 0.3%;
to (1992): U.K. 20.7%; Belgium-
Luxembourg 12.3%; Spain 9.2%; U.S.
8.1%; France 6.4%; Germany 4.3%.

Religious Affiliation

Protestant 28.7%
Traditional beliefs 12.6%
Muslim 6.6%
Other 2.5%
Roman Catholic 49.6%

The crested crane symbol was selected by the British for Uganda. The flag, established for independence on Oct. 9, 1962, was based on the flag of the ruling Uganda People's Congress (which has three black-yellow-red stripes), with the addition of the crane in the center. Black stands for the people, yellow for sunshine, and red for brotherhood.

©2000, Encyclopædia Britannica, Inc.

UKRAINE

Scale 1 : 19,690,000

| 0 | 80 | 160 mi |
| 0 | 120 | 240 km |

Ethnic Composition

Ukrainian 72.6%
Russian 22.2%
Other 5.2%

Official name: Ukraine.
Head of government: Prime Minister.
Official language: Ukrainian.
Monetary unit: hryvnia.
Area: 233,100 sq mi (603,700 sq km).
Population (1996): 51,273,000.
GNP per capita (1994): U.S.$1,570.
Principal exports (1995): ferrous metals 36.2%; machinery 11.8%; mineral commodities 10.6%; chemicals 9.7%; food 8.5% *to:* Russia 43.5%; U.S. 4.8%; Germany 4.1%; Belarus 3.7%.

The first national flag of Ukraine, adopted in 1848, had equal stripes of yellow over blue and was based on the coat of arms of the city of Lviv. In 1918 the stripes were reversed to reflect the symbolism of blue skies over golden wheat fields. A red Soviet banner flew from 1949, but it was replaced by the blue-yellow bicolor on Jan. 28, 1992.

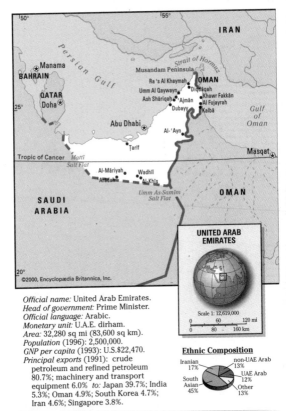

Official name: United Arab Emirates.
Head of government: Prime Minister.
Official language: Arabic.
Monetary unit: U.A.E. dirham.
Area: 32,280 sq mi (83,600 sq km).
Population (1996): 2,500,000.
GNP per capita (1993): U.S.$22,470.
Principal exports (1991): crude
petroleum and refined petroleum
80.7%; machinery and transport
equipment 6.0% *to:* Japan 39.7%; India
5.3%; Oman 4.9%; South Korea 4.7%;
Iran 4.6%; Singapore 3.8%.

Ethnic Composition

Iranian 17%
non-UAE Arab 13%
UAE Arab 12%
Other 13%
South Asian 45%

On Dec. 2, 1971, six small Arab states formed the United Arab
Emirates, and a seventh state joined on Feb. 11, 1972. The flag
took its colors from the Arab Revolt flag of 1917. The colors
are included in a 13th-century poem which speaks of green
Arab lands defended in black battles by blood-red swords of
Arabs whose deeds are pure white.

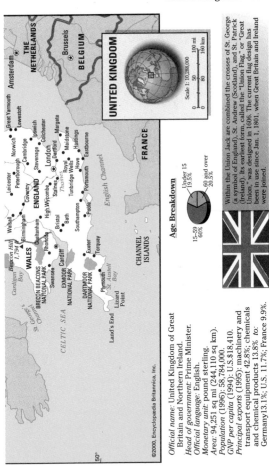

THE NETHERLANDS

Amsterdam

Brussels

BELGIUM

Great Yarmouth

Lowestoft

UNITED KINGDOM

Scale 1: 10,288,000

| 0 | 50 | 100 mi |
| 0 | 80 | 160 km |

Within the Union Jack are combined the crosses of St. George (a symbol of England), St. Andrew (Scotland), and St. Patrick (Ireland). Its earliest form, called the "Union Flag," or "Great Union," was designed in 1606. The current flag design has been in use since Jan. 1, 1801, when Great Britain and Ireland were joined.

Norwich

Ipswich Colchester

Leicester Peterborough Cambridge

Coventry Stevenage Margate

Birmingham High Wycombe London Maidstone Dartford

Walsall Royal Hastings

Cheltenham Tunbridge Wells Eastbourne

Rhondda Southampton Hove Portsmouth

Bristol Bath Poole

Swansea

ENGLAND

WALES

Cardiff

Cardigan Beacon Hill
Bay 1,794

BRECON BEACONS
NATIONAL PARK

EXMOOR
NATIONAL PARK

Exeter Torquay

DARTMOOR
NATIONAL PARK

Plymouth St. Austell
Bay

Land's End Lizard Point

CELTIC SEA

St. George's
Channel

Thames

English Channel

FRANCE

CHANNEL
ISLANDS

50°

Age Breakdown

Under 15
19.5%

60 and over
20.5%

15–59
60%

Official name: United Kingdom of Great Britain and Northern Ireland.
Head of government: Prime Minister.
Official language: English.
Monetary unit: pound sterling.
Area: 94,251 sq mi (244,110 sq km).
Population (1996): 58,784,000.
GNP per capita (1994): U.S.$18,410.
Principal exports (1995): machinery and transport equipment 42.8%; chemicals and chemical products 13.8% *to:* Germany13.1%; U.S. 11.7%; France 9.9%.

©2000, Encyclopædia Britannica, Inc.

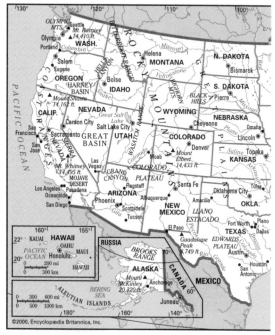

Official name: United States of America.
Head of government: President.
Official language: none.
Monetary unit: dollar.
Area: 3,675,031 sq mi (9,518,323 sq km).
Population (1996): 265,455,000.
GNP per capita (1995): U.S.$27,515.
Principal exports (1995): machinery and transport equipment 48.2%, of which motor vehicles and parts 13.2%; electrical machinery 11.2%; chemicals and related products 10.6%; food and live animals 6.7% *to:* Canada 21.6%; Japan 11.0%; Mexico 7.8%; United Kingdom 4.9%; South Korea 4.4%; Germany 3.8%; Taiwan 3.4%; The Netherlands 2.8%; Singapore 2.6%; France 2.4%; Hong Kong 2.4%; Belgium 2.2%.

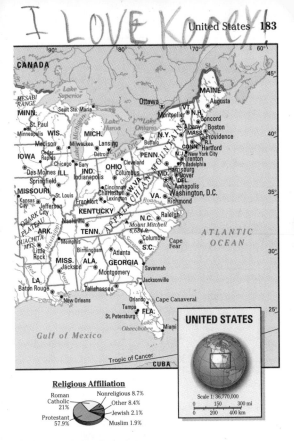

CANADA

Lake Superior

MESABI RANGE

MINN.
St. Paul
Minneapolis
WIS.
Madison
Milwaukee
IOWA
Cedar Rapids
Des Moines
Springfield
MISSOURI
Kansas City
Jefferson City
St. Louis
ARK.
Little Rock
OZARK PLATEAU
OUACHITA MTS.
LA.
Baton Rouge
New Orleans

Sault Ste. Marie
MICH.
Lansing
Detroit
Chicago
Gary
IND.
Indianapolis
ILL.
OHIO
Columbus
Cincinnati
KENTUCKY
Nashville
Frankfort
Lexington
TENN.
Memphis
MISS.
Jackson
ALA.
Birmingham
Montgomery
Tallahassee
GEORGIA
Atlanta

Lake Michigan
Lake Huron
Lake Erie
Lake Ontario
Cleveland
Buffalo
PENN.
Harrisburg
Pittsburgh
W.VA.
Charleston
VA.
Richmond
Roanoke
N.C.
Raleigh
Mount Mitchell 6,684 ft.
S.C.
Columbia
Cape Fear

Ottawa
MAINE
Augusta
Montpelier
VT.
N.H.
Concord
Albany
N.Y.
MASS.
Boston
Providence
R.I.
CONN.
Hartford
New York City
N.J.
Philadelphia
Trenton
DEL.
Dover
MD.
Annapolis
Washington, D.C.

ATLANTIC OCEAN

Savannah
Jacksonville
Orlando
Cape Canaveral
Tampa
St. Petersburg
FLA.
Lake Okeechobee
Miami

Gulf of Mexico

Tropic of Cancer
CUBA

UNITED STATES

Scale 1: 36,770,000

| 0 | 150 | 300 mi |
| 0 | 200 | 400 km |

Religious Affiliation

Roman Catholic 21%
Protestant 57.9%
Nonreligious 8.7%
Other 8.4%
Jewish 2.1%
Muslim 1.9%

The Stars and Stripes has white stars corresponding to the states of the union (50 since July 4, 1960), as well as stripes for the 13 original states. The first unofficial national flag, hoisted on Jan. 1, 1776, had the British Union flag in the canton. The official flag dates to June 14, 1777; its design was standardized in 1912 and 1934.

©2000, Encyclopædia Britannica, Inc.

URUGUAY

Scale 1: 10,810,000

| 0 | 50 | 100 mi |
| 0 | 80 | 160 km |

Racial Composition

White 86%

Mestizo 8%

Mulatto or Black 6%

Official name: Oriental Republic of Uruguay.
Head of government: President.
Official language: Spanish.
Monetary unit: peso.
Area: 68,037 sq mi (176,215 sq km).
Population (1996): 3,140,000.
GNP per capita (1994): U.S.$4,650.
Principal exports (1995): live animals and live-animal products 26.6%; textiles and textile products 20.0%; vegetable products 14.6% *to (1994):* Brazil 25.7%; Argentina 20.0%; U.S. 6.8%.

The flag adopted on Dec. 16, 1828, combined symbols of Argentina with the flag pattern of the United States. It was last altered on July 11, 1830. On the canton is the golden "Sun of May," which was seen on May 25, 1810, as a favorable omen for anti-Spanish forces in Buenos Aires, Arg. The stripes are for the original Uruguayan departments.

KAZAKSTAN

Official name: Republic of Uzbekistan.
Head of government: Prime Minister.
Official language: Uzbek.
Monetary unit: sum.
Area: 172,700 sq mi (447,400 sq km).
Population (1996): 23,206,000.
GNP per capita (1994): U.S.$950.
Principal exports (1995): light industrial
products 34.7%; oil and gas 15.1%;
machine-building equipment 5.9%;
food products 5.8% *to:* Russia 53.4%;
Kazakstan 16.1%; Tajikistan 9.6%;
Turkmenistan 9.0%; Kyrgyzstan 3.4%.

The flag of the former Soviet republic was legalized on Nov. 18, 1991. The blue is for water but also recalls the 14th-century ruler Timur. The green is for nature, fertility, and new life. The white is for peace and purity; red is for human life force. The stars are for the months and the Zodiac, while the moon is for the new republic and Islam.

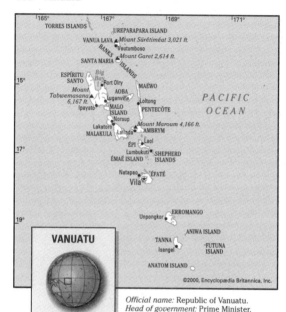

Official name: Republic of Vanuatu.
Head of government: Prime Minister.
Official languages: Bislama; French;
English.
Monetary unit: vatu.
Area: 4,707 sq mi (12,190 sq km).
Population (1996): 172,000.
GNP per capita (1994): U.S.$1,150.
Principal exports (1994): copra 30.7%;
beef and veal 15.5%; timber 10.6%;
cacao beans and preparations 7.8%
to (1993): EU 32.0%; Japan 29.0%;
Australia 11.0%; New Caledonia 7.0%.

Religious Affiliation

Roman Catholic 14.5%
Anglican 14%
Seventh-day Adventist 8.2%
Presbyterian 35.8%
Other 27.5%

The flag was hoisted upon independence from France and
Britain, on July 30, 1980. Black is for the soil and the people,
green for vegetation, and red for local religious traditions
such as the sacrifice of pigs. On the triangle are two crossed
branches and a full-round pig's tusk, a holy symbol. The horizontal "Y" is for peace and Christianity.

Official name: Republic of Venezuela.
Head of government: President.
Official language: Spanish.
Monetary unit: bolívar.
Area: 352,144 sq mi (912,050 sq km).
Population (1996): 22,311,000.
GNP per capita (1994): U.S.$2,760.
Principal exports (1994): crude
   petroleum and petroleum products
   75.2%; basic metal manufactures 9.0%
   to: U.S. 52.8%; Colombia 7.2%;
   Netherlands Antilles 6.4%; Suriname
   5.4%; Brazil 3.5%; Germany 2.1%.

The Venezuelan flag was adopted on March 18, 1864. Yellow
was originally said to stand for the gold of the New World,
separated by the blue of the Atlantic Ocean from "bloody
Spain," symbolized by red. The stars are for the original
seven provinces. In the upper hoist corner, the national arms
are added to flags which serve the government.

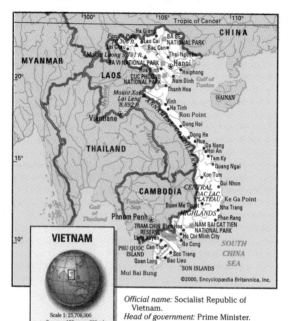

Official name: Socialist Republic of
Vietnam.
Head of government: Prime Minister.
Official language: Vietnamese.
Monetary unit: dong.
Area: 127,816 sq mi (331,041 sq km).
Population (1996): 76,151,000.
GNP per capita (1994): U.S.$190.
Principal exports (1994): crude
  petroleum 24.1%; fish and fish
  products 13.6%; agricultural and
  forestry products 13.3%; rice 11.9%
to (1995): Japan 28.5%; Germany 9.4%.

On Sept. 29, 1945, Vietnamese communists adopted the red
flag in use today. On July 4, 1976, following the defeat of the
American-sponsored government in the south, the flag
became official throughout the nation. The five points of the
star are said to stand for the proletariat, peasantry, military,
intellectuals, and petty bourgeoisie.

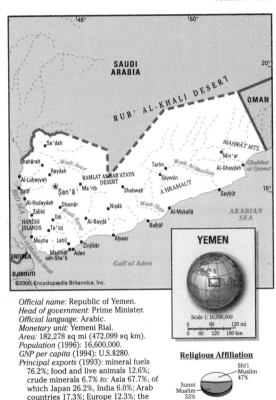

Official name: Republic of Yemen.
Head of government: Prime Minister.
Official language: Arabic.
Monetary unit: Yemeni Rial.
Area: 182,278 sq mi (472,099 sq km).
Population (1996): 16,600,000.
GNP per capita (1994): U.S.$280.
Principal exports (1993): mineral fuels
76.2%; food and live animals 12.6%;
crude minerals 6.7% *to:* Asia 67.7%, of
which Japan 26.2%, India 6.0%; Arab
countries 17.3%; Europe 12.3%; the
Americas 1.0%; Africa 0.7%.

YEMEN

Scale 1: 16,096,000

0   60   120 mi

0   60   120   180 km

Religious Affiliation

Shi'i
Muslim
47%

Sunni
Muslim
53%

Revolutions broke out in North Yemen in 1962 and in South
Yemen in 1967. In 1990 the two states unified, and that May 23
the tricolor was adopted, its design influenced by the former
United Arab Republic. The black is for the dark days of the
past, white for the bright future, and red for the blood shed
for independence and unity.

Official name: Federal Republic of Yugoslavia.
Head of government: Prime Minister.
Official language: Serbo-Croatian.
Monetary unit: Yugoslav dinar.
Area: 39,449 sq mi (102,173 sq km).
Population (1996): 10,473,000.
GNP per capita (1995): U.S.$1,510.
Principal exports (1992): manufactured goods 47.2%; machinery and transport equipment 17.2%; food and live animals 17.0% *to:* former U.S.S.R. 21.1%; Germany 16.3%; Italy 12.0%.

YUGOSLAVIA

Scale 1: 8,452,000

| 0 | 40 | 80 mi |
| 0 | 60 | 120 km |

Ethnic Composition

Serb 62.6%
Albanian 16.5%
Other 15.9%
Montenegrin 5%

The Pan-Slavic colors (blue, white, and red) have been in the flag from Oct. 31, 1918. A central star was introduced after World War II, under the leadership of Josip Broz Tito. In 1991 the country broke up, leaving only Serbia and Montenegro united, and the constitution of April 27, 1992, maintained the tricolor but omitted the star.

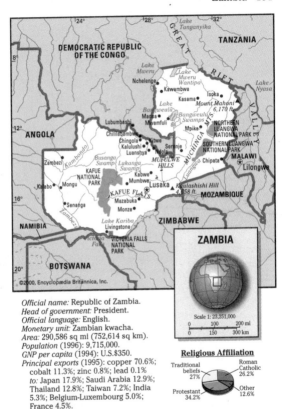

Official name: Republic of Zambia.
Head of government: President.
Official language: English.
Monetary unit: Zambian kwacha.
Area: 290,586 sq mi (752,614 sq km).
Population (1996): 9,715,000.
GNP per capita (1994): U.S.$350.
Principal exports (1995): copper 70.6%;
cobalt 11.3%; zinc 0.8%; lead 0.1%
to: Japan 17.9%; Saudi Arabia 12.9%;
Thailand 12.8%; Taiwan 7.2%; India
5.3%; Belgium-Luxembourg 5.0%;
France 4.5%.

ZAMBIA

Scale 1: 23,251,000

| 0 | 100 | 200 mi |

| 0 | 150 | 300 km |

Religious Affiliation

Traditional
beliefs
27%

Roman
Catholic
26.2%

Protestant
34.2%

Other
12.6%

Zambia separated from Britain on Oct. 24, 1964. Its flag, based
on the flag of the United National Independence Party, has a
green background for agriculture, red for the freedom struggle, black for the African people, and orange for copper. The
orange eagle appeared in the colonial coat of arms of 1939. It
symbolizes freedom and success.

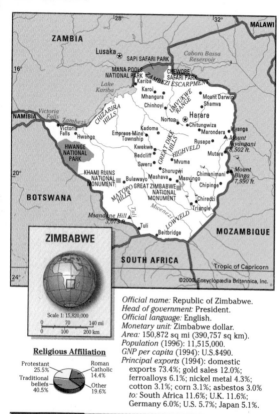

Official name: Republic of Zimbabwe.
Head of government: President.
Official language: English.
Monetary unit: Zimbabwe dollar.
Area: 150,872 sq mi (390,757 sq km).
Population (1996): 11,515,000.
GNP per capita (1994): U.S.$490.
Principal exports (1994): domestic
exports 73.4%; gold sales 12.0%;
ferroalloys 6.1%; nickel metal 4.3%;
cotton 3.1%; corn 3.1%; asbestos 3.0%
to: South Africa 11.6%; U.K. 11.6%;
Germany 6.0%; U.S. 5.7%; Japan 5.1%.

Religious Affiliation

Protestant
25.5%

Roman
Catholic
14.4%

Traditional
beliefs
40.5%

Other
19.6%

On April 18, 1980, elections brought the black majority to
power under the current flag. The black color is for the ethnic majority, while red is for blood, green for agriculture, yellow for mineral wealth, and white for peace and progress. At
the hoist is a red star (for socialism) and the ancient
"Zimbabwe Bird" from the Great Zimbabwe ruins.

List of Selected Cities

AFGHANISTAN . . . . pg. 1

Adraskan	33°39' N, 062°16' E
Almār	35°50' N, 064°32' E
Anār Darreh	32°46' N, 061°39' E
Andkhvoy	36°56' N, 065°08' E
Āqchah	36°56' N, 066°11' E
Baghlān	36°13' N, 068°46' E
Bāghrān	33°04' N, 065°05' E
Bagrām	34°58' N, 069°17' E
Bālā Bolūk	32°38' N, 062°28' E
Bāmīān (Bāmyān)	34°50' N, 067°50' E
Barg-e Matāl	35°40' N, 071°21' E
Bāzār-e Panjvā'ī	31°32' N, 065°28' E
Chaghchārān	34°31' N, 065°15' E
Chahār Borjak	30°17' N, 062°03' E
Chakhānsūr	31°10' N, 062°04' E
Delārām	32°11' N, 063°25' E
Do Qal'eh	32°08' N, 061°27' E
Dowlatābād	36°26' N, 064°55' E
Dūrāj	37°56' N, 070°43' E
Eslām Qal'eh	34°40' N, 061°04' E
Farāh (Farrah, Ferah)	32°22' N, 062°07' E
Feyzābād (Faizābād)	37°06' N, 070°34' E
Ghaznī	33°33' N, 068°26' E
Ghūrīān	34°21' N, 061°30' E
Gīzāb	33°23' N, 066°16' E
Golestān	32°37' N, 063°39' E
Golrān	35°06' N, 061°41' E
Gowmal Kalay	32°31' N, 068°51' E
Herāt (Harāt)	34°20' N, 062°12' E
Jabal os Sarāj	35°07' N, 069°14' E
Jalālābād	34°26' N, 070°28' E
Jaldak	31°58' N, 066°43' E
Jawand	35°04' N, 064°09' E
Kabul	34°31' N, 069°12' E
Kajakī	32°16' N, 065°05' E
Kandahār (Qandahār)	31°35' N, 065°45' E
Khadīr	33°55' N, 065°56' E
Khānābād	36°41' N, 069°07' E
Kholm	36°42' N, 067°41' E
Khowst	33°22' N, 069°57' E
Kondūz (Qonduz)	36°45' N, 068°51' E
Koshk	34°57' N, 062°28' E
Kūhestānāt	35°49' N, 065°52' E
Lashkar Gāh (Bust)	31°35' N, 064°21' E
Maḥmūd-e Rāqī	35°01' N, 069°20' E
Mazār-e Sharif	36°42' N, 067°06' E
Nāvor	33°53' N, 067°57' E
Orgūn	32°57' N, 069°11' E
Orūzgān	32°56' N, 066°38' E
Owbeh	34°22' N, 063°10' E
Palālak	30°14' N, 062°54' E
Pol-e 'Alam	33°59' N, 069°02' E

Porchaman	33°08' N, 063°51' E
Qalāt	32°07' N, 066°54' E
Qal'eh-ye Now	34°59' N, 063°08' E
Sar-e Pol	36°14' N, 065°55' E
Sayghān	35°11' N, 067°42' E
Shāh Jūy	32°31' N, 067°25' E
Shahrak	34°06' N, 064°18' E
Shīndand (Sabzevār)	33°18' N, 062°08' E
Shīr Khān	37°11' N, 068°36' E
Yangī Qal'eh	37°28' N, 069°36' E
Zaranj	30°58' N, 061°53' E

ALBANIA . . . . pg. 2

Berat	40°42' N, 019°57' E
Burrel	41°36' N, 020°01' E
Cërrik	41°02' N, 019°57' E
Çorovodë	40°30' N, 020°13' E
Durrës	41°19' N, 019°26' E
Elbasan	41°06' N, 020°05' E
Ersekë	40°22' N, 020°40' E
Fier	40°43' N, 019°34' E
Gjirokastër	40°05' N, 020°10' E
Gramsh	40°52' N, 020°11' E
Himarë	40°07' N, 019°44' E
Kavajë	41°11' N, 019°33' E
Korçë (Koritsa)	40°37' N, 020°46' E
Krujë	41°30' N, 019°48' E
Kukës	42°05' N, 020°24' E
Laç	41°38' N, 019°43' E
Lezhë	41°47' N, 019°39' E
Librazhd	41°11' N, 020°19' E
Lushnje	40°56' N, 019°42' E
Patos	40°38' N, 019°39' E
Përmet	40°14' N, 020°21' E
Peshkopi	41°41' N, 020°25' E
Pogradec	40°54' N, 020°39' E
Pukë	42°03' N, 019°54' E
Rrëshen	41°47' N, 019°54' E
Sarandë	39°52' N, 020°00' E
Shkodër (Scutari)	42°05' N, 019°30' E
Tepelenë	40°19' N, 020°01' E
Tiranë (Tirana)	41°20' N, 019°50' E
Vlorë	40°27' N, 019°30' E
Vorë	41°23' N, 019°40' E

ALGERIA . . . . pg. 3

Adrar (Timmi)	27°54' N, 000°17'W
Aïn Beïda (Daoud)	35°48' N, 007°24' E
Algiers (or Al-Jaza'ir)	36°47' N, 003°03' E
Annaba (Bone)	36°54' N, 007°46' E
Batna	35°34' N, 006°11' E
Béchar (Colomb-Bechar)	31°37' N, 002°13' W
Bejaïa (Bougie)	36°45' N, 005°05' E
Beni Abbès	30°08' N, 002°10' W
Biskra (Beskra)	34°51' N, 005°44' E
Bordj Bou Arréridj	36°04' N, 004°47' E

Chief (El-Asnam or
   Orleansville) . . . . 36°10′ N, 001°20′ E
Constantine (Qacentina) . . 36°22′ N, 006°37′ E
Djelfa . . . . 34°40′ N, 003°15′ E
El-Oued . . . . 33°20′ N, 006°53′ E
Ghardaïa . . . . 32°29′ N, 003°40′ E
In Salah (Aïn Salah) . . . . . 27°13′ N, 002°28′ E
Kenadsa . . . . 31°34′ N, 002°26′ E
Médéa (Lemdiyya) . . . . . . 36°16′ N, 002°45′ E
Mostaganem
   (Mestghanem) . . . . 35°56′ N, 000°05′ E
Oran (Wahran) . . . . 35°42′ N, 000°38′ W
Ouargla (Warqla) . . . . 31°57′ N, 005°20′ E
Saïda . . . . 34°50′ N, 000°09′ E
Sétif (Stif) . . . . 36°12′ N, 005°24′ E
Sidi Bel Abbés . . . . 35°12′ N, 000°38′ W
Skikda (Philippeville) . . . . 36°52′ N, 006°54′ E
Souk-Ahras . . . . 36°17′ N, 007°57′ E
Tamanrasset
   (Fort Laperrine) . . . . 22°47′ N, 005°31′ W
Tébessa (Tbessa or
   Theveste) . . . . 35°24′ N, 008°07′ E
Tiaret
   (Tihert or Tagdempt) . . . 35°22′ N, 001°19′ E
Tindouf . . . . 27°42′ N, 008°09′ W
Tlemcen (Tlemsen) . . . . . . 34°52′ N, 001°19′ W
Touggourt . . . . 33°06′ N, 006°04′ E

ANDORRA . . . . pg. 4

Andorra la Vella . . . . 42°30′ N, 001°30′ E
Canillo . . . . 42°34′ N, 001°35′ E
Encamp . . . . 42°32′ N, 001°35′ E
La Massana . . . . 42°33′ N, 001°31′ E
Les Escaldes . . . . 42°30′ N, 001°32′ E
Ordino . . . . 42°34′ N, 001°30′ E
Sant Julià de Lòria . . . . . 42°28′ N, 001°30′ E
Soldeu . . . . 42°35′ N, 001°40′ E

ANGOLA . . . . pg. 5

Benguela (São Félipe
   de Benguela) . . . . 12°35′ S, 013°24′ E
Caála (Robert Williams) . 12°51′ S, 015°34′ E
Cabinda . . . . 05°33′ S, 012°12′ E
Cacolo . . . . 10°08′ S, 019°16′ E
Caconda . . . . 13°44′ S, 015°04′ E
Caluquembe . . . . 13°52′ S, 014°26′ E
Camacupa (General
   Machado) . . . . 12°01′ S, 017°29′ E
Cangamba . . . . 13°41′ S, 019°52′ E
Catumbela . . . . 12°26′ S, 013°33′ E
Cubal . . . . 13°02′ S, 014°15′ E
Cuchi . . . . 14°39′ S, 016°54′ E
Damba . . . . 06°41′ S, 015°08′ E
Gabela . . . . 10°51′ S, 014°22′ E
Ganda (Mariano
   Machado) . . . . 13°01′ S, 014°38′ E
Huambo (Nova Lisboa) . . 12°46′ S, 015°44′ E
Kuito (Silva Porto) . . . . . 12°23′ S, 016°56′ E

Lobito . . . . 12°21′ S, 013°33′ E
Luanda (São Paulo de
   Luanda) . . . . 08°49′ S, 013°15′ E
Luau . . . . 10°42′ S, 022°14′ E
Lubango (Sá da Bandeira) . 14°55′ S, 013°30′ E
Lucapa . . . . 08°25′ S, 020°45′ E
Luena (Vila Luso) . . . . . . 11°47′ S, 019°55′ E
Malanje . . . . 09°32′ S, 016°20′ E
Mavinga . . . . 15°48′ S, 020°21′ E
M'banza Congo
   (São Salvador) . . . . 06°16′ S, 014°15′ E
Menongue (Serpa Pinto) . 14°40′ S, 017°42′ E
Namibe (Moçâmedes,
   or Mossamedes) . . . . . . 15°10′ S, 012°09′ E
N'dalatando
   (Dalatando, or Salazar) . 09°18′ S, 014°55′ E
Negage . . . . 07°46′ S, 015°16′ E
Nóqui . . . . 05°51′ S, 013°26′ E
Ondjiva . . . . 17°04′ S, 015°44′ E
Porto Amboim . . . . 10°44′ S, 013°45′ E
Quimbele . . . . 06°31′ S, 016°13′ E
Saurimo
   (Henrique de Carvalho) . 09°39′ S, 020°24′ E
Soyo . . . . 06°08′ S, 012°22′ E
Sumbe (Novo Redondo) . . 11°12′ S, 013°50′ E
Tombua (Porto
   Alexandre) . . . . 15°48′ S, 011°51′ E
Uíge (Carmona) . . . . 07°37′ S, 015°03′ E
Waku Kungo
   (Santa Comba) . . . . 11°21′ S, 015°07′ E

ANTIGUA AND BARBUDA . . . . pg. 6

Codrington . . . . 17°38′ N, 061°50′ W
St. John's . . . . 17°06′ N, 061°51′ W

ARGENTINA . . . . . . pg. 7

Avellaneda . . . . 29°07′ S, 059°40′ W
Bahía Blanca . . . . 38°43′ S, 062°17′ W
Buenos Aires . . . . 34°36′ S, 058°27′ W
Comodoro Rivadavia . . . 45°52′ S, 067°30′ W
Concordia . . . . 31°24′ S, 058°02′ W
Córdoba . . . . 31°24′ S, 064°11′ W
Corrientes . . . . 27°28′ S, 058°50′ W
Formosa . . . . 26°11′ S, 058°11′ W
La Plata . . . . 34°55′ S, 057°57′ W
La Rioja . . . . 29°26′ S, 066°51′ W
Luján . . . . 34°34′ S, 059°07′ W
Mar del Plata . . . . 38°00′ S, 057°33′ W
Mercedes . . . . 33°40′ S, 065°28′ W
Neuquén . . . . 38°57′ S, 068°04′ W
Paraná . . . . 31°44′ S, 060°32′ W
Posadas . . . . 27°23′ S, 055°53′ W
Rawson . . . . 43°18′ S, 065°06′ W
Resistencia . . . . 27°27′ S, 058°59′ W
Río Gallegos . . . . 51°38′ S, 069°13′ W

Salta	24°47′ S, 065°25′ W
San Miguel de Tucumán	26°49′ S, 065°13′ W
San Rafael	34°36′ S, 068°20′ W
Santa Fe	31°38′ S, 060°42′ W
Santa Rosa	36°37′ S, 064°17′ W
Santiago del Estero	27°47′ S, 064°16′ W
Tandil	37°19′ S, 059°09′ W
Tigre	34°25′ S, 058°34′ W
Ushuaia	54°48′ S, 068°18′ W
Viedma	40°48′ S, 063°00′ W
Villa María	32°25′ S, 063°15′ W

ARMENIA . . . . .pg. 8

Abovyan	40°15′ N, 044°35′ E
Alaverdi	41°08′ N, 044°39′ E
Ararat	39°50′ N, 044°42′ E
Artashat (Artaxata)	39°57′ N, 044°33′ E
Artik	40°37′ N, 043°59′ E
Charentsavan	40°24′ N, 044°38′ E
Dilijan	40°44′ N, 044°52′ E
Ejmiadzin (Echmiadzin)	40°10′ N, 044°18′ E
Goris (Geryusy)	39°30′ N, 046°23′ E
Gyumri (Kumayri, Alexandropol, or Leninakan)	40°48′ N, 043°50′ E
Hoktemberyan (Oktemberyan)	40°09′ N, 044°02′ E
Hrazdan (Razdan)	40°29′ N, 044°46′ E
Ijevan	40°51′ N, 045°09′ E
Kamo (Nor-Bayazet)	40°21′ N, 045°08′ E
Kapan	39°12′ N, 046°24′ E
Sevan	40°32′ N, 044°56′ E
Spitak	40°49′ N, 044°16′ E
Stepanavan	41°01′ N, 044°23′ E
Vanadzor	40°48′ N, 044°30′ E
Yerevan (Erevan)	40°11′ N, 044°30′ E

AUSTRALIA . . . . . . .pg. 9

Adelaide	34°56′ S, 138°36′ E
Alice Springs	23°42′ S, 133°53′ E
Bowral	34°28′ S, 150°25′ E
Brisbane	27°30′ S, 153°01′ E
Broken Hill	31°57′ S, 141°26′ E
Bunbury	33°20′ S, 115°38′ E
Bundaberg	24°51′ S, 152°21′ E
Cairns	16°55′ S, 145°46′ E
Canberra	35°20′ S, 149°10′ E
Darwin	12°28′ S, 130°50′ E
Devonport	41°10′ S, 146°21′ E
Geelong	38°09′ S, 144°21′ E
Geraldton	28°46′ S, 114°36′ E
Gladstone	23°51′ S, 151°15′ E
Gold Coast	28°06′ S, 153°27′ E
Goulburn	34°45′ S, 149°43′ E
Hobart	42°55′ S, 147°20′ E
Kalgoorlie-Boulder	30°45′ S, 121°28′ E
Lismore	28°48′ S, 153°16′ E
Mackay	21°09′ S, 149°12′ E

Maryborough	25°32′ S, 152°42′ E
Melbourne	37°50′ S, 145°00′ E
Mount Gambier	37°50′ S, 140°46′ E
Mount Isa	20°44′ S, 139°30′ E
Newcastle	32°55′ S, 151°45′ E
Perth	31°56′ S, 115°50′ E
Port Macquarie	31°26′ S, 152°55′ E
Rockingham	32°17′ S, 115°43′ E
Sydney	33°53′ S, 151°12′ E
Toowoomba	27°33′ S, 151°58′ E
Warrnambool	38°23′ S, 142°29′ E
Whyalla	33°02′ S, 137°35′ E
Wollongong	34°25′ S, 150°54′ E

AUSTRIA . . . . .pg. 10

Amstetten	48°07′ N, 014°52′ E
Baden	48°01′ N, 016°14′ E
Branau [am Inn]	48°16′ N, 013°02′ E
Bregenz	47°30′ N, 009°46′ E
Bruck [an der Leitha]	47°25′ N, 015°17′ E
Dornbirn	47°25′ N, 009°44′ E
Eisenstadt	47°51′ N, 016°31′ E
Feldkirch	47°14′ N, 009°36′ E
Freistadt	48°30′ N, 014°30′ E
Fürstenfeld	47°03′ N, 016°05′ E
Gmünd	48°46′ N, 014°59′ E
Gmunden	47°55′ N, 013°48′ E
Graz	47°04′ N, 015°27′ E
Hallein	47°41′ N, 013°06′ E
Innsbruck	47°16′ N, 011°24′ E
Kapfenberg	47°26′ N, 015°18′ E
Klagenfurt	46°38′ N, 014°18′ E
Klosterneuburg	48°18′ N, 016°19′ E
Köflach	47°04′ N, 015°05′ E
Krems an der Donau	48°25′ N, 015°36′ E
Kufstein	47°35′ N, 012°10′ E
Laa [an der Thaya]	48°43′ N, 016°23′ E
Landeck	47°08′ N, 010°34′ E
Leibnitz	46°46′ N, 015°32′ E
Leoben (Donawitz)	47°23′ N, 015°06′ E
Leonding	48°16′ N, 014°15′ E
Liezen	47°34′ N, 014°14′ E
Linz	48°18′ N, 014°18′ E
Neunkirchen	47°43′ N, 016°05′ E
Oberwart	47°17′ N, 016°12′ E
Radenthein	46°48′ N, 013°43′ E
Salzburg	47°48′ N, 013°02′ E
Sankt Pölten	48°12′ N, 015°38′ E
Schrems	48°47′ N, 015°04′ E
Steyr	48°03′ N, 014°25′ E
Telfs	47°18′ N, 011°04′ E
Ternitz	47°43′ N, 016°02′ E
Traun	48°13′ N, 014°14′ E
Trofaiach	47°25′ N, 015°00′ E
Vienna (Wien)	48°12′ N, 016°22′ E
Villach	46°36′ N, 013°50′ E
Vöcklabruck	48°01′ N, 013°39′ E
Völkermarkt	46°39′ N, 014°38′ E
Weiner Neustadt	47°48′ N, 016°15′ E
Wolfsberg	46°50′ N, 014°50′ E

AZERBAIJAN .....pg. 11

Ağcabädi	40°02′ N,	047°28′ E
Ağdam	39°59′ N,	046°57′ E
Ağstafa	41°07′ N,	045°27′ E
Ağsu	40°34′ N,	048°24′ E
Äli-Bayramlı	39°55′ N,	048°56′ E
Astara	38°26′ N,	048°53′ E
Baku (Bakı)	40°23′ N,	049°51′ E
Balakän	41°43′ N,	046°24′ E
Bärdä	40°24′ N,	047°10′ E
Daĺkäsän	40°32′ N,	046°07′ E
Däväçi	41°12′ N,	048°59′ E
Füzuli	39°36′ N,	047°09′ E
Gäncä (Gyandzha, Gandzha, Kirovabad, or Yelizavetpol)	40°41′ N,	046°22′ E
Göyçay	40°39′ N,	047°45′ E
İmişli	40°47′ N,	048°09′ E
İsmayıllı	40°47′ N,	048°09′ E
Kürdämir	40°21′ N,	048°11′ E
Länkäran	38°45′ N,	048°50′ E
Masallı	39°03′ N,	048°40′ E
Mingäçevir (Mingechaur)	40°45′ N,	047°03′ E
Nakhichevan (Naxcivan)	39°12′ N,	045°24′ E
Neftçala	39°23′ N,	049°16′ E
Ordubad	38°54′ N,	046°01′ E
Qäbälä (Kutkashen)	40°58′ N,	047°52′ E
Qax	41°25′ N,	046°55′ E
Qazax	41°05′ N,	045°22′ E
Qazimämmäd	40°03′ N,	048°56′ E
Şäki (Sheki, Nukha)	41°12′ N,	047°12′ E
Şalyan	39°35′ N,	048°59′ E
Şamaxı	40°38′ N,	048°39′ E
Şämkir	40°50′ N,	046°02′ E
Siyäzän	41°04′ N,	049°02′ E
Sumqayıt	40°36′ N,	049°38′ E
Tovuz	40°59′ N,	045°36′ E
Ucar	40°31′ N,	047°39′ E
Xaçmaz	41°28′ N,	048°48′ E
Xankändi (Stepanakert)	39°50′ N,	046°46′ E
Xudat	41°38′ N,	048°41′ E
Yevlax	40°37′ N,	047°09′ E
Zaqatala	41°38′ N,	046°39′ E

BAHAMAS, THE .pg. 12

Dunmore Town	25°30′ N,	076°39′ W
Freeport	26°32′ N,	078°42′ W
Matthew Town	20°57′ N,	073°40′ W
Nassau	25°05′ N,	077°21′ W
Old Bight	24°15′ N,	075°21′ W
West End	26°41′ N,	078°58′ W

BAHRAIN ....pg. 13

Ad Dūr	25°59′ N,	050°37′ E
Al-Ḥadd	26°15′ N,	050°39′ E

Al Jasrah	26°10′ N,	050°27′ E
Al Mālikīyah	37°10′ N,	042°08′ E
Al-Muharraq	26°16′ N,	050°37′ E
Ar-Rifāʿ	26°07′ N,	050°33′ E
Ar-Rifāʿash-Sharqī	26°07′ N,	050°34′ E
Ar-Rumaythah	25°55′ N,	050°33′ E
ʿAwālī	26°05′ N,	050°33′ E
Bārbaār	26°14′ N,	050°29′ E
Madīnat Ḥamad	26°08′ N,	050°30′ E
Madīnat ʿĪsā	26°10′ N,	050°33′ E
Manama	26°13′ N,	050°35′ E

BANGLADESH ....pg. 14

Azmiriganj	24°33′ N,	091°14′ E
Bāgerhāt	22°40′ N,	089°48′ E
Bājitpur	24°13′ N,	090°57′ E
Barisāl	22°42′ N,	090°22′ E
Bhairab Bāzar	24°04′ N,	090°58′ E
Bogra	24°51′ N,	089°22′ E
Brāhmanbāria	23°59′ N,	091°07′ E
Chālna Port (Mongla Port)	22°28′ N,	089°35′ E
Chāndpur	23°13′ N,	090°39′ E
Chaumuhāni (Chowmohani)	22°56′ N,	091°07′ E
Chittagong	22°20′ N,	091°50′ E
Chuadānga	23°38′ N,	088°51′ E
Comilla (Kumillā)	23°27′ N,	091°12′ E
Cox's Bāzar	21°26′ N,	091°59′ E
Dhaka (Dacca or Dhakal)	23°43′ N,	090°25′ E
Dinājpur	25°38′ N,	088°38′ E
Farīdpur	23°36′ N,	089°50′ E
Gopālpur	24°50′ N,	090°06′ E
Ishurdi (Ishurda)	24°08′ N,	089°05′ E
Jamālpur	24°55′ N,	089°56′ E
Jessore	23°10′ N,	089°13′ E
Jhenida	23°33′ N,	089°10′ E
Khulna	22°48′ N,	089°33′ E
Kishorganj	24°26′ N,	090°46′ E
Kurigrām	25°49′ N,	089°39′ E
Kushtia	23°55′ N,	089°07′ E
Lākshām	23°14′ N,	091°08′ E
Lakshmipur	22°57′ N,	090°50′ E
Lālmanir Hāt (Lalmonirhat)	25°54′ N,	089°27′ E
Mādārīpur	23°10′ N,	090°12′ E
Mymensingh (Nasirābād)	24°45′ N,	090°24′ E
Naogaon	24°47′ N,	088°56′ E
Nārāyanganj	23°37′ N,	090°30′ E
Narsinghdi (Narsingdi)	23°55′ N,	090°43′ E
Nawābganj	24°36′ N,	088°17′ E
Noākhāli (Sudhārām)	22°49′ N,	091°06′ E
Pābna (Pubna)	24°00′ N,	089°15′ E
Patuākhāli	22°21′ N,	090°21′ E
Rājshāhi	24°22′ N,	088°36′ E
Rāngāmāti	22°38′ N,	092°12′ E
Rangpur	25°45′ N,	089°15′ E
Saidpur	25°47′ N,	088°54′ E
Sātkhira	22°43′ N,	089°06′ E
Sherpur	24°41′ N,	089°25′ E

Sherpur	25°01' N, 090°01' E
Sirajganj (Seraganj)	24°27' N, 089°43' E
Sylhet	24°54' N, 091°52' E
Tangail	24°15' N, 089°55' E

BARBADOS ......pg. 15

Bennetts	13°10' N, 059°36' W
Bridgetown	13°06' N, 059°37' W
Holetown	13°11' N, 059°39' W
Marchfield	13°07' N, 059°28' W
Massiah	13°10' N, 059°29' W
Oistins	13°04' N, 059°32' W
Portland	13°16' N, 059°36' W
Prospect	13°08' N, 059°36' W
Speightstown	13°15' N, 059°39' W
Westmoreland	13°13' N, 059°37' W

BELARUS ......pg. 16

Baranovichi	53°08' N, 026°02' E
Beloözersk (Beloozyorsk)	52°28' N, 025°10' E
Bobruysk	53°09' N, 029°14' E
Borisov (Barysaw)	54°15' N, 028°30' E
Braslav	55°38' N, 027°02' E
Brest (Brest-Litovsk)	52°06' N, 023°42' E
Bykhov	53°31' N, 030°15' E
Chashniki	54°52' N, 029°10' E
Cherikov	53°34' N, 031°23' E
Cherven	53°42' N, 028°26' E
Dobrush	52°25' N, 031°19' E
Dokshitsy	54°54' N, 027°46' E
Drogichin	52°11' N, 025°09' E
Dyatlovo	53°28' N, 025°24' E
Dzerzhinsk	53°41' N, 027°08' E
Gantsevichi	52°45' N, 026°26' E
Glubokoye	55°08' N, 027°41' E
Gorki	54°17' N, 030°59' E
Gorodok	55°28' N, 029°59' E
Grodno (Hrodna)	53°41' N, 023°50' E
Homyel' (Gomel)	52°25' N, 031°00' E
Kletsk	53°04' N, 026°38' E
Klimovichi	53°37' N, 031°58' E
Kobrin	52°13' N, 024°21' E
Kossovo	52°45' N, 025°09' E
Kostyukovichi	53°20' N, 032°03' E
Lepel	54°53' N, 028°42' E
Lida	53°53' N, 025°18' E
Luninets	52°15' N, 026°48' E
Mahilyow (Mogilyov, Mahilyou)	53°54' N, 030°21' E
Malorita	51°47' N, 024°05' E
Minsk (Mensk)	53°54' N, 027°34' E
Molodechno (Maladzyechna)	54°19' N, 026°51' E
Mosty	53°25' N, 024°32' E
Mozyr (Mazyr)	52°03' N, 029°16' E
Mstislavl	54°02' N, 031°44' E
Narovlya	51°48' N, 029°30' E
Nesvizh	53°13' N, 026°40' E

Novolukomi	54°39' N, 029°13' E
Orsha	54°31' N, 030°26' E
Oshmyany	54°25' N, 025°56' E
Osipovichi	53°18' N, 028°38' E
Petrikov	52°08' N, 028°30' E
Pinsk	52°07' N, 026°07' E
Polotsk (Polatsk)	55°29' N, 028°47' E
Pruzhany	52°33' N, 024°28' E
Rechitsa (Rechytsa)	52°22' N, 030°23' E
Slutsk	53°01' N, 027°33' E
Soligorsk (Salihorsk)	52°48' N, 027°32' E
Starye Dorogi	53°02' N, 028°16' E
Stolbtsy	53°29' N, 026°44' E
Stolin	51°53' N, 026°51' E
Svetlogorsk (Svetlahorsk)	52°38' N, 029°46' E
Verkhnedvinsk	55°47' N, 027°56' E
Vetka	52°33' N, 031°10' E
Vileyka	54°30' N, 026°55' E
Vitebsk (Vitsyebsk)	55°12' N, 030°11' E
Volkovysk	53°10' N, 024°28' E
Vysokoye	52°22' N, 023°22' E
Yelsk	51°48' N, 029°09' E
Zaslavl	54°00' N, 027°17' E
Zhitkovichi	52°14' N, 027°52' E
Zhodino	54°06' N, 028°21' E

BELGIUM ......pg. 17

Aalst (Alost)	50°56' N, 004°02' E
Aalter	51°05' N, 003°27' E
Antwerp (Antwerpen, Anvers)	51°13' N, 004°25' E
Arlon (Aarlen)	49°41' N, 005°49' E
Ath	50°38' N, 003°47' E
Athus	49°34' N, 005°50' E
Bastogne	50°00' N, 005°43' E
Bouillon	49°48' N, 005°04' E
Boussu	50°26' N, 003°48' E
Braine-l'Alleud	50°41' N, 004°22' E
Brecht	51°21' N, 004°38' E
Bree	51°08' N, 005°36' E
Brugge (Bruges)	51°13' N, 003°14' E
Brussels (Brussel, Bruxelles)	50°50' N, 004°20' E
Charleroi	50°25' N, 004°26' E
Ciney	50°18' N, 005°06' E
Couvin	50°03' N, 004°29' E
Dinant	50°16' N, 004°55' E
Eeklo	51°11' N, 003°34' E
Enghien (Edingen)	50°42' N, 004°02' E
Eupen	50°38' N, 006°02' E
Florenville	49°42' N, 005°18' E
Geel (Gheel)	51°10' N, 005°00' E
Genk (Genck)	50°58' N, 005°30' E
Ghent (Gand, Gent)	51°03' N, 003°43' E
Hasselt	50°56' N, 005°20' E
Ixelles (Elsene)	50°50' N, 004°22' E
Kapellen	51°19' N, 004°26' E
Kortrijk (Courtrai)	50°50' N, 003°16' E
La Louvière	50°28' N, 004°11' E

Liège (Luttich)	50°38′ N, 005°34′ E
Louvain (Leuven)	50°53′ N, 004°42′ E
Marche-en-Famenne	50°12′ N, 005°20′ E
Mechelen (Malines)	51°02′ N, 004°28′ E
Mons (Bergen)	50°27′ N, 003°56′ E
Mouscron (Moeskroen)	50°44′ N, 003°13′ E
Namur (Namen)	50°28′ N, 004°52′ E
Neerpelt	51°13′ N, 005°25′ E
Ostend (Oostende)	51°13′ N, 002°55′ E
Peer	51°08′ N, 005°28′ E
Péruwelz	50°31′ N, 003°35′ E
Philippeville	50°12′ N, 004°32′ E
Riemst	50°48′ N, 005°36′ E
Roeselare (Roulers)	50°57′ N, 003°08′ E
Saint-Hubert	50°01′ N, 005°23′ E
Schaerbeek (Schaarbeek)	50°51′ N, 004°23′ E
Seraing	50°36′ N, 005°29′ E
Sint-Niklaas	51°10′ N, 004°08′ E
Spa	50°30′ N, 005°52′ E
Spy	50°29′ N, 004°42′ E
Staden	50°59′ N, 003°01′ E
Tessenderlo	51°04′ N, 005°05′ E
Thuin	50°20′ N, 004°17′ E
Tienen	50°48′ N, 004°57′ E
Torhout	51°04′ N, 003°06′ E
Tournai (Doornik)	50°36′ N, 003°23′ E
Turnhout	51°19′ N, 004°57′ E
Uccle (Ukkel)	50°48′ N, 004°19′ E
Verviers	50°35′ N, 005°52′ E
Wanze	50°32′ N, 005°13′ E
Waremme	50°41′ N, 005°15′ E
Waterloo	50°43′ N, 004°23′ E
Zwijndrecht	51°13′ N, 004°20′ E

BELIZE .... pg. 18

Belize City	17°30′ N, 088°12′ W
Belmopan	17°15′ N, 088°46′ W
Benque Viejo	17°05′ N, 089°08′ W
Bermudian Landing	17°33′ N, 088°31′ W
Corozal	18°24′ N, 088°24′ W
Dangriga (Stann Creek)	16°58′ N, 088°13′ W
Monkey River	16°22′ N, 088°29′ W
Orange Walk	18°06′ N, 088°33′ W
Pembroke Hall	18°17′ N, 088°27′ W
Punta Gorda	16°07′ N, 088°48′ W
San Ignacio (El Cayo)	17°10′ N, 89°04′ W

BENIN .... pg. 19

Abomey	07°11′ N, 001°59′ E
Cotonou	06°21′ N, 002°26′ E
Djougou	09°42′ N, 001°40′ E
Kandi	11°08′ N, 002°56′ E
Natitingou	10°19′ N, 001°22′ E
Parakou	09°21′ N, 002°37′ E
Porto-Novo	06°29′ N, 002°37′ E
Savalou	07°56′ N, 001°58′ E
Savè	08°02′ N, 002°29′ E

BHUTAN .... pg. 20

Bumthang (Byakar or Jakar)	27°32′ N, 090°43′ E
Chhukha	27°04′ N, 089°35′ E
Chima Kothi	27°03′ N, 089°35′ E
Chirang	27°04′ N, 090°06′ E
Dagana (Taga)	27°03′ N, 089°55′ E
Deothang (Dewangiri)	26°52′ N, 091°28′ E
Domphu (Damphu)	27°01′ N, 090°08′ E
Gaylegphug (Gelekphu, Hatsar or Hatsar)	26°51′ N, 090°29′ E
Ha	27°22′ N, 089°17′ E
Kanglung (Kanglum)	27°16′ N, 091°30′ E
Lhuntsi	27°39′ N, 091°09′ E
Mongar	27°15′ N, 091°12′ E
Paro	27°26′ N, 089°25′ E
Pema Gatsel	26°59′ N, 091°26′ E
Phuntsholing	26°52′ N, 089°26′ E
Punakha	27°37′ N, 089°52′ E
Samchi (Tori Bari)	26°53′ N, 089°07′ E
Samdrup Jongkhar	26°47′ N, 091°30′ E
Shemgang	27°12′ N, 090°38′ E
Shompangkha (Sarbhang)	26°52′ N, 090°16′ E
Sibsoo	27°01′ N, 088°55′ E
Tashigang	27°20′ N, 091°32′ E
Thimphu	27°28′ N, 089°38′ E
Tongsa	27°31′ N, 090°30′ E
Wangdü Phodrang	27°29′ N, 089°54′ E

BOLIVIA .... pg. 21

Apolo	14°43′ S, 068°31′ W
Benavides	12°38′ S, 067°20′ W
Bermejo	22°44′ S, 064°21′ W
Camargo	20°39′ S, 065°13′ W
Camiri	20°03′ S, 063°31′ W
Caranavi	15°46′ S, 067°36′ W
Chulumani	16°24′ S, 067°31′ W
Cobija	11°02′ S, 068°44′ W
Cochabamba	17°24′ S, 066°09′ W
Concepción	16°15′ S, 062°04′ W
Copacabana	16°10′ S, 069°05′ W
Corocoro	17°12′ S, 068°29′ W
Cuevo	20°27′ S, 063°32′ W
El Carmen	18°49′ S, 058°33′ W
Fortaleza	10°37′ S, 066°13′ W
Guayaramerin	10°48′ S, 065°23′ W
Huacaya	20°45′ S, 063°43′ W
Huachacalla	18°45′ S, 068°17′ W
Ixiamas	13°45′ S, 068°09′ W
La Esperanza	14°34′ S, 062°10′ W
La Horquilla	12°34′ S, 064°25′ W
La Paz	16°30′ S, 068°09′ W
Llallagua	18°25′ S, 066°38′ W
Llica	19°52′ S, 068°16′ W
Loreto	15°13′ S, 064°40′ W
Magdalena	13°20′ S, 064°08′ W
Monteagudo	19°49′ S, 063°59′ W
Montero	17°20′ S, 063°15′ W

Oruro	17°59' S, 067°09' W
Porvenir	11°15' S, 068°41' W
Potosí	19°35' S, 065°45' W
Puerto Acosta	15°32' S, 069°15' W
Puerto Rico	11°05' S, 067°38' W
Punata	17°33' S, 065°50' W
Quetena	22°10' S, 067°25' W
Quillacollo	17°26' S, 066°17' W
Reyes	14°19' S, 067°23' W
Riberalta	10°59' S, 066°06' W
Roboré	18°20' S, 059°45' W
Samaipata	18°09' S, 063°52' W
San Ignacio	16°23' S, 060°59' W
San José	17°51' S, 060°47' W
San Matías	16°22' S, 058°24' W
San Pablo	15°41' S, 063°15' W
San Ramón	13°17' S, 064°43' W
Santa Cruz	17°48' S, 063°10' W
Santiago	19°22' S, 060°51' W
Siglo Veinte	18°22' S, 066°38' W
Sucre	19°02' S, 065°17' W
Tarabuco	19°10' S, 064°57' W
Tarija	21°31' S, 064°45' W
Tiahuanacu (Tiwanacu)	16°33' S, 068°42' W
Trinidad	14°47' S, 064°47' W
Tupiza	21°27' S, 065°43' W
Uyuni	20°28' S, 066°50' W
Villazón	22°06' S, 065°36' W
Yacuíba	22°02' S, 063°45' W

BOSNIA AND HERZEGOVINA . . . pg. 22

Banja Luka	44°46' N, 017°10' E
Bihać	44°49' N, 015°52' E
Bijeljina	44°45' N, 019°13' E
Bosanska Gradiška	45°09' N, 017°15' E
Bosanski Šamac	45°04' N, 018°28' E
Brčko	44°52' N, 018°49' E
Derventa	44°59' N, 017°55' E
Goražde	43°40' N, 018°59' E
Jablanica	43°39' N, 017°45' E
Jajce	44°21' N, 017°17' E
Kladanj	44°14' N, 018°42' E
Ključ	44°32' N, 016°47' E
Konjic	43°39' N, 017°58' E
Mostar	43°21' N, 017°49' E
Prijedor	44°59' N, 016°42' E
Sanski Most	44°50' N, 018°25' E
Sarajevo	44°06' N, 019°18' E
Srebrenica	44°14' N, 017°40' E
Travnik	44°14' N, 017°40' E
Tuzla	44°33' N, 018°41' E
Vareš	44°10' N, 018°20' E
Zenica	44°13' N, 017°55' E

BOTSWANA . . . . . . pg. 23

Francistown	21°13' S, 027°31' E

Gaborone	24°40' S, 025°54' E
Ghanzi	21°34' S, 021°47' E
Kanye	24°59' S, 025°21' E
Kasane	17°49' S, 025°09' E
Letlhakane	21°25' S, 025°35' E
Lobatse	25°13' S, 025°40' E
Mahalapye	23°04' S, 026°50' E
Maun	19°59' S, 023°25' E
Mochudi	24°25' S, 026°09' E
Orapa	21°17' S, 025°22' E
Palapye (Palapye Road)	22°33' S, 027°08' E
Ramotswa	24°52' S, 025°49' E
Selebi-Phikwe	22°01' S, 027°50' E
Serowe	22°23' S, 026°43' E
Shashe	21°26' S, 027°27' E
Tlokweng	24°32' S, 025°58' E
Tshabong	26°03' S, 022°27' E
Tshane	24°05' S, 021°54' E

BRAZIL . . . . pg. 24

Aracaju	10°55' S, 037°04' W
Belém (Pará)	01°27' S, 048°29' W
Belo Horizonte	19°55' S, 043°56' W
Boa Vista	02°49' N, 060°30' W
Brasília	15°47' S, 047°55' W
Campina Grande	07°13' S, 035°53' W
Campo Grande	20°27' S, 054°37' W
Canoas	29°56' S, 051°11' W
Caxias do Sul	29°10' S, 051°11' W
Curitiba	25°25' S, 049°15' W
Duque de Caxias	22°47' S, 043°18' W
Florianópolis	27°35' S, 048°34' W
Fortaleza	03°43' S, 038°30' W
Goiânia	16°40' S, 049°16' W
Itabuna	14°48' S, 039°16' W
João Pessoa	07°07' S, 034°52' W
Macapá	00°02' N, 051°03' W
Maceió	09°40' S, 035°43' W
Manaus	03°08' S, 060°01' W
Natal	05°47' S, 035°13' W
Nova Iguaçu	22°45' S, 043°27' W
Novo Hamburgo	29°41' S, 051°08' W
Passo Fundo	28°15' S, 052°24' W
Pôrto Alegre	30°04' S, 051°11' W
Pôrto Velho	08°46' S, 063°54' W
Recife	08°03' S, 034°54' W
Rio Branco	09°58' S, 067°48' W
Rio de Janeiro	22°54' S, 043°14' W
Rio Grande	32°02' S, 052°05' W
Salvador	12°59' S, 038°31' W
Santarém	02°26' S, 054°42' W
Santo André	23°40' S, 046°31' W
São Gonçalo	22°51' S, 043°04' W
São José do Rio Prêto	20°48' S, 049°23' W
São Luís	02°31' S, 044°16' W
São Paulo	23°32' S, 046°37' W
Tefé	03°22' S, 064°42' W
Teresina	05°05' S, 042°49' W
Vitória	20°19' S, 040°21' W

BRUNEI . . . . .pg. 25

Badas.	04°36' N,	114°27' E
Bandar Seri Begawan		
(Brunei)	04°53' N,	114°56' E
Bangar	04°43' N,	115°04' E
Kuala Belait	04°36' N,	114°14' E
Labi	04°23' N,	114°27' E
Labu.	04°45' N,	115°11' E
Muara	05°02' N,	115°04' E
Seria.	04°37' N,	114°19' E
Sukang.	04°19' N,	114°37' E
Tutong.	04°48' N,	114°39' E

BULGARIA . . . . . .pg. 26

Balchik.	43°25' N,	028°10' E
Berkovitsa	43°14' N,	023°07' E
Blagoevgrad	42°01' N,	023°06' E
Burgas.	42°30' N,	027°28' E
Dimitrovgrad.	42°03' N,	025°36' E
Dobrich (Tolbukhin) . . .	43°34' N,	027°50' E
Dulovo	43°49' N,	027°09' E
Gabrovo.	42°52' N,	025°19' E
Grudovo	42°21' N,	027°10' E
Kazanlŭk	42°37' N,	025°24' E
Khaskovo.	41°56' N,	025°33' E
Kŭrdzhali	41°39' N,	025°22' E
Kyustendil	42°17' N,	022°41' E
Lom	43°49' N,	023°14' E
Lovech.	43°08' N,	024°43' E
Montana		
(Mikhaylovgrad)	43°25' N,	023°13' E
Nikopol	43°42' N,	024°54' E
Pazardzhik.	42°12' N,	024°20' E
Pernik (Dimitrovo)	42°36' N,	023°02' E
Petrich.	41°24' N,	023°13' E
Pleven	43°25' N,	024°37' E
Plovdiv	42°09' N,	024°45' E
Razgrad	43°32' N,	026°31' E
Ruse.	43°50' N,	025°57' E
Shumen (Kolarovgrad) . .	43°16' N,	026°55' E
Silistra	44°07' N,	027°16' E
Sliven	42°40' N,	026°19' E
Sofia.	42°41' N,	023°19' E
Stara Zagora	42°25' N,	025°38' E
Troyan	42°53' N,	024°43' E
Varna	43°13' N,	027°55' E
Veliko Tŭrnovo	43°04' N,	025°39' E
Velingrad.	42°01' N,	024°00' E
Vidin	43°59' N,	022°52' E
Vratsa (Vraca)	43°12' N,	023°33' E
Vrŭv	44°11' N,	022°44' E
Yambol	42°29' N,	026°30' E

BURKINA FASO . . .pg. 27

Banfora	10°38' N,	004°46' W
Bobo-Dioulasso.	11°12' N,	004°18' W

Boulsa	12°39' N,	000°34' W
Dédougou	12°28' N,	003°28' W
Diébougou	10°58' N,	003°15' W
Dori	14°02' N,	000°02' W
Fada Ngourma.	12°04' N,	000°21' W
Faramana.	12°03' N,	004°40' W
Gaoua	10°20' N,	003°11' W
Kaya	13°05' N,	001°05' W
Koudougou	12°15' N,	002°22' W
Koupéla	12°11' N,	000°21' W
Léo	11°06' N,	002°06' W
Nouna	12°44' N,	003°52' W
Orodara	10°59' N,	004°55' W
Ouagadougou	12°22' N,	001°31' W
Ouahigouya	13°35' N,	002°25' W
Pô.	11°10' N,	001°09' W
Réo.	12°19' N,	002°28' W
Tenkodogo	11°47' N,	000°22' W
Yako.	12°58' N,	002°16' W

BURUNDI . . . . .pg. 28

Bubanza.	03°06' S,	029°23' E
Bujumbura	03°23' S,	029°22' E
Bururi	03°57' S,	029°37' E
Gitega	03°26' S,	029°56' E
Muramvya	03°16' S,	029°37' E
Ngozi	02°54' S,	029°50' E
Nyanza-Lac	04°21' S,	029°36' E

CAMBODIA . . . . . .pg. 29

Ânlóng Vêng	14°14' N,	104°05' E
Bă Kêv	13°42' N,	107°12' E
Battambang		
(Batdâmbâng)	13°06' N,	103°12' E
Chbar.	12°46' N,	107°10' E
Chôăm Khsant	14°13' N,	104°56' E
Chŏng Kal	13°57' N,	103°35' E
Kâmpóng Cham	12°00' N,	105°27' E
Kâmpóng Chhnăng	12°15' N,	104°40' E
Kâmpóng Kdei.	13°07' N,	104°21' E
Kâmpóng Saôm		
(Sihanoukville)	10°38' N,	103°30' E
Kâmpóng Spoe	11°27' N,	104°32' E
Kâmpóng Thum	12°42' N,	104°54' E
Kâmpot (Kâmpôt).	10°37' N,	104°11' E
Krâchéh (Kratie).	12°29' N,	106°01' E
Krâkôr	12°32' N,	104°12' E
Krŏng Kaôh Kŏng	11°37' N,	102°59' E
Lumphăt (Lomphat) . . .	13°30' N,	106°59' E
Mémôt	11°49' N,	106°11' E
Moŭng Roessei	12°46' N,	103°27' E
Ôdŏngk	11°48' N,	104°45' E
Péam Prus	12°19' N,	103°09' E
Phnom Penh (Phnum Penh		
or Pnom Penh)	11°33' N,	104°55' E
Phnum Tbêng Méanchey .	13°49' N,	104°58' E
Phsar Réam (Ream)	10°30' N,	103°37' E

Prey Vêng . . . . 11°29′ N, 105°19′ E
Pursat (Poŭthĭsăt) . . . . . 12°32′ N, 103°55′ E
Rôvĭĕng Tbong . . . . 13°21′ N, 105°07′ E
Săndăn . . . . 12°42′ N, 106°01′ E
Senmonorom . . . . 12°27′ N, 107°12′ E
Siĕmpang . . . . 14°07′ N, 106°23′ E
Siem Reap (Siĕmréab) . . 13°22′ N, 103°51′ E
Sĭsŏphŏn . . . . 13°35′ N, 102°59′ E
Stoeng Trêng
(Stung Treng) . . . . . . 13°31′ N, 105°58′ E
Svay Chék . . . . 13°48′ N, 102°58′ E
Takêv (Takéo) . . . . 10°59′ N, 104°47′ E
Tăng Krăsăng . . . . 12°34′ N, 105°03′ E
Virôchey . . . . 13°59′ N, 106°49′ E

CAMEROON . . . . . pg. 30

Bafang . . . . 05°09′ N, 010°11′ E
Bafia . . . . 04°45′ N, 011°14′ E
Bafoussam . . . . 05°28′ N, 010°25′ E
Bamenda . . . . 05°56′ N, 010°10′ E
Banyo . . . . 06°45′ N, 011°49′ E
Batibo . . . . 05°50′ N, 009°52′ E
Batouri . . . . 04°26′ N, 014°22′ E
Bertoua . . . . 04°35′ N, 013°41′ E
Bétaré-Oya . . . . 05°36′ N, 014°05′ E
Douala . . . . 04°03′ N, 009°42′ E
Ebolowa . . . . 02°54′ N, 011°09′ E
Edéa . . . . 03°48′ N, 010°08′ E
Eséka . . . . 03°39′ N, 010°46′ E
Foumban . . . . 05°43′ N, 010°55′ E
Garoua . . . . 09°18′ N, 013°24′ E
Guider . . . . 09°56′ N, 013°57′ E
Kaélé . . . . 10°07′ N, 014°27′ E
Kribi . . . . 02°57′ N, 009°55′ E
Kumba . . . . 04°38′ N, 009°25′ E
Loum . . . . 04°43′ N, 009°44′ E
Mamfe . . . . 05°46′ N, 009°17′ E
Maroua . . . . 10°36′ N, 014°20′ E
Mbalmayo . . . . 03°31′ N, 011°30′ E
Meiganga . . . . 06°31′ N, 014°18′ E
Mora . . . . 11°03′ N, 014°09′ E
Ngaoundéré . . . . 07°19′ N, 013°35′ E
Nkambe . . . . 06°38′ N, 010°40′ E
Nkongsamba . . . . 04°57′ N, 009°56′ E
Obala . . . . 04°10′ N, 011°32′ E
Sangmélima . . . . 02°56′ N, 011°59′ E
Tcholliré . . . . 08°24′ N, 014°10′ E
Tibati . . . . 06°28′ N, 012°38′ E
Wum . . . . 06°23′ N, 010°24′ E
Yagoua . . . . 10°20′ N, 015°14′ E
Yaoundé . . . . 03°52′ N, 011°31′ E
Yokadouma . . . . 03°31′ N, 015°03′ E

CANADA . . . . pg. 31

Amos . . . . 48°35′ N, 078°07′ W
Arctic Bay . . . . 73°02′ N, 085°11′ W
Baie-Comeau . . . . 49°13′ N, 068°09′ W
Baker Lake . . . . 64°15′ N, 096°00′ W

Banff . . . . 51°10′ N, 115°34′ W
Barrie . . . . 44°24′ N, 079°40′ W
Battleford . . . . 52°44′ N, 108°19′ W
Beauport . . . . 46°52′ N, 071°11′ W
Bonavista . . . . 48°39′ N, 053°07′ W
Brandon . . . . 49°50′ N, 099°57′ W
Bridgewater . . . . 44°23′ N, 064°31′ W
Brooks . . . . 50°35′ N, 111°53′ W
Buchans . . . . 48°49′ N, 056°52′ W
Burlington . . . . 43°19′ N, 079°47′ W
Burnaby . . . . 49°16′ N, 122°57′ W
Calgary . . . . 51°03′ N, 114°05′ W
Cambridge Bay . . . . 69°03′ N, 105°05′ W
Camrose . . . . 53°01′ N, 112°50′ W
Carbonear . . . . 47°44′ N, 053°13′ W
Carmacks . . . . 62°05′ N, 136°17′ W
Charlesbourg . . . . 46°51′ N, 071°16′ W
Charlottetown . . . . 46°14′ N, 063°08′ W
Chatham . . . . 42°24′ N, 082°11′ W
Chibougamau . . . . 49°55′ N, 074°22′ W
Chicoutimi . . . . 48°26′ N, 071°04′ W
Churchill . . . . 58°46′ N, 094°10′ W
Churchill Falls . . . . 53°33′ N, 064°01′ W
Cranbrook . . . . 49°30′ N, 115°46′ W
Dartmouth . . . . 44°40′ N, 063°34′ W
Dauphin . . . . 51°09′ N, 100°03′ W
Dawson . . . . 64°04′ N, 139°26′ W
Dawson Creek . . . . 55°46′ N, 120°14′ W
Duck Lake . . . . 52°49′ N, 106°14′ W
Edmonton . . . . 53°33′ N, 113°28′ W
Elliot Lake . . . . 46°23′ N, 082°42′ W
Enderby . . . . 50°33′ N, 119°09′ W
Eskimo Point . . . . 61°07′ N, 094°03′ W
Esterhazy . . . . 50°39′ N, 102°05′ W
Estevan . . . . 49°08′ N, 102°59′ W
Faro . . . . 62°14′ N, 133°20′ W
Fernie . . . . 49°30′ N, 115°04′ W
Flin Flon . . . . 54°46′ N, 101°53′ W
Fogo . . . . 49°43′ N, 054°17′ W
Fort Liard . . . . 60°15′ N, 123°28′ W
Fort MacLeod . . . . 49°43′ N, 113°25′ W
Fort McMurray . . . . 56°44′ N, 111°23′ W
Fort McPherson . . . . 67°27′ N, 134°53′ W
Fort Qu'Appelle . . . . 50°46′ N, 103°48′ W
Fort St. John . . . . 56°15′ N, 120°51′ W
Fort Smith . . . . 60°00′ N, 111°53′ W
Fredericton . . . . 45°58′ N, 066°39′ W
Gagnon . . . . 51°53′ N, 068°10′ W
Gander . . . . 48°57′ N, 054°37′ W
Gaspe . . . . 48°50′ N, 064°29′ W
Glace Bay . . . . 46°12′ N, 059°57′ W
Granby . . . . 45°24′ N, 072°43′ W
Grand Bank . . . . 47°06′ N, 055°46′ W
Grande Prairie . . . . 55°10′ N, 118°48′ W
Grand Falls . . . . 48°56′ N, 055°40′ W
Grimshaw . . . . 56°11′ N, 117°36′ W
Grise Fiord . . . . 76°25′ N, 082°55′ W
Haines Junction . . . . 60°45′ N, 137°30′ W
Halifax . . . . 44°39′ N, 063°36′ W
Hamilton . . . . 43°15′ N, 079°51′ W
Happy Valley-Goose Bay . . 53°19′ N, 060°20′ W

Harbour Grace . . . . 47°42' N, 053°13' W
Hay River . . . . 60°49' N, 115°47' W
Inuvik . . . . 68°21' N, 133°43' W
Iqaluit (Frobisher Bay) . . 63°45' N, 068°31' W
Iroquois Falls . . . . 48°46' N, 080°41' W
Jasper . . . . 52°53' N, 118°05' W
Joliette . . . . 46°01' N, 073°27' W
Jonquiere . . . . 48°25' N, 071°13' W
Kamloops . . . . 50°40' N, 120°19' W
Kapuskasing . . . . 49°25' N, 082°26' W
Kelowna . . . . 49°53' N, 119°29' W
Kenora . . . . 49°47' N, 094°29' W
Kindersley . . . . 51°28' N, 109°10' W
Kirkland Lake . . . . 48°09' N, 080°02' W
Kitchener . . . . 43°27' N, 080°29' W
Kuujjuaq (Fort-Chimo) . 58°06' N, 068°25' W
La Baie . . . . 48°20' N, 070°52' W
Labrador City . . . . 52°57' N, 066°55' W
La Tuque . . . . 47°26' N, 072°47' W
Lethbridge . . . . 49°42' N, 112°49' W
Lewisporte . . . . 49°14' N, 055°03' W
Liverpool . . . . 44°02' N, 064°43' W
Lloydminster . . . . 53°17' N, 110°00' W
London . . . . 42°59' N, 081°14' W
Longueuil . . . . 45°32' N, 073°30' W
Lynn Lake . . . . 56°51' N, 101°03' W
Maple Creek . . . . 49°55' N, 109°29' W
Marystown . . . . 47°10' N, 055°09' W
Mayo . . . . 63°36' N, 135°54' W
Medicine Hat . . . . 50°03' N, 110°40' W
Mississauga . . . . 43°35' N, 079°39' W
Moncton . . . . 46°07' N, 064°48' W
Montmagny . . . . 46°59' N, 070°33' W
Montreal . . . . 45°30' N, 073°36' W
Moose Jaw . . . . 50°24' N, 105°32' W
Mount Pearl . . . . 47°31' N, 052°47' W
Nanaimo . . . . 49°10' N, 123°56' W
Nelson . . . . 49°30' N, 117°17' W
Nepean . . . . 45°16' N, 075°46' W
New Liskeard . . . . 47°30' N, 079°40' W
Niagara Falls . . . . 43°06' N, 079°04' W
Nickel Centre . . . . 46°34' N, 080°49' W
Nipawin . . . . 53°22' N, 104°00' W
North Battleford . . . . . . 52°47' N, 108°17' W
North Bay . . . . 46°19' N, 079°28' W
North West River . . . . . 53°32' N, 060°08' W
Old Crow . . . . 67°34' N, 139°50' W
Oshawa . . . . 43°54' N, 078°51' W
Ottawa . . . . 45°25' N, 075°42' W
Pangnirtung . . . . 66°08' N, 065°43' W
Parry Sound . . . . 45°21' N, 080°02' W
Peace River . . . . 56°14' N, 117°17' W
Perce . . . . 48°32' N, 064°13' W
Peterborough . . . . 44°18' N, 078°19' W
Pine Point . . . . 60°50' N, 114°28' W
Portage la Prairie . . . . . 49°59' N, 098°18' W
Port Alberni . . . . 49°14' N, 124°48' W
Port Hawkesbury . . . . . 45°37' N, 061°21' W
Prince Albert . . . . 53°12' N, 105°46' W
Prince George . . . . 53°55' N, 122°45' W
Prince Rupert . . . . 54°19' N, 130°19' W

Quebec . . . . 46°49' N, 071°14' W
Quesnel . . . . 53°00' N, 122°30' W
Rae-Edzo . . . . 62°50' N, 116°03' W
Rankin Inlet . . . . 62°49' N, 092°05' W
Red Deer . . . . 52°16' N, 113°48' W
Regina . . . . 50°27' N, 104°37' W
Resolute Bay . . . . 74°41' N, 094°54' W
Revelstoke . . . . 50°59' N, 118°12' W
Rimouski . . . . 48°26' N, 068°33' W
Roberval . . . . 48°31' N, 072°13' W
Ross River . . . . 61°59' N, 132°26' W
Sachs Harbour . . . . 72°00' N, 125°13' W
Saint Albert . . . . 53°38' N, 113°38' W
Sainte-Foy . . . . 46°47' N, 071°17' W
Saint John . . . . 45°16' N, 066°03' W
Saint John's . . . . 47°34' N, 052°43' W
Saskatoon . . . . 52°07' N, 106°38' W
Sault Ste. Marie . . . . . . 46°31' N, 084°20' W
Scarborough . . . . 43°47' N, 079°15' W
Schefferville . . . . 54°48' N, 066°50' W
Selkirk . . . . 50°09' N, 096°52' W
Senneterre . . . . 48°23' N, 077°14' W
Sept-Îles . . . . 50°12' N, 066°23' W
Shawinigan . . . . 46°33' N, 072°45' W
Shelburne . . . . 43°46' N, 065°19' W
Sherbrooke . . . . 45°25' N, 071°54' W
Snow Lake . . . . 54°53' N, 100°02' W
Springdale . . . . 49°30' N, 056°04' W
Sturgeon Falls . . . . 46°22' N, 079°55' W
Sudbury . . . . 46°30' N, 081°00' W
Surrey . . . . 49°06' N, 122°47' W
Swan River . . . . 52°07' N, 101°16' W
Sydney . . . . 46°09' N, 060°11' W
Teslin . . . . 60°10' N, 132°43' W
The Pas . . . . 53°50' N, 101°15' W
Thompson . . . . 55°45' N, 097°52' W
Thunder Bay . . . . 48°24' N, 089°19' W
Timmins . . . . 48°28' N, 081°20' W
Toronto . . . . 43°39' N, 079°23' W
Trois-Rivieres . . . . 46°21' N, 072°33' W
Truro . . . . 45°22' N, 063°16' W
Tuktoyaktuk . . . . 69°27' N, 133°02' W
Val-d'Or . . . . 48°06' N, 077°47' W
Vancouver . . . . 49°15' N, 123°07' W
Vernon . . . . 50°16' N, 119°16' W
Victoria . . . . 48°26' N, 123°22' W
Wabush . . . . 52°55' N, 066°52' W
Watson Lake . . . . 60°04' N, 128°42' W
Weyburn . . . . 49°40' N, 103°51' W
Whitehorse . . . . 60°43' N, 135°03' W
Williams Lake . . . . 52°08' N, 122°09' W
Windsor . . . . 42°18' N, 083°01' W
Windsor . . . . 44°59' N, 064°08' W
Winnipeg . . . . 49°53' N, 097°09' W
Yarmouth . . . . 43°50' N, 066°07' W
Yellowknife . . . . 62°27' N, 114°22' W
Yorkton . . . . 51°13' N, 102°28' W

CAPE VERDE . . . . . pg. 32

Mindelo . . . . 16°53' N, 025°00' W

Porto Novo	17°01′ N, 025°04′ W
Praia	14°55′ N, 023°31′ W
São Filipe	14°54′ N, 024°31′ W

CENTRAL AFRICAN REPUBLIC . . . . pg. 33

Alindao	05°02′ N, 021°13′ E
Baboua	05°48′ N, 014°49′ E
Bambari	05°45′ N, 020°40′ E
Bangassou	04°44′ N, 022°49′ E
Bangui	04°22′ N, 018°35′ E
Batangafo	07°18′ N, 018°18′ E
Berbérati	04°16′ N, 015°47′ E
Bimbo	04°18′ N, 018°33′ E
Birao	10°17′ N, 022°47′ E
Boda	04°19′ N, 017°28′ E
Bossangoa	06°29′ N, 017°27′ E
Bossembélé	05°16′ N, 017°39′ E
Bouar	05°57′ N, 015°36′ E
Bouca	06°30′ N, 018°17′ E
Bozoum	06°19′ N, 016°23′ E
Bria	06°32′ N, 021°59′ E
Carnot	04°56′ N, 015°52′ E
Dekóa	06°19′ N, 019°04′ E
Ippy	06°15′ N, 021°12′ E
Kaga Bandoro	06°59′ N, 019°11′ E
Mbaïki	03°53′ N, 018°00′ E
Mobaye	04°19′ N, 021°11′ E
Mouka	07°16′ N, 021°52′ E
Ndélé	08°24′ N, 020°39′ E
Nola	03°32′ N, 016°04′ E
Obo	05°24′ N, 026°30′ E
Ouadda	08°04′ N, 022°24′ E
Ouanda Djallé	08°54′ N, 022°48′ E
Sibut	05°44′ N, 019°05′ E
Zinga	03°43′ N, 018°35′ E

CHAD . . . . pg. 34

Abéché	13°49′ N, 020°49′ E
Adre	13°28′ N, 022°12′ E
Am Dam	12°46′ N, 020°29′ E
Am Timan	11°02′ N, 020°17′ E
Am Zoer	14°13′ N, 021°23′ E
Aozou	21°49′ N, 017°25′ E
Arada	15°01′ N, 020°40′ E
Ati	13°13′ N, 018°20′ E
Biltine	14°32′ N, 020°55′ E
Bol	13°28′ N, 014°43′ E
Bongor	10°17′ N, 015°22′ E
Doba	08°39′ N, 016°51′ E
Gélengdeng	10°56′ N, 015°32′ E
Goré	07°55′ N, 016°38′ E
Goz Beïda	12°13′ N, 021°25′ E
Koro Toro	16°05′ N, 018°30′ E
Laï	09°24′ N, 016°18′ E
Largeau (Faya-Largeau)	17°55′ N, 019°07′ E
Mao	14°07′ N, 015°19′ E

Massenya	11°24′ N, 016°10′ E
Mongo	12°11′ N, 018°42′ E
Moundou	08°34′ N, 016°05′ E
N'Djamena (Fort Lamy)	12°07′ N, 015°03′ E
Pala	09°22′ N, 014°54′ E
Sarh (Fort-Archambault)	09°09′ N, 018°23′ E

CHILE . . . . pg. 35

Antofagasta	23°39′ S, 070°24′ W
Arica	18°29′ S, 070°20′ W
Castro	42°29′ S, 073°46′ W
Chillán	36°36′ S, 072°07′ W
Chuquicamata	22°19′ S, 068°56′ W
Colhaique	45°34′ S, 072°04′ W
Concepción	36°50′ S, 073°03′ W
Copiapó	27°22′ S, 070°20′ W
Coquimbo	29°58′ S, 071°21′ W
Iquique	20°13′ S, 070°10′ W
La Serena	29°54′ S, 071°16′ W
Porvenir	53°18′ S, 070°22′ W
Potrerillos	26°26′ S, 069°29′ W
Puerto Aisén	45°24′ S, 072°42′ W
Puerto Montt	41°28′ S, 072°57′ W
Punta Arenas	53°09′ S, 070°55′ W
Purranque	40°55′ S, 073°10′ W
San Pedro	33°54′ S, 071°28′ W
Santiago	33°27′ S, 070°40′ W
Talca	35°26′ S, 071°40′ W
Talcahuano	36°43′ S, 073°07′ W
Temuco	38°44′ S, 072°36′ W
Tocopilla	22°05′ S, 070°12′ W
Valdivia	39°48′ S, 073°14′ W
Valparaíso	33°02′ S, 071°38′ W
Viña del Mar	33°02′ S, 071°34′ W

CHINA . . . . pg. 36-7

Anshan	41°07′ N, 122°57′ E
Beijing	39°56′ N, 116°24′ E
Changchun	43°52′ N, 125°21′ E
Changsha	28°12′ N, 112°58′ E
Chengdu	30°40′ N, 104°04′ E
Chongqing (locally Yuzhou)	29°34′ N, 106°35′ E
Dalian (Lüda)	38°55′ N, 121°39′ E
Fushun	41°52′ N, 123°53′ E
Fuzhou	26°05′ N, 119°18′ E
Guangzhou	23°07′ N, 113°15′ E
Guiyang	26°35′ N, 106°43′ E
Haikou	20°03′ N, 110°19′ E
Hangzhou	30°15′ N, 120°10′ E
Harbin	45°45′ N, 126°39′ E
Hefei	31°51′ N, 117°17′ E
Hohhot	40°47′ N, 111°37′ E
Jinan	36°40′ N, 117°00′ E
Kunming	25°04′ N, 102°41′ E
Lanzhou	36°03′ N, 103°41′ E
Lhasa	29°39′ N, 091°06′ E
Nanchang	28°41′ N, 115°53′ E

Nanjing	32°03′ N, 118°47′ E
Nanning	22°49′ N, 108°19′ E
Qingdao	36°04′ N, 120°19′ E
Shanghai	31°14′ N, 121°28′ E
Shaoxing	30°00′ N, 120°35′ E
Shenyang	41°48′ N, 123°27′ E
Shijiazhuang	38°03′ N, 114°29′ E
Tai'an	36°12′ N, 117°07′ E
Taiyuan	37°52′ N, 112°33′ E
Tianjin	39°08′ N, 117°12′ E
Ürümqi	43°48′ N, 087°35′ E
Wuhan	30°35′ N, 114°16′ E
Xi'an	34°16′ N, 108°54′ E
Xining	36°37′ N, 101°46′ E
Yinchuan	38°28′ N, 106°19′ E
Zhengzhou	34°45′ N, 113°40′ E

COLOMBIA ......pg. 38

Armenia	04°31′ N, 075°41′ W
Barranquilla	10°59′ N, 074°48′ W
Bello	06°20′ N, 075°33′ W
Bisinaca	04°30′ N, 069°40′ W
Bogotá	04°36′ N, 074°05′ W
Bolívar	01°50′ N, 076°58′ W
Bucaramanga	07°08′ N, 073°09′ W
Buenaventura	03°53′ N, 077°04′ W
Cali	03°27′ N, 076°31′ W
Caranacoa	02°25′ N, 068°57′ W
Cartagena	10°25′ N, 075°32′ W
Cúcuta	07°54′ N, 072°31′ W
Duitama	05°50′ N, 073°02′ W
El Dorado	01°11′ N, 071°52′ W
El Yopal	05°21′ N, 072°23′ W
Florencia	01°36′ N, 075°36′ W
Ibagué	04°27′ N, 075°14′ W
Macují	00°24′ N, 073°07′ W
Magangué	09°14′ N, 074°45′ W
Manizales	05°05′ N, 075°32′ W
Matarca	00°30′ S, 072°38′ W
Medellín	06°15′ N, 075°35′ W
Mitú	01°08′ N, 070°03′ W
Montería	08°46′ N, 075°53′ W
Ocaña	08°15′ N, 073°20′ W
Palmira	03°32′ N, 076°16′ W
Pasto	01°13′ N, 077°17′ W
Pereira	04°49′ N, 075°43′ W
Popayán	02°27′ N, 076°36′ W
Puerto Berrío	06°29′ N, 074°24′ W
Puerto Carreño	06°12′ N, 067°22′ W
Puerto Inírida	03°51′ N, 067°55′ W
Quibdó	05°42′ N, 076°40′ W
Riohacha	11°33′ N, 072°55′ W
San José de Guaviare	02°35′ N, 072°38′ W
San Martín	03°42′ N, 073°42′ W
Santa Marta	11°15′ N, 074°13′ W
Sincelejo	09°18′ N, 075°24′ W
Sogamoso	05°43′ N, 072°56′ W
Tuluá	04°06′ N, 076°11′ W
Tumaco	01°49′ N, 078°46′ W

Tunja	05°31′ N, 073°22′ W
Urrao	06°20′ N, 076°11′ W
Valledupar	10°29′ N, 073°15′ W
Villa Rosario	07°50′ N, 072°28′ W
Villavicencio	04°09′ N, 073°37′ W
Zipaquirá	05°02′ N, 074°00′ W

COMOROS ......pg. 39

Fomboni	12°18′ S, 043°46′ E
Mitsamiouli	11°22′ S, 043°21′ E
Moroni	11°41′ S, 043°16′ E
Mutsamudu	12°10′ S, 044°25′ E

CONGO, DEMOCRATIC REPUBLIC OF THE ......pg. 40

Aketi	02°44′ N, 023°46′ E
Banana	06°01′ S, 012°24′ E
Bandundu	03°19′ S, 017°22′ E
Beni	00°30′ N, 029°28′ E
Boende	00°13′ S, 020°52′ E
Boma	05°51′ S, 013°03′ E
Buta	02°48′ N, 024°44′ E
Butembo	00°09′ N, 029°17′ E
Gandajika	06°45′ S, 023°57′ E
Gemena	03°15′ N, 019°46′ E
Ilebo	04°19′ S, 020°35′ E
Isiro	02°46′ N, 027°37′ E
Kabinda	06°08′ S, 024°29′ E
Kalemi (Albertville)	05°56′ S, 029°12′ E
Kamina	08°44′ S, 025°00′ E
Kananga (Luluabourg)	05°54′ S, 022°25′ E
Kikwit	05°02′ S, 018°49′ E
Kindu	02°57′ S, 025°56′ E
Kinshasa (Leopoldville)	04°18′ S, 015°18′ E
Kisangani (Stanleyville)	00°30′ N, 025°12′ E
Kolwezi	10°43′ S, 025°28′ E
Kutu	02°44′ S, 018°09′ E
Likasi	10°59′ S, 026°44′ E
Lubumbashi (Elisabethville)	11°40′ N, 027°28′ E
Manono	07°18′ S, 027°25′ E
Matadi	05°49′ S, 013°27′ E
Mbandaka	00°04′ N, 018°16′ E
Mbanza-Ngungu	05°15′ S, 014°52′ E
Mbuji-Mayi	06°09′ S, 023°36′ E
Mwene-Ditu	07°03′ S, 023°27′ E
Samba	04°38′ S, 026°22′ E
Tshikapa	06°25′ S, 020°48′ E
Yangambi	00°47′ N, 024°28′ E

CONGO, REPUBLIC OF THE . . . . pg. 41

Brazzaville	04°16′ S,	015°17′ E
Djambala	02°33′ S,	014°45′ E
Gamboma	01°53′ S,	015°51′ E
Impfondo	01°37′ N,	018°04′ E
Kayes	04°25′ S,	011°41′ E
Liranga	00°40′ S,	017°36′ E
Loubomo	04°12′ N,	012°41′ E
Madingou	04°09′ S,	013°34′ E
Makabana	02°48′ S,	012°29′ E
Makoua	00°01′ N,	015°39′ E
Mossendjo	02°57′ S,	012°44′ E
Mpouya	02°37′ S,	16°013′ E
Nkayi	04°11′ S,	013°18′ E
Ouesso	01°37′ N,	016°04′ E
Owando	00°29′ S,	015°55′ E
Pointe-Noire	04°48′ S,	011°51′ E
Sibiti	03°41′ S,	013°21′ E
Souanké	02°05′ N,	014°03′ E
Zanaga	02°15′ S,	013°50′ E

COSTA RICA . . . . . pg. 42

Alajuela	10°01′ N,	084°13′ W
Cañas	10°26′ N,	085°06′ W
Desamparados	09°54′ N,	084°05′ W
Golfito	08°39′ N,	083°09′ W
Heredia	10°00′ N,	084°07′ W
Ipís	09°58′ N,	084°01′ W
La Cruz	11°04′ N,	085°38′ W
Liberia	10°38′ N,	085°26′ W
Miramar	10°06′ N,	084°44′ W
Nicoya	10°09′ N,	085°27′ W
Puerto Limón (Limón)	10°00′ N,	083°02′ W
Puntarenas	09°58′ N,	084°50′ W
Quesada	10°20′ N,	084°26′ W
San Isidro	09°23′ N,	083°42′ W
San José	09°56′ N,	084°05′ W
San Ramón	10°05′ N,	084°28′ W
Santa Cruz	10°16′ N,	085°35′ W
Siquirres	10°06′ N,	083°31′ W
Tilarán	10°28′ N,	084°58′ W

CROATIA . . . . pg. 43

Bjelovar	45°54′ N,	016°51′ E
Đakovo	45°19′ N,	018°25′ E
Dubrovnik	42°39′ N,	018°07′ E
Jasenovac	45°16′ N,	016°54′ E
Karlovac	45°29′ N,	015°33′ E
Knin	44°02′ N,	016°12′ E
Makarska	43°18′ N,	017°02′ E
Nin	44°14′ N,	015°11′ E
Opatija	45°20′ N,	014°19′ E
Osijek	45°33′ N,	018°42′ E

Ploče	43°04′ N,	017°26′ E
Pula	44°52′ N,	013°50′ E
Sesvete	45°50′ N,	016°10′ E
Rijeka	45°21′ N,	014°24′ E
Sisak	45°29′ N,	016°22′ E
Slavonski Brod	45°09′ N,	018°02′ E
Slavonska Požega (Požega)	45°20′ N,	017°41′ E
Split	43°31′ N,	016°26′ E
Trogir	43°32′ N,	016°15′ E
Varaždin	46°18′ N,	016°20′ E
Vinkovci	45°17′ N,	018°49′ E
Vukovar	45°21′ N,	019°00′ E
Zadar	44°07′ N,	015°15′ E
Zagreb	45°48′ N,	016°00′ E

CUBA . . . . pg. 44

Banes	20°58′ N,	075°43′ W
Baracoa	20°21′ N,	074°30′ W
Bayamo	20°23′ N,	076°39′ W
Camagüey	21°23′ N,	077°55′ W
Cárdenas	23°02′ N,	081°12′ W
Ciego de Avila	21°51′ N,	078°46′ W
Cienfuegos	22°09′ N,	080°27′ W
Colón	22°43′ N,	080°54′ W
Florida	21°32′ N,	078°14′ W
Guantánamo	20°08′ N,	075°12′ W
Guïnes	22°50′ N,	082°02′ W
Havana (La Habana)	23°08′ N,	082°22′ W
Holguín	20°53′ N,	076°15′ W
Jagüey Grande	22°32′ N,	081°08′ W
Jovellanos	22°48′ N,	081°12′ W
Las Tunas	20°58′ N,	076°57′ W
Manzanillo	20°21′ N,	077°07′ W
Matanzas	23°03′ N,	081°35′ W
Mayarí	20°40′ N,	075°41′ W
Morón	22°06′ N,	078°38′ W
Nueva Gerona	21°53′ N,	082°48′ W
Nuevitas	21°33′ N,	077°16′ W
Palma Soriano	20°13′ N,	076°00′ W
Pinar del Río	22°25′ N,	083°42′ W
Placetas	22°19′ N,	079°40′ W
Puerto Padre	21°12′ N,	076°36′ W
Sagua la Grande	22°49′ N,	080°05′ W
San Antonio de los Baños	22°53′ N,	082°30′ W
Sancti Spíritus	21°56′ N,	079°27′ W
Santa Clara	22°24′ N,	079°58′ W
Santa Cruz del Sur	20°43′ N,	078°00′ W
Santiago de Cuba	20°01′ N,	075°49′ W

CYPRUS . . . . pg. 45

Akanthou	35°22′ N,	033°45′ E
Akrotiri	34°36′ N,	032°57′ E
Athna	35°03′ N,	033°47′ E
Ayios Amvrosios	35°20′ N,	033°35′ E
Ayios Theodhoros	34°48′ N,	033°23′ E
Famagusta	35°07′ N,	033°57′ E

Kalokhorio.	34°55' N,	033°32' E
Kouklia	34°42' N,	032°34' E
Kyrenia	35°20' N,	033°19' E
Larnaca	34°55' N,	033°38' E
Laxia	35°06' N,	033°22' E
Leonarisso	35°28' N,	034°08' E
Limassol	34°40' N,	033°02' E
Livadhia	35°24' N,	034°02' E
Liveras	35°23' N,	032°57' E
Mari	34°44' N,	033°18' E
Morphou	35°12' N,	032°59' E
Nicosia (Lefkosia)	35°10' N,	033°22' E
Ora.	34°51' N,	033°12' E
Ormidhia	34°59' N,	033°47' E
Pakhna.	34°46' N,	032°48' E
Pano Lakatamia	35°06' N,	033°18' E
Paphos	34°45' N,	032°25' E
Paralimni	35°02' N,	033°59' E
Patriki	35°22' N,	033°59' E
Perivolia	34°49' N,	033°35' E
Pomos	35°09' N,	032°33' E
Prastio.	35°10' N,	033°45' E
Trikomo	35°17' N,	033°52' E
Tsadha.	34°50' N,	032°28' E
Varosha	35°06' N,	033°57' E
Vroisha	35°04' N,	032°40' E
Yialoussa	35°32' N,	034°11' E

CZECH REPUBLIC

Břeclav	48°46' N,	016°53' E
Brno.	49°12' N,	016°38' E
Česká Lípa.	50°41' N,	014°33' E
České Budějovice.	48°59' N,	014°28' E
Český Těšín	49°45' N,	018°37' E
Cheb	50°04' N,	012°22' E
Chomutov	50°27' N,	013°26' E
Děčín	50°47' N,	014°13' E
Frýdek Místek	49°41' N,	018°21' E
Havířov	49°47' N,	018°22' E
Havlíčkův Brod	49°37' N,	015°35' E
Hodonín.	48°52' N,	017°08' E
Hradec Králové.	50°13' N,	015°50' E
Jablonec	50°43' N,	015°11' E
Jihlava	49°24' N,	015°35' E
Karlovy Vary	50°13' N,	012°54' E
Karviná	49°52' N,	018°33' E
Kladno	50°09' N,	014°06' E
Kolín	50°02' N,	015°12' E
Krnov.	50°06' N,	017°43' E
Kroměříž	49°18' N,	017°24' E
Liberec	50°47' N,	015°03' E
Litvínov	50°36' N,	013°37' E
Mladá Boleslav	50°25' N,	014°54' E
Most.	50°32' N,	013°39' E
Nový Jičín	49°36' N,	018°01' E
Olomouc	49°35' N,	017°15' E
Opava	49°57' N,	017°55' E
Orlová	49°51' N,	018°25' E

Ostrava	49°50' N,	018°17' E
Pardubice	50°02' N,	015°47' E
Písek	49°18' N,	014°09' E
Plzeň	49°45' N,	013°22' E
Prague (Praha)	50°05' N,	014°28' E
Přerov	49°27' N,	017°27' E
Příbram	49°42' N,	014°01' E
Prostějov	49°28' N,	017°07' E
Šumperk	49°58' N,	016°58' E
Tábor.	49°25' N,	014°40' E
Teplice.	50°38' N,	013°50' E
Třebíč	49°13' N,	015°53' E
Trinec	49°41' N,	018°39' E
Trutnov	50°34' N,	015°54' E
Uherské Hradiště	49°04' N,	017°27' E
Ústí nad Labem.	50°40' N,	014°02' E
Valašské Meziříčí	49°28' N,	017°58' E
Vsetín	49°20' N,	018°00' E
Žďár nad Sázavou	49°35' N,	015°56' E
Zlín.	49°13' N,	017°40' E
Znojmo	48°51' N,	016°03' E

DENMARK

Ålborg (Aalborg).	57°03' N,	009°56' E
Århus (Aarhus).	56°09' N,	010°13' E
Ärs	56°48' N,	009°32' E
Brønderslev	57°16' N,	009°58' E
Brørup	55°29' N,	009°01' E
Copenhagen (København)	55°40' N,	012°35' E
Esbjerg	55°28' N,	008°27' E
Fakse	55°15' N,	012°08' E
Fredericia	55°35' N,	009°46' E
Frederiksberg	55°41' N,	012°32' E
Frederikshavn	57°26' N,	010°32' E
Gilleleje	56°07' N,	012°19' E
Give	55°51' N,	009°15' E
Grenå	56°25' N,	010°53' E
Hadsund	56°43' N,	010°07' E
Helsingør	56°02' N,	012°37' E
Herning	56°08' N,	008°59' E
Hillerød	55°56' N,	012°19' E
Hirtshals	57°35' N,	009°58' E
Hjørring	57°28' N,	009°59' E
Holstebro	56°21' N,	008°38' E
Hornslet.	56°19' N,	010°20' E
Horsens	55°52' N,	009°52' E
Jyderup	55°40' N,	011°26' E
Klarup	57°01' N,	010°03' E
Køge.	55°27' N,	012°11' E
Kolding	55°29' N,	009°29' E
Lemvig.	56°32' N,	008°18' E
Løgstør	56°58' N,	009°15' E
Næstved	55°14' N,	011°46' E
Nakskov.	54°50' N,	011°09' E
Nykøbing	54°46' N,	011°53' E
Nykøbing	55°55' N,	011°41' E
Nykøbing	56°48' N,	008°52' E
Odense	55°24' N,	010°23' E
Ølgod	55°49' N,	008°37' E

Otterup	55°31' N, 010°24' E
Padborg	54°49' N, 009°22' E
Randers	56°28' N, 010°03' E
Ribe	55°21' N, 008°46' E
Ringkøbing	56°05' N, 008°15' E
Rønne	55°39' N, 012°05' E
Roskilde	55°06' N, 014°42' E
Rudkøbing	57°44' N, 010°36' E
Skagen	56°34' N, 009°02' E
Skive	55°57' N, 008°30' E
Skjern	55°24' N, 011°22' E
Slagelse	55°24' N, 011°22' E
Sønderborg	54°55' N, 009°47' E
Struer	56°29' N, 008°37' E
Svendborg	55°03' N, 010°37' E
Thisted	56°57' N, 008°42' E
Tilst	56°12' N, 010°07' E
Toftlund	55°11' N, 009°04' E
Tønder	54°56' N, 008°54' E
Varde	55°38' N, 008°29' E
Vejle	55°42' N, 009°32' E
Viborg	56°26' N, 009°24' E
Vodskov	57°06' N, 010°02' E
Vordingborg	55°01' N, 011°55' E

DJIBOUTI . . . . pg. 48

Ali Sabih	11°10' N, 042°42' E
Dikhil	11°06' N, 042°23' E
Djibouti	11°36' N, 043°09' E
Tadjoura	11°47' N, 042°53' E

DOMINICA . . . . pg. 49

Castle Bruce	15°26' N, 061°16' W
Colihaut	15°30' N, 061°29' W
La Plaine	15°20' N, 061°15' W
Marigot	15°32' N, 061°18' W
Portsmouth	15°35' N, 061°28' W
Rosalie	15°22' N, 061°16' W
Roseau	15°18' N, 061°24' W
Saint Joseph	15°24' N, 061°26' W
Salibia	15°29' N, 061°16' W
Soufrière	15°13' N, 061°22' W
Vieille Case	15°36' N, 061°24' W

DOMINICAN REPUBLIC . . . . pg. 50

Azua	18°27' N, 070°44' W
Baní	18°17' N, 070°20' W
Barahona	18°12' N, 071°06' W
Bayaguana	18°58' N, 069°00' W
Bonao	18°56' N, 070°25' W
Cotuí	19°03' N, 070°09' W
Dajabón	19°33' N, 071°42' W
Duvergé	18°22' N, 071°31' W

El Seibo	18°46' N, 069°02' W
Enriquillo	17°54' N, 071°14' W
Higüey	18°37' N, 068°42' W
Jimaní	18°28' N, 071°51' W
La Romana	18°25' N, 068°58' W
La Vega	19°13' N, 070°31' W
Las Matas	18°52' N, 071°31' W
Mao	19°34' N, 071°05' W
Miches	18°59' N, 069°03' W
Moca	19°24' N, 070°31' W
Montecristi	19°52' N, 071°39' W
Nagua (Julia Molina)	19°23' N, 069°50' W
Neiba	18°28' N, 071°25' W
Pedernales	18°02' N, 071°45' W
Puerto Plata	19°48' N, 070°41' W
Sabaneta	19°28' N, 071°20' W
Salcedo	19°23' N, 070°25' W
Samaná	19°13' N, 069°19' W
San Cristóbal	18°25' N, 070°06' W
San Francisco de Macorís	19°18' N, 070°15' W
San Juan	18°48' N, 071°14' W
San Pedro de Macorís	18°27' N, 069°18' W
Sánchez	19°14' N, 069°36' W
Santiago	19°27' N, 070°42' W
Santo Domingo	18°28' N, 069°54' W

ECUADOR . . . . pg. 51

Ambato	01°15' S, 078°37' W
Azogues	02°44' S, 078°50' W
Babahoyo	01°49' S, 079°31' W
Balzar	01°22' S, 079°54' W
Cuenca	02°53' S, 078°59' W
Esmeraldas	00°59' N, 079°42' W
General Leonidas Plaza Gutiérrez	02°58' S, 078°25' W
Girón	03°10' S, 079°08' W
Guayaquil	02°10' S, 079°54' W
Huaquillas	03°29' S, 080°14' W
Ibarra	00°21' N, 078°07' W
Jipijapa	01°20' S, 080°35' W
Latacunga	00°56' S, 078°37' W
Loja	04°00' S, 079°13' W
Macará	04°23' S, 079°57' W
Macas	02°19' S, 078°07' W
Machala	03°16' S, 079°58' W
Manta	00°57' S, 080°44' W
Milagro	02°07' S, 079°36' W
Muisne	00°36' N, 080°02' W
Naranjal	02°40' S, 079°37' W
Otavalo	00°14' N, 078°16' W
Pasaje	03°20' S, 079°49' W
Piñas	03°40' S, 079°39' W
Portoviejo	01°03' S, 080°27' W
Puerto Francisco de Orellana (Coca)	00°28' S, 076°58' W
Puyo	01°28' S, 077°59' W
Quevedo	01°02' S, 079°27' W
Quito	00°13' S, 078°30' W
Riobamba	01°40' S, 078°38' W
Salinas	02°13' S, 080°58' W

San Gabriel	00°36′ N, 077°49′ W
San Lorenzo	01°17′ N, 078°50′ W
Santo Domingo de los Colorados (Santo Domingo)	00°15′ S, 079°09′ W
Tena	00°59′ S, 077°49′ W
Tulcán	00°48′ N, 077°43′ W
Valdez	01°15′ N, 079°00′ W
Yantzaza	03°51′ S, 078°45′ W
Zamora	04°04′ S, 078°58′ W
Zaruma	03°41′ S, 079°37′ W

EGYPT ....pg. 52

Akhmīm	26°34′ N, 031°44′ E
Al-'Arīsh	31°08′ N, 033°48′ E
Alexandria (Al-Iskandarīyah)	31°12′ N, 029°54′ E
Al-Fayyūm	29°19′ N, 030°50′ E
Al-Khārijah	25°26′ N, 030°33′ E
Al-Maḥallah al-Kubrā	30°58′ N, 031°10′ E
Al-Manṣūrah	31°03′ N, 031°23′ E
Al-Ma'sarah	25°30′ N, 029°04′ E
Al-Minyā	28°06′ N, 030°45′ E
Aswān	24°05′ N, 032°53′ E
Asyut	27°11′ N, 031°11′ E
Aṭ-Ṭur	28°14′ N, 033°37′ E
Az-Zāqazīq	30°35′ N, 031°31′ E
Banhā	30°28′ N, 031°11′ E
Banī Suwayf	29°05′ N, 031°05′ E
Cairo (Al-Qāhirah)	30°03′ N, 031°15′ E
Damanhūr	31°02′ N, 030°28′ E
Damietta (Dumyāṭ)	31°25′ N, 031°48′ E
Giza (Al-Jīzah)	30°01′ N, 031°13′ E
Jirjā	26°20′ N, 031°53′ E
Luxor (Al-Uqsur)	25°41′ N, 032°39′ E
Mallawī	27°44′ N, 030°50′ E
Matruh	31°21′ N, 027°14′ E
Port Said (Būr Sa'īd)	31°16′ N, 032°18′ E
Qinā	26°10′ N, 032°43′ E
Sawhāj	26°33′ N, 031°42′ E
Shibīn al-Kawm	30°33′ N, 031°01′ E
Suez (As-Suways)	29°58′ N, 032°33′ E
Ṭanṭā	30°47′ N, 031°00′ E

EL SALVADOR ...pg. 53

Acajutla	13°35′ N, 089°50′ W
Chalatenango	14°02′ N, 088°56′ W
Chalchuapa	13°59′ N, 089°41′ W
Cojutepeque	13°43′ N, 088°56′ W
Ilobasco	13°51′ N, 088°51′ W
Izalco	13°45′ N, 089°40′ W
La Unión	13°20′ N, 087°51′ W
Nueva San Salvador (Santa Tecla)	13°41′ N, 089°17′ W
San Francisco (San Francisco Gotera)	13°42′ N, 088°06′ W
San Miguel	13°29′ N, 088°11′ W
San Salvador	13°42′ N, 089°12′ W
Santa Ana	13°59′ N, 089°34′ W
San Vincente	13°38′ N, 088°48′ W
Sensuntepeque	13°52′ N, 088°38′ W
Sonsonate	13°43′ N, 089°44′ W
Usulatán	13°21′ N, 088°27′ W
Zacatecoluca	13°20′ N, 088°52′ W

EQUATORIAL GUINEA ....pg. 54

Bata	01°51′ N, 009°45′ E
Kogo	01°05′ N, 009°42′ E
Malabo (Santa Isabel)	03°21′ N, 008°40′ E
Mbini	01°34′ N, 009°37′ E
Mikomeseng	02°08′ N, 010°37′ E
Niefang	01°51′ N, 010°15′ E
San Antonio de Ureca	03°16′ N, 008°32′ E

ERITREA ....pg. 55

Akordat	15°33′ N, 037°53′ E
Aseb (Assab)	13°00′ N, 042°44′ E
Asmara (Asmera)	15°20′ N, 038°56′ E
Keren	15°47′ N, 038°28′ E
Massawa (Mitsiwa)	15°36′ N, 039°28′ E
Nakfa	16°40′ N, 038°29′ E

ESTONIA ....pg. 56

Abja-Paluoja	58°08′ N, 025°21′ E
Ambla	59°11′ N, 025°51′ E
Antsla	57°50′ N, 026°32′ E
Haapsalu	58°56′ N, 023°33′ E
Järva-Jaani	59°02′ N, 025°53′ E
Järvakandi	58°47′ N, 024°49′ E
Jõgeva	58°45′ N, 026°24′ E
Käina	58°50′ N, 022°47′ E
Kallaste	58°39′ N, 027°09′ E
Kärdla	59°00′ N, 022°45′ E
Kehra	59°20′ N, 025°20′ E
Keila	59°18′ N, 024°25′ E
Kilingi-Nõmme	58°09′ N, 024°58′ E
Kiviõli	59°21′ N, 026°57′ E
Kohtla-Järve	59°24′ N, 027°15′ E
Kunda	59°29′ N, 026°32′ E
Kuressaare (Kingissepa)	58°15′ N, 022°28′ E
Lavassaare	58°31′ N, 024°22′ E
Līhula (Lihula)	58°41′ N, 023°50′ E
Loksa	59°35′ N, 025°42′ E
Maardu	59°25′ N, 024°59′ E
Märjamaa	58°54′ N, 024°26′ E
Mõisaküla	58°06′ N, 025°11′ E
Mustla	58°14′ N, 025°52′ E
Narva	59°23′ N, 028°12′ E
Nuia	58°06′ N, 025°33′ E
Orissaare	58°34′ N, 023°05′ E

Otepää	58°03′ N, 026°30′ E
Paide	58°54′ N, 025°33′ E
Paldiski	59°20′ N, 024°06′ E
Pärnu	58°24′ N, 024°32′ E
Põlva	58°03′ N, 027°03′ E
Püssi	59°22′ N, 027°03′ E
Rakvere	59°22′ N, 026°20′ E
Räpina	58°06′ N, 027°27′ E
Rapla	59°01′ N, 024°47′ E
Saue	59°18′ N, 024°34′ E
Sindi	58°24′ N, 024°40′ E
Suure-Jaani	58°33′ N, 025°28′ E
Tallinn	59°25′ N, 024°45′ E
Tapa	59°16′ N, 025°58′ E
Tartu	58°23′ N, 026°43′ E
Tootsi	58°34′ N, 024°49′ E
Tõrva	58°00′ N, 025°56′ E
Türi	58°48′ N, 025°26′ E
Valga	57°47′ N, 026°02′ E
Viivikonna	59°19′ N, 027°42′ E
Viljandi	58°24′ N, 025°36′ E
Võsu	59°35′ N, 025°58′ E

ETHIOPIA ....pg. 57

Addis Ababa (Adis Abeba)	09°02′ N, 038°42′ E
Adigrat	14°17′ N, 039°28′ E
Adwa (Adowa or Aduwa)	14°10′ N, 038°54′ E
Agaro	07°51′ N, 036°39′ E
Akaki	09°05′ N, 039°00′ E
Aksum	14°08′ N, 038°43′ E
Alamata	12°25′ N, 039°33′ E
Arba Minch (Arba Mench)	06°02′ N, 037°33′ E
Bahir Dar	11°36′ N, 037°23′ E
Debre Markos	10°21′ N, 037°44′ E
Debre Zeyit	08°45′ N, 038°59′ E
Dembidollo	08°32′ N, 034°48′ E
Dese (Dase)	11°08′ N, 039°38′ E
Dire Dawa	09°35′ N, 041°52′ E
Finchaa	09°33′ N, 037°21′ E
Gonder	12°36′ N, 037°28′ E
Gore	08°09′ N, 035°32′ E
Harer (Harar)	09°19′ N, 042°07′ E
Jijiga	09°21′ N, 042°48′ E
Jima (Jimma)	07°40′ N, 036°50′ E
Kembolcha (Kombolcha)	11°05′ N, 039°44′ E
Kibre Mengist	05°53′ N, 038°59′ E
Lalibela	12°02′ N, 039°02′ E
Mekele	13°30′ N, 039°28′ E
Metu	08°18′ N, 035°35′ E
Nazret	08°33′ N, 039°16′ E
Nekemte	09°05′ N, 036°33′ E
Sodo	06°54′ N, 037°45′ E
Weldya	11°50′ N, 039°41′ E
Yirga Alem	06°45′ N, 038°25′ E

FIJI ....pg. 58

Ba	17°33′ S, 177°41′ E

Lami	18°07′ S, 178°25′ E
Lautoka	17°37′ S, 177°28′ E
Nadi	17°48′ S, 177°25′ E
Suva	18°08′ S, 178°25′ E

FINLAND ....pg. 59

Espoo (Esbo)	60°13′ N, 024°40′ E
Forssa	60°49′ N, 023°38′ E
Hämeenlinna (Tavastehus)	61°00′ N, 024°27′ E
Hanko	59°50′ N, 022°57′ E
Haukipudas	65°11′ N, 025°21′ E
Heinola	61°13′ N, 026°02′ E
Helsinki	60°10′ N, 024°58′ E
Ilmajoki	62°44′ N, 022°34′ E
Ivalo	68°39′ N, 027°36′ E
Jämsä	61°52′ N, 025°12′ E
Joensuu	62°36′ N, 029°46′ E
Jyväskylä	62°14′ N, 025°44′ E
Kangasala	61°28′ N, 024°05′ E
Kaskinen	62°23′ N, 021°13′ E
Kemi	65°44′ N, 024°34′ E
Kittilä	67°40′ N, 024°54′ E
Kotka	60°28′ N, 026°55′ E
Kouvola	60°52′ N, 026°42′ E
Kuhmo	64°08′ N, 029°31′ E
Kuopio	62°54′ N, 027°41′ E
Lahti	60°58′ N, 025°40′ E
Lappeenranta (Villmanstrand)	61°04′ N, 028°11′ E
Lapua	62°57′ N, 023°00′ E
Lohja	60°15′ N, 024°05′ E
Mariehamn (Maarianhamina)	60°06′ N, 019°57′ E
Mikkeli (Sankt Michel)	61°41′ N, 027°15′ E
Nivala	63°55′ N, 024°58′ E
Nurmes	63°33′ N, 029°07′ E
Oulu (Uleåborg)	65°01′ N, 025°28′ E
Pello	66°47′ N, 023°55′ E
Pietarsaari	63°40′ N, 022°42′ E
Pori (Björneborg)	61°29′ N, 021°47′ E
Posio	66°06′ N, 028°09′ E
Raahe	64°41′ N, 024°29′ E
Rauma	61°08′ N, 021°30′ E
Rovaniemi	66°30′ N, 025°43′ E
Salla	66°50′ N, 028°40′ E
Salo	60°23′ N, 023°08′ E
Sotkamo	64°08′ N, 028°25′ E
Tampere (Tammerfors)	61°30′ N, 023°45′ E
Turku (Åbo)	60°27′ N, 022°17′ E
Vaasa (Vasa)	63°06′ N, 021°36′ E
Vantaa (Vanda)	60°18′ N, 024°51′ E

FRANCE ....pg. 60

Ajaccio	41°55′ N, 008°44′ E
Amiens	49°54′ N, 002°18′ E
Angers	47°28′ N, 000°33′ W

Annecy	45°54′ N, 006°07′ E
Auch	43°39′ N, 000°35′ E
Aurillac	44°55′ N, 002°27′ E
Auxerre	47°48′ N, 003°34′ E
Avignon	43°57′ N, 004°49′ E
Bar-le-Duc	48°47′ N, 005°10′ E
Bastia	42°42′ N, 009°27′ E
Beauvais	49°26′ N, 002°05′ E
Belfort	47°38′ N, 006°52′ E
Bonifacio	41°23′ N, 009°09′ E
Bordeaux	44°50′ N, 000°34′ W
Bourges	47°05′ N, 002°24′ E
Brest	48°24′ N, 004°29′ W
Caen	49°11′ N, 000°21′ W
Cahors	44°26′ N, 001°26′ E
Calais	50°57′ N, 001°50′ E
Charleville-Mézières	49°46′ N, 004°43′ E
Chartres	48°27′ N, 001°30′ E
Clermont-Ferrand	45°47′ N, 003°05′ E
Colmar	48°05′ N, 007°22′ E
Dijon	47°19′ N, 005°01′ E
Dunkirk (Dunkerque)	51°03′ N, 002°22′ E
Épinal	48°11′ N, 006°27′ E
Grenoble	45°10′ N, 005°43′ E
Guéret	46°10′ N, 001°52′ E
La Rochelle	46°10′ N, 001°09′ W
Le Havre	49°30′ N, 000°08′ E
Le Mans	48°00′ N, 000°12′ E
Lille	50°38′ N, 003°04′ E
Limoges	45°45′ N, 001°20′ E
Lyon	45°45′ N, 004°51′ E
Marseille	43°18′ N, 005°24′ E
Metz	49°08′ N, 006°10′ E
Mont-de-Marsan	43°53′ N, 000°30′ W
Moulins	46°34′ N, 003°20′ E
Nancy	48°41′ N, 006°12′ E
Nantes	47°13′ N, 001°33′ W
Nevers	46°59′ N, 003°10′ E
Nice	43°42′ N, 007°15′ E
Nîmes	43°50′ N, 004°21′ E
Niort	46°19′ N, 000°28′ W
Orléans	47°55′ N, 001°54′ E
Paris	48°52′ N, 002°20′ E
Pau	43°18′ N, 000°22′ W
Périgueux	45°11′ N, 000°43′ E
Perpignan	42°41′ N, 002°53′ E
Poitiers	46°35′ N, 000°20′ E
Quimper	48°00′ N, 004°06′ W
Rennes	48°05′ N, 001°41′ W
Saint-Brieuc	48°31′ N, 002°47′ W
Strasbourg	48°35′ N, 007°45′ E
Tarbes	43°14′ N, 000°05′ E
Toulon	43°07′ N, 005°56′ E
Toulouse	43°36′ N, 001°26′ E
Tours	47°23′ N, 000°41′ E
Troyes	48°18′ N, 004°05′ E
Tulle	45°16′ N, 001°46′ E
Valence	44°56′ N, 004°54′ E
Vannes	47°40′ N, 002°45′ W
Versailles	48°48′ N, 002°08′ E
Vesoul	47°38′ N, 006°10′ E

GABON . . . . pg. 61

Bitam	02°05′ N, 011°29′ E
Booué	00°06′ S, 011°56′ E
Fougamou	01°13′ S, 010°36′ E
Franceville	01°38′ S, 013°35′ E
Kango	00°09′ N, 010°08′ E
Koula-Moutou	01°08′ S, 012°29′ E
Lambaréné	00°42′ S, 010°13′ E
Lastoursville	00°49′ S, 012°42′ E
Léconi	01°35′ S, 014°14′ E
Libreville	00°23′ N, 009°27′ E
Makokou	00°34′ N, 012°52′ E
Mayumba	03°25′ S, 010°39′ E
Mekambo	01°01′ N, 013°56′ E
Mimongo	01°38′ S, 011°39′ E
Minvoul	02°09′ N, 012°08′ E
Mitzic	00°47′ N, 011°34′ E
Mouila	01°52′ S, 011°01′ E
Ndjolé	00°11′ S, 010°45′ E
Okondja	00°41′ S, 013°47′ E
Omboué	01°34′ S, 009°15′ E
Ovendo	00°17′ N, 009°30′ E
Oyem	01°37′ N, 011°35′ E
Port-Gentil	00°43′ S, 008°47′ E
Setté Cama	02°32′ S, 009°45′ E
Tchibanga	02°51′ S, 011°02′ E

GAMBIA, THE . . . . pg. 62

Banjul	13°27′ N, 016°35′ W
Basse Santa Su	13°19′ N, 014°13′ W
Brikama	13°16′ N, 016°39′ W
Georgetown	13°32′ N, 014°46′ W
Mansa Konko	13°28′ N, 015°33′ W
Serekunda	13°26′ N, 016°34′ W
Yundum	13°20′ N, 016°41′ W

GEORGIA . . . . pg. 63

Akhalk'alak'i	41°24′ N, 043°29′ E
Batumi	41°38′ N, 041°38′ E
Chiat'ura	42°19′ N, 043°18′ E
Gagra	43°20′ N, 040°15′ E
Gardabani	41°28′ N, 045°05′ E
Gori	41°58′ N, 044°07′ E
Gudaut'a	43°06′ N, 040°38′ E
Khashuri	41°59′ N, 043°36′ E
K'obulet'i	41°50′ N, 041°45′ E
Kutaisi	42°15′ N, 042°40′ E
Marneuli	41°27′ N, 044°48′ E
Och'amch'ire	42°43′ N, 041°28′ E
Pot'i	42°09′ N, 041°40′ E
Rustavi	41°33′ N, 045°03′ E
Samtredia	42°11′ N, 042°20′ E
Sokhumi	43°00′ N, 041°02′ E
Tbilisi (Tiflis)	41°42′ N, 044°45′ E
T'elavi	41°55′ N, 045°28′ E

Tqibuli	42°22′ N,	042°59′ E
Tqvarch'eli (Tkvarchely)	42°51′ N,	041°41′ E
Ts'khinvali (Staliniri)	42°14′ N,	043°58′ E
Tsqaltubo	42°20′ N,	042°34′ E
Zugdidi	42°30′ N,	041°53′ E

GERMANY . . . . .pg. 64

Aachen	50°46′ N,	006°06′ E
Augsburg	48°22′ N,	010°53′ E
Aurich	53°28′ N,	007°29′ E
Baden-Baden	48°45′ N,	008°15′ E
Berlin	52°31′ N,	013°22′ E
Bielefeld	52°02′ N,	008°32′ E
Bonn	50°44′ N,	007°06′ E
Brandenburg	52°25′ N,	012°33′ E
Bremen	53°05′ N,	008°48′ E
Bremerhaven	53°33′ N,	008°35′ E
Chemnitz		
(Karl-Marx-Stadt)	50°50′ N,	012°55′ E
Cologne (Köln)	50°56′ N,	006°57′ E
Cottbus	51°46′ N,	014°20′ E
Dessau	51°50′ N,	012°15′ E
Dortmund	51°31′ N,	007°27′ E
Dresden	51°03′ N,	013°45′ E
Duisburg	51°26′ N,	006°45′ E
Düsseldorf	51°13′ N,	006°46′ E
Erfurt	50°59′ N,	011°02′ E
Erlangen	49°36′ N,	011°01′ E
Essen	51°27′ N,	007°01′ E
Frankfurt am Main	50°07′ N,	008°41′ E
Freiburg	48°00′ N,	007°51′ E
Göttingen	51°32′ N,	009°56′ E
Halle	51°30′ N,	012°00′ E
Hamburg	53°33′ N,	010°00′ E
Hannover	52°22′ N,	009°43′ E
Heidelberg	49°25′ N,	008°42′ E
Jena	50°56′ N,	011°35′ E
Kassel	51°19′ N,	009°30′ E
Kiel	54°20′ N,	010°08′ E
Leipzig	51°18′ N,	012°20′ E
Lübeck	53°52′ N,	010°42′ E
Magdeburg	52°10′ N,	011°40′ E
Mainz	50°00′ N,	008°15′ E
Mannheim	49°29′ N,	008°28′ E
Munich	48°09′ N,	011°35′ E
Nürnberg (Nuremberg)	49°27′ N,	011°05′ E
Oldenburg	53°08′ N,	010°53′ E
Osnabrück	52°16′ N,	008°03′ E
Potsdam	52°24′ N,	013°04′ E
Regensburg	49°01′ N,	012°06′ E
Rostock	54°05′ N,	012°08′ E
Saarbrücken	49°14′ N,	007°00′ E
Schwerin	53°38′ N,	011°23′ E
Siegen	50°52′ N,	008°02′ E
Stuttgart	48°46′ N,	009°11′ E
Ulm	48°24′ N,	010°00′ E
Wiesbaden	50°05′ N,	008°15′ E
Würzburg	49°48′ N,	009°56′ E
Zwickau	50°44′ N,	012°30′E

GHANA . . . . .pg. 65

Accra	05°33′ N,	000°13′ E
Anloga	05°48′ N,	000°54′ E
Awaso	06°14′ N,	002°16′ W
Axim	04°52′ N,	002°14′ W
Bawku	11°03′ N,	000°15′ W
Bolgatanga	10°47′ N,	000°51′ W
Cape Coast	05°06′ N,	001°15′ W
Damongo	09°05′ N,	001°49′ W
Dunkwa	05°58′ N,	001°47′ W
Koforidua	05°14′ N,	001°20′ W
Kumasi	06°41′ N,	001°37′ W
Mampong	07°04′ N,	001°24′ W
Obuasi	06°12′ N,	001°40′ W
Prestea	05°26′ N,	002°09′ W
Salaga	08°33′ N,	000°31′ W
Sekondi-Takoradi	04°53′ N,	001°45′ W
Sunyani	07°20′ N,	002°20′ W
Swedru	05°32′ N,	000°42′ W
Tamale	09°24′ N,	000°50′ W
Tarkwa	05°18′ N,	001°59′ W
Tema	05°37′ N,	000°01′ W
Wa	10°03′ N,	002°29′ W
Yendi	09°26′ N,	000°01′ W

GREECE . . . . .pg. 66

Alexandroúpolis		
(Alexandhroupolis)	40°51′ N,	025°52′ E
Ándros	37°50′ N,	024°56′ E
Árgos	37°38′ N,	022°44′ E
Árta	39°09′ N,	020°59′ E
Áyios Nikólaos	35°11′ N,	025°43′ E
Drama	41°09′ N,	024°09′ E
Edessa (Edhessa)	40°48′ N,	022°03′ E
Ermoúpolis		
(Hermoúpolis)	37°27′ N,	024°56′ E
Flórina	40°47′ N,	021°24′ E
Hydra (Ídhra)	37°21′ N,	023°28′ E
Igoumenítsa	39°30′ N,	020°16′ E
Ioánnina (Yannina)	39°40′ N,	020°50′ E
Íos	36°44′ N,	025°17′ E
Iráklion		
(Candia or Heraklion)	35°20′ N,	025°08′ E
Kalamariá	40°35′ N,	022°58′ E
Kalamata (Kalámai)	37°02′ N,	022°07′ E
Kálimnos	36°57′ N,	026°59′ E
Karditsa	39°22′ N,	021°55′ E
Kariaí	40°15′ N,	024°15′ E
Karpenísion	38°55′ N,	021°47′ E
Katerini	40°16′ N,	022°30′ E
Kavála		
(Kaválla or Neapolis)	40°56′ N,	024°25′ E
Kéa	37°38′ N,	024°21′ E
Kérkira	39°36′ N,	019°55′ E
Khalkís (Chalcis)	38°28′ N,	023°36′ E
Khaniá (Canea)	35°31′ N,	024°02′ E
Khíos (Chios)	38°22′ N,	026°08′ E

Kilkís	41°00′ N, 022°52′ E
Komotiní	41°07′ N, 025°24′ E
Lamía	38°54′ N, 022°26′ E
Lárissa (Lárisa)	39°38′ N, 022°25′ E
Laurium (Lávrion)	37°43′ N, 024°03′ E
Mégara	38°00′ N, 023°21′ E
Mesolóngion (Missolonghi)	38°22′ N, 021°26′ E
Mitilíni (Mytilene)	39°06′ N, 026°33′ E
Monemvasía	36°41′ N, 023°03′ E
Náuplia (Navplion)	37°34′ N, 022°48′ E
Náxos	37°06′ N, 025°23′ E
Néa Ionía	38°02′ N, 023°45′ E
Pátrai	38°15′ N, 021°44′ E
Piraeus (Piraievs)	37°57′ N, 028°38′ E
Préveza	38°57′ N, 020°45′ E
Pylos (Pílos)	36°55′ N, 021°42′ E
Pyrgos (Pírgos)	37°41′ N, 021°27′ E
Réthimnon	35°22′ N, 024°28′ E
Rhodes (Ródhos)	36°26′ N, 028°13′ E
Sámos	37°45′ N, 026°58′ E
Samothráki	40°29′ N, 025°31′ E
Sérrai	41°05′ N, 023°33′ E
Sparta (Spárti)	37°05′ N, 022°26′ E
Thásos	40°47′ N, 024°43′ E
Thebes (Thívai)	38°19′ N, 023°19′ E
Thessaloníki (Salonika)	40°38′ N, 022°56′ E
Tríkala	39°33′ N, 021°46′ E
Trípolis	37°31′ N, 022°22′ E
Vólos	39°22′ N, 022°57′ E
Yíthion (Gíthion)	36°45′ N, 022°34′ E
Xánthi	41°08′ N, 024°53′ E
Zákinthos	37°47′ N, 020°54′ E

GRENADA . . . . .pg. 67

Birch Grove	12°07′ N, 061°40′ W
Concord	12°07′ N, 061°44′ W
Corinth	12°02′ N, 061°40′ W
Gouyave	12°10′ N, 061°44′ W
Grand Anse	12°01′ N, 061°45′ W
Grenville	12°07′ N, 061°37′ W
Hillsborough	12°29′ N, 061°28′ W
La Poterie	12°10′ N, 061°36′ W
Rose Hill	12°12′ N, 061°37′ W
St. George's	12°03′ N, 061°45′ W
Sauteurs	12°14′ N, 061°38′ W
Victoria	12°12′ N, 061°42′ W

GUATEMALA . . . . .pg. 68

Amatitlán	14°29′ N, 090°37′ W
Antigua Guatemala (Antigua)	14°34′ N, 090°44′ W
Champerico	14°18′ N, 091°55′ W
Coatepeque	14°42′ N, 091°52′ W
Cobán	15°29′ N, 090°22′ W
Cuilapa (Cuajiniquilapa)	14°17′ N, 090°18′ W

El Estor	15°32′ N, 089°21′ W
Escuintla	14°18′ N, 090°47′ W
Esquipulas	14°34′ N, 089°21′ W
Flores	16°56′ N, 089°53′ W
Gualán	15°08′ N, 089°22′ W
Guatemala City (Guatemala)	14°38′ N, 090°31′ W
Huehuetenango	15°20′ N, 091°28′ W
Jalapa	14°38′ N, 089°59′ W
Jutiapa	14°17′ N, 089°54′ W
Mazatenango	14°32′ N, 091°30′ W
Poptún	16°21′ N, 089°26′ W
Pueblo Nuevo Tiquisate	14°17′ N, 091°22′ W
Puerto Barrios	15°43′ N, 088°36′ W
Puerto San José	13°55′ N, 090°49′ W
Quezaltenango	14°50′ N, 091°31′ W
Salamá	15°06′ N, 090°16′ W
San Benito	16°55′ N, 089°54′ W
San Cristóbal Verapaz	15°23′ N, 090°24′ W
Santa Cruz del Quiché	15°02′ N, 091°08′ W
Sololá	14°46′ N, 091°11′ W
Todos Santos Cuchumatán	15°31′ N, 091°37′ W
Villa Nueva	14°31′ N, 090°35′ W
Zacapa	14°58′ N, 089°32′ W
Zunil	14°47′ N, 091°29′ W

GUINEA . . . . .pg. 69

Beyla	08°41′ N, 008°38′ W
Boffa	10°10′ N, 014°02′ W
Boké	10°56′ N, 014°18′ W
Conakry	09°31′ N, 013°43′ W
Dabola	10°45′ N, 011°07′ W
Dalaba	10°42′ N, 012°15′ W
Dinguiraye	11°18′ N, 010°43′ W
Faranah	10°02′ N, 010°44′ W
Forécariah	09°26′ N, 013°06′ W
Fria	10°27′ N, 013°32′ W
Gaoual	11°45′ N, 013°12′ W
Guéckédou	08°33′ N, 010°09′ W
Kankan	10°23′ N, 009°18′ W
Kérouané	09°16′ N, 009°01′ W
Kindia	10°04′ N, 012°51′ W
Kissidougou	09°11′ N, 010°06′ W
Kouroussa	10°39′ N, 009°53′ W
Labé	11°19′ N, 012°17′ W
Macenta	08°33′ N, 009°28′ W
Mamou	10°23′ N, 012°05′ W
Nzérékoré	07°45′ N, 008°49′ W
Pita	11°05′ N, 012°24′ W
Siguiri	11°25′ N, 009°10′ W
Télimélé	10°54′ N, 013°02′ W
Tougué	11°27′ N, 011°41′ W

GUINEA-BISSAU . .pg. 70

Bafatá	12°10′ N, 014°40′ W
Bambadinca	12°02′ N, 014°52′ W
Bedanda	11°21′ N, 015°07′ W

Béli . . . . 11°51' N, 013°56' W
Bissau . . . . 11°51' N, 015°35' W
Bissorã . . . . 12°03' N, 015°26' W
Bolama . . . . 11°35' N, 015°28' W
Buba . . . . 11°35' N, 015°00' W
Bula . . . . 12°07' N, 015°43' W
Buruntuma . . . . 12°26' N, 013°39' W
Cacheu . . . . 12°16' N, 016°10' W
Catió . . . . 11°17' N, 015°15' W
Empada . . . . 11°33' N, 015°14' W
Farim . . . . 12°29' N, 015°13' W
Fulacunda . . . . 11°46' N, 015°10' W
Gabú (Nova Lamego) . . . . 12°17' N, 014°13' W
Galomaro . . . . 11°57' N, 014°38' W
Jolmete . . . . 12°13' N, 015°52' W
Madina do Boé . . . . 11°45' N, 014°13' W
Mansôa . . . . 12°04' N, 015°19' W
Nhacra . . . . 11°58' N, 015°33' W
Piche . . . . 12°20' N, 013°57' W
Pirada . . . . 12°40' N, 014°10' W
Quebo . . . . 11°20' N, 014°56' W
Quinhámel . . . . 11°53' N, 015°51' W
Safim . . . . 11°57' N, 015°39' W
Sangonhá . . . . 11°10' N, 014°53' W
São Domingos . . . . 12°24' N, 016°12' W
Teixeira Pinto . . . . 12°04' N, 016°02' W
Tite . . . . 11°47' N, 015°24' W
Xitole . . . . 11°44' N, 014°49' W

GUYANA . . . . . . .pg. 71

Apoteri . . . . 04°02' N, 058°34' W
Bartica . . . . 06°24' N, 058°37' W
Charity. . . . . 07°24' N, 058°36' W
Corriverton . . . . 05°52' N, 057°10' W
Georgetown . . . . 06°48' N, 058°10' W
Isherton . . . . 02°19' N, 059°22' W
Ituni . . . . 05°30' N, 058°14' W
Karasabai . . . . 04°02' N, 059°32' W
Karmuda Village . . . . 05°38' N, 060°18' W
Lethem . . . . 03°23' N, 059°48' W
Linden . . . . 06°00' N, 058°18' W
Mabaruma . . . . 08°12' N, 059°47' W
Mahaicony Village . . . . . . 06°36' N, 057°48' W
Matthews Ridge . . . . 07°30' N, 060°10' W
New Amsterdam . . . . 06°15' N, 057°31' W
Orinduik . . . . 04°42' N, 060°01' W
Parika . . . . 06°52' N, 058°25' W
Port Kaituma . . . . 07°44' N, 059°53' W
Rose Hall . . . . 06°16' N, 057°21' W
Suddie . . . . 07°07' N, 058°29' W
Vreed en Hoop . . . . 06°48' N, 058°11' W

HAITI . . . . .pg. 72

Anse-d'Hainault . . . . 18°30' N, 074°27' W
Cap-Haïtien . . . . 19°45' N, 072°12' W
Desdunes . . . . 19°17' N, 072°39' W
Gonaïves . . . . 19°27' N, 072°41' W
Grand Goâve . . . . 18°26' N, 072°46' W

Hinche . . . . 19°09' N, 072°01' W
Jean Rabel . . . . 18°15' N, 072°40' W
Lascahobas . . . . 18°50' N, 071°56' W
Léogâne . . . . 18°31' N, 072°38' W
Limbé . . . . 19°42' N, 072°24' W
Miragoâne . . . . 18°27' N, 073°06' W
Mirebalais . . . . 18°55' N, 072°06' W
Môle Saint-Nicolas . . . . . . 19°48' N, 073°23' W
Ouanaminthe . . . . 19°33' N, 071°44' W
Pétionville . . . . 18°31' N, 072°17' W
Petite Rivière de
   l'Artibonite . . . . 19°08' N, 072°29' W
Port-au-Prince . . . . 18°32' N, 072°20' W
Roseaux . . . . 18°36' N, 074°01' W
Saint-Louis du Nord . . . . . 19°56' N, 072°43' W
Saint-Michel de l'Atalaye . . 19°22' N, 072°20' W
Thomasique . . . . 19°05' N, 071°50' W
Trou du Nord . . . . 19°38' N, 072°01' W
Verrettes . . . . 19°03' N, 072°28' W

HONDURAS . . . . . .pg. 73

Amapala . . . . 13°17' N, 087°39' W
Catacamas . . . . 14°48' N, 085°54' W
Choloma . . . . 15°37' N, 087°57' W
Choluteca . . . . 13°18' N, 087°12' W
Comayagua . . . . 14°27' N, 087°38' W
Danlí . . . . 14°02' N, 086°35' W
El Paraíso . . . . 15°01' N, 088°59' W
El Progreso . . . . 15°24' N, 087°48' W
Gracias . . . . 14°35' N, 088°35' W
Guaimaca . . . . 14°32' N, 086°49' W
Intibucá . . . . 14°19' N, 088°10' W
Juticalpa . . . . 14°39' N, 086°12' W
La Ceiba . . . . 15°47' N, 086°48' W
La Esperanza . . . . 14°18' N, 088°11' W
La Lima . . . . 15°26' N, 087°55' W
La Paz . . . . 14°19' N, 087°41' W
Morazán . . . . 15°19' N, 087°36' W
Nacaome . . . . 13°32' N, 087°29' W
Olanchito . . . . 15°30' N, 086°34' W
Puerto Cortés . . . . 15°50' N, 087°50' W
Puerto Lempira . . . . 15°16' N, 083°46' W
San Lorenzo . . . . 13°25' N, 087°27' W
San Marcos de Colón . . . . 13°26' N, 086°48' W
San Pedro Sula . . . . 15°30' N, 088°02' W
Santa Bárbara . . . . 14°55' N, 088°14' W
Santa Rita . . . . 15°12' N, 087°53' W
Signatapeque . . . . 14°36' N, 087°57' W
Talanga . . . . 14°24' N, 087°05' W
Tegucigalpa . . . . 14°06' N, 087°13' W
Trujillo . . . . 15°55' N, 86°00' W
Yoro . . . . 15°08' N, 087°08' W
Yuscarán . . . . 13°56' N, 086°51' W

HUNGARY . . . . . . .pg. 74

Baja . . . . 46°11' N, 018°58' E
Balmazújváros . . . . 47°37' N, 021°21' E
Barcs . . . . 45°58' N, 017°28' E

Békéscsaba . . . . 46°41′ N, 021°06′ E
Berettyóújfalu . . . . 47°13′ N, 021°33′ E
Budapest . . . . 47°30′ N, 019°05′ E
Cegléd . . . . 47°10′ N, 019°48′ E
Debrecen . . . . 47°32′ N, 021°38′ E
Dunaújváros
  (Sztálinváros) . . . . 46°59′ N, 018°56′ E
Eger . . . . 47°54′ N, 020°23′ E
Esztergom . . . . 47°48′ N, 018°45′ E
Fertőd (Eszterháza) . . . . . . 47°37′ N, 016°52′ E
Gyomaendrőd . . . . 46°56′ N, 020°50′ E
Gyöngyös . . . . 47°47′ N, 019°56′ E
Győr . . . . 47°41′ N, 017°38′ E
Gyula . . . . 46°39′ N, 021°17′ E
Hódmezővásárhely . . . . . . 46°25′ N, 020°20′ E
Kalocsa . . . . 46°32′ N, 019°00′ E
Kaposvár . . . . 46°22′ N, 017°48′ E
Kazincbarcika . . . . 48°15′ N, 020°38′ E
Kecskemét . . . . 46°54′ N, 019°42′ E
Keszthely . . . . 46°46′ N, 017°15′ E
Kisvárda . . . . 48°13′ N, 022°05′ E
Körmend . . . . 47°01′ N, 016°36′ E
Kőszeg . . . . 47°23′ N, 016°33′ E
Lenti . . . . 46°37′ N, 016°33′ E
Makó . . . . 46°13′ N, 020°29′ E
Marcali . . . . 46°35′ N, 017°25′ E
Miskolc . . . . 48°06′ N, 020°47′ E
Mohács . . . . 45°59′ N, 018°42′ E
Nagyatád . . . . 46°13′ N, 017°22′ E
Nagykanizsa . . . . 46°27′ N, 016°59′ E
Nagykőrös . . . . 47°02′ N, 019°47′ E
Nyírbátor . . . . 47°50′ N, 022°08′ E
Nyíregyháza . . . . 47°57′ N, 021°43′ E
Orosháza . . . . 46°34′ N, 020°40′ E
Ózd . . . . 48°13′ N, 020°18′ E
Paks . . . . 46°38′ N, 018°52′ E
Pápa . . . . 47°20′ N, 017°28′ E
Pécs . . . . 46°05′ N, 018°14′ E
Salgótarján . . . . 48°07′ N, 019°49′ E
Sarkad . . . . 46°45′ N, 021°23′ E
Sárospatak . . . . 48°19′ N, 021°35′ E
Sátoraljaújhely . . . . 48°24′ N, 021°40′ E
Siklós . . . . 45°51′ N, 018°18′ E
Sopron . . . . 47°41′ N, 016°36′ E
Szeged . . . . 46°15′ N, 020°10′ E
Szeghalom . . . . 47°02′ N, 021°10′ E
Székesfehérvár . . . . 47°12′ N, 018°25′ E
Szekszárd . . . . 46°21′ N, 018°43′ E
Szigetvár . . . . 46°03′ N, 017°48′ E
Szolnok . . . . 47°11′ N, 020°12′ E
Szombathely . . . . 47°14′ N, 016°37′ E
Tamási . . . . 46°38′ N, 018°17′ E
Tatabánya . . . . 47°34′ N, 018°25′ E
Vác . . . . 47°47′ N, 019°08′ E
Veszprém . . . . 47°06′ N, 017°55′ E
Zalaegerszeg . . . . 46°50′ N, 016°51′ E

ICELAND . . . . pg. 75

Akureyri . . . . 65°40′ N, 018°06′ W
Reykjavík . . . . 64°09′ N, 021°57′ W

Vestmannaeyjar . . . . 62°26′ N, 020°16′ W

INDIA . . . . pg. 76

Agra . . . . 27°11′ N, 078°01′ E
Ahmadabad
  (Ahmedabad) . . . . 23°02′ N, 072°37′ E
Ahmadnāgar
  (Ahmednagar) . . . . 19°05′ N, 074°44′ E
Allahabad . . . . 25°27′ N, 081°51′ E
Amritsar . . . . 31°35′ N, 074°53′ E
Āsānsol . . . . 23°41′ N, 086°59′ E
Balurghat . . . . 25°13′ N, 088°46′ E
Bangalore . . . . 12°59′ N, 077°35′ E
Baroda (Vadodara) . . . . 22°18′ N, 073°12′ E
Bathinda (Bhatinda) . . . . . . 30°12′ N, 074°57′ E
Bhilwara . . . . 25°21′ N, 074°38′ E
Bhiwandi . . . . 19°18′ N, 073°04′ E
Bhopal . . . . 23°16′ N, 077°24′ E
Bombay (Mumbai) . . . . 18°58′ N, 072°50′ E
Calcutta . . . . 22°32′ N, 088°22′ E
Cochin . . . . 09°58′ N, 076°14′ E
Coimbatore . . . . 11°00′ N, 076°58′ E
Cuddapah . . . . 14°28′ N, 078°49′ E
Dehra Dun . . . . 30°19′ N, 078°02′ E
Delhi . . . . 28°40′ N, 077°13′ E
Eluru (Ellore) . . . . 16°42′ N, 081°06′ E
Gangānagar
  (Śri Gangānagar) . . . . 29°55′ N, 073°53′ E
Guntur . . . . 16°18′ N, 080°27′ E
Gwalior . . . . 26°13′ N, 078°10′ E
Howrah (Haora) . . . . 22°35′ N, 088°20′ E
Hubli-Dharwad . . . . 15°21′ N, 075°10′ E
Hyderabad . . . . 17°23′ N, 078°28′ E
Imphal . . . . 24°49′ N, 093°57′ E
Indore . . . . 22°43′ N, 075°50′ E
Jabalpur (Jubbulpore) . . . . . 23°10′ N, 079°57′ E
Jaipur . . . . 26°55′ N, 075°49′ E
Jammu . . . . 32°44′ N, 074°52′ E
Jamnagar . . . . 22°28′ N, 070°04′ E
Jodhpur . . . . 26°17′ N, 073°02′ E
Jūnāgadh . . . . 21°31′ N, 070°28′ E
Kanpur (Cawnpore) . . . . . . 26°28′ N, 080°21′ E
Khambhat (Cambay) . . . . . . 22°18′ N, 072°37′ E
Kota (Kotah) . . . . 25°11′ N, 075°50′ E
Longju . . . . 28°45′ N, 093°35′ E
Lucknow . . . . 26°51′ N, 080°55′ E
Ludhiana . . . . 30°54′ N, 075°51′ E
Madras (Chennai) . . . . 13°05′ N, 080°17′ E
Madurai (Madura) . . . . 09°56′ N, 078°07′ E
Malegaon . . . . 20°33′ N, 074°32′ E
Meerut . . . . 28°59′ N, 077°42′ E
Nagpur . . . . 21°09′ N, 079°06′ E
New Delhi . . . . 28°36′ N, 077°12′ E
Patna . . . . 25°36′ N, 085°07′ E
Pune (Poona) . . . . 18°32′ N, 073°52′ E
Puri . . . . 19°48′ N, 085°51′ E
Quilon . . . . 08°53′ N, 076°36′ E
Raipur . . . . 21°14′ N, 081°38′ E
Rajkot . . . . 22°18′ N, 070°47′ E
Sambalpur . . . . 21°27′ N, 083°58′ E

Shiliguri (Siliguri) . . . . 26°42' N, 088°26' E
Sholapur (Solapur) . . . . 17°41' N, 075°55' E
Sibsāgar . . . . 26°59' N, 094°38' E
Srinagar . . . . 34°05' N, 074°49' E
Surat . . . . 21°10' N, 072°50' E
Thanjavur (Tanjore) . . . . 10°48' N, 079°09' E
Tiruppur (Tirupper) . . . . 11°06' N, 077°21' E
Vadodara (Baroda) . . . . 22°18' N, 073°12' E
Vārānasi (Banāras,
Benares). . . . . 25°20' N, 083°00' E
Vishākhapatnam
(Visākhāpatam) . . . . 17°42' N, 083°18' E

INDONESIA . . . . . . pg. 77

Ambon . . . . 03°43' S, 128°12' E
Balikpapan . . . . 01°17' S, 116°50' E
Banda Aceh (Kuta Raja) . . . . 05°34' N, 095°20' E
Bandung . . . . 06°54' S, 107°36' E
Banjarmasin . . . . 03°20' S, 114°35' E
Cilacap. . . . . 07°44' S, 109°00' E
Jakarta. . . . . 06°10' S, 106°48' E
Jambi . . . . 01°36' S, 103°37' E
Kendari . . . . 03°57' S, 122°35' E
Kupang . . . . 10°10' S, 123°35' E
Malang. . . . . 07°59' S, 112°37' E
Manado . . . . 01°29' N, 124°51' E
Mataram . . . . 08°35' S, 116°07' E
Medan . . . . 03°35' N, 098°40' E
Padang. . . . . 00°57' S, 100°21' E
Palembang . . . . 02°55' S, 104°45' E
Palu . . . . 00°53' S, 119°53' E
Samarinda . . . . 00°30' S, 117°09' E
Semarang. . . . . 06°58' S, 110°25' E
Surabaya . . . . 07°15' S, 112°45' E
Ujungpandang. . . . . 05°07' S, 119°24' E

IRAN . . . . pg. 78

Ahvāz. . . . . 31°19' N, 048°42' E
Āmol . . . . 36°28' N, 052°21' E
Arāk . . . . 34°05' N, 049°41' E
Ardabīl. . . . . 38°15' N, 048°18' E
Bakhtarān . . . . 34°19' N, 047°04' E
Bandar 'Abbās. . . . . 27°11' N, 056°17' E
Behbahān . . . . 30°35' N, 050°14' E
Bīrjand . . . . 32°53' N, 059°13' E
Būshehr . . . . 28°59' N, 050°50' E
Dārāb . . . . 28°45' N, 054°34' E
Dezfūl. . . . . 32°23' N, 048°24' E
Eṣfahān . . . . 32°40' N, 051°38' E
Gorgān. . . . . 36°50' N, 054°29' E
Hamadān . . . . 34°48' N, 048°30' E
Kāshān . . . . 33°59' N, 051°29' E
Kāzerūn . . . . 29°37' N, 051°38' E
Kermān . . . . 30°17' N, 057°05' E
Khorramābād . . . . 33°30' N, 048°20' E
Khvoy . . . . 38°33' N, 044°58' E
Mahābād . . . . 36°45' N, 045°43' E
Mashhad . . . . 36°18' N, 059°36' E

Orūmīyeh . . . . 37°33' N, 045°04' E
Qā'en . . . . 33°44' N, 059°11' E
Qom . . . . 34°39' N, 050°54' E
Quchan . . . . 37°06' N, 058°30' E
Rafsanjān . . . . 30°24' N, 056°00' E
Rasht . . . . 37°16' N, 049°36' E
Sanandaj . . . . 35°19' N, 047°00' E
Shīrāz . . . . 29°36' N, 052°32' E
Tabrīz. . . . . 38°05' N, 046°18' E
Tehrān . . . . 35°40' N, 051°26' E
Yazd. . . . . 31°53' N, 054°22' E
Zāhedān. . . . . 29°30' N, 060°52' E
Zanjan . . . . 36°40' N, 048°29' E

IRAQ . . . . pg. 79

Ad-Diwaniyah . . . . 31°59' N, 044°56' E
Al-'Amarah . . . . 31°50' N, 047°09' E
Al-Gharrāf . . . . 31°21' N, 046°17' E
Al-Hillah . . . . 32°29' N, 044°25' E
Al-Khāliṣ . . . . 33°49' N, 044°32' E
Al-Kūt. . . . . 32°30' N, 045°49' E
Al-Maḥmūdiya. . . . . 33°03' N, 044°21' E
Al-Majarr al-Kabir . . . . 31°34' N, 047°00' E
'Ānah . . . . 34°28' N, 041°56' E
An-Najaf . . . . 31°59' N, 044°20' E
An-Nashwah . . . . 30°49' N, 047°36' E
An-Nasiriyah . . . . 31°02' N, 046°16' E
Ar-Ramādī . . . . 33°25' N, 043°17' E
Ar-Ruṭbah . . . . 33°02' N, 040°17' E
As-Samawah . . . . 31°18' N, 045°17' E
As-Sulaymaniyah . . . . 35°33' N, 045°26' E
Aş-Şuwayrah . . . . 32°55' N, 044°47' E
Baghdad . . . . 33°21' N, 044°25' E
Ba'qubah . . . . 33°45' N, 044°38' E
Barzān . . . . 36°55' N, 044°03' E
Basra (Al-Basrah) . . . . 30°30' N, 047°47' E
Dibs . . . . 35°40' N, 044°04' E
Hīt . . . . 33°38' N, 042°49' E
Irbil
(Arbela, Arbil, or Erbil) . . 36°11' N, 044°01' E
Jalūlā' . . . . 34°16' N, 045°10' E
Karbala'. . . . . 32°36' N, 044°02' E
Khānaqin. . . . . 34°21' N, 045°22' E
Kirkuk . . . . 35°28' N, 044°23' E
Mosul (Al-Mawsil). . . . . 36°20' N, 043°08' E
Qal'at Dizah . . . . 36°11' N, 045°07' E
Sinjār . . . . 36°19' N, 041°52' E
Tall Kayf . . . . 36°29' N, 043°08' E
Tikrīt . . . . 34°36' N, 043°42' E
Ṭūz Khurmātū
(Touz Hourmato) . . . . 34°53' N, 044°38' E
Zummār . . . . 36°47' N, 042°38' E

IRELAND . . . . pg. 80

Arklow
(An tinbhear Mor) . . . . . . 52°48' N, 006°09' W
Athlone . . . . 53°26' N, 007°57' W
Ballina . . . . 54°07' N, 009°10' W

Ballycastle . . . . 54°17′ N, 009°22′ W
Ballycotton . . . . 51°50′ N, 008°01′ W
Ballymote . . . . 54°05′ N, 008°31′ W
Ballyvaghan . . . . 53°07′ N, 009°09′ W
Bandon
  (Droichead na Bandan) . 51°45′ N, 008°44′ W
Bantry . . . . 51°41′ N, 009°27′ W
Belmullet . . . . 54°13′ N, 010°00′ W
Blarney . . . . 51°56′ N, 008°34′ W
Boyle . . . . 53°58′ N, 008°18′ W
Bray (Bre) . . . . 53°12′ N, 006°06′ W
Buncrana . . . . 55°08′ N, 007°27′ W
Carlow (Ceatharlach) . . . 52°50′ N, 006°56′ W
Carndonagh . . . . 55°15′ N, 007°16′ W
Carrick on Shannon . . . . . 53°57′ N, 008°05′ W
Castlebar . . . . 53°51′ N, 009°18′ W
Castletownbere . . . . 51°39′ N, 009°55′ W
Cavan (Cabhan, An) . . . . . 54°00′ N, 007°22′ W
Charleville (Rath Luirc) . . 52°21′ N, 008°41′ W
Clifden . . . . 53°29′ N, 010°01′ W
Clonakilty . . . . 51°37′ N, 008°53′ W
Clonmel (Cluain Meala) . . 52°21′ N, 007°42′ W
Cobh . . . . 51°51′ N, 008°17′ W
Cork (Corcaigh) . . . . 51°54′ N, 008°28′ W
Dingle . . . . 52°08′ N, 010°15′ W
Donegal . . . . 54°39′ N, 008°07′ W
Drogheda
  (Droichead Atha) . . . . . 53°43′ N, 006°21′ W
Dublin . . . . 53°20′ N, 006°15′ W
Dundalk (Dun Dealgan) . . 54°00′ N, 006°25′ W
Dungarvan . . . . 52°05′ N, 007°37′ W
Ennis (Inis) . . . . 52°51′ N, 008°59′ W
Enniscorthy . . . . 52°30′ N, 006°34′ W
Ennistimon . . . . 52°56′ N, 009°18′ W
Galway (Gaillimh) . . . . . . 53°17′ N, 009°03′ W
Gort . . . . 53°04′ N, 008°49′ W
Kenmare . . . . 51°53′ N, 009°35′ W
Kilkee . . . . 52°41′ N, 009°38′ W
Kilkenny
  (Cill Chainnigh) . . . . . . 52°39′ N, 007°15′ W
Killarney (Cill Airne) . . . . 52°03′ N, 009°31′ W
Letterkenny . . . . 54°57′ N, 007°44′ W
Lifford . . . . 54°50′ N, 007°29′ W
Limerick (Luimneach) . . . 52°40′ N, 008°37′ W
Listowel . . . . 52°27′ N, 009°29′ W
Longford . . . . 53°44′ N, 007°48′ W
Loughrea . . . . 53°12′ N, 008°34′ W
Mallow . . . . 52°08′ N, 008°38′ W
Monaghan . . . . 54°15′ N, 006°58′ W
Naas (Nas, An) . . . . 53°13′ N, 006°40′ W
New Ross (Ros Mhic
  Thriuin) . . . . 52°23′ N, 006°56′ W
Portlaoise (Maryborough,
  Portlaoighise) . . . . 53°02′ N, 007°18′ W
Portumna . . . . 53°05′ N, 008°13′ W
Roscommon . . . . 53°38′ N, 008°11′ W
Rosslare . . . . 52°17′ N, 006°23′ W
Shannon . . . . 52°42′ N, 008°52′ W
Sligo . . . . 54°16′ N, 008°28′ W
Swords . . . . 53°27′ N, 006°13′ W
Tralee . . . . 52°16′ N, 009°43′ W

Trim . . . . 53°33′ N, 006°48′ W
Tullamore . . . . 53°16′ N, 007°29′ W
Waterford (Port Lairge) . . 52°15′ N, 007°06′ W
Westport . . . . 53°48′ N, 009°33′ W
Wexford (Loch Garman) . . 52°20′ N, 006°28′ W
Wicklow (Cill Mhantain) . 52°59′ N, 006°03′ W
Youghal . . . . 51°57′ N, 007°51′ W

ISRAEL . . . . pg. 81

'Arad . . . . 31°15′ N, 035°13′ E
Ashdod . . . . 31°49′ N, 034°39′ E
Ashqelon . . . . 31°40′ N, 034°35′ E
Bat Yam . . . . 32°01′ N, 034°45′ E
Beersheba
  (Be'er Sheva') . . . . 31°14′ N, 034°47′ E
Bet She'an . . . . 32°30′ N, 035°30′ E
Bet Shemesh . . . . 31°45′ N, 035°00′ E
Dimona . . . . 31°04′ N, 035°02′ E
Elat . . . . 29°33′ N, 034°57′ E
'En Yahav . . . . 30°38′ N, 035°11′ E
Hadera . . . . 32°26′ N, 034°55′ E
Haifa (Hefa) . . . . 32°50′ N, 035°00′ E
Hazeva . . . . 30°48′ N, 035°15′ E
Herzliyya . . . . 32°10′ N, 034°51′ E
Holon . . . . 32°01′ N, 034°46′ E
Jerusalem
  (Yerushalayim) . . . . 31°46′ N, 035°14′ E
Karmi'el . . . . 32°55′ N, 035°18′ E
Nazareth (Nazerat) . . . . . 32°42′ N, 035°18′ E
Netanya . . . . 32°20′ N, 034°51′ E
Nir Yizhaq . . . . 31°14′ N, 034°22′ E
Petah Tiqwa . . . . 32°05′ N, 034°53′ E
Qiryat Ata . . . . 32°48′ N, 035°06′ E
Qiryat Shemona . . . . 33°13′ N, 035°34′ E
Rama . . . . 32°56′ N, 035°22′ E
Rehovot . . . . 31°54′ N, 034°49′ E
Tel Aviv-Yafo . . . . 32°04′ N, 034°46′ E

ITALY . . . . pg. 82

Agrigento (Girgenti) . . . . 37°19′ N, 013°34′ E
Ancona . . . . 43°38′ N, 013°30′ E
Aosta . . . . 45°44′ N, 007°20′ E
Arezzo . . . . 43°25′ N, 011°53′ E
Bari . . . . 41°08′ N, 016°51′ E
Bologna . . . . 44°29′ N, 011°20′ E
Bolzano . . . . 46°31′ N, 011°22′ E
Brescia . . . . 45°33′ N, 010°15′ E
Cagliari . . . . 39°13′ N, 009°07′ E
Catania . . . . 37°30′ N, 015°06′ E
Catanzaro . . . . 38°54′ N, 016°35′ E
Crotone . . . . 39°05′ N, 017°08′ E
Cuneo (Coni) . . . . 44°23′ N, 007°32′ E
Fermo . . . . 43°09′ N, 013°43′ E
Florence (Firenze or
  Florentia) . . . . 43°46′ N, 011°15′ E
Foggia . . . . 41°27′ N, 015°34′ E
Genoa (Genova) . . . . 44°25′ N, 008°57′ E
Grosseto . . . . 42°46′ N, 011°08′ E

Iglesias. . . . . 39°19′ N, 008°32′ E
Latina. . . . . 41°28′ N, 012°52′ E
Manfredonia. . . . . 41°38′ N, 015°55′ E
Marsala. . . . . 37°48′ N, 012°26′ E
Milan (Milano) . . . . 45°28′ N, 009°12′ E
Naples (Napoli or
    Neapolis) . . . . 40°50′ N, 014°15′ E
Oristano . . . . 39°54′ N, 008°36′ E
Padua (Padova) . . . . 45°25′ N, 011°53′ E
Palermo. . . . . 38°07′ N, 013°22′ E
Perugia (Perusia) . . . . 43°08′ N, 012°22′ E
Pescara . . . . 42°28′ N, 014°13′ E
Piombino. . . . . 42°55′ N, 010°32′ E
Pisa . . . . 43°43′ N, 010°23′ E
Porto Torres. . . . . 40°50′ N, 008°24′ E
Potenza . . . . 40°38′ N, 015°48′ E
Ragusa. . . . . 36°55′ N, 014°44′ E
Ravenna. . . . . 44°25′ N, 012°12′ E
Rome (Roma) . . . . 41°54′ N, 012°29′ E
Salerno . . . . 40°41′ N, 014°47′ E
San Remo . . . . 43°49′ N, 007°46′ E
Sassari . . . . 40°43′ N, 008°34′ E
Siena . . . . 43°19′ N, 011°21′ E
Syracuse (Siracusa) . . . . 37°04′ N, 015°18′ E
Taranto (Taras or
    Tarentum) . . . . 40°28′ N, 017°14′ E
Trapani . . . . 38°01′ N, 012°29′ E
Trento . . . . 46°04′ N, 011°08′ E
Trieste. . . . . 45°40′ N, 013°46′ E
Turin (Torino). . . . . 45°03′ N, 007°40′ E
Udine . . . . 46°03′ N, 013°14′ E
Venice (Venezia). . . . . 45°27′ N, 012°21′ E
Verona. . . . . 45°27′ N, 011°00′ E

IVORY COAST . . . . pg. 83

Abengourou . . . . 06°44′ N, 003°29′ W
Abidjan . . . . 05°19′ N, 004°02′ W
Aboisso . . . . 05°28′ N, 003°12′ W
Adzopé . . . . 06°06′ N, 003°52′ W
Agboville . . . . 05°56′ N, 004°13′ W
Anyama . . . . 05°30′ N, 004°03′ W
Arrah . . . . 06°40′ N, 003°58′ W
Biankouma . . . . 07°44′ N, 007°37′ W
Bondoukou . . . . 08°02′ N, 002°48′ W
Bouaflé . . . . 06°59′ N, 005°45′ W
Bouaké. . . . . 07°41′ N, 005°02′ W
Bouna . . . . 09°16′ N, 003°00′ W
Boundiali . . . . 09°31′ N, 006°29′ W
Daloa . . . . 06°53′ N, 006°27′ W
Daoukro . . . . 07°03′ N, 003°58′ W
Dimbokro . . . . 06°39′ N, 004°42′ W
Divo . . . . 05°50′ N, 005°22′ W
Duékoué . . . . 06°45′ N, 007°21′ W
Ferkéssédougou . . . . 09°36′ N, 005°12′ W
Gagnoa . . . . 06°08′ N, 005°56′ W
Grand-Bassam . . . . 05°12′ N, 003°44′ W
Guiglo . . . . 06°33′ N, 007°29′ W
Katiola . . . . 08°08′ N, 005°06′ W
Kong . . . . 09°09′ N, 004°37′ W
Korhogo . . . . 09°27′ N, 005°38′ W

Lakota . . . . 05°51′ N, 005°41′ W
Man . . . . 07°24′ N, 007°33′ W
Odienné. . . . . 09°30′ N, 007°34′ W
Oumé . . . . 06°23′ N, 005°25′ W
San-Pédro . . . . 04°44′ N, 006°37′ W
Sassandra . . . . 04°57′ N, 006°05′ W
Séguéla . . . . 07°57′ N, 006°40′ W
Sinfra . . . . 06°37′ N, 005°55′ W
Tabou . . . . 04°25′ N, 007°21′ W
Tengréla . . . . 10°26′ N, 006°20′ W
Tortiya . . . . 08°46′ N, 005°41′ W
Yamoussoukro . . . . 06°49′ N, 005°17′ W

JAMAICA . . . . pg. 84

Annotto Bay . . . . 18°16′ N, 076°46′ W
Kingston . . . . 17°58′ N, 076°48′ W
Lucea . . . . 18°27′ N, 078°10′ W
Mandeville. . . . . 18°02′ N, 077°30′ W
May Pen. . . . . 17°58′ N, 077°14′ W
Montego Bay. . . . . 18°28′ N, 077°55′ W
Port Antonio . . . . 18°11′ N, 076°28′ W
St. Ann's Bay . . . . 18°26′ N, 077°08′ W
Savanna-la-Mar . . . . 18°13′ N, 078°08′ W
Spanish Town . . . . 17°59′ N, 076°57′ W

JAPAN . . . . pg. 85

Akita . . . . 39°43′ N, 140°07′ E
Aomori. . . . . 40°49′ N, 140°45′ E
Asahikawa . . . . 43°46′ N, 142°22′ E
Chiba . . . . 35°36′ N, 140°07′ E
Fukui . . . . 36°04′ N, 136°13′ E
Fukuoka . . . . 33°35′ N, 130°24′ E
Fukushima . . . . 37°45′ N, 140°28′ E
Funabashi . . . . 35°42′ N, 139°59′ E
Gifu . . . . 35°25′ N, 136°45′ E
Hachinohe . . . . 40°30′ N, 141°29′ E
Hakodate . . . . 41°45′ N, 140°43′ E
Hiroshima . . . . 34°24′ N, 132°27′ E
Hofu . . . . 34°03′ N, 131°34′ E
Iwaki . . . . 37°05′ N, 140°50′ E
Kagoshima . . . . 31°36′ N, 130°33′ E
Kanazawa . . . . 36°34′ N, 136°39′ E
Kawasaki . . . . 35°32′ N, 139°43′ E
Kita-Kyushu. . . . . 33°50′ N, 130°50′ E
Kōbe . . . . 34°41′ N, 135°10′ E
Kōchi . . . . 33°33′ N, 133°33′ E
Kumamoto. . . . . 32°48′ N, 130°43′ E
Kushiro . . . . 42°54′ N, 140°45′ E
Kutchan. . . . . 42°54′ N, 140°45′ E
Kyōto . . . . 35°00′ N, 135°45′ E
Matsue. . . . . 35°28′ N, 133°04′ E
Matsuyama . . . . 33°50′ N, 132°45′ E
Mito . . . . 36°22′ N, 140°28′ E
Miyazaki . . . . 31°52′ N, 131°25′ E
Morioka . . . . 39°42′ N, 141°09′ E
Muroran . . . . 42°18′ N, 140°59′ E
Nagano . . . . 36°39′ N, 138°11′ E
Nagasaki . . . . 32°48′ N, 129°55′ E

Nagoya. . . . . 35°10' N, 136°55' E
Naha. . . . . 26°13' N, 127°40' E
Niigata. . . . . 37°55' N, 139°03' E
Obihiro. . . . . 42°55' N, 143°12' E
Okayama. . . . . 34°39' N, 133°55' E
Ōsaka. . . . . 34°40' N, 135°30' E
Otaru. . . . . 43°13' N, 141°00' E
Sakai. . . . . 34°35' N, 135°28' E
Sapporo. . . . . 43°03' N, 141°21' E
Sendai. . . . . 31°49' N, 130°18' E
Shizuoka. . . . . 34°58' N, 138°23' E
Tokyo. . . . . 35°42' N, 139°46' E
Tomakomai. . . . . 42°38' N, 141°36' E
Tottori. . . . . 35°30' N, 134°14' E
Toyama. . . . . 36°41' N, 137°13' E
Utsunomiya. . . . . 36°33' N, 139°52' E
Wakayama. . . . . 34°13' N, 135°11' E
Wakkanai. . . . . 45°25' N, 141°40' E
Yaizu. . . . . 34°52' N, 138°20' E
Yamagata. . . . . 38°15' N, 140°20' E
Yokohama. . . . . 35°27' N, 139°39' E

JORDAN . . . . pg. 86

Adir. . . . . 31°12' N, 035°46' E
Al-'Aqabah. . . . . 29°31' N, 035°00' E
Al-Faydah. . . . . 32°35' N, 038°13' E
Al-Ḥiṣn. . . . . 32°29' N, 035°53' E
Al-Karak. . . . . 31°11' N, 035°42' E
Al-Mafraq. . . . . 32°21' N, 036°12' E
Al-Mazra'ah. . . . . 31°16' N, 035°31' E
Al-Mudawwarah. . . . . 29°19' N, 035°59' E
Al-Qaṭrānah. . . . . 31°15' N, 036°03' E
Amman ('Ammān). . . . . 31°57' N, 035°56' E
Ar-Ramthā. . . . . 32°34' N, 036°00' E
Ash-Shawbak. . . . . 30°32' N, 035°34' E
Aṣ Ṣalt. . . . . 32°03' N, 035°44' E
Aṭ-Ṭafīlah. . . . . 30°50' N, .035°36' E
Az-Zarqā`. . . . . 32°05' N, 036°06' E
Bā'ir. . . . . 30°46' N, 036°41' E
Dhāt Ra's. . . . . 31°00' N, 035°46' E
Irbid. . . . . 32°33' N, 035°51' E
Ma'ān. . . . . 30°12' N, 035°44' E
Ma'dabā. . . . . 31°43' N, 035°48' E
Maḥaṭṭat al-Ḥafīf. . . . . 32°12' N, 037°08' E
Maḥaṭṭat al-Jufūr. . . . . 32°30' N, 038°12' E
Ṣuwaylih. . . . . 32°02' N, 035°50' E

KAZAKSTAN . . . pg. 87

Almaty (Alma-Ata). . . . . 43°15' N, 076°57' E
Aqtau (Aktau, or
    Shevchenko). . . . . 43°39' N, 051°12' E
Aqtöbe (Aktyubinsk). . . . . . . 50°17' N, 057°10' E
Arqalyq. . . . . 50°13' N, 066°50' E
Astana (Akmola,
    Akmolinsk, Aqmola,
    or Tselinograd). . . . . 51°10' N, 071°30' E
Atyraū (Atenau, Gurjev, or
    Guryev). . . . . 47°07' N, 051°53' E

Ayaguz. . . . . 47°56' N, 080°23' E
Balqash (Balkhash or
    Balchas). . . . . 46°49' N, 075°00' E
Dzhezkazgan. . . . . 47°47' N, 067°46' E
Kokchetav. . . . . 53°17' N, 069°30' E
Leninogor (Leninogorsk
    or Ridder). . . . . 50°22' N, 083°32' E
Oral (Uralsk). . . . . 51°14' N, 051°22' E
Öskemen
    (Ust-Kamenogorsk). . . . . . 49°58' N, 082°40' E
Panfilov (Zharkent). . . . . 44°10' N, 080°01' E
Pavlodar. . . . . 52°18' N, 076°57' E
Petropavl
    (Petropavlovsk). . . . . 54°52' N, 069°06' E
Qaraghandy
    (Karaganda). . . . . 49°50' N, 073°10' E
Qostanay (Kustanay). . . . . . . 53°10' N, 063°35' E
Qyzylorda (Kzyl-Orda). . . . . . 44°48' N, 065°28' E
Rūdnyy (Rudny). . . . . 52°57' N, 063°07' E
Semey (Semipalatinsk). . . . . . 50°28' N, 080°13' E
Shchūchinsk. . . . . 52°56' N, 070°12' E
Shymkent (Chimkent or
    Cimkent). . . . . 42°18' N, 069°36' E
Taldyqorghan (Taldy
    -Kurgan). . . . . 45°00' N, 078°24' E
Talghar. . . . . 43°19' N, 077°15' E
Termirtaū
    (Samarkand). . . . . 50°05' N, 072°56' E
Türkistan. . . . . 43°20' N, 068°15' E
Tyuratam (Turaram or
    Leninsk). . . . . 45°40' N, 063°20' E
Zhambyl (Dzhambul). . . . . . . 42°54' N, 071°22' E
Zhangatas. . . . . 43°34' N, 069°45' E
Zhetiqara. . . . . 52°11' N, 061°12' E
Zhezqazghan. . . . . 47°47' N, 067°46' E
Zyryan. . . . . 49°43' N, 084°20' E

KENYA . . . . pg. 88

Bungoma. . . . . 00°34' N, 034°34' E
Busia. . . . . 00°28' N, 034°06' E
Eldoret. . . . . 00°31' N, 035°17' E
Embu. . . . . 00°32' S, 037°27' E
Garissa. . . . . 00°28' S, 039°38' E
Isiolo. . . . . 00°21' N, 037°35' E
Kisii. . . . . 00°41' S, 034°46' E
Kisumu. . . . . 00°06' S, 034°45' E
Lamu. . . . . 02°16' S, 040°54' E
Lodwar. . . . . 03°07' N, 035°36' E
Machakos. . . . . 01°31' S, 037°16' E
Malindi. . . . . 03°13' S, 040°07' E
Mandera. . . . . 03°56' N, 041°52' E
Maralal. . . . . 01°06' N, 036°42' E
Marsabit. . . . . 02°20' N, 037°59' E
Meru. . . . . 00°03' N, 037°39' E
Mombasa. . . . . 04°03' N, 039°40' E
Murang'a. . . . . 00°43' N, 037°09' E
Nairobi. . . . . 01°17' S, 036°49' E
Nakuru. . . . . 00°17' S, 036°04' E
Nanyuki. . . . . 00°01' N, 037°04' E

Wajir . . . . 01°45′ N, 040°04′ E

KIRIBATI . . . . pg. 89

Bairiki . . . . 01°20′ N, 173°01′ E

KUWAIT . . . . pg. 90

Al-Aḥmadī . . . . 29°05′ N, 048°04′ E
Al-Jahrah . . . . 29°20′ N, 047°40′ E
Ash-Shu'aybah . . . . 29°03′ N, 048°08′ E
Ḥawallī . . . . 29°19′ N, 048°02′ E
Kuwait . . . . 29°20′ N, 047°59′ E
Umm Qasar . . . . 30°02′ N, 047°55′ E

KYRGYZSTAN . . . . pg. 91

Bishkek (Frunze) . . . . 42°54′ N, 074°36′ E
Dzhalal-Abad . . . . 40°56′ N, 073°00′ E
Irkeshtam . . . . 39°41′ N, 073°55′ E
Kara-Balta . . . . 42°50′ N, 073°52′ E
Karakol (Przhevalsk) . . . . . . 42°33′ N, 078°18′ E
Kök-Janggak . . . . 41°02′ N, 073°12′ E
Kyzyl-Kyya . . . . 40°16′ N, 072°08′ E
Mayly-Say . . . . 41°17′ N, 072°24′ E
Naryn . . . . 41°26′ N, 075°58′ E
Osh . . . . 40°32′ N, 072°48′ E
Sülüktü . . . . 39°56′ N, 069°34′ E
Talas . . . . 42°32′ N, 072°14′ E
Tash-Kömür . . . . 41°21′ N, 072°14′ E
Tokmok . . . . 42°52′ N, 075°18′ E
Ysyk-Kül (Rybachye) . . . . . . 42°26′ N, 076°12′ E

LAOS . . . . pg. 92

Attapu . . . . 14°48′ N, 106°50′ E
Ban Houayxay . . . . 20°18′ N, 100°26′ E
Champasak . . . . 14°53′ N, 105°52′ E
Louang Namtha . . . . 20°57′ N, 101°25′ E
Louangphrabang . . . . 19°52′ N, 102°08′ E
Muang Khammouan
  (Muang Thakhek) . . . . 17°24′ N, 104°48′ E
Muang Pek . . . . 19°35′ N, 103°19′ E
Muang Xaignabouri
  (Sayaboury) . . . . 19°15′ N, 101°45′ E
Muang Xay . . . . 20°42′ N, 101°59′ E
Pakxé . . . . 15°07′ N, 105°47′ E
Phôngsali . . . . 21°41′ N, 102°06′ E
Saravan . . . . 15°43′ N, 106°25′ E
Savannakhét . . . . 16°33′ N, 104°45′ E
Vientiane
  (Viangchan) . . . . 17°58′ N, 102°36′ E
Xam Nua . . . . 20°25′ N, 104°02′ E

LATVIA . . . . pg. 93

Aizpute . . . . 56°43′ N, 021°36′ E

Alūksne . . . . 57°25′ N, 027°03′ E
Auce . . . . 56°28′ N, 022°53′ E
Balvi . . . . 57°08′ N, 027°15′ E
Bauska . . . . 56°24′ N, 024°11′ E
Cēsis . . . . 57°18′ N, 025°15′ E
Daugavpils . . . . 55°53′ N, 026°32′ E
Dobele . . . . 56°37′ N, 023°16′ E
Gulbene . . . . 57°11′ N, 026°45′ E
Ilūkste . . . . 55°58′ N, 026°18′ E
Jaunjelgava . . . . 56°37′ N, 025°05′ E
Jēkabpils . . . . 56°29′ N, 025°51′ E
Jelgava . . . . 56°39′ N, 023°42′ E
Jūrmala . . . . 56°58′ N, 023°34′ E
Kandava . . . . 57°02′ N, 022°46′ E
Kārsava . . . . 56°47′ N, 027°40′ E
Ķegums . . . . 56°44′ N, 024°43′ E
Krāslava . . . . 55°54′ N, 027°10′ E
Liepāja . . . . 56°31′ N, 021°01′ E
Limbaži . . . . 57°31′ N, 024°42′ E
Ludza . . . . 56°33′ N, 027°43′ E
Malta . . . . 56°23′ N, 027°07′ E
Mazsalace . . . . 57°52′ N, 025°03′ E
Ogre . . . . 56°49′ N, 024°36′ E
Piltene . . . . 57°13′ N, 021°40′ E
Preili . . . . 56°18′ N, 026°43′ E
Priekule . . . . 56°33′ N, 021°19′ E
Rēzekne . . . . 56°30′ N, 027°19′ E
Riga (Rīga) . . . . 56°57′ N, 024°06′ E
Rujiena . . . . 57°54′ N, 025°19′ E
Sabile . . . . 57°03′ N, 022°35′ E
Salacgrīva . . . . 57°45′ N, 024°21′ E
Saldus . . . . 56°40′ N, 022°30′ E
Sigulda . . . . 57°09′ N, 024°51′ E
Stučka . . . . 56°35′ N, 025°12′ E
Talsi . . . . 57°15′ N, 022°36′ E
Valdemārpils . . . . 57°22′ N, 022°35′ E
Valmiera . . . . 57°33′ N, 025°24′ E
Ventspils . . . . 57°24′ N, 021°31′ E
Viesīte . . . . 56°21′ N, 025°33′ E
Vilaka . . . . 57°11′ N, 027°41′ E
Viļāni . . . . 56°33′ N, 026°57′ E
Zilupe . . . . 56°23′ N, 028°07′ E

LEBANON . . . . pg. 94

Ad-Dāmūr . . . . 33°44′ N, 035°27′ E
Al-'Abdah . . . . 34°31′ N, 035°58′ E
Al-Batrūn . . . . 34°15′ N, 035°39′ E
Al-Hirmil . . . . 34°23′ N, 036°23′ E
Al-Labwah . . . . 34°12′ N, 036°21′ E
Al-Qubayyāt . . . . 34°34′ N, 036°17′ E
Amyūn . . . . 34°18′ N, 035°49′ E
An-Nabaṭīyah at-Taḥtā . . . . . 33°23′ N, 035°29′ E
Aṣ-Ṣarafand . . . . 33°27′ N, 035°18′ E
Baalbek (Ba'labakk) . . . . 34°00′ N, 036°12′ E
B'aqlīn . . . . 33°41′ N, 035°33′ E
Beirut (Bayrut) . . . . 33°53′ N, 035°30′ E
Bḥamdūn . . . . 33°48′ N, 035°39′ E
Bint Jubayl . . . . 33°07′ N, 035°26′ E
Bsharri . . . . 34°15′ N, 036°01′ E

En-Nāqūrah	33°07' N,	035°08' E
Ghazir	34°01' N,	035°40' E
Ghazzah	33°40' N,	035°49' E
Ghūmāh	34°13' N,	035°42' E
Halbā	34°33' N,	036°05' E
Haṣbayya	33°24' N,	035°41' E
Ḥimlāyā	33°56' N,	035°42' E
Ihdin	34°17' N,	035°58' E
Jubayl (Byblos)	34°07' N,	035°39' E
Jubb Jannin	33°37' N,	035°47' E
Jūniyah	33°59' N,	035°58' E
Jwayyā	33°14' N,	035°19' E
Khaldah	33°47' N,	035°29' E
Marj 'Uyūn	33°22' N,	035°35' E
Shḥim	33°37' N,	035°29' E
Shikkā	34°20' N,	035°44' E
Sidon (Sayda)	33°33' N,	035°22' E
Tripoli (Tarabulus)	34°26' N,	035°51' E
Tyre (Ṣūr)	33°16' N,	035°11' E
Zaḥlah	33°51' N,	035°53' E
Zgharta	34°24' N,	035°54' E

LESOTHO ......pg. 95

Butha-Buthe	28°45' S,	028°15' E
Libono	28°38' S,	028°35' E
Mafeteng	29°49' S,	027°15' E
Maseru	29°19' S,	027°29' E
Mohales Hoek	30°09' S,	027°28' E
Mokhotlong	29°22' S,	029°02' E
Qacha's Nek	30°08' S,	028°41' E
Quthing	30°24' S,	027°43' E
Roma	29°27' S,	027°42' E
Teyateyaneng	29°09' S,	027°44' E

LIBERIA ......pg. 96

Bentol	06°26' N,	010°36' W
Bopolu	06°54' N,	010°46' W
Buchanan (Grand Bassa)	05°53' N,	010°03' W
Careysburg	06°24' N,	010°33' W
Gbarnga	07°00' N,	009°29' W
Grand Cess (Grand Sesters)	04°34' N,	008°13' W
Greenville (Sino)	05°00' N,	009°02' W
Harbel	06°16' N,	010°21' W
Harper	04°22' N,	007°43' W
Kle	06°42' N,	010°53' W
Monrovia	06°19' N,	010°48' W
Robertsport	06°45' N,	011°22' W
Saniquellie (Sangbui)	07°22' N,	008°43' W
Tubmanburg (Vaitown)	06°52' N,	010°49' W
Voinjama	08°25' N,	009°45' W
Yekepa	07°35' N,	008°32' W
Zorzor	07°47' N,	009°26' W
Zwedru (Tchien)	06°04' N,	008°08' W

LIBYA ....pg. 97

Al-Bayḍā (Baida or Zāwiyat al-Bayḍā)	32°46' N,	021°43' E
Al-Kufrah	24°10' N,	023°15' E
Al-Marj (Barce)	32°30' N,	020°50' E
Al-'Uwaynāt (Sardalas)	25°48' N,	010°33' E
As-Sidrah (Es-Sidre)	30°39' N,	018°22' E
Awbāri (Ubari)	26°35' N,	012°46' E
Az-Zuwaytinah	30°58' N,	020°07' E
Benghazi (Banghazi or Bengasi)	32°07' N,	020°04' E
Dahra	29°30' N,	017°50' E
Darnah (Dērna)	32°46' N,	022°39' E
Ghadāmis (Ghadames)	30°08' N,	009°30' E
Ghaddūwah (Goddua)	26°26' N,	014°18' E
Gharyān (Garian)	32°10' N,	013°01' E
Ghāt	24°58' N,	010°11' E
Marādah	29°14' N,	019°13' E
Miṣrātah (Misurata)	32°23' N,	015°06' E
Murzuq	25°55' N,	013°55' E
Sabhā (Sebha)	27°02' N,	014°26' E
Sarīr	27°30' N,	022°30' E
Surt (Sirte)	31°13' N,	016°35' E
Tarabulus, see Tripoli		
Tāzirbū	25°45' N,	021°00' E
Tobruk (Ṭubruq)	32°05' N,	023°59' E
Tripoli (Ṭarābulus)	32°54' N,	013°11' E
Waddān	29°10' N,	016°08' E
Wāw al-Kabīr	25°20' N,	016°43' E
Zalṭan (Zelten)	32°57' N,	011°52' E
Zlīṭan (Zliten)	32°28' N,	014°34' E
Zuwārah (Zuāra)	32°56' N,	012°06' E

LIECHTENSTEIN . pg. 98

Balzers	47°04' N,	009°32' E
Eschen	47°13' N,	009°32' E
Mauren	47°13' N,	009°33' E
Schaan	47°10' N,	009°31' E
Triesen	47°07' N,	009°32' E
Vaduz	47°09' N,	009°31' E

LITHUANIA ......pg. 99

Alytus	54°24' N,	024°03' E
Anykščiai	55°32' N,	025°06' E
Birštonas	54°37' N,	024°02' E
Biržai	56°12' N,	024°45' E
Druskininkai	54°01' N,	023°58' E
Gargždai	55°43' N,	021°24' E
Ignalina	55°21' N,	026°10' E
Jonava	55°05' N,	024°17' E
Joniškis	56°14' N,	023°37' E
Jurbarkas	55°04' N,	022°46' E
Kaunas	54°54' N,	023°54' E
Kazlų Rūda	54°46' N,	023°30' E
Kėdainiai	55°17' N,	023°58' E

Kelmé	55°38' N,	022°56' E
Klaipéda	55°43' N,	021°07' E
Kuršénai	56°00' N,	022°56' E
Lazdijai	54°14' N,	023°31' E
Marijampolé (Kapsukas)	54°34' N,	023°21' E
Mažeikiai	56°19' N,	022°20' E
Naujoji Akmené	56°19' N,	022°54' E
Neringa	55°22' N,	021°04' E
Pagégiai	55°09' N,	021°54' E
Pakruojis	58°58' N,	023°52' E
Palanga	55°55' N,	021°03' E
Pandélys	56°01' N,	025°13' E
Panevéžys	55°44' N,	024°21' E
Pasvalys	56°04' N,	024°24' E
Plungé	55°55' N,	021°51' E
Priekulé	55°33' N,	021°19' E
Radviliškis	55°49' N,	023°32' E
Ramygala	55°31' N,	024°18' E
Raseiniai	55°22' N,	023°07' E
Rokiškis	55°58' N,	025°35' E
Šalčininkai	54°18' N,	025°23' E
Šiauliai	55°56' N,	023°19' E
Šilalé	55°28' N,	022°12' E
Šiluté	55°21' N,	021°29' E
Širvintos	55°03' N,	024°57' E
Skuodas	56°16' N,	021°32' E
Tauragé	55°15' N,	022°17' E
Telšiai	55°59' N,	022°15' E
Trakai	54°38' N,	024°56' E
Utena	55°30' N,	025°36' E
Varéna	54°13' N,	024°34' E
Vilkaviškis	54°39' N,	023°02' E
Vilkija	55°03' N,	023°35' E
Vilnius	54°41' N,	025°19' E
Zarasai	55°44' N,	026°15' E

LUXEMBOURG ..pg. 100

Bains (Modorf-les-Bains)	49°30' N,	006°17' E
Bettembourg	49°31' N,	006°06' E
Capellen	49°39' N,	005°59' E
Clervaux	50°03' N,	006°02' E
Diekirch	49°52' N,	006°10' E
Differdange	49°31' N,	005°53' E
Dudelange	49°28' N,	006°06' E
Echternach	49°49' N,	006°25' E
Esch-sur-Alzette	49°30' N,	005°59' E
Ettelbruck	49°51' N,	006°07' E
Grevenmacher	49°41' N,	006°27' E
Hesperange	49°34' N,	006°09' E
Junglinster	49°43' N,	006°15' E
Lorentzweiler	49°42' N,	006°09' E
Luxembourg	49°36' N,	006°08' E
Mamer	49°38' N,	006°02' E
Mersch	49°45' N,	006°06' E
Niederanven	49°39' N,	006°16' E
Pétange	49°33' N,	005°53' E
Rambrouch	49°50' N,	005°51' E
Redange	49°46' N,	005°53' E

Remich	49°32' N,	006°22' E
Sanem	49°33' N,	005°56' E
Schifflange	49°30' N,	006°01' E
Vianden	49°56' N,	006°13' E
Walfedange	49°39' N,	006°08' E
Wiltz	49°58' N,	005°56' E
Wincrange	50°03' N,	005°55' E
Wormeldange	49°37' N,	006°25' E

MACEDONIA ....pg. 101

Bitola	41°02' N,	021°20' E
Gostivar	41°48' N,	020°54' E
Kavadarci	41°26' N,	022°00' E
Kičevo	41°31' N,	020°57' E
Kočani	41°55' N,	022°25' E
Kruševo	41°22' N,	021°15' E
Kumanovo	42°08' N,	021°43' E
Ohrid	41°07' N,	020°48' E
Prilep	41°21' N,	021°34' E
Skopje (Skoplje)	42°00' N,	021°29' E
Štip	41°44' N,	022°12' E
Strumica	41°26' N,	022°39' E
Tetovo	42°01' N,	020°59' E
Tito Veles	41°42' N,	021°48' E

MADAGASCAR ..pg. 102

Ambanja	13°41' S,	048°27' E
Ambatondrazaka	17°50' S,	048°25' E
Andapa	14°39' S,	049°39' E
Ankarana (Sosumav)	13°05' S,	048°55' E
Antalaha	14°53' S,	050°17' E
Antananarivo (Tananarive)	18°55' S,	047°31' E
Antsirabe	19°51' S,	047°02' E
Antsiranana (Diégo-Suarez)	12°16' S,	049°17' E
Antsohihy	14°52' S,	047°59' E
Fianarantsoa	21°26' S,	047°05' E
Ihosy	22°24' S,	046°07' E
Maevatanana	16°57' S,	046°50' E
Mahabo	20°23' S,	044°40' E
Mahajanga (Majunga)	15°43' S,	046°19' E
Mahanoro	19°54' S,	048°48' E
Mananjary	21°13' S,	048°20' E
Maroantsetra	15°26' S,	049°44' E
Marovoay	16°06' S,	046°38' E
Morombe	21°44' S,	043°21' E
Morondava	20°17' S,	044°17' E
Port-Bergé (Boriziny)	15°33' S,	047°40' E
Toamasina (Tamatave)	18°10' S,	049°23' E
Tôlañaro (Faradofay, Fort-Dauphin or Taolanaro)	25°02' S,	047°00' E
Toliara (Toliary or Tulear)	23°21' S,	043°40' E
Vangaindrano	23°21' S,	047°36' E
Vatomandry	19°20' S,	048°59' E

MALAWI . . . . pg. 103

Balaka	14°59' S,	034°57' E
Blantyre	15°47' S,	035°00' E
Chikwawa	16°03' S,	034°48' E
Cholo (Thyolo)	16°04' S,	035°08' E
Dedza	14°22' S,	034°20' E
Dowa	13°39' S,	033°56' E
Karonga	09°56' S,	033°56' E
Kasungu	13°02' S,	033°29' E
Lilongwe	13°59' S,	033°47' E
Mangoche (Fort Johnson)	14°28' S,	035°16' E
Mchinji (Fort Manning)	13°48' S,	032°54' E
Monkey Bay	14°05' S,	034°55' E
Mzimba	11°54' S,	033°36' E
Mzuzu	11°27' S,	033°55' E
Nkhata Bay	11°36' S,	034°18' E
Nkhota Kota (Kota Kota)	12°55' S,	034°18' E
Nsanje (Port Herald)	16°55' S,	035°16' E
Salima	13°47' S,	034°26' E
Zomba	15°23' S,	035°20' E

MALAYSIA . . . . pg. 104

Alor Setar	06°07' N,	100°22' E
Batu Pahat	01°51' N,	102°56' E
Bau	01°25' N,	110°09' E
Bentong	03°32' N,	101°55' E
Bintulu	03°10' N,	113°02' E
Butterworth	05°25' N,	100°24' E
George Town (Pinang)	05°25' N,	100°20' E
Ipoh	04°35' N,	101°05' E
Johor Baharu	01°28' N,	103°45' E
Kangar	06°26' N,	100°12' E
Kelang (Klang)	03°02' N,	101°27' E
Keluang	02°02' N,	103°19' E
Kota Baharu	06°08' N,	102°15' E
Kota Kinabalu (Jesselton)	05°59' N,	116°04' E
Kota Tinggi	01°44' N,	103°54' E
Kuala Dungun (Dungun)	04°47' N,	103°26' E
Kuala Lumpur	03°10' N,	101°42' E
Kuala Terengganu	05°20' N,	103°08' E
Kuantan	03°48' N,	103°20' E
Kuching	01°33' N,	110°20' E
Lundu	01°40' N,	109°51' E
Melaka (Malacca)	02°12' N,	102°15' E
Miri	04°23' N,	113°59' E
Muar (Bandar Maharani)	02°02' N,	102°34' E
Petaling Jaya	03°05' N,	101°39' E
Sandakan	05°50' N,	118°07' E
Sarikei	02°07' N,	111°31' E
Seremban	02°43' N,	101°56' E
Sibu	02°18' N,	111°49' E
Song	02°01' N,	112°33' E
Sri Aman (Simanggang)	01°15' N,	111°26' E

Taiping	04°51' N,	100°44' E
Tawau	04°15' N,	117°54' E
Teluk Intan (Telok Anson)	04°02' N,	101°01' E
Victoria (Labuan)	05°17' N,	115°15' E

MALDIVES . . . . . . pg. 105

Male	04°10' N,	073°30' E

MALI . . . . pg. 106

Ansongo	15°40' N,	000°30' E
Bafoulabé	13°48' N,	010°50' W
Bamako	12°39' N,	008°00' W
Diamou	14°05' N,	011°16' W
Diré	16°16' N,	003°24' W
Gao	16°16' N,	000°03' W
Goundam	16°25' N,	003°40' W
Kalana	10°47' N,	008°12' W
Kangaba	11°56' N,	008°25' W
Kayes	14°27' N,	011°26' W
Kolokani	13°35' N,	008°02' W
Koro	14°04' N,	003°05' W
Labbezanga	14°57' N,	000°42' E
Ménaka	15°55' N,	002°24' E
Mopti	14°30' N,	004°12' W
Nara	15°10' N,	007°17' W
Niafounké	15°56' N,	004°00' W
Nioro Du Sahel	15°14' N,	009°35' W
San	13°18' N,	004°54' W
Ségou	13°27' N,	006°16' W
Sikasso	11°19' N,	005°40' W
Taoudenni	22°40' N,	003°59' W
Timbuktu	16°46' N,	003°01' W

MALTA . . . . pg. 107

Birkirkara	35°54' N,	014°28' E
Hamrun	35°53' N,	014°29' E
Mosta	35°55' N,	014°26' E
Rabat	35°53' N,	014°24' E
Valletta (Valeta)	35°54' N,	014°31' E
Żabbar	35°52' N,	014°32' E
Żebbug	35°52' N,	014°26' E
Żejtun	35°51' N,	014°32' E

MARSHALL ISLANDS . . . . pg. 108

Majuro	07°09' N,	171°12' E

MAURITANIA pg.109

Akjoujt	19°45' N,	014°23' W
Aleg	17°03' N,	013°55' W
Atar	20°31' N,	013°03' W

Ayoûn el 'Atroûs.	16°40′ N, 009°37′ W
Bir Mogreïn	25°14′ N, 011°35′ W
Bogué (Boghé)	16°35′ N, 014°16′ W
Boutilimit	17°33′ N, 014°42′ W
Chinguetti	20°27′ N, 012°22′ W
Guérou	16°48′ N, 011°50′ W
Kaédi	16°09′ N, 013°30′ W
Kiffa	16°37′ N, 011°24′ W
Maghama	15°31′ N, 012°51′ W
M'Bout	16°02′ N, 012°35′ W
Mederdra	16°55′ N, 015°39′ W
Néma	16°37′ N, 007°15′ W
Nouadhibou	20°54′ N, 017°04′ W
Nouakchott	18°06′ N, 015°57′ W
Rosso	16°30′ N, 015°49′ W
Sélibaby	15°10′ N, 012°11′ W
Tichit	18°28′ N, 009°30′ W
Tidjikdja	18°33′ N, 011°25′ W
Timbédra	16°15′ N, 008°10′ W
Zouïrât	22°42′ N, 012°30′ W

MEXICO . . . . .pg. 110

Acapulco	16°51′ N, 099°55′ W
Aguascalientes	21°53′ N, 102°18′ W
Caborca	30°37′ N, 112°06′ W
Campeche	19°51′ N, 090°32′ W
Cananea	30°57′ N, 110°18′ W
Cancún	21°05′ N, 086°46′ W
Carmen	18°38′ N, 091°50′ W
Casas Grandes	30°22′ N, 107°57′ W
Chetumal	18°30′ N, 088°18′ W
Chihuahua	28°38′ N, 106°05′ W
Ciudad Acuña (Las Vacas)	29°18′ N, 100°55′ W
Ciudad Juárez	31°44′ N, 106°29′ W
Ciudad Obregón	27°29′ N, 109°56′ W
Ciudad Victoria	23°44′ N, 099°08′ W
Colima	19°14′ N, 103°43′ W
Culiacán	24°48′ N, 107°24′ W
Durango	24°02′ N, 104°40′ W
Guadalajara	20°40′ N, 103°20′ W
Guadalupe	25°41′ N, 100°15′ W
Guaymas	27°56′ N, 110°54′ W
Hermosillo	29°04′ N, 110°58′ W
Jiménez	27°08′ N, 104°55′ W
Juchitán	16°26′ N, 095°01′ W
La Paz	24°10′ N, 110°18′ W
León	21°07′ N, 101°40′ W
Matamoros	25°53′ N, 097°30′ W
Matehuala	23°39′ N, 100°39′ W
Mazatlán	23°13′ N, 106°25′ W
Mérida	20°58′ N, 089°37′ W
Mexicali	32°40′ N, 115°29′ W
Mexico City (Ciudad de Mexico)	19°24′ N, 099°09′ W
Minatitlán	17°59′ N, 094°31′ W
Monterrey	25°40′ N, 100°19′ W
Morelia	19°42′ N, 101°07′ W
Nuevo Laredo	27°30′ N, 099°31′ W

Oaxaca	17°03′ N, 096°43′ W
Poza Rica	20°33′ N, 097°27′ W
Puebla	19°03′ N, 098°12′ W
Saltillo	25°25′ N, 101°00′ W
San Felipe	31°00′ N, 114°52′ W
San Ignacio	27°27′ N, 112°51′ W
Tampico	22°13′ N, 097°51′ W
Tijuana	32°32′ N, 117°01′ W
Torreón	25°33′ N, 103°26′ W
Tuxtla	16°45′ N, 093°07′ W
Veracruz	19°12′ N, 096°08′ W
Villahermosa	17°59′ N, 092°55′ W
Zapopan	20°43′ N, 103°24′ W

MICRONESIA, FEDERATED STATES OF . . . . .pg. 111

Colonia	09°31′ N, 138°08′ E
Kosrae	05°19′ N, 162°59′ E
Palikir	06°59′ N, 158°08′ E
Weno	07°26′ N, 151°52′ E

MOLDOVA . . . . . .pg. 112

Bălți	47°46′ N, 027°56′ E
Calaras	47°16′ N, 028°19′ E
Căușeni	46°38′ N, 029°25′ E
Chișinău	47°00′ N, 028°50′ E
Ciadâr-Lunga	46°03′ N, 028°50′ E
Comrat (Komrat)	46°18′ N, 028°39′ E
Drochia	48°02′ N, 027°48′ E
Dubăsari	47°07′ N, 029°10′ E
Fălești (Faleshty)	47°34′ N, 027°42′ E
Florești	47°53′ N, 028°17′ E
Hâncești (Kotovsk)	46°50′ N, 028°36′ E
Kagul	45°54′ N, 028°11′ E
Leova (Leovo)	46°28′ N, 028°15′ E
Orhei (Orgeyev)	47°22′ N, 028°49′ E
Rîbnița	47°45′ N, 029°00′ E
Rezina	47°45′ N, 028°58′ E
Soroca (Soroki)	48°09′ N, 028°18′ E
Tighina	46°49′ N, 029°29′ E
Tiraspol	46°50′ N, 029°37′ E
Ungheni	47°12′ N, 027°48′ E

MONGOLIA . . . . . .pg. 113

Altay	46°20′ N, 096°18′ E
Arvayheer	46°15′ N, 102°48′ E
Baruun-Urt	46°42′ N, 113°15′ E
Bulgan	48°45′ N, 103°34′ E
Choybalsan (Bayan Tumen)	48°04′ N, 114°30′ E
Choyr	46°18′ N, 108°20′ E
Dalandzadgad	43°34′ N, 104°25′ E
Darhan	49°29′ N, 105°55′ E

Dariganga . . . . 45°18′ N, 113°52′ E
Dzüünharaa . . . . 48°52′ N, 106°28′ E
Erdenet . . . . 49°02′ N, 104°05′ E
Ereen . . . . 49°15′ N, 112°29′ E
Hanh . . . . 51°30′ N, 100°40′ E
Hatgal . . . . 50°26′ N, 100°09′ E
Hovd (Jirgalanta) . . . . . 48°01′ N, 091°38′ E
Mörön . . . . 49°38′ N, 100°10′ E
Öndörhaan (Tsetsen
　Khan) . . . . 47°19′ N, 110°39′ E
Saynshand . . . . 44°52′ N, 110°09′ E
Sühbaatar . . . . 50°15′ N, 106°12′ E
Tes . . . . 49°41′ N, 095°48′ E
Tosontsengel . . . . 48°47′ N, 098°15′ E
Tsetserleg . . . . 47°30′ N, 101°27′ E
Tümentsogt . . . . 47°27′ N, 112°15′ E
Ulaanbaatar . . . . 47°55′ N, 106°53′ E
Uliastay . . . . 47°45′ N, 096°49′ E

MOROCCO . . . . . .pg. 114

Agadir . . . . 30°24′ N, 009°36′ W
Asilah (Arzila or Arcila) . 35°28′ N, 006°02′ W
Beni Mellal . . . . 32°20′ N, 006°21′ W
Berkane . . . . 34°56′ N, 002°20′ W
Boudenib . . . . 31°57′ N, 003°36′ W
Boulemane . . . . 33°22′ N, 004°45′ W
Casablanca
　(Ad-Dār al-Bayḍā′
　or Dar el-Beida) . . . . . 33°37′ N, 007°35′ W
El Jadida (Mazagan) . . . . 33°15′ N, 008°30′ W
El-Kelaa des Srarhna . . . 32°03′ N, 007°24′ W
Er-Rachidia
　(Ksar es-Souk) . . . . . . 31°56′ N, 004°26′ W
Fès (Fez) . . . . 34°02′ N, 004°59′ W
Figuig . . . . 32°06′ N, 001°14′ W
Guelmim (Goulimine) . . . 28°56′ N, 010°04′ W
Kenitra (Mina Hassan Tani
　or Port-Lyautey) . . . . . 34°16′ N, 006°36′ W
Khouribga . . . . 32°53′ N, 006°54′ W
Larache (El-Araish) . . . . 35°12′ N, 006°09′ W
Marrakech . . . . 31°38′ N, 008°00′ W
Meknès . . . . 33°54′ N, 005°33′ W
Mohammedia (Fedala) . . . 33°42′ N, 007°24′ W
Nador . . . . 35°11′ N, 002°56′ W
Ouarzazate . . . . 30°55′ N, 006°55′ W
Oued Zem . . . . 32°52′ N, 006°34′ W
Oujda . . . . 34°40′ N, 001°54′ W
Rabat (Ribat) . . . . 34°02′ N, 006°50′ W
Safi (Asfi) . . . . 32°18′ N, 009°14′ W
Salé (Sla) . . . . 34°04′ N, 006°48′ W
Settat . . . . 33°00′ N, 007°37′ W
Tangier (Tanger) . . . . . . 35°48′ N, 005°48′ W
Tan-Tan . . . . 28°26′ N, 011°06′ W
Taounate . . . . 34°33′ N, 004°39′ W
Tarfaya . . . . 27°57′ N, 012°55′ W
Tata . . . . 29°45′ N, 007°59′ W
Taza . . . . 34°13′ N, 004°01′ W
Tétouan (Tetuan) . . . . . . 35°34′ N, 005°22′ W
Zagora . . . . 30°19′ N, 005°50′ W

MOZAMBIQUE . .pg. 115

Angoche . . . . 16°15′ S, 039°54′ E
Beira . . . . 19°50′ S, 034°52′ E
Chimoio (Vila Pery) . . . . 19°08′ S, 033°29′ E
Chokwe . . . . 24°32′ S, 032°59′ E
Inhambane . . . . 23°52′ S, 035°23′ E
Lichinga . . . . 13°18′ S, 035°14′ E
Maputo (Lourenço
　Marques) . . . . 25°58′ S, 032°34′ E
Massinga . . . . 23°20′ S, 035°22′ E
Memba . . . . 14°12′ S, 040°32′ E
Moçambique
　(Mozambique) . . . . . . 15°03′ S, 040°45′ E
Mocubúri . . . . 14°39′ S, 038°54′ E
Mopeia Velha . . . . 17°59′ S, 035°43′ E
Morrumbene . . . . 23°39′ S, 035°20′ E
Nacala . . . . 14°33′ S, 040°40′ E
Namapa . . . . 13°43′ S, 039°50′ E
Nampula . . . . 15°09′ S, 039°18′ E
Panda . . . . 24°03′ S, 034°43′ E
Pemba . . . . 12°57′ S, 040°30′ E
Quelimane . . . . 17°51′ S, 036°52′ E
Quissico . . . . 24°43′ S, 034°45′ E
Tete . . . . 16°10′ S, 033°36′ E
Vila da Manhiça . . . . . . 25°24′ S, 032°48′ E
Vila da Mocimboa
　da Praia . . . . 11°20′ S, 040°21′ E
Vila do Chinde (Chinde) . 18°34′ S, 036°27′ E
Xai Xai (Joaõ Belo) . . . . 25°04′ S, 033°39′ E

MYANMAR . . . . . .pg. 116

Allanmyo . . . . 19°22′ N, 095°13′ E
Bassein (Pathein) . . . . . 16°47′ N, 094°44′ E
Bhamo . . . . 24°16′ N, 097°14′ E
Chauk . . . . 20°53′ N, 094°49′ E
Henzada . . . . 17°38′ N, 095°28′ E
Homalin . . . . 24°52′ N, 094°55′ E
Kale . . . . 16°05′ N, 097°54′ E
Katha . . . . 24°11′ N, 096°21′ E
Kawthaung . . . . 09°59′ N, 098°33′ E
Kēng Tung . . . . 21°17′ N, 099°36′ E
Kyaikkami . . . . 16°04′ N, 097°34′ E
Kyaukpyu (Ramree) . . . . 19°05′ N, 093°52′ E
Labutta . . . . 16°09′ N, 094°46′ E
Loi-kaw . . . . 19°41′ N, 097°13′ E
Magwe (Magwa) . . . . . . 20°09′ N, 094°55′ E
Mandalay . . . . 22°00′ N, 096°05′ E
Mergui . . . . 12°26′ N, 098°36′ E
Minbu . . . . 20°11′ N, 094°53′ E
Monywa . . . . 22°07′ N, 095°08′ E
Moulmein (Mawlamyine) . 16°30′ N, 097°38′ E
Myitkyina . . . . 25°23′ N, 097°24′ E
Palaw . . . . 12°58′ N, 098°39′ E
Pegu (Bago) . . . . 17°20′ N, 096°29′ E
Prome (Pye) . . . . 18°49′ N, 095°13′ E
Putao . . . . 27°21′ N, 097°24′ E

Sagaing	21°52′ N, 095°59′ E
Shwebo	22°34′ N, 095°42′ E
Sittwe (Akyab)	16°46′ N, 096°15′ E
Syriam	20°47′ N, 097°02′ E
Taunggyi	20°47′ N, 097°02′ E
Tavoy (Dawei)	14°05′ N, 098°12′ E
Tenasserim	12°05′ N, 099°01′ E
Thaton	16°55′ N, 097°22′ E
Tonzang	23°36′ N, 093°42′ E
Toungoo	18°56′ N, 096°26′ E
Yangon (Rangoon)	16°47′ N, 096°10′ E

NAMIBIA .... pg. 117

Aranos	24°08′ S, 019°07′ E
Bagani	18°07′ S, 021°38′ E
Gobabis	22°27′ S, 018°58′ E
Grootfontein	19°34′ S, 018°07′ E
Karasburg	28°01′ S, 018°45′ E
Karibib	21°56′ S, 015°50′ E
Keetmanshoop	26°35′ S, 018°08′ E
Khorixas	20°22′ S, 014°58′ E
Lüderitz	26°38′ S, 015°09′ E
Maltahöhe	24°50′ S, 016°59′ E
Mariental	24°38′ S, 017°58′ E
Okahandja	21°59′ S, 016°55′ E
Omaruru	21°26′ S, 015°56′ E
Ondangwa (Ondangua)	17°55′ S, 015°57′ E
Opuwo	18°04′ S, 013°51′ E
Oranjemund	28°33′ S, 016°26′ E
Oshakati	17°47′ S, 015°41′ E
Otjimbingwe	22°21′ S, 016°08′ E
Otjiwarongo	20°27′ S, 016°39′ E
Outjo	20°07′ S, 016°09′ E
Rehoboth	17°56′ S, 019°46′ E
Rundu	22°41′ S, 014°32′ E
Swakopmund	19°14′ S, 017°43′ E
Tsumeb	22°00′ S, 015°36′ E
Usakos	22°57′ S, 014°30′ E
Walvis Bay	22°57′ S, 014°30′ E
Warmbad	28°27′ S, 018°44′ E
Windhoek	22°35′ S, 017°05′ E

NEPAL .... pg. 118

Bāglūṅg	28°16′ N, 083°36′ E
Banepa	27°38′ N, 085°31′ E
Bhairahawā	27°30′ N, 083°27′ E
Bhaktapur (Bhadgaon)	27°41′ N, 085°25′ E
Bhojpur	27°10′ N, 087°03′ E
Biratnagar	26°29′ N, 087°17′ E
Birendranagar	28°46′ N, 081°38′ E
Birganj	27°00′ N, 084°52′ E
Dailekh	28°50′ N, 081°44′ E
Dandeldhūrā	29°18′ N, 080°35′ E
Ilām	26°54′ N, 087°56′ E
Jājarkot	28°42′ N, 082°12′ E
Jalésvar	26°38′ N, 085°48′ E
Jomosom	28°47′ N, 083°44′ E
Jumlā	29°17′ N, 082°10′ E

Kathmandu	27°43′ N, 085°19′ E
Lahān	26°43′ N, 086°29′ E
Lalitpur (Patan)	27°40′ N, 085°20′ E
Lumbini (Rummin-dei)	27°29′ N, 083°17′ E
Mahendranagar	28°55′ N, 080°20′ E
Mustāng	29°11′ N, 083°58′ E
Nepālganj	28°03′ N, 081°37′ E
Pokharā	28°14′ N, 083°59′ E
Sallyān	28°22′ N, 082°10′ E
Simikot	29°58′ N, 081°50′ E
Taplejūng	27°21′ N, 087°40′ E

NETHERLANDS, THE .... pg. 119

Alkmaar	52°38′ N, 004°45′ E
Almelo	52°21′ N, 006°40′ E
Amersfoort	52°09′ N, 005°23′ E
Amstelveen	52°18′ N, 004°52′ E
Amsterdam	52°21′ N, 004°55′ E
Apeldoorn	52°13′ N, 005°58′ E
Arnhem	51°59′ N, 005°55′ E
Assen	53°00′ N, 006°33′ E
Bergen op Zoom	51°30′ N, 004°18′ E
Breda	51°34′ N, 004°48′ E
Delft	52°00′ N, 004°22′ E
Den Helder	52°58′ N, 004°46′ E
Deventer	52°15′ N, 006°12′ E
Dordrecht (Dort or Dordt)	51°48′ N, 004°40′ E
Drachten	53°06′ N, 006°06′ E
Ede	52°02′ N, 005°40′ E
Eindhoven	51°27′ N, 005°28′ E
Emmen	52°47′ N, 006°54′ E
Enschede	52°13′ N, 006°54′ E
Geleen	50°58′ N, 005°50′ E
Gendringen	51°52′ N, 006°23′ E
Groningen	53°13′ N, 006°33′ E
Haarlem	52°22′ N, 004°39′ E
Heerenveen	52°57′ N, 005°56′ E
Heerlen	50°54′ N, 005°59′ E
Helmond	51°29′ N, 005°40′ E
Hengelo	52°16′ N, 006°48′ E
Hilversum	52°14′ N, 005°11′ E
Hoofddorp (Haarlemmermeer)	52°18′ N, 004°42′ E
Hoorn	52°39′ N, 005°04′ E
IJmuiden	52°28′ N, 004°36′ E
Langedijk	52°42′ N, 004°49′ E
Leeuwarden (Ljouwert)	53°12′ N, 005°47′ E
Leiden (Leyden)	52°09′ N, 004°30′ E
Lelystad	52°31′ N, 005°29′ E
Maastricht	50°51′ N, 005°41′ E
Meppel	52°42′ N, 006°12′ E
Middelburg	51°30′ N, 003°37′ E
Nieuwegein	52°02′ N, 005°06′ E
Nijmegen (Nimwegen)	51°50′ N, 005°52′ E
Ommen	52°31′ N, 006°26′ E
Oostburg	51°20′ N, 003°30′ E
Oss	51°46′ N, 005°32′ E

Purmerend . . . . 52°31′ N, 004°57′ E
Ridderkerk . . . . 51°52′ N, 004°36′ E
Roermond . . . . 51°12′ N, 006°00′ E
Roosendaal . . . . 51°32′ N, 004°28′ E
Rosmalen . . . . 51°43′ N, 005°22′ E
Rotterdam . . . . 51°55′ N, 004°30′ E
Schiedam . . . . 51°55′ N, 004°24′ E
's-Hertogenbosch (Den
  Bosch or Bois-le-Duc) . 51°42′ N, 005°19′ E
Sneek (Snits) . . . . 53°02′ N, 005°40′ E
Soest . . . . 52°11′ N, 005°18′ E
Steenwijk . . . . 52°47′ N, 006°07′ E
Stein. . . . . 50°58′ N, 005°46′ E
Terneuzen . . . . 51°20′ N, 003°50′ E
The Hague ('s-Gravenhage,
  Den Haag, or La Haye) . 52°05′ N, 004°18′ E
Tholen . . . . 51°32′ N, 004°13′ E
Tilburg. . . . . 51°33′ N, 005°07′ E
Utrecht . . . . 52°05′ N, 005°08′ E
Veenendaal . . . . 52°02′ N, 005°33′ E
Venlo . . . . 51°22′ N, 006°10′ E
Vlaardingen . . . . 51°55′ N, 004°21′ E
Vlissingen (Flushing) . . . 51°27′ N, 003°35′ E
Zaanstad . . . . 52°27′ N, 004°50′ E
Zoetermeer . . . . 52°03′ N, 004°30′ E
Zwolle . . . . 52°30′ N, 006°05′ E

NEW ZEALAND . . pg. 120

Auckland . . . . 36°52′ S, 174°46′ E
Blenheim . . . . 41°31′ S, 173°57′ E
Cheviot . . . . 42°49′ S, 173°16′ E
Christchurch . . . . 43°32′ S, 172°39′ E
Dunedin . . . . 45°53′ S, 170°29′ E
East Coast Bays . . . . . . 36°45′ S, 174°45′ E
Gisborne . . . . 38°39′ S, 178°01′ E
Greymouth . . . . 42°27′ S, 171°12′ E
Hamilton . . . . 37°47′ S, 175°16′ E
Hastings . . . . 39°39′ S, 176°50′ E
Invercargill . . . . 46°25′ S, 168°22′ E
Lower Hutt . . . . 41°13′ S, 174°56′ E
Manukau . . . . 36°57′ S, 174°56′ E
Milford Sound . . . . 44°41′ S, 167°55′ E
Napier . . . . 39°31′ S, 176°54′ E
Nelson . . . . 41°17′ S, 173°17′ E
New Plymouth . . . . 39°04′ S, 174°04′ E
Oamaru . . . . 45°06′ S, 170°58′ E
Paeroa . . . . 37°23′ S, 175°40′ E
Palmerston North . . . . . 40°21′ S, 175°37′ E
Porirua . . . . 41°08′ S, 174°51′ E
Rotorua . . . . 38°10′ S, 176°14′ E
Takapuna. . . . . 36°47′ S, 174°45′ E
Tauranga . . . . 37°42′ S, 176°08′ E
Timaru . . . . 44°24′ S, 171°14′ E
Upper Hutt . . . . 41°08′ S, 175°03′ E
Waihi . . . . 37°24′ S, 175°56′ E
Wanganui . . . . 39°56′ S, 175°02′ E
Wellington . . . . 41°18′ S, 174°47′ E
Westport . . . . 41°45′ S, 171°36′ E
Whangarei . . . . 35°43′ S, 174°20′ E

NICARAGUA . . . .pg. 121

Bluefields. . . . . 12°00′ N, 083°45′ W
Chinandega. . . . . 12°37′ N, 087°09′ W
Esquipulas. . . . . 12°40′ N, 085°47′ W
Estelí . . . . 13°05′ N, 086°21′ W
Granada . . . . 11°56′ N, 085°57′ W
Juigalpa . . . . 12°05′ N, 085°24′ W
León. . . . . 12°26′ N, 086°53′ W
Managua . . . . 12°09′ N, 086°17′ W
Masaya . . . . 11°58′ N, 086°06′ W
Matagalpa . . . . 12°55′ N, 085°55′ W
Nandaime . . . . 11°45′ N, 086°03′ W
Ocotal . . . . 13°38′ N, 086°29′ W
Puerto Cabezas . . . . 14°02′ N, 083°23′ W
San Carlos . . . . 11°07′ N, 084°47′ W
San Juan del Norte
  (Greytown) . . . . 10°55′ N, 083°42′ W
San Juan del Sur . . . . . . 11°15′ N, 085°52′ W
Somoto . . . . 13°29′ N, 086°35′ W
Waspam . . . . 14°44′ N, 083°58′ W

NIGER . . . . .pg. 122

Agadez . . . . 16°58′ N, 007°59′ E
Ayorou. . . . . 14°44′ N, 000°55′ E
Bilma . . . . 18°41′ N, 012°56′ E
Dakoro . . . . 14°31′ N, 006°46′ E
Diffa . . . . 13°19′ N, 012°37′ E
Dogondoutchi . . . . 13°38′ N, 004°02′ E
Dosso . . . . 13°03′ N, 003°12′ E
Filingué . . . . 14°21′ N, 003°19′ E
Gaya . . . . 11°53′ N, 003°27′ E
Gouré . . . . 13°58′ N, 010°18′ E
I-n-Gall . . . . 16°47′ N, 006°56′ E
Keïta . . . . 14°46′ N, 005°46′ E
Kolo . . . . 13°19′ N, 002°20′ E
Madaoua . . . . 14°06′ N, 006°26′ E
Magaria . . . . 13°00′ N, 008°54′ E
Maradi . . . . 13°29′ N, 007°06′ E
Mayahi. . . . . 13°58′ N, 007°40′ E
Nguigmi . . . . 14°15′ N, 013°07′ E
Niamey . . . . 13°31′ N, 002°07′ E
Tahoua . . . . 14°54′ N, 005°16′ E
Tânout . . . . 14°58′ N, 008°53′ E
Zinder . . . . 13°48′ N, 008°59′ E

NIGERIA . . . . .pg. 123

Aba . . . . 05°07′ N, 007°22′ E
Abuja . . . . 09°15′ N, 006°56′ E
Ado-Ekiti . . . . 07°38′ N, 005°13′ E
Asari . . . . 10°31′ N, 012°18′ E
Awka . . . . 06°13′ N, 007°05′ E
Azare . . . . 11°41′ N, 010°12′ E
Bauchi . . . . 10°19′ N, 009°50′ E
Benin City . . . . 06°20′ N, 005°38′ E
Bida . . . . 09°05′ N, 006°01′ E
Birnin Kebbi . . . . 12°28′ N, 004°12′ E

Biu	10°37′ N, 012°12′ E
Calabar	04°57′ N, 008°19′ E
Deba Habe	10°13′ N, 011°23′ E
Dikwa	12°02′ N, 013°55′ E
Dukku	10°49′ N, 010°46′ E
Ede	07°44′ N, 004°26′ E
Enugu	06°26′ N, 007°29′ E
Funtua	11°32′ N, 007°19′ E
Garko	11°39′ N, 008°48′ E
Gashua	12°52′ N, 011°03′ E
Gboko	07°19′ N, 009°00′ E
Gombe	10°17′ N, 011°10′ E
Gumel	12°38′ N, 009°23′ E
Gusau	12°10′ N, 006°40′ E
Ibadan	07°23′ N, 003°54′ E
Ibi	08°11′ N, 009°45′ E
Idah	07°06′ N, 006°44′ E
Ife	07°28′ N, 004°34′ E
Ifon	06°55′ N, 005°46′ E
Ikerre	07°30′ N, 005°14′ E
Ila	08°01′ N, 004°54′ E
Ilorin	08°30′ N, 004°33′ E
Iwo	07°38′ N, 004°11′ E
Jega	12°13′ N, 004°23′ E
Jimeta	09°17′ N, 012°28′ E
Jos	09°55′ N, 008°54′ E
Kaduna	10°31′ N, 007°26′ E
Kano	12°00′ N, 008°31′ E
Katsina	13°00′ N, 007°36′ E
Kaura Namoda	12°36′ N, 006°35′ E
Keffi	08°51′ N, 007°52′ E
Kishi	09°05′ N, 003°51′ E
Kumo	10°03′ N, 011°13′ E
Lafia	08°29′ N, 008°31′ E
Lafiagi	08°52′ N, 005°25′ E
Lagos	06°27′ N, 003°23′ E
Lere	09°43′ N, 009°21′ E
Mada	12°09′ N, 006°56′ E
Maiduguri	11°51′ N, 013°09′ E
Makurdi	07°44′ N, 008°32′ E
Minna	09°37′ N, 006°33′ E
Mubi	10°16′ N, 013°16′ E
Mushin	06°32′ N, 003°22′ E
Ngurtuwa	13°05′ N, 013°34′ E
Nguru	12°53′ N, 010°28′ E
Nsukka	06°52′ N, 007°23′ E
Ogbomosho	08°08′ N, 004°16′ E
Omoko	05°21′ N, 006°39′ E
Onitsha	06°10′ N, 006°47′ E
Opobo Town	04°31′ N, 007°32′ E
Oron	04°50′ N, 008°14′ E
Oshogbo	07°46′ N, 004°34′ E
Oyo	07°51′ N, 003°56′ E
Pindiga	09°59′ N, 010°54′ E
Port Harcourt	04°46′ N, 007°01′ E
Potiskum	11°43′ N, 011°04′ E
Sapele	05°55′ N, 005°42′ E
Shaki	08°40′ N, 003°23′ E
Sokoto	13°04′ N, 005°15′ E
Ugep	05°48′ N, 008°05′ E
Umuahia	05°32′ N, 007°29′ E

Uyo	05°03′ N, 007°56′ E
Warri	05°31′ N, 005°45′ E
Wukari	07°51′ N, 009°47′ E
Zaria	11°04′ N, 007°42′ E

NORTH KOREA .pg. 124

Anju	39°36′ N, 125°40′ E
Ch'ŏngjin	41°46′ N, 129°49′ E
Cho'san	40°50′ N, 125°48′ E
Haeju	38°02′ N, 125°42′ E
Hamhŭng	39°54′ N, 127°32′ E
Hŭich'ŏn	40°10′ N, 126°17′ E
Hyangsan	40°03′ N, 126°10′ E
Hyesan	41°24′ N, 128°10′ E
Ich'ŏn	38°29′ N, 126°53′ E
Kaesŏng	37°58′ N, 126°33′ E
Kanggye	40°58′ N, 126°36′ E
Kimch'aek (Songjin)	40°41′ N, 129°12′ E
Kŭmch'on	38°09′ N, 126°29′ E
Kusŏng	39°59′ N, 125°15′ E
Kyŏngwŏn	42°49′ N, 130°09′ E
Manp'o	41°09′ N, 126°17′ E
Myŏngch'ŏn	41°04′ N, 129°26′ E
Najin	42°15′ N, 130°18′ E
Namp'o	38°44′ N, 125°24′ E
P'anmunjŏm	37°57′ N, 126°40′ E
Puryŏng	42°04′ N, 129°43′ E
P'yŏngsŏng	39°15′ N, 125°52′ E
P'yŏngyang	39°01′ N, 125°45′ E
Sariwŏn	38°30′ N, 125°45′ E
Sinp'o	40°02′ N, 128°12′ E
Sinŭiju	40°06′ N, 124°24′ E
Songnim	38°44′ N, 125°38′ E
Taegwan	40°13′ N, 125°12′ E
Tanch'ŏn	40°28′ N, 128°55′ E
Tŏkch'ŏn	39°45′ N, 126°18′ E
T'ongch'ŏn	38°57′ N, 127°52′ E
Unggi	42°20′ N, 130°24′ E
Wŏnsan	39°10′ N, 127°26′ E

NORWAY ....pg. 125

Ålesund	62°28′ N, 006°09′ E
Alta	69°58′ N, 023°15′ E
Båtsfjord	70°38′ N, 029°44′ E
Bergen	60°23′ N, 005°20′ E
Bodø	67°17′ N, 014°23′ E
Brønnøysund	65°28′ N, 012°13′ E
Drammen	59°44′ N, 010°15′ E
Elverum	60°53′ N, 011°34′ E
Evje	58°36′ N, 007°51′ E
Fauske	67°15′ N, 015°24′ E
Finnsnes	69°14′ N, 017°59′ E
Flekkefjord	58°17′ N, 006°41′ E
Hamar	60°48′ N, 011°06′ E
Hammerfest	70°40′ N, 023°42′ E
Hareid	62°22′ N, 006°02′ E
Harstad	68°47′ N, 016°33′ E
Haugesund	59°25′ N, 005°18′ E

Hermansverk . . . . 61°11′ N, 006°51′ E
Karasjok . . . . 69°27′ N, 025°30′ E
Kautokeino . . . . 68°59′ N, 023°08′ E
Kolsås . . . . 59°55′ N, 010°31′ E
Kongsvinger . . . . 60°12′ N, 012°00′ E
Kristiansund . . . . 63°07′ N, 007°45′ E
Lillehammer . . . . 61°08′ N, 010°30′ E
Måløy . . . . 61°56′ N, 005°07′ E
Mandal . . . . 58°02′ N, 007°27′ E
Molde . . . . 62°44′ N, 007°11′ E
Mosjøen . . . . 65°50′ N, 013°12′ E
Narvik . . . . 68°26′ N, 017°25′ E
Nordfold . . . . 67°46′ N, 015°12′ E
Oslo (Christiania,
　Kristiania) . . . . 59°55′ N, 010°45′ E
Sandnessjøen . . . . 66°01′ N, 012°38′ E
Sarpsborg . . . . 59°17′ N, 011°07′ E
Skien . . . . 59°12′ N, 009°36′ E
Skjervøy . . . . 70°02′ N, 020°59′ E
Stavanger . . . . 58°58′ N, 005°45′ E
Steinkjer . . . . 64°01′ N, 011°30′ E
Svolvær . . . . 68°14′ N, 014°34′ E
Tønsberg . . . . 59°17′ N, 010°25′ E
Tromsø . . . . 69°40′ N, 018°58′ E
Trondheim . . . . 63°25′ N, 010°25′ E
Vadsø . . . . 70°05′ N, 029°46′ E
Vardø . . . . 70°22′ N, 031°06′ E

OMAN . . . . pg. 126

Al-Maṣna'ah . . . . 23°47′ N, 057°38′ E
Ar-Rustaq . . . . 23°24′ N, 057°26′ E
Bahlā' (Bahlah) . . . . 22°58′ N, 057°18′ E
Barkā' . . . . 23°43′ N, 057°53′ E
Ḍank . . . . 23°33′ N, 056°16′ E
Duqm . . . . 19°39′ N, 057°42′ E
Haymā' . . . . 19°56′ N, 056°19′ E
Ibrā' . . . . 22°43′ N, 058°32′ E
Khabura . . . . 23°59′ N, 057°08′ E
Khaṣab . . . . 26°12′ N, 056°15′ E
Khawr Rawrī (Khor Rori) . 17°02′ N, 054°27′ E
Maṭraḥ . . . . 23°37′ N, 058°34′ E
Mirbāṭ . . . . 17°00′ N, 054°41′ E
Muscat (Masqaṭ) . . . . 23°37′ N, 058°35′ E
Nizvā (Nazwah) . . . . 22°56′ N, 057°32′ E
Qurayyāt . . . . 23°15′ N, 058°54′ E
Rakhyūt . . . . 16°44′ N, 053°20′ E
Ṣalālah . . . . 17°00′ N, 054°06′ E
Shināṣ . . . . 24°46′ N, 056°28′ E
Ṣuḥār . . . . 24°22′ N, 056°45′ E
Ṣūr . . . . 22°34′ N, 059°32′ E
Ṭāqah . . . . 17°02′ N, 054°24′ E
Thamarīt . . . . 17°39′ N, 054°02′ E

PAKISTAN . . . . pg. 127

Badīn . . . . 24°39′ N, 068°50′ E
Bahāwalnagar . . . . 29°59′ N, 073°16′ E
Bannu . . . . 32°59′ N, 070°36′ E
Chitrāl . . . . 35°51′ N, 071°47′ E

Dādu . . . . 26°44′ N, 067°47′ E
Dera Ghazi Khan . . . . 30°03′ N, 070°38′ E
Dera Ismail Khan . . . . 31°50′ N, 070°54′ E
Faisalabad (Lyallpur) . . . . 31°25′ N, 073°05′ E
Gujranwala . . . . 32°09′ N, 074°11′ E
Gwadar . . . . 25°07′ N, 062°19′ E
Hyderabad . . . . 25°22′ N, 068°22′ E
Islamabad . . . . 33°42′ N, 073°10′ E
Karachi . . . . 24°52′ N, 067°03′ E
Khuzdār . . . . 27°48′ N, 066°37′ E
Kotri . . . . 25°22′ N, 068°18′ E
Larkana . . . . 27°33′ N, 068°13′ E
Las Bela . . . . 26°14′ N, 066°19′ E
Loralai . . . . 30°22′ N, 068°36′ E
Mardan . . . . 34°12′ N, 072°02′ E
Mianwali . . . . 32°35′ N, 071°33′ E
Mīrpur Khās . . . . 25°32′ N, 069°00′ E
Multan . . . . 30°11′ N, 071°29′ E
Nawabshah . . . . 26°15′ N, 068°25′ E
Panjgūr . . . . 26°58′ N, 064°06′ E
Peshawar . . . . 34°01′ N, 071°33′ E
Pishīn . . . . 30°35′ N, 067°00′ E
Quetta . . . . 30°12′ N, 067°00′ E
Raḥīmyār Khān . . . . 28°25′ N, 070°18′ E
Rawalpindi . . . . 33°36′ N, 073°04′ E
Sahiwal (Montgomery) . . . 30°40′ N, 073°06′ E
Sargodha . . . . 32°05′ N, 072°40′ E
Sūi . . . . 28°37′ N, 069°19′ E
Sukkur . . . . 27°42′ N, 068°52′ E
Thatta . . . . 24°45′ N, 067°55′ E
Turbat . . . . 25°59′ N, 063°04′ E
Wāh . . . . 33°48′ N, 072°42′ E
Zhob (Fort Sandeman) . . . 31°20′ N, 069°27′ E

PALAU . . . . pg. 128

Airai . . . . 07°22′ N, 134°33′ E
Klouklubed . . . . 07°02′ N, 134°15′ E
Koror . . . . 07°20′ N, 134°29′ E
Melekeok . . . . 07°29′ N, 134°38′ E
Meyungs . . . . 07°20′ N, 134°27′ E
Ngardmau . . . . 07°37′ N, 134°36′ E

PANAMA . . . . pg. 129

Aguadulce . . . . 08°15′ N, 080°33′ W
Almirante . . . . 09°18′ N, 082°24′ W
Antón . . . . 08°24′ N, 080°16′ W
Boquete . . . . 08°47′ N, 082°26′ W
Cañazas . . . . 09°06′ N, 078°10′ W
Capira . . . . 08°45′ N, 079°53′ W
Changuinola . . . . 09°26′ N, 082°31′ W
Chepo . . . . 09°10′ N, 079°06′ W
Chitré . . . . 07°58′ N, 080°26′ W
Colón . . . . 09°22′ N, 079°54′ W
David . . . . 08°26′ N, 082°26′ W
Guararé . . . . 07°49′ N, 080°17′ W
La Chorrera . . . . 08°53′ N, 079°47′ W
La Concepción . . . . 08°31′ N, 082°37′ W
La Palma . . . . 08°25′ N, 078°09′ W

Las Cumbres	09°05′ N, 079°32′ W
Las Lajas	08°15′ N, 081°52′ W
Las Tablas	07°46′ N, 080°17′ W
Ocú	07°57′ N, 080°47′ W
Panama City (Panamá)	08°58′ N, 079°32′ W
Pedregal	09°04′ N, 079°26′ W
Penonomé	08°31′ N, 080°22′ W
Portobelo (Puerto Bello)	09°33′ N, 079°39′ W
Puerto Armuelles	08°17′ N, 082°52′ W
San Miguelito	09°02′ N, 079°30′ E
Santiago	08°06′ N, 080°59′ W
Soná	08°01′ N, 081°19′ W
Yaviza (Yavisa)	08°11′ N, 077°41′ W

PAPUA NEW GUINEA . . . . pg. 130

Aitape	03°08′ S, 142°21′ E
Alotau	10°20′ S, 150°25′ E
Ambunti	04°14′ S, 142°50′ E
Arawa	06°13′ S, 155°33′ E
Baimuru	07°30′ S, 144°49′ E
Balimo	08°03′ S, 142°57′ E
Bogia	04°16′ S, 144°54′ E
Buin	06°50′ S, 155°44′ E
Bulolo	07°12′ S, 146°39′ E
Bwagaoia	10°42′ S, 152°50′ E
Daru	09°05′ S, 143°12′ E
Finschhafen	06°36′ S, 147°51′ E
Goroka	06°05′ S, 145°23′ E
Kandrian	06°13′ S, 149°33′ E
Kavieng	02°34′ S, 150°48′ E
Kerema	07°58′ S, 145°46′ E
Kikori	07°25′ S, 144°15′ E
Kimbe	05°33′ S, 150°09′ E
Kiunga	06°07′ S, 141°18′ E
Kupiano	10°05′ S, 148°11′ E
Lae	06°44′ S, 147°00′ E
Lorengau	02°01′ S, 147°16′ E
Losuia	08°32′ S, 151°04′ E
Madang	05°13′ S, 145°48′ E
Mt. Hagen	05°52′ S, 144°13′ E
Namatanai	03°40′ S, 152°27′ E
Popondetta	08°46′ S, 148°14′ E
Port Moresby	09°29′ S, 147°11′ E
Rabaul	04°12′ S, 152°11′ E
Saidor	05°38′ S, 146°28′ E
Samarai	10°37′ S, 150°40′ E
Tari	05°42′ S, 142°57′ E
Vanimo	02°41′ S, 141°18′ E
Wewak	03°33′ S, 143°38′ E

PARAGUAY . . . . . . pg. 131

Asunción	25°16′ S, 057°40′ W
Caacupé	25°23′ S, 057°09′ W
Caaguazú	25°26′ S, 056°02′ W
Caazapá	26°09′ S, 056°24′ W
Capitán Pablo Lagerenza	19°55′ S, 060°47′ W

Ciudad del Este (Puerto Presidente Stroessner)	25°31′ S, 054°37′ W
Concepción	23°25′ S, 057°17′ W
Encarnación	27°20′ S, 055°54′ W
Filadelfia	22°21′ S, 060°02′ W
Fuerto Olimpo	21°02′ S, 057°54′ W
General Eugenio A. Garay	20°31′ S, 062°08′ W
Luque	25°16′ S, 057°34′ W
Mariscal Estigarribia	22°02′ S, 060°38′ W
Paraguarí	25°38′ S, 057°09′ W
Pedro Juan Caballero	22°34′ S, 055°37′ W
Pilar	26°52′ S, 058°23′ W
Pozo Colorado	23°26′ S, 058°58′ W
Salto del Guairá	24°05′ S, 054°20′ W
San Juan Bautista	26°38′ S, 057°10′ W
San Lázaro	22°10′ S, 057°58′ W
Villarica	25°45′ S, 056°26′ W

PERU . . . . pg. 132

Abancay	13°35′ S, 072°55′ W
Acomayo	13°55′ S, 071°41′ W
Arequipa	16°24′ S, 071°33′ W
Ayabaca	04°38′ S, 079°43′ W
Ayacucho	13°07′ S, 074°13′ W
Ayaviri	14°52′ S, 070°35′ W
Bagua	05°40′ S, 078°31′ W
Barranca	10°45′ S, 077°46′ W
Cajamarca	07°10′ S, 078°31′ W
Callao	12°04′ S, 077°09′ W
Castilla	05°12′ S, 080°38′ W
Cerro de Pasco	10°41′ S, 076°16′ W
Chiclayo	06°46′ S, 079°51′ W
Chimbote	09°05′ S, 078°36′ W
Contamana	07°15′ S, 074°54′ W
Cuzco	13°31′ S, 071°59′ W
Espinar	14°47′ S, 071°29′ W
Huacho	11°07′ S, 077°37′ W
Huancayo	12°04′ S, 075°14′ W
Huánuco	09°55′ S, 076°14′ W
Huaraz	09°32′ S, 077°32′ W
Huarmey	10°04′ S, 078°10′ W
Ica	14°04′ S, 075°42′ W
Iñapari	10°57′ S, 069°35′ W
Iquitos	03°46′ S, 073°15′ W
Juliaca	15°30′ S, 070°08′ W
Lagunas	05°14′ S, 075°38′ W
Lima	12°03′ S, 077°03′ W
Macusani	14°05′ S, 070°26′ W
Miraflores	12°07′ S, 077°02′ W
Moquegua	17°12′ S, 070°56′ W
Moyobamba	06°03′ S, 076°58′ W
Nauta	04°32′ S, 073°33′ W
Pampas	12°24′ S, 074°54′ W
Pisco	13°42′ S, 076°13′ W
Piura	05°12′ S, 080°38′ W
Pucallpa	08°23′ S, 074°32′ W
Puerto Maldonado	12°36′ S, 069°11′ W
Puno	15°50′ S, 070°02′ W
Requena	04°58′ S, 073°50′ W

San Juan	15°21′ S, 075°10′ W
Tacna	18°01′ S, 070°15′ W
Tarapoto	06°30′ S, 076°25′ W
Trujillo	08°07′ S, 079°02′ W
Tumbes	03°34′ S, 080°28′ W

PHILIPPINES . . . . . pg. 133

Angeles	15°09′ N, 120°35′ E
Aparri	18°22′ N, 121°39′ E
Bacolod	10°40′ N, 122°56′ E
Balabac	07°59′ N, 117°04′ E
Batangas	13°45′ N, 121°03′ E
Bayombong	16°29′ N, 121°09′ E
Borongan	11°37′ N, 125°26′ E
Butuan	08°54′ N, 125°35′ E
Cagayan de Oro	08°29′ N, 124°39′ E
Caloocan	14°39′ N, 120°58′ E
Cavite	14°29′ N, 120°55′ E
Cebu	10°18′ N, 123°54′ E
Daet	14°05′ N, 122°55′ E
Dagupan	16°03′ N, 120°20′ E
Dipolog	08°35′ N, 123°20′ E
Dumaguete	09°18′ N, 123°18′ E
General Santos	06°07′ N, 125°10′ E
Iligan	08°14′ N, 124°14′ E
Iloilo City	10°42′ N, 122°33′ E
Isabela	06°42′ N, 121°58′ E
Jolo	06°03′ N, 121°00′ E
Laoag	12°34′ N, 125°00′ E
Lucena	13°56′ N, 121°37′ E
Manila	14°35′ N, 121°00′ E
Masbate	12°22′ N, 123°36′ E
Mati	06°57′ N, 126°13′ E
Naga (Nueva Caceres)	13°37′ N, 123°11′ E
Ormoc	11°00′ N, 124°37′ E
Ozamiz	08°08′ N, 123°50′ E
Pandan	14°03′ N, 124°10′ E
Puerto Princesa	09°44′ N, 118°44′ E
Quezon City	14°38′ N, 121°00′ E
Romblon	12°35′ N, 122°15′ E
Roxas (Capiz)	11°35′ N, 122°45′ E
Surigao	09°45′ N, 125°30′ E
Tagbilaran	09°39′ N, 123°51′ E
Tuguegarao	17°37′ N, 121°44′ E
Zamboanga	06°54′ N, 122°04′ E

POLAND . . . . pg. 134

Biała Podlaska	52°02′ N, 023°08′ E
Białystok	53°08′ N, 023°09′ E
Bielsko-Biała	49°49′ N, 019°02′ E
Bydgoszcz	53°09′ N, 018°00′ E
Ciechanów	52°53′ N, 020°37′ E
Częstochowa	50°48′ N, 019°07′ E
Dąbrova Górnicza	50°20′ N, 019°12′ E
Elbląg	54°10′ N, 019°23′ E
Gdańsk (Danzig)	54°21′ N, 018°40′ E
Gdynia	54°30′ N, 018°33′ E
Gorzów Wielkopolski	52°44′ N, 015°14′ E

Grudziądz	53°29′ N, 018°46′ E
Iława	53°36′ N, 019°34′ E
Inowrocław	52°48′ N, 018°16′ E
Kalisz	51°45′ N, 018°05′ E
Katowice	50°16′ N, 019°01′ E
Kielce	50°50′ N, 020°40′ E
Konin	52°13′ N, 018°16′ E
Koszalin	54°12′ N, 016°11′ E
Kraków	50°05′ N, 019°55′ E
Krosno	49°41′ N, 021°47′ E
Legnica	51°12′ N, 016°12′ E
Leszno	51°51′ N, 016°35′ E
Łódź	51°45′ N, 019°28′ E
Łomża	53°11′ N, 022°05′ E
Lublin	51°15′ N, 022°34′ E
Malbork	54°02′ N, 019°03′ E
Mogilno	52°40′ N, 017°58′ E
Nidzica	53°22′ N, 020°26′ E
Nowy Sącz	49°38′ N, 020°43′ E
Olsztyn	53°47′ N, 020°29′ E
Opole	50°40′ N, 017°57′ E
Ostrołęka	53°05′ N, 021°34′ E
Piła	53°09′ N, 016°45′ E
Pińczów	50°32′ N, 020°32′ E
Piotrków Trybunalski	51°24′ N, 019°41′ E
Pisz	53°38′ N, 021°48′ E
Poznań	52°25′ N, 016°58′ E
Radom	51°25′ N, 021°09′ E
Rybnik	50°07′ N, 018°32′ E
Rzeszów	50°03′ N, 022°00′ E
Siedlce	52°10′ N, 022°18′ E
Słupsk	54°27′ N, 017°02′ E
Suwałki	54°06′ N, 022°56′ E
Szczecin (Stettin)	53°25′ N, 014°35′ E
Tarnobrzeg	50°35′ N, 021°41′ E
Tarnów	50°01′ N, 020°59′ E
Tczew	54°06′ N, 018°48′ E
Tomaszów Mazowiecki	51°32′ N, 020°01′ E
Toruń	53°02′ N, 018°36′ E
Tuchola	53°35′ N, 017°51′ E
Tychy	50°08′ N, 018°59′ E
Wałbrzych	50°46′ N, 016°17′ E
Warsaw (Warszawa)	52°15′ N, 021°00′ E
Włocławek	52°39′ N, 019°05′ E
Wrocław (Breslau)	51°06′ N, 017°02′ E
Zabrze	50°19′ N, 018°47′ E
Zamość	50°43′ N, 023°15′ E
Zielona Góra	51°56′ N, 015°30′ E

PORTUGAL . . . . . pg. 135

Alcobaça	39°33′ N, 008°59′ W
Almada	38°41′ N, 009°09′ W
Amadora	38°45′ N, 009°14′ W
Aveiro	40°38′ N, 008°39′ W
Barreiro	38°40′ N, 009°04′ W
Batalha	39°39′ N, 008°50′ W
Beja	38°01′ N, 007°52′ W
Braga	41°33′ N, 008°26′ W
Bragança	41°49′ N, 006°45′ W
Castelo Branco	39°49′ N, 007°30′ W

Chaves	41°44′ N, 007°28′ W
Coimbra	40°12′ N, 008°25′ W
Elvas	38°53′ N, 007°10′ W
Évora	38°34′ N, 007°54′ W
Faro	37°01′ N, 007°56′ W
Fátima	39°37′ N, 008°39′ W
Figueira da Foz	40°09′ N, 008°52′ W
Guarda	40°32′ N, 007°16′ W
Guimarães	41°27′ N, 008°18′ W
Leiria	39°45′ N, 008°48′ W
Lisbon (Lisboa)	38°43′ N, 009°08′ W
Nazaré	39°36′ N, 009°04′ W
Odivelas	38°47′ N, 009°11′ W
Oeiras	38°41′ N, 009°19′ W
Portalegre	39°17′ N, 007°26′ W
Portimão (Vila Nova de Portimão)	37°08′ N, 008°32′ W
Porto (Oporto)	41°09′ N, 008°37′ W
Póvoa de Varzim	41°23′ N, 008°46′ W
Queluz	38°45′ N, 009°15′ W
Santarém	39°14′ N, 008°41′ W
Setúbal	38°32′ N, 008°54′ W
Sines	37°57′ N, 008°52′ W
Tomar	39°36′ N, 008°25′ W
Torres Vedras	39°06′ N, 009°16′ W
Urgeiriça	40°30′ N, 007°53′ W
Viana do Castelo	41°42′ N, 008°50′ W
Vila do Conde	41°21′ N, 008°45′ W
Vila Franca de Xira	38°57′ N, 008°59′ W
Vila Nova de Gaia	41°08′ N, 008°37′ W
Vila Real	41°18′ N, 007°45′ W
Viseu	40°39′ N, 007°55′ W

QATAR . . . . pg. 136

Al-Wakrah	25°10′ N, 051°36′ E
Ar Rayyān	25°18′ N, 051°27′ E
Ar-Ruways	26°08′ N, 051°13′ E
Doha (ad-Dawhah)	25°17′ N, 051°32′ E
Dukhān	25°25′ N, 050°47′ E
Musay'id	25°00′ N, 051°33′ E
Umm Bāb	25°09′ N, 050°50′ E

ROMANIA . . . . . . pg. 137

Alba Iulia (Gyulafehérvár)	46°04′ N, 023°35′ E
Alexandria	43°59′ N, 025°20′ E
Arad	46°11′ N, 021°19′ E
Bacău	46°34′ N, 026°54′ E
Baia Mare	47°40′ N, 023°35′ E
Bârlad	46°14′ N, 027°40′ E
Bistrița	47°08′ N, 024°29′ E
Botoșani	47°45′ N, 026°40′ E
Brăila	45°16′ N, 027°59′ E
Brașov (Orașul Stalin)	45°38′ N, 025°35′ E
Bucharest	44°26′ N, 026°06′ E
Buzău	45°09′ N, 026°50′ E
Calafat	43°59′ N, 022°56′ E
Călărași	44°12′ N, 027°20′ E

Cluj-Napoca	46°46′ N, 023°36′ E
Constanța	44°11′ N, 028°39′ E
Craiova	44°19′ N, 023°48′ E
Dej	47°09′ N, 023°52′ E
Deva	45°53′ N, 022°54′ E
Drobeta-Turnu Severin	44°38′ N, 022°40′ E
Focșani	45°42′ N, 027°11′ E
Galați (Galatz)	45°27′ N, 028°03′ E
Giurgiu	43°53′ N, 025°58′ E
Hunedoara	45°45′ N, 022°54′ E
Iași (Jassy)	47°10′ N, 027°36′ E
Lugoj	45°41′ N, 021°55′ E
Mangalia	43°48′ N, 028°35′ E
Medgidia	44°15′ N, 028°17′ E
Mediaș	46°10′ N, 024°21′ E
Mizil	45°01′ N, 026°27′ E
Onești (Gheorghe Gheorghiu Dej)	46°15′ N, 026°45′ E
Oradea (Nagyvárad)	47°04′ N, 021°56′ E
Petroșani	45°25′ N, 023°22′ E
Piatra-Neamț	46°55′ N, 026°20′ E
Pitești	44°51′ N, 024°52′ E
Ploiești (Ploești)	44°57′ N, 026°01′ E
Reșița	45°18′ N, 021°55′ E
Roman	46°55′ N, 026°55′ E
Satu Mare	47°48′ N, 022°53′ E
Sebeș	45°58′ N, 023°34′ E
Slatina	44°26′ N, 024°22′ E
Suceava	47°38′ N, 026°15′ E
Țăndărei	44°39′ N, 027°40′ E
Târgoviște	44°56′ N, 025°27′ E
Targu Jiu	45°03′ N, 023°17′ E
Târgu Mureș	46°33′ N, 024°34′ E
Tecuci	45°52′ N, 027°25′ E
Timișoara	45°45′ N, 021°13′ E
Tulcea	45°10′ N, 028°48′ E
Turda	46°34′ N, 023°47′ E
Vaslui	46°38′ N, 027°44′ E
Zalau	47°12′ N, 023°03′ E

RUSSIA . . . . pg. 138-9

Abakan	53°43′ N, 091°26′ E
Aginskoye	51°06′ N, 114°32′ E
Anadyr (Novo-Mariinsk)	64°45′ N, 177°29′ E
Angarsk	52°34′ N, 103°54′ E
Birobidzhan	48°48′ N, 132°57′ E
Biysk (Bisk)	52°34′ N, 085°15′ E
Cheboksary	56°09′ N, 047°15′ E
Chelyabinsk	55°10′ N, 061°24′ E
Cherepovets	59°08′ N, 037°54′ E
Chita	52°03′ N, 113°30′ E
Dudinka	69°25′ N, 086°15′ E
Gorno-Altaysk (Ulala, or Oyrot-Tura)	51°58′ N, 085°58′ E
Grozny	43°20′ N, 045°42′ E
Izhevsk (Ustinov)	56°51′ N, 053°14′ E
Kaluga	54°31′ N, 036°16′ E
Kazan	55°45′ N, 049°08′ E

Khanty-Mansiysk		
(Ostyako-Vogulsk)	61°00' N,	069°06' E
Kirovsk	67°37' N,	033°40' E
Komsomol'sk-na-Amure	50°35' N,	137°02' E
Krasnoyarsk	56°01' N,	092°50' E
Kudymkar	59°01' N,	054°39' E
Kurgan	55°26' N,	065°18' E
Kyzyl (Khem-Beldyr)	51°42' N,	094°27' E
Magadan	59°34' N,	150°48' E
Makhachkala	42°58' N,	047°30' E
Maykop (Maikop)	44°35' N,	040°10' E
Moscow (Moskva)	55°45' N,	037°35' E
Murmansk	68°58' N,	033°05' E
Nal'chik	43°29' N,	043°37' E
Nar'yan-Mar	67°39' N,	053°00' E
Nizhnekamsk	55°36' N,	051°47' E
Nizhny Novgorod		
(Gorky)	56°20' N,	044°00' E
Novgorod	58°31' N,	031°17' E
Novokuznetsk		
(Kuznetsk,		
or Stalinsk)	53°45' N,	087°06' E
Novosibirsk	55°02' N,	082°55' E
Omsk	55°00' N,	073°24' E
Orenburg (Chkalov)	51°45' N,	055°06' E
Orsk	51°12' N,	058°34' E
Palana	59°07' N,	159°58' E
Penza	53°13' N,	045°00' E
Perm' (Molotov)	58°00' N,	056°15' E
Petropavlovsk-		
Kamchatsky	53°01' N,	158°39' E
Petrozavodsk	61°49' N,	034°20' E
Rostov-na-Donu		
(Rostov-on-Don)	47°14' N,	039°42' E
St. Petersburg		
(Leningrad,		
or Sankt Peterburg)	59°55' N,	030°15' E
Salavat	53°21' N,	055°55' E
Salekhard	66°33' N,	066°40' E
Samara (Kuybyshev)	53°12' N,	050°09' E
Saransk	54°11' N,	045°11' E
Saratov	51°34' N,	046°02' E
Smolensk	54°47' N,	032°03' E
Syktyvkar	61°40' N,	050°48' E
Tomsk	56°30' N,	084°58' E
Tver' (Kalinin)	56°52' N,	035°55' E
Tyumen'	57°09' N,	065°26' E
Ufa	55°45' N,	055°56' E
Ulan-Ude	51°50' N,	107°37' E
Ussuriysk	43°48' N,	131°59' E
Ust'-Ordinsky	52°48' N,	104°45' E
Vladimir	56°10' N,	040°25' E
Vladivostok	43°08' N,	131°54' E
Voigograd (Stalingrad,		
or Tsaritsyn)	48°45' N,	044°25' E
Vologda	59°13' N,	039°54' E
Voronezh	51°38' N,	039°12' E
Yakutsk	62°00' N,	129°40' E
Yaroslavl	57°37' N,	039°52' E
Yekaterinburg		
(Sverdlovsk)	56°51' N,	060°36' E

Yuzhno-Sakhalinsk	46°57' N,	142°44' E

RWANDA . . . . .pg. 140

Butare	02°36' S,	029°44' E
Gisenyi	01°42' S,	029°15' E
Kigali	01°57' S,	030°04' E
Ruhengeri	01°30' S,	029°38' E

SAINT KITTS AND NEVIS . . . . .pg. 141

Basseterre	17°18' N,	062°43' W
Brown Hill	17°08' N,	062°33' W
Cayon	17°22' N,	062°43' W
Challengers	17°18' N,	062°47' W
Charlestown	17°08' N,	062°37' W
Cotton Ground	17°11' N,	062°36' W
Half Way Tree	17°20' N,	062°49' W
Mansion	17°22' N,	062°46' W
Monkey Hill Village	17°19' N,	062°43' W
Newcastle	17°13' N,	062°34' W
New River	17°09' N,	062°32' W
Newton Ground	17°23' N,	062°51' W
Old Road Town	17°19' N,	062°48' W
Sadlers	17°24' N,	062°49' W
Saint Paul's	17°24' N,	062°49' W
Sandy Point Town	17°22' N,	062°50' W
Verchild's	17°20' N,	062°48' W
Zetlands	17°08' N,	062°34' W

SAINT LUCIA . . .pg. 142

Anse La Raye	13°57' N,	061°03' W
Canaries	13°55' N,	061°04' W
Castries	14°01' N,	061°00' W
Dauphin	14°03' N,	060°55' W
Dennery	13°55' N,	060°54' W
Grande Anse	14°01' N,	061°45' W
Gros Islet	14°05' N,	060°58' W
Laborie	13°45' N,	061°00' W
Micoud	13°50' N,	060°54' W
Praslin	13°53' N,	060°54' W
Sans Soucis	13°59' N,	061°01' W
Soufrière	13°52' N,	061°04' W

SAINT VINCENT AND THE GRENADINES . . . .pg. 143

Ashton	12°36' N,	061°27' W
Barrouallie	13°14' N,	061°17' W
Calliaqua	13°08' N,	061°12' W
Chateaubelair	13°17' N,	061°15' W
Georgetown	13°16' N,	061°08' W
Kingstown	13°09' N,	061°14' W

SAMOA ....pg. 144

Apia	13°50′ S,	171°44′ W
Fa'aala	13°45′ S,	172°16′ W
Faleasi'u	13°48′ S,	171°54′ W
Le'auva'a	13°48′ S,	171°51′ W
Lotofaga	13°59′ S,	171°50′ W
Matavai (Asau)	13°28′ S,	172°35′ W
Safotu	13°27′ S,	172°24′ W
Sagone	13°39′ S,	172°35′ W
Samatau	13°54′ S,	172°02′ W
Sili	13°43′ S,	172°21′ W
Si'umu	14°01′ S,	171°47′ W
Solosolo	13°51′ S,	171°36′ W

SAN MARINO ....pg. 145

San Marino	43°56′ N,	012°25′ E

SÃO TOMÉ AND PRÍNCIPE .. pg. 146

Infante Don Henrique	01°34′ N,	007°25′ E
Neves	00°22′ N,	006°33′ E
Porto Alegre	00°02′ N,	006°32′ E
Santana	00°16′ N,	006°45′ E
Santo Amaro	00°22′ N,	006°42′ E
Santo António	01°39′ N,	007°25′ E
São Tomé	00°20′ N,	006°44′ E
Trindade	00°15′ N,	006°40′ E

SAUDI ARABIA .. pg. 147

Abhā	18°13′ N,	042°30′ E
Abqaiq (Buqayq)	25°56′ N,	049°40′ E
Ad-Dammām	26°26′ N,	050°07′ E
'Afif	23°55′ N,	042°56′ E
Al-Bāhah	20°01′ N,	041°28′ E
Al-Badi'	22°02′ N,	046°34′ E
Al-Bātin Hafar	28°27′ N,	045°58′ E
Al-Bi'ār	22°39′ N,	039°40′ E
Al-Hā'ir	24°23′ N,	046°50′ E
Al-Hufūf	25°22′ N,	049°34′ E
Al-Ju'aydah	19°40′ N,	041°34′ E
Al-Jubayl	27°01′ N,	049°40′ E
Al-Khubar	26°17′ N,	050°12′ E
Al-Mish'āb	28°12′ N,	048°36′ E
Al-Mubarraz	25°25′ N,	049°35′ E
Al-Qatīf	26°33′ N,	050°00′ E
Al-Qunfudhah	19°08′ N,	041°05′ E
Al-Ulā	26°38′ N,	037°55′ E
Ar'ar	30°59′ N,	041°02′ E
As-Safrā'	24°02′ N,	038°56′ E
As-Sulayyil	20°27′ N,	045°34′ E
At-Ta'if	21°16′ N,	040°25′ E
Az-Zilfi	26°18′ N,	044°48′ E
Badanah	30°59′ N,	040°58′ E
Birkah	23°48′ N,	038°50′ E

Buraydah	26°20′ N,	043°59′ E
Buraykah	22°21′ N,	039°20′ E
Hā'il	27°33′ N,	041°42′ E
Halabān	23°29′ N,	044°23′ E
Harajah	17°56′ N,	043°21′ E
Jidda (Jiddah)	21°29′ N,	039°12′ E
Jizān (Qīzān)	16°54′ N,	042°32′ E
Khamīs Mushayt	18°18′ N,	042°44′ E
Khawsh	18°59′ N,	041°55′ E
Laylā	22°17′ N,	046°45′ E
Madā'in Sālih	26°48′ N,	037°57′ E
Mecca (Makkah)	21°27′ N,	039°49′ E
Medina (al-Madinah; Yathrib)	24°28′ N,	039°36′ E
Miskah	24°49′ N,	042°56′ E
Muṣābih	18°42′ N,	042°01′ E
Na'jān	24°05′ N,	047°10′ E
Najrān	17°26′ N,	044°15′ E
Qanā	27°47′ N,	041°25′ E
Rābigh	22°48′ N,	039°02′ E
Rafhā'	29°38′ N,	043°30′ E
Ras Tanura	26°42′ N,	050°06′ E
Riyadh (ar-Riyad)	24°38′ N,	046°43′ E
Sahwah	19°19′ N,	042°08′ E
Sakākah	29°59′ N,	040°12′ E
Shidād	21°19′ N,	040°03′ E
Tabūk	28°23′ N,	036°35′ E
Taymā'	27°38′ N,	038°29′ E
Turayf	31°41′ N,	038°39′ E
'Usfan	21°55′ N,	039°22′ E
Yanbu	24°05′ N,	038°03′ E
Zahrān	17°40′ N,	043°30′ E
Zalim	22°43′ N,	042°10′ E

SENEGAL ....pg. 148

Bakel	14°54′ N,	012°27′ W
Bignona	12°49′ N,	016°14′ W
Dagana	16°31′ N,	015°30′ W
Dakar	14°40′ N,	017°26′ W
Diourbel	14°40′ N,	016°15′ W
Fatick	14°20′ N,	016°25′ W
Joal	14°10′ N,	016°51′ W
Kaffrine	14°06′ N,	015°33′ W
Kaolack	14°09′ N,	016°04′ W
Kédougou	12°33′ N,	012°11′ W
Kolda	12°53′ N,	014°57′ W
Koungheul	13°59′ N,	014°48′ W
Linguère	15°24′ N,	015°07′ W
Louga	15°37′ N,	016°13′ W
Mbacké	14°48′ N,	015°55′ W
Mbour	14°24′ N,	016°58′ W
Mékhé	15°07′ N,	016°38′ W
Podor	16°40′ N,	014°57′ W
Richard-Toll	16°28′ N,	015°41′ W
Saint Louis	16°02′ N,	016°30′ W
Sédhiou	12°44′ N,	015°33′ W
Tambacounda	13°47′ N,	013°40′ W
Thiès	14°48′ N,	016°56′ W
Tivaouane	14°57′ N,	016°49′ W

Vélingara	13°09' N, 014°07' W
Ziguinchor	12°35' N, 016°16' W

SEYCHELLES . . . .pg. 149

Victoria	04°37' S, 055°27' E

SIERRA LEONE . .pg. 150

Bo	07°58' N, 011°45' W
Bonthe	07°32' N, 012°30' W
Freetown	08°30' N, 013°15' W
Kabala	09°35' N, 011°33' W
Kailahun	08°17' N, 010°34' W
Kambia	09°07' N, 012°55' W
Kenema	07°52' N, 011°12' W
Koidu-New Sembehun	08°38' N, 010°59' W
Lunsar	08°41' N, 012°32' W
Magburaka	08°43' N, 011°57' W
Makeni	08°53' N, 012°03' W
Mongeri	08°19' N, 011°44' W
Moyamba	08°10' N, 012°26' W
Pepel	08°35' N, 013°03' W
Port Loko	08°46' N, 012°47' W
Pujehun	07°21' N, 011°42' W
Sulima	06°58' N, 011°35' W

SINGAPORE . . . . .pg. 151

Singapore	01°16' N, 103°50' E

SLOVAKIA . . . . .pg. 152

Banská Bystrica	48°44' N, 019°09' E
Bardejov	49°17' N, 021°17' E
Bratislava	48°09' N, 017°07' E
Čadca	49°26' N, 018°47' E
Fil'akovo	48°16' N, 019°50' E
Humenné	48°56' N, 021°55' E
Komárno	47°46' N, 018°08' E
Košice	48°42' N, 021°15' E
Levice	48°13' N, 018°36' E
Liptovský Mikuláš	49°05' N, 019°37' E
Lučenec	48°20' N, 019°40' E
Martin	49°04' N, 018°56' E
Michalovce	48°45' N, 021°56' E
Nitra	48°19' N, 018°05' E
Nové Zámky	47°59' N, 018°10' E
Partizánske	48°38' N, 018°23' E
Piešťany	48°36' N, 017°50' E
Poprad	49°03' N, 020°18' E
Považská Bystrica	49°07' N, 018°27' E
Prešov	49°00' N, 021°15' E
Prievidza	48°46' N, 018°38' E
Rimavská Sobota	48°23' N, 020°02' E
Rožňava	48°40' N, 020°32' E
Skalica	48°51' N, 017°14' E
Spišská Nová Ves	48°57' N, 020°34' E
Topol'čany	48°34' N, 018°11' E
Trebišov	48°38' N, 021°43' E
Trenčín	48°54' N, 018°02' E
Trnava	48°22' N, 017°36' E
Žilina	49°13' N, 018°44' E
Zvolen	48°35' N, 019°08' E

SLOVENIA . . . . .pg. 153

Celje	46°14' N, 015°16' E
Hrastnik	46°09' N, 015°06' E
Idrija	46°00' N, 014°02' E
Javornik	46°14' N, 014°18' E
Jesenice	46°27' N, 014°04' E
Kočevje	45°39' N, 014°51' E
Koper	45°33' N, 013°44' E
Kranj	46°14' N, 014°22' E
Krško	45°58' N, 015°29' E
Ljubljana	46°02' N, 014°30' E
Maribor	46°33' N, 015°39' E
Murska Sobota	46°40' N, 016°10' E
Novo Mesto	45°48' N, 015°10' E
Postojna	45°47' N, 014°14' E
Ptuj	46°25' N, 015°52' E
Trbovlje	46°10' N, 015°03' E
Velenje	46°22' N, 015°07' E
Zagorje	46°08' N, 015°00' E

SOLOMON ISLANDS . . . . .pg. 154

Buala	08°08' S, 159°35' E
Honiara	09°26' S, 159°57' E
Kirakira	10°27' S, 161°55' E
Lata	10°44' S, 165°54' E
Maravovo	09°17' S, 159°38' E
Munda	08°19' S, 157°15' E
Sahalu	09°44' S, 160°31' E
Sasamungga	07°02' S, 156°47' E
Takwa	08°22' S, 160°48' E

SOMALIA . . . . .pg. 155

Baardheere (Bardera)	02°20' N, 042°17' E
Baraawe (Brava)	01°06' N, 044°03' E
Baydhabo (Baidoa)	03°07' N, 043°39' E
Beledweyne (Belet Uen)	04°45' N, 045°12' E
Berbera	10°25' N, 045°02' E
Boosaaso (Bender Cassim)	11°17' N, 049°11' E
Burao (Burco)	09°31' N, 045°32' E
Buulobarde (Bulo Burti)	03°51' N, 045°34' E
Eyl	07°58' N, 049°49' E
Hargeysa	09°35' N, 044°04' E
Hobyo (Obbia)	05°21' N, 048°32' E
Jamaame (Giamama or Jamame or Margherita)	00°04' N, 042°45' E

Jawhar (Giohar)	02°46' N, 045°31' E
Kismaayo (Chisimayu)	00°22' S, 042°32' E
Marka (Merca)	01°43' N, 044°53' E
Mogadishu (Mogadiscio or Mogadisho)	02°04' N, 045°22' E
Seylac (Zeila)	11°21' N, 043°29' E
Xaafun	10°25' N, 051°16' E

SOUTH AFRICA . . pg. 156

Bellville	33°54' S, 018°38' E
Bisho	32°53' S, 027°24' E
Bloemfontein	29°08' S, 026°10' E
Calvinia	31°28' S, 019°47' E
Cape Town (Kaapstad)	33°55' S, 018°25' E
Durban (Port Natal)	29°51' S, 031°01' E
East London	33°02' S, 027°55' E
George	33°58' S, 022°27' E
Germiston	26°13' S, 028°11' E
Hopefield	33°04' S, 018°21' E
Johannesburg	26°12' S, 028°05' E
Kimberley	28°45' S, 024°46' E
Klerksdorp	26°52' S, 026°40' E
Krugersdorp	26°06' S, 027°46' E
Kuruman	27°28' S, 023°26' E
Ladysmith	28°33' S, 029°47' E
Margate	30°51' S, 030°22' E
Newcastle	27°45' S, 029°56' E
Oudtshoorn	33°35' S, 022°12' E
Pietermaritzburg	29°37' S, 030°23' E
Port Elizabeth	33°58' S, 025°35' E
Port Nolloth	29°15' S, 016°52' E
Pretoria	25°45' S, 028°10' E
Queenstown	31°54' S, 026°53' E
Rustenburg	25°40' S, 027°15' E
Seshego	23°51' S, 029°23' E
Soweto	26°16' S, 027°52' E
Stellenbosch	33°46' S, 025°24' E
Uitenhage	28°27' S, 021°15' E
Upington	26°42' S, 027°49' E
Vanderbijlpark	27°59' S, 026°42' E
Welkom	27°59' S, 026°42' E
Worcester	33°39' S, 019°26' E

SOUTH KOREA . pg. 157

Andong	36°34' N, 128°44' E
Anyang	37°23' N, 126°55' E
Ch'ang won	35°16' N, 128°37' E
Cheju	33°31' N, 126°32' E
Chŏngju	36°38' N, 127°30' E
Chŏnju	35°49' N, 127°09' E
Ch'unch'ŏn	37°52' N, 127°44' E
Inch'ŏn	37°28' N, 126°38' E
Iri	35°56' N, 126°57' E
Kumi	36°08' N, 128°20' E
Kunsan	35°59' N, 126°43' E
Kwangju	35°10' N, 126°55' E
Kyŏngju	35°50' N, 129°13' E
Masan	35°11' N, 128°34' E

Mokp'o	34°47' N, 126°23' E
P'ohang	36°02' N, 129°22' E
Pusan	35°06' N, 129°03' E
Samch'ŏnp'o	34°55' N, 128°04' E
Seoul (Sŏul)	37°34' N, 127°00' E
Sŏsan	36°47' N, 126°27' E
Sunch'ŏn	34°57' N, 127°29' E
Suwŏn	37°16' N, 127°01' E
T'aebaek	37°10' N, 128°59' E
Taech'ŏn	36°21' N, 126°36' E
Taegu (Daegu or Taiku)	35°52' N, 128°35' E
Taejon	36°20' N, 127°26' E
Uijŏngbu	37°44' N, 127°02' E
Ulsan	35°33' N, 129°19' E
Wŏnju	37°21' N, 127°58' E

SPAIN . . . . pg. 158

Albacete	38°59' N, 001°51' W
Alcalá de Henares	40°29' N, 003°22' W
Algeciras	36°08' N, 005°30' W
Alicante (Alacant)	38°21' N, 000°29' W
Avilés	43°33' N, 005°55' W
Badajoz	38°53' N, 006°58' W
Barcelona	41°23' N, 002°11' E
Bilbao	43°15' N, 002°58' W
Burgos	42°21' N, 003°42' W
Cáceres	39°29' N, 006°22' W
Cádiz (Cadiz)	36°32' N, 006°18' W
Cartagena	37°36' N, 000°59' W
Castellón de la Plana	39°59' N, 000°02' W
Ciudad Real	38°59' N, 003°56' W
Cordova (Córdoba)	37°53' N, 004°46' W
Cuenca	40°04' N, 002°08' W
Elche (Elx)	38°15' N, 000°42' W
Ferrol (El Ferrol del Caudillo)	43°29' N, 008°14' W
Gernika-Lumo (Guernica y Luno)	43°19' N, 002°41' W
Getafe	40°18' N, 003°43' W
Gijón	43°32' N, 005°40' W
Granada	37°11' N, 003°36' W
Huelva	37°16' N, 006°57' W
Jaén	37°46' N, 003°47' W
La Coruña (A Coruña)	43°22' N, 008°23' W
León	42°36' N, 005°34' W
Lérida (Lleida)	41°37' N, 000°37' E
L'Hospitalet de Llobregat	41°22' N, 002°08' E
Logroño	42°28' N, 002°27' W
Lugo	43°00' N, 007°34' W
Madrid	40°24' N, 003°41' W
Málaga	36°43' N, 004°25' W
Mérida	38°55' N, 006°20' W
Murcia	37°59' N, 001°07' W
Palencia	42°01' N, 004°32' W
Pamplona (Iruña)	42°49' N, 001°38' W
Salamanca	40°58' N, 005°39' W
San Fernando	36°28' N, 006°12' W
Santander	43°28' N, 003°48' W

Santiago
de Compostela........ 42°53′ N, 008°33′ W
Saragossa (Zaragoza)... 41°38′ N, 000°53′ W
Segovia .... 40°57′ N, 004°07′ W
Seville (Sevilla) .... 37°23′ N, 005°59′ W
Soria .... 41°46′ N, 002°28′ W
Tarragona .... 41°07′ N, 001°15′ E
Terrassa (Tarrasa) ..... 41°34′ N, 002°01′ E
Teruel .... 40°21′ N, 001°06′ W
Toledo .... 39°52′ N, 004°01′ W
Valencia............. 39°28′ N, 000°22′ W
Valladolid .... 41°39′ N, 004°43′ W
Vigo .... 42°14′ N, 008°43′ W
Vitoria (Gasteiz) ...... 42°51′ N, 002°40′ W

SRI LANKA . . . . . pg. 159

Ambalangoda .... 06°14′ N, 080°03′ E
Anuradhapura. .... 08°21′ N, 080°23′ E
Badulla .... 06°59′ N, 081°03′ E
Batticaloa .... 07°43′ N, 081°42′ E
Beruwala .... 06°29′ N, 079°59′ E
Chavakachcheri .... 09°39′ N, 080°09′ E
Colombo .... 06°56′ N, 079°51′ E
Dehiwala–
Mount Lavinia .... 06°51′ N, 079°52′ E
Eravur .... 07°46′ N, 081°36′ E
Galle................ 06°02′ N, 080°13′ E
Gampola .... 07°10′ N, 080°34′ E
Hambantota .... 06°07′ N, 081°07′ E
Jaffna .... 09°40′ N, 080°00′ E
Kalutara .... 06°35′ N, 079°58′ E
Kandy .... 07°18′ N, 080°38′ E
Kankesanturai .... 09°49′ N, 080°02′ E
Kegalla .... 07°15′ N, 080°21′ E
Kilinochchi .... 09°24′ N, 080°24′ E
Kotte .... 06°54′ N, 079°54′ E
Kurunegala .... 07°30′ N, 080°22′ E
Madampe .... 07°30′ N, 079°50′ E
Mannar .... 08°59′ N, 079°54′ E
Moratuwa .... 06°46′ N, 079°53′ E
Mullaittivu .... 09°16′ N, 080°49′ E
Mutur................ 08°27′ N, 081°16′ E
Negombo .... 07°13′ N, 079°50′ E
Nuwara Eliya .... 06°58′ N, 080°46′ E
Point Pedro .... 09°50′ N, 080°14′ E
Polonnaruwa .... 07°56′ N, 081°00′ E
Puttalam .... 08°02′ N, 079°49′ E
Ratnapura .... 06°41′ N, 080°24′ E
Tangalla.............. 06°01′ N, 080°48′ E
Trincomalee .... 08°34′ N, 081°14′ E
Vavuniya .... 08°45′ N, 080°30′ E
Watugedara .... 06°15′ N, 080°03′ E
Weligama............. 05°58′ N, 080°25′ E
Yala .... 06°22′ N, 081°31′ E

SUDAN . . . . pg. 160

Ad-Damazin
(Ed–Damazin) .... 11°46′ N, 034°21′ E

Ad-Dāmir .... 17°35′ N, 033°58′ E
Ad-Duwaym
(Ed-Dueim)......... 14°00′ N, 032°19′ E
Al-Fūlah .... 11°48′ N, 028°24′ E
Al-Fashir (El Fasher) ... 13°38′ N, 025°21′ E
Al-Junaynah (Geneina) .. 13°27′ N, 022°27′ E
Al-Mijlad .... 11°02′ N, 027°44′ E
Al-Qadārif (Gedaref) ... 14°02′ N, 035°24′ E
Al-Ubbayid (El-Obeid) .. 13°11′ N, 030°13′ E
An-Nuhūd (An-Nahūd) .. 12°42′ N, 028°26′ E
ʿAṭbarah .... 17°42′ N, 033°59′ E
Bor................. 06°12′ N, 031°33′ E
Dunqulah (Dongola) .... 19°10′ N, 030°29′ E
Juba .... 04°51′ N, 031°37′ E
Kāduqlī .... 11°01′ N, 029°43′ E
Kas................. 12°30′ N, 024°17′ E
Kassalā .... 15°28′ N, 036°24′ E
Khartoum .... 15°36′ N, 032°32′ E
Khartoum North .... 15°38′ N, 032°33′ E
Kūstī .... 13°10′ N, 032°40′ E
Malakāl .... 09°31′ N, 031°39′ E
Marawi.............. 18°29′ N, 031°49′ E
Nagichot .... 04°16′ N, 033°34′ E
Nāṣir .... 08°36′ N, 033°04′ E
Nyala .... 12°03′ N, 024°53′ E
Omdurman .... 15°38′ N, 032°30′ E
Port Sudan .... 19°37′ N, 037°14′ E
Rumbek .... 06°48′ N, 029°41′ E
Sannār .... 13°33′ N, 033°38′ E
Sawākin .... 19°07′ N, 037°20′ E
Shandi .... 16°42′ N, 033°26′ E
Wadi Halfaʿ .... 21°48′ N, 031°21′ E
Wad Madanī .... 14°24′ N, 033°32′ E
Wāw (Wau) .... 07°42′ N, 028°00′ E

SURINAME . . . . . pg. 161

Albina .... 05°30′ N, 054°03′ W
Benzdorp............. 03°41′ N, 054°05′ W
Bitagron .... 05°10′ N, 056°06′ W
Brokopondo .... 05°04′ N, 054°58′ W
Brownsweg .... 05°01′ N, 055°10′ W
Goddo .... 04°01′ N, 055°28′ W
Groningen .... 05°48′ N, 055°28′ W
Meerzorg .... 05°49′ N, 055°09′ W
Nieuw Amsterdam ..... 05°53′ N, 055°05′ W
Nieuw Nickerie .... 05°57′ N, 056°59′ W
Onverwacht........... 05°36′ N, 055°12′ W
Paramaribo .... 05°50′ N, 055°10′ W
Totness .... 05°53′ N, 056°19′ W
Zanderij .... 05°27′ N, 055°12′ W

SWAZILAND . . . . . pg. 162

Hlatikulu .... 26°58′ S, 031°19′ E
Kadake............... 26°13′ S, 031°02′ E
Manzini (Bremersdorp) . 26°29′ S, 031°22′ E
Mbabane .... 26°19′ S, 031°08′ E
Nhlangono............ 27°07′ S, 031°12′ E
Piggs Peak .... 25°58′ S, 031°15′ E

Siteki (Stegi) . . . . 26°27′ S, 031°57′ E

SWEDEN . . . . .pg. 163

Älvsbyn . . . . 65°40′ N, 021°00′ E
Falun . . . . 60°36′ N, 015°38′ E
Gävle . . . . 60°40′ N, 017°10′ E
Göteborg . . . . 57°43′ N, 011°58′ E
Halmstad . . . . 56°39′ N, 012°50′ E
Haparanda . . . . 65°50′ N, 024°10′ E
Hudiksvall . . . . 61°44′ N, 017°07′ E
Jönköping . . . . 57°47′ N, 014°11′ E
Karlskrona . . . . 56°10′ N, 015°35′ E
Karlstad . . . . 59°22′ N, 013°30′ E
Kiruna . . . . 67°51′ N, 020°13′ E
Kristianstad . . . . 56°02′ N, 014°08′ E
Linköping . . . . 58°25′ N, 015°37′ E
Luleå . . . . 65°34′ N, 022°10′ E
Lycksele . . . . 64°36′ N, 018°40′ E
Malmberget . . . . 67°10′ N, 020°40′ E
Malmö . . . . 55°36′ N, 013°00′ E
Mariestad . . . . 58°43′ N, 013°51′ E
Mora . . . . 61°00′ N, 014°33′ E
Örebro . . . . 59°17′ N, 015°13′ E
Örnsköldsvik . . . . 63°18′ N, 018°43′ E
Östersund . . . . 63°11′ N, 014°39′ E
Piteå . . . . 65°20′ N, 021°30′ E
Skellefteå . . . . 64°46′ N, 020°57′ E
Söderhamn . . . . 61°18′ N, 017°03′ E
Stockholm . . . . 59°20′ N, 018°03′ E
Strömsund . . . . 63°51′ N, 015°35′ E
Sundsvall . . . . 62°23′ N, 017°18′ E
Umeå . . . . 63°50′ N, 020°15′ E
Uppsala . . . . 59°52′ N, 017°38′ E
Vänersborg . . . . 58°22′ N, 012°19′ E
Västerås . . . . 59°37′ N, 016°33′ E
Växjö . . . . 56°53′ N, 014°49′ E
Vetanlda . . . . 57°26′ N, 015°04′ E
Visby . . . . 57°38′ N, 018°18′ E
Ystad . . . . 55°25′ N, 013°49′ E

SWITZERLAND .pg. 164

Aarau . . . . 47°23′ N, 008°03′ E
Altdorf . . . . 46°53′ N, 008°39′ E
Arbon . . . . 47°31′ N, 009°26′ E
Appenzell . . . . 47°20′ N, 009°24′ E
Arosa . . . . 46°47′ N, 009°40′ E
Baden . . . . 47°28′ N, 008°18′ E
Basel . . . . 47°35′ N, 007°32′ E
Bellinzona . . . . 46°12′ N, 009°01′ E
Bern . . . . 46°55′ N, 007°28′ E
Biel (Bienne) . . . . 47°10′ N, 007°15′ E
Chur (Coire) . . . . 46°51′ N, 009°30′ E
Davos . . . . 46°49′ N, 009°50′ E
Delémont . . . . 47°22′ N, 007°20′ E
Frauenfeld . . . . 47°33′ N, 008°54′ E
Fribourg (Freiburg) . . . . . 46°48′ N, 007°09′ E
Geneva . . . . 46°12′ N, 006°10′ E
Glarus . . . . 47°02′ N, 009°04′ E

Grindelwald . . . . 46°37′ N, 008°03′ E
Gstaad . . . . 46°28′ N, 007°17′ E
Herisau . . . . 47°24′ N, 009°16′ E
Interlaken . . . . 46°41′ N, 007°51′ E
La Chaux-de-Fonds . . . . . 47°08′ N, 006°51′ E
Lausanne . . . . 46°32′ N, 006°40′ E
Liestal . . . . 47°28′ N, 007°44′ E
Locarno (Luggarus) . . . . . 46°10′ N, 008°48′ E
Lucerne (Luzern) . . . . 47°05′ N, 008°16′ E
Lugano (Lauis) . . . . 46°00′ N, 008°58′ E
Montreux . . . . 46°26′ N, 006°55′ E
Neuchatel (Neuenburg) . . 47°00′ N, 006°58′ E
Saint Gall
(Sankt Gallen) . . . . 47°28′ N, 009°24′ E
Saint Moritz
(San Murezzan,
Saint-Moritz,
or Sankt Moritz) . . . . . . 46°30′ N, 009°50′ E
Sarnen . . . . 46°54′ N, 008°14′ E
Schaffhausen . . . . 47°42′ N, 008°38′ E
Sion (Sitten) . . . . 46°14′ N, 007°21′ E
Solothurn (Soleure) . . . . . 47°14′ N, 007°31′ E
Stans . . . . 46°58′ N, 008°21′ E
Thun (Thoune) . . . . 46°45′ N, 007°37′ E
Vevey . . . . 46°27′ N, 006°51′ E
Winterthur . . . . 47°30′ N, 008°45′ E
Zermatt . . . . 46°01′ N, 007°45′ E
Zug . . . . 47°10′ N, 008°31′ E
Zürich . . . . 47°22′ N, 008°33′ E

SYRIA . . . . .pg. 165

Al-Bāb . . . . 36°22′ N, 037°31′ E
Al-Hasakah . . . . 36°29′ N, 040°45′ E
Al-Mayādin . . . . 35°01′ N, 040°27′ E
Al-Qāmishli
(Al-Kamishly) . . . . 37°02′ N, 041°14′ E
Aleppo (Ḥalab) . . . . 36°12′ N, 037°10′ E
Ar-Raqqah (Rakka) . . . . . 35°57′ N, 039°01′ E
As-Safirah . . . . 36°04′ N, 037°22′ E
As-Suwaydā′ . . . . 32°42′ N, 036°34′ E
A′zāz (I′zaz) . . . . 36°35′ N, 037°03′ E
Damascus . . . . 33°30′ N, 036°18′ E
Dar′ā . . . . 32°37′ N, 036°06′ E
Dayr az-Zawr . . . . 35°20′ N, 040°09′ E
Dūmā (Douma) . . . . 33°35′ N, 036°24′ E
Ḥamāh (Hama) . . . . 35°08′ N, 036°45′ E
Ḥimṣ (Homs) . . . . 34°44′ N, 036°43′ E
Idlib . . . . 35°55′ N, 036°38′ E
Jablah (Jableh) . . . . 35°21′ N, 035°55′ E
Jarābulus . . . . 36°49′ N, 038°01′ E
Latakia (Al-Lādhiqīyah) . . 35°31′ N, 035°47′ E
Ma′arrat an-Nu′mān . . . . 35°38′ N, 036°40′ E
Ma′lūlā . . . . 33°50′ N, 036°33′ E
Manbij (Manbej) . . . . 36°31′ N, 037°57′ E
Mukharram al-Fawqānī . . 34°49′ N, 037°05′ E
Ra′s al-′Ayn . . . . 36°51′ N, 040°04′ E
Salamīyah . . . . 35°01′ N, 037°03′ E
Tadmur . . . . 34°33′ N, 038°17′ E
Ṭarṭūs . . . . 34°53′ N, 035°53′ E

TAIWAN . . . . pg. 166

Chang-hua	24°05′ N, 120°32′ E
Ch'ao-chou	22°33′ N, 120°32′ E
Ch'e-ch'eng	22°05′ N, 120°42′ E
Chia-i	23°29′ N, 120°27′ E
Ch'ih-shang	23°07′ N, 121°12′ E
Chi-lung	25°08′ N, 121°44′ E
Chung-hsing Hsin-ts'un . . .	23°57′ N, 120°41′ E
Chu-tung	24°44′ N, 121°05′ E
Erh-lin	23°54′ N, 120°22′ E
Feng-lin	23°45′ N, 121°26′ E
Feng-shan	22°38′ N, 120°21′ E
Feng-yüan	24°15′ N, 120°43′ E
Hsin-chu	24°48′ N, 120°58′ E
Hsin-ying	23°18′ N, 120°19′ E
Hua-lien	23°59′ N, 121°36′ E
I-lan	24°46′ N, 121°45′ E
Kang-shan	22°48′ N, 120°17′ E
Kao-hsiung	22°38′ N, 120°17′ E
Lan-yü	22°02′ N, 121°33′ E
Lo-tung	24°41′ N, 121°46′ E
Lu-kang	24°03′ N, 120°25′ E
Lü-tao	22°40′ N, 121°28′ E
Miao-li	24°34′ N, 120°49′ E
Nan-t'ou	23°55′ N, 120°41′ E
Pan-ch'iao	25°01′ N, 121°27′ E
P'ing-tung	22°40′ N, 120°29′ E
San-ch'ung	25°04′ N, 121°30′ E
Su-ao	24°36′ N, 121°51′ E
T'ai-chung	24°09′ N, 120°41′ E
T'ai-nan	23°00′ N, 120°12′ E
Taipei (T'ai-pei)	25°03′ N, 121°30′ E
T'ai-tung	22°45′ N, 121°09′ E
T'ao-yüan	25°00′ N, 121°18′ E
Tung-ho	22°58′ N, 121°18′ E
Yüan-lin	23°58′ N, 120°34′ E
Yung-k'ang	23°02′ N, 120°15′ E

TAJIKISTAN . . . . . pg. 167

Dushanbe	38°33′ N, 068°48′ E
Kalininobod	37°52′ N, 068°55′ E
Khorugh	37°30′ N, 071°36′ E
Khujand (Leninabad, or	
Khojand)	40°17′ N, 069°37′ E
Kofarniqon	
(Ordzhonikidzeābad) . . .	38°34′ N, 069°01′ E
Kŭlob	37°55′ N, 069°46′ E
Norak	38°23′ N, 069°21′ E
Qayroqqum	40°16′ N, 069°49′ E
Qŭrghonteppa	37°50′ N, 068°47′ E
Uroteppa	39°55′ N, 069°01′ E

TANZANIA . . . . . pg. 168

Arusha	03°22′ S, 036°41′ E
Bagamoyo	06°26′ S, 038°54′ E
Bukoba	01°20′ S, 031°49′ E

Chake Chake	05°15′ S, 039°46′ E
Dar es Salaam	06°48′ S, 039°17′ E
Dodoma	06°11′ S, 035°45′ E
Ifakara	08°08′ S, 036°41′ E
Iringa	07°46′ S, 035°42′ E
Kigoma	04°52′ S, 029°38′ E
Korogwe	05°09′ S, 038°29′ E
Lindi	10°00′ S, 039°43′ E
Mbeya	08°54′ S, 033°27′ E
Mkoani	05°22′ S, 039°39′ E
Morogoro	06°49′ S, 037°40′ E
Moshi	03°21′ S, 037°20′ E
Mpwapwa	06°21′ S, 036°29′ E
Mtwara	10°16′ S, 040°11′ E
Musoma	01°30′ S, 033°48′ E
Mwanza	02°31′ S, 032°54′ E
Newala	10°56′ S, 039°18′ E
Pangani	09°32′ S, 035°31′ E
Shinyanga	03°40′ S, 033°26′ E
Singida	04°49′ S, 034°45′ E
Songea	10°41′ S, 035°39′ E
Sumbawanga	07°58′ S, 031°37′ E
Tabora	05°01′ S, 032°48′ E
Tanga	05°04′ S, 039°06′ E
Tunduru	11°07′ S, 037°21′ E
Wete	05°04′ S, 039°43′ E
Zanzibar	06°10′ S, 039°11′ E

THAILAND . . . . . . pg. 169

Bangkok (Krung Thep)	13°45′ N, 100°31′ E
Chanthaburi	
(Chantabun)	12°36′ N, 102°09′ E
Chiang Mai (Chiengmai) . .	18°47′ N, 098°59′ E
Chon Buri	13°22′ N, 100°59′ E
Hat Yai (Haad Yai)	07°01′ N, 100°28′ E
Khon Kaen	16°26′ N, 102°50′ E
Mae Sot	16°43′ N, 098°34′ E
Nakhon Phanom	17°24′ N, 104°47′ E
Nakhon Ratchasima	
(Khorat)	14°58′ N, 102°07′ E
Nakhon Sawan	15°41′ N, 100°07′ E
Nakhon Si Thammarat	08°26′ N, 099°58′ E
Nan	18°47′ N, 100°47′ E
Nong Khai	17°52′ N, 102°44′ E
Nonthaburi	13°50′ N, 100°29′ E
Pathum Thani	14°01′ N, 100°32′ E
Pattaya	12°54′ N, 100°51′ E
Phichit	16°26′ N, 100°22′ E
Phitsanulok	16°50′ N, 100°15′ E
Phra Nakhon Si Ayutthaya	
(Ayutthaya)	14°21′ N, 100°33′ E
Phuket	07°53′ N, 098°24′ E
Roi Et	16°03′ N, 103°40′ E
Sakon Nakhon	17°10′ N, 104°09′ E
Samut Prakan	13°36′ N, 100°36′ E
Samut Sakhon	
(Samut Sakorn)	13°32′ N, 100°17′ E
Sara Buri	14°32′ N, 100°55′ E
Trang	07°33′ N, 099°36′ E
Trat	12°14′ N, 102°30′ E

Ubon Ratchathani. . . . . 15°14' N, 104°54' E
Udon Thani . . . . 17°26' N, 102°46' E
Uthai Thani . . . . 15°22' N, 100°03' E
Yala . . . . 06°33' N, 101°18' E

TOGO . . . . .pg. 170

Aného . . . . 06°14' N, 001°36' E
Atakpamé . . . . 07°32' N, 001°08' E
Bassar . . . . 09°15' N, 000°47' E
Blitta . . . . 08°19' N, 000°59' E
Dapaong . . . . 10°52' N, 000°12' E
Kara (Lama Kara) . . . . 09°33' N, 001°12' E
Lomé . . . . 06°08' N, 001°13' E
Palimé . . . . 09°21' N, 002°37' E
Sokodé . . . . 08°59' N, 001°08' E
Tsévié . . . . 06°25' N, 001°13' E

TONGA . . . . .pg. 171

Nuku'alofa . . . . 21°08' N, 175°12' E

TRINIDAD AND TOBAGO . . . . . . .pg. 172

Arima . . . . 10°38' N, 061°17' W
Arouca . . . . 10°38' N, 061°20' W
Chaguanas . . . . 10°31' N, 061°25' W
Charlotteville . . . . 11°19' N, 060°33' W
Couva . . . . 10°25' N, 061°27' W
Point Fortin . . . . 10°11' N, 061°41' W
Port of Spain . . . . 10°39' N, 061°31' W
Princes Town . . . . 10°16' N, 061°23' W
Rio Claro . . . . 10°18' N, 061°11' W
Roxborough . . . . 11°15' N, 060°35' W
San Fernando . . . . 10°17' N, 061°28' W
Sangre Grande . . . . 10°35' N, 061°07' W
Scarborough . . . . 11°11' N, 060°44' W
Siparia . . . . 10°08' N, 061°30' W
Tunapuna . . . . 10°38' N, 061°23' W

TUNISIA . . . . .pg. 173

Al-Ḥammāmāt
  (Hammamet) . . . . 36°24' N, 010°37' E
Al-Mahdīyah (Mahdia) . . . . 35°30' N, 011°04' E
Al-Metlaoui . . . . 34°20' N, 008°24' E
Al-Muknīn (Moknine) . . . . 35°38' N, 010°54' E
Al-Munastīr (Monastir or
  Ruspina) . . . . 35°47' N, 010°50' E
Al-Qaṣrayn (Kasserine) . . . 35°11' N, 008°48' E
Al-Qayrawān (Kairouan
  or Qairouan) . . . . 35°41' N, 010°07' E
Bājah (Béja) . . . . 36°44' N, 009°11' E
Banzart (Bizerte) . . . . 37°17' N, 009°52' E
Ḥammām al-Anf
  (Hammam-lif) . . . . 36°44' N, 010°20' E
Jarjīs (Zarzis) . . . . 33°30' N, 011°07' E

Madanīn (Medenine) . . . . . 33°21' N, 010°30' E
Makthar . . . . 35°51' N, 009°12' E
Manzil Bū Ruqaybah
  (Ferryville or Menzel-
  Bourguiba) . . . . 37°10' N, 009°48' E
Nābul (Nabeul or
  Neapolis) . . . . 36°27' N, 010°44' E
Naftah (Nefta) . . . . 33°52' N, 007°53' E
Qābis
  (Gabes or Tacape) . . . . . . 33°53' N, 010°07' E
Qafṣah (Gafsa) . . . . 34°25' N, 008°48' E
Qiblī (Kebili) . . . . 33°42' N, 008°58' E
Safāqis (Sfax) . . . . 34°44' N, 010°46' E
Sūsah
  (Sousa or Sousse) . . . . . . 35°49' N, 010°38' E
Tawzar (Tozeur) . . . . 33°55' N, 008°08' E
Tunis (Tunis) . . . . 36°48' N, 010°11' E
Zaghwān (Zaghouan) . . . . . 36°24' N, 010°09' E

TURKEY . . . . .pg. 174

Adana . . . . 37°01' N, 035°18' E
Afyon . . . . 38°45' N, 030°33' E
Amasya . . . . 40°39' N, 035°51' E
Ankara (Angora) . . . . 39°56' N, 032°52' E
Antakya (Antioch) . . . . 36°14' N, 036°07' E
Antalya
  (Attalia or Hatay) . . . . . . 36°53' N, 030°42' E
Artvin . . . . 41°11' N, 041°49' E
Aydın . . . . 37°51' N, 027°51' E
Balıkesir. . . . . 39°39' N, 027°53' E
Bandırma (Panderma) . . . . . 40°20' N, 027°58' E
Batman . . . . 37°52' N, 041°07' E
Bursa (Brusa) . . . . 40°11' N, 029°04' E
Çorum . . . . 40°33' N, 034°58' E
Denizli . . . . 37°46' N, 029°06' E
Diyarbakır (Amida) . . . . 37°55' N, 040°14' E
Elâzığ . . . . 38°41' N, 039°14' E
Erzincan . . . . 39°44' N, 039°29' E
Erzurum . . . . 39°55' N, 041°17' E
Eskişehir . . . . 39°46' N, 030°32' E
Gaziantep . . . . 37°05' N, 037°22' E
Iğdır . . . . 39°56' N, 044°02' E
İskenderun
  (Alexandretta) . . . . 36°35' N, 036°10' E
Isparta (Hamid-Abad) . . . . . 37°46' N, 030°33' E
Istanbul
  (Constantinople) . . . . 41°01' N, 028°58' E
İzmir (Smyrna) . . . . 38°25' N, 027°09' E
İzmit. . . . . 40°46' N, 029°55' E
Kahramanmaraş
  (Maraş) . . . . 37°36' N, 036°55' E
Karabük . . . . 41°12' N, 032°37' E
Karaman . . . . 37°11' N, 033°14' E
Kars . . . . 40°37' N, 043°05' E
Kayseri (Caesarea) . . . . 38°43' N, 035°30' E
Kırıkkale . . . . 39°50' N, 033°31' E
Konya (Iconium) . . . . 37°52' N, 032°31' E
Kütahya . . . . 39°25' N, 029°59' E
Manisa . . . . 38°36' N, 027°26' E
Mardin . . . . 37°18' N, 040°44' E

Mersin	36°48′ N, 034°38′ E
Muğla	37°12′ N, 028°22′ E
Nevşehir	38°38′ N, 034°43′ E
Niğde	37°59′ N, 034°42′ E
Ordu	41°00′ N, 037°53′ E
Samsun (Amisus)	41°17′ N, 036°20′ E
Sinop	42°01′ N, 035°09′ E
Sivas (Sebastia)	39°45′ N, 037°02′ E
Trabzon (Trapezus or Trebizond)	41°00′ N, 039°43′ E
Urfa	37°08′ N, 038°46′ E
Uşak (Ushak)	38°41′ N, 029°25′ E
Van	38°30′ N, 043°23′ E
Yalova	40°39′ N, 029°15′ E
Yozgat	39°50′ N, 034°48′ E
Zonguldak	41°27′ N, 031°49′ E

TURKMENISTAN pg. 175

Ashgabat (Ashkhabad)	37°57′ N, 058°23′ E
Bayramaly	37°37′ N, 062°10′ E
Büzmeyin	38°05′ N, 058°12′ E
Chärjew	39°06′ N, 063°34′ E
Cheleken	39°26′ N, 053°07′ E
Chirchiq	41°29′ N, 069°35′ E
Dashhowuz	41°50′ N, 059°58′ E
Gowurdak	37°50′ N, 066°04′ E
Kerki	37°50′ N, 065°12′ E
Mary (Merv)	37°36′ N, 061°50′ E
Nebitdag	39°30′ N, 054°22′ E
Türkmenbashy (Krasnovodsk)	40°00′ N, 053°00′ E
Yolöten	37°18′ N, 062°21′ E

TUVALU . . . . pg. 176

Fongafale	08°31′ S, 179°13′ E

UGANDA . . . . pg. 177

Entebbe	00°04′ N, 032°28′ E
Gulu	02°47′ N, 032°18′ E
Jinja	00°26′ N, 033°12′ E
Kabarole	00°39′ N, 030°16′ E
Kampala	00°19′ N, 032°35′ E
Masaka	00°20′ S, 031°44′ E
Mbale	01°05′ N, 034°10′ E
Soroti	01°43′ N, 033°37′ E
Tororo	00°42′ N, 034°11′ E

UKRAINE . . . . pg. 178

Alchevsk	48°30′ N, 038°47′ E
Berdyansk	46°45′ N, 036°47′ E
Berdychiv	49°54′ N, 028°35′ E
Bila Tserkva	49°47′ N, 030°07′ E
Cherkasy	49°26′ N, 032°04′ E

Chernihiv	51°30′ N, 031°18′ E
Chernivtsi	48°18′ N, 025°56′ E
Chornobyl (Chernobyl)	51°16′ N, 030°14′ E
Dnipropetrovs′k	48°27′ N, 034°59′ E
Donetsk	48°00′ N, 037°48′ E
Kerch	45°21′ N, 036°28′ E
Kharkiv	50°00′ N, 036°15′ E
Khmelnytskyy	49°25′ N, 027°00′ E
Kiev (Kyyiv)	50°26′ N, 030°31′ E
Korosten	50°57′ N, 028°39′ E
Kovel	51°13′ N, 024°43′ E
Krasny Luch	48°08′ N, 038°56′ E
Kryvyy Rih	47°55′ N, 033°21′ E
Luhansk	48°34′ N, 039°20′ E
Lutsk	50°45′ N, 025°20′ E
Lviv	49°50′ N, 024°00′ E
Makiyivka	48°02′ N, 037°58′ E
Marhanets	47°38′ N, 034°38′ E
Mariupol	47°06′ N, 037°33′ E
Melitopol	46°50′ N, 035°22′ E
Mykolayiv	46°58′ N, 032°00′ E
Myrhorod	49°58′ N, 033°36′ E
Novhorod-Siverskyy	52°00′ N, 033°16′ E
Odessa	46°28′ N, 030°44′ E
Pavlograd	48°31′ N, 035°52′ E
Poltava	49°35′ N, 034°34′ E
Pryluky	50°36′ N, 032°24′ E
Rivne	50°37′ N, 026°15′ E
Rubizhne	49°01′ N, 038°23′ E
Sevastopol	44°36′ N, 033°32′ E
Shostka	51°52′ N, 033°29′ E
Simferopol	44°57′ N, 034°06′ E
Sumy	50°54′ N, 034°48′ E
Syeverodonets′k	48°58′ N, 038°26′ E
Uzhhorod	48°37′ N, 022°18′ E
Vinnytsya	49°14′ N, 028°29′ E
Voznesensk	47°33′ N, 031°20′ E
Yevpatoriya	45°12′ N, 033°22′ E
Zaporizhzhya	47°49′ N, 035°11′ E
Zhytomyr	50°15′ N, 028°40′ E

UNITED ARAB EMIRATES . . . . . . pg. 179

Abu Dhabi	24°28′ N, 054°22′ E
ʿAjmān	25°25′ N, 055°27′ E
Al-ʿAyn	24°13′ N, 055°46′ E
Al-Fujayrah	25°08′ N, 056°21′ E
Al-Khīs	23°00′ N, 054°12′ E
Al-Māriyah	23°08′ N, 053°44′ E
ʿArādah	22°59′ N, 053°26′ E
Ash-Shāriqah	25°22′ N, 055°23′ E
Diqdāqah	25°40′ N, 055°58′ E
Dubayy	25°16′ N, 055°18′ E
Kalbā	025°05′ N, 056°22′ E
Khawr Fakkān	25°21′ N, 056°22′ E
Ra′s Al-Khaymah	25°47′ N, 055°57′ E
Tarīf	24°03′ N, 053°46′ E
Umm Al-Qaywayn	25°35′ N, 055°34′ E
Wadhīl	23°03′ N, 054°08′ E

UNITED KINGDOM . . . . . pg. 180-1

Aberdeen	57°09′ N, 002°08′ W
Barrow-in-Furness	54°07′ N, 003°14′ W
Bath	51°23′ N, 002°22′ W
Belfast	54°35′ N, 005°56′ W
Birmingham	52°29′ N, 001°51′ W
Bradford	53°47′ N, 001°45′ W
Bristol	51°26′ N, 002°35′ W
Cambridge	52°12′ N, 000°09′ E
Cardiff	51°29′ N, 003°11′ W
Carlisle	54°53′ N, 002°57′ W
Cheltenham	51°54′ N, 002°05′ W
Colchester	51°54′ N, 000°54′ E
Coventry	52°24′ N, 001°31′ W
Darlington	54°32′ N, 001°34′ W
Dartford	51°26′ N, 000°12′ W
Derby	52°55′ N, 001°28′ W
Derry (Londonderry)	55°00′ N, 007°20′ W
Dundee	56°29′ N, 003°02′ W
Dunfermline	56°04′ N, 003°26′ W
Eastbourne	50°47′ N, 000°16′ E
Edinburgh	55°57′ N, 003°10′ W
Exeter	50°43′ N, 003°31′ W
Glasgow	55°52′ N, 004°15′ W
Great Yarmouth	52°36′ N, 001°44′ E
Grimsby	53°34′ N, 000°05′ W
Hamilton	55°47′ N, 004°02′ W
Harrogate	54°00′ N, 001°32′ W
Hartlepool	54°41′ N, 001°13′ W
Hastings	50°52′ N, 000°35′ E
High Wycombe	51°38′ N, 000°45′ W
Hove	50°50′ N, 000°11′ W
Ipswich	52°03′ N, 001°09′ E
Kilmarnock	55°36′ N, 004°30′ W
King's Lynn	52°45′ N, 000°24′ E
Kingston upon Hull	53°45′ N, 000°20′ W
Leeds	53°48′ N, 001°32′ W
Leicester	52°38′ N, 001°08′ W
Lincoln	53°14′ N, 000°32′ W
Liverpool	53°25′ N, 002°57′ W
London	51°30′ N, 000°07′ W
Lowestoft	52°28′ N, 001°45′ E
Maidstone	51°16′ N, 000°32′ E
Manchester	53°29′ N, 002°15′ W
Margate	51°23′ N, 001°23′ E
Newcastle upon Tyne	54°58′ N, 001°36′ W
Newtownabbey	54°40′ N, 005°57′ W
Norwich	52°38′ N, 001°18′ E
Nottingham	52°58′ N, 001°10′ W
Paisley	55°50′ N, 004°25′ W
Peterborough	52°35′ N, 000°14′ W
Plymouth	50°23′ N, 004°09′ W
Poole	50°43′ N, 001°59′ W
Portsmouth	50°49′ N, 001°04′ W
Rhondda	51°39′ N, 003°29′ W
Royal Tunbridge Wells	51°08′ N, 000°16′ E
Sheffield	53°23′ N, 001°28′ W
South Shields	54°59′ N, 001°26′ W
Southampton	50°55′ N, 001°24′ W
Staines	51°26′ N, 000°30′ W
Stevenage	51°54′ N, 000°12′ W
Stoke-on-Trent	53°01′ N, 002°11′ W
Swansea	51°38′ N, 003°58′ W
Torquay	50°29′ N, 003°32′ W
Walsall	52°35′ N, 001°59′ W
Warrington	53°24′ N, 002°36′ W
York	53°57′ N, 001°06′ W

UNITED STATES
. . . . pg. 182-3

Aberdeen, S.D.	45°28′ N, 098°29′ W
Aberdeen, Wash.	46°59′ N, 123°50′ W
Abilene, Kan.	38°55′ N, 097°13′ W
Abilene, Tex.	32°28′ N, 099°43′ W
Ada, Okla.	34°46′ N, 096°41′ W
Akron, Ohio	41°05′ N, 081°31′ W
Alamogordo, N.M.	32°54′ N, 105°57′ W
Alamosa, Colo.	37°28′ N, 105°52′ W
Albany, Ga.	31°35′ N, 084°10′ W
Albany, N.Y.	42°39′ N, 073°45′ W
Albuquerque, N.M.	35°05′ N, 106°39′ W
Alexandria, La.	31°18′ N, 092°27′ W
Alexandria, Va.	38°48′ N, 077°03′ W
Alliance, Neb.	42°06′ N, 102°52′ W
Alpena, Mich.	45°04′ N, 083°27′ W
Alton, Ill.	38°53′ N, 090°11′ W
Alturas, Calif.	41°29′ N, 120°32′ W
Altus, Okla.	34°38′ N, 099°20′ W
Amarillo, Tex.	35°13′ N, 101°50′ W
Americus, Ga.	32°04′ N, 084°14′ W
Anaconda, Mont.	46°08′ N, 112°57′ W
Anchorage, Alaska	61°13′ N, 149°54′ W
Andalusia, Ala.	31°18′ N, 086°29′ W
Ann Arbor, Mich.	42°17′ N, 083°45′ W
Annapolis, Md.	38°59′ N, 076°30′ W
Appleton, Wis.	44°16′ N, 088°25′ W
Arcata, Calif.	40°52′ N, 124°05′ W
Arlington, Tex.	32°44′ N, 097°07′ W
Arlington, Va.	38°53′ N, 077°07′ W
Asheville, N.C.	35°36′ N, 082°33′ W
Ashland, Ky.	38°28′ N, 082°38′ W
Ashland, Wis.	46°35′ N, 090°53′ W
Aspen, Colo.	39°11′ N, 106°49′ W
Astoria, Ore.	46°11′ N, 123°50′ W
Athens, Ga.	33°57′ N, 083°23′ W
Atlanta, Ga.	33°45′ N, 084°23′ W
Atlantic City, N.J.	39°21′ N, 074°27′ W
Augusta, Ga.	33°28′ N, 081°58′ W
Augusta, Me.	44°19′ N, 069°47′ W
Aurora, Colo.	39°43′ N, 104°49′ W
Austin, Minn.	43°40′ N, 092°58′ W
Austin, Tex.	30°17′ N, 097°45′ W
Baker, Mont.	46°22′ N, 104°17′ W
Baker, Ore.	44°47′ N, 117°50′ W
Bakersfield, Calif.	35°23′ N, 119°01′ W
Baltimore, Md.	39°17′ N, 076°37′ W
Bangor, Me.	44°48′ N, 068°46′ W

Ely, Minn.	47°55′ N, 091°51′ W
Ely, Nev.	39°15′ N, 114°54′ W
Emporia, Kan.	38°25′ N, 096°11′ W
Enid, Okla.	36°24′ N, 097°53′ W
Erie, Pa.	42°08′ N, 080°05′ W
Escanaba, Mich.	45°45′ N, 087°04′ W
Escondido, Calif.	33°07′ N, 117°05′ W
Eugene, Ore.	44°05′ N, 123°04′ W
Eunice, La.	30°30′ N, 092°25′ W
Eureka, Calif.	40°47′ N, 124°09′ W
Eustis, Fla.	28°51′ N, 081°41′ W
Evanston, Wyo.	41°16′ N, 110°58′ W
Everett, Wash.	47°59′ N, 122°12′ W
Fairbanks, Alaska.	64°51′ N, 147°45′ W
Falls City, Neb.	40°03′ N, 095°36′ W
Fargo, N.D.	46°53′ N, 096°48′ W
Farmington, N.M.	36°44′ N, 108°12′ W
Fayetteville, Ark.	36°03′ N, 094°09′ W
Fayetteville, N.C.	35°03′ N, 078°53′ W
Fergus Falls, Minn.	46°17′ N, 096°04′ W
Flagstaff, Ariz.	35°12′ N, 111°39′ W
Flint, Mich.	43°01′ N, 083°41′ W
Florence, S.C.	34°12′ N, 079°46′ W
Fort Bragg, Calif.	39°26′ N, 123°48′ W
Fort Collins, Colo.	40°35′ N, 105°05′ W
Fort Dodge, Ia.	42°30′ N, 094°11′ W
Fort Lauderdale, Fla.	26°07′ N, 080°08′ W
Fort Madison, Ia.	40°38′ N, 091°27′ W
Fort Myers, Fla.	26°39′ N, 081°53′ W
Fort Pierce, Fla.	27°26′ N, 080°19′ W
Fort Smith, Ark.	35°23′ N, 094°25′ W
Fort Wayne, Ind.	41°04′ N, 085°09′ W
Fort Worth, Tex.	32°45′ N, 097°18′ W
Frankfort, Ky.	38°12′ N, 084°52′ W
Freeport, Ill.	42°17′ N, 089°36′ W
Freeport, Tex.	28°57′ N, 095°21′ W
Fremont, Neb.	41°26′ N, 096°30′ W
Fresno, Calif.	36°44′ N, 119°47′ W
Gadsden, Ala.	34°01′ N, 086°01′ W
Gainesville, Fla.	29°40′ N, 082°20′ W
Gainesville, Ga.	34°17′ N, 083°49′ W
Galena, Alaska.	64°44′ N, 156°56′ W
Gallup, N.M.	35°31′ N, 108°45′ W
Galveston, Tex.	29°18′ N, 094°48′ W
Garden City, Kan.	37°58′ N, 100°52′ W
Garland, Tex.	32°54′ N, 096°38′ W
Gary, Ind.	41°36′ N, 087°20′ W
Georgetown, S.C.	33°23′ N, 079°17′ W
Gillette, Wyo.	44°18′ N, 105°30′ W
Glasgow, Ky.	37°00′ N, 085°55′ W
Glasgow, Mont.	48°12′ N, 106°38′ W
Glendive, Mont.	47°07′ N, 104°43′ W
Glenwood Springs, Colo.	39°33′ N, 107°19′ W
Goliad, Tex.	28°40′ N, 097°23′ W
Goodland, Kan.	39°21′ N, 101°43′ W
Grand Forks, N.D.	47°55′ N, 097°03′ W
Grand Island, Neb.	40°55′ N, 098°21′ W
Grand Junction, Colo.	39°04′ N, 108°33′ W
Grand Rapids, Mich.	42°58′ N, 085°40′ W
Granite Falls, Minn.	44°49′ N, 095°33′ W
Great Falls, Mont.	47°30′ N, 111°17′ W
Greeley, Colo.	40°25′ N, 104°42′ W
Green Bay, Wis.	44°31′ N, 088°00′ W
Greensboro, N.C.	36°04′ N, 079°48′ W
Greenville, Ala.	31°50′ N, 086°38′ W
Greenville, Miss.	33°24′ N, 091°04′ W
Greenwood, S.C.	34°12′ N, 082°10′ W
Griffin, Ga.	33°15′ N, 084°16′ W
Gulfport, Miss.	30°22′ N, 089°06′ W
Guymon, Okla.	36°41′ N, 101°29′ W
Hampton, Va.	37°02′ N, 076°21′ W
Hannibal, Mo.	39°42′ N, 091°22′ W
Harlingen, Tex.	26°12′ N, 097°42′ W
Harrisburg, Pa.	40°16′ N, 076°53′ W
Hartford, Conn.	41°46′ N, 072°41′ W
Hattiesburg, Miss.	31°20′ N, 089°17′ W
Helena, Mont.	46°36′ N, 112°02′ W
Henderson, Nev.	36°02′ N, 114°59′ W
Hialeah, Fla.	25°51′ N, 080°16′ W
Hilo, Hawaii	19°44′ N, 155°05′ W
Hobbs, N.M.	32°42′ N, 103°08′ W
Hollywood, Fla.	26°01′ N, 080°09′ W
Honokaa, Hawaii	20°05′ N, 155°28′ W
Honolulu, Hawaii	21°19′ N, 157°52′ W
Hope, Ark.	33°40′ N, 093°36′ W
Hot Springs, Ark.	34°31′ N, 093°03′ W
Houghton, Mich.	47°07′ N, 088°34′ W
Houston, Tex.	29°46′ N, 095°22′ W
Hugo, Okla.	34°01′ N, 095°31′ W
Huntsville, Ala.	34°44′ N, 086°35′ W
Hutchinson, Kan.	38°05′ N, 097°56′ W
Idaho Falls, Idaho	43°30′ N, 112°02′ W
Independence, Mo.	39°05′ N, 094°24′ W
Indianapolis, Ind.	39°46′ N, 086°09′ W
International Falls, Minn.	48°36′ N, 093°25′ W
Iron Mountain, Mich.	45°49′ N, 088°04′ W
Ironwood, Mich.	46°27′ N, 090°09′ W
Ithaca, N.Y.	42°26′ N, 076°30′ W
Jackson, Miss.	32°18′ N, 090°12′ W
Jackson, Tenn.	35°37′ N, 088°49′ W
Jacksonville, Fla.	30°20′ N, 081°39′ W
Jacksonville, N.C.	34°45′ N, 077°26′ W
Jamestown, N.Y.	42°06′ N, 079°14′ W
Jefferson City, Mo.	38°34′ N, 092°10′ W
Jersey City, N.J.	40°44′ N, 074°04′ W
Joliet, Ill.	41°32′ N, 088°05′ W
Jonesboro, Ark.	35°50′ N, 090°42′ W
Jonesboro, Ga.	33°31′ N, 084°22′ W
Juneau, Alaska	58°20′ N, 134°27′ W
Kaktovik, Alaska	70°08′ N, 143°38′ W
Kalamazoo, Mich.	42°17′ N, 085°35′ W
Kalispell, Mont.	48°12′ N, 114°19′ W
Kansas City, Kan.	39°07′ N, 094°38′ W
Kansas City, Mo.	39°06′ N, 094°35′ W
Kapaa, Hawaii	22°05′ N, 159°19′ W
Kearney, Neb.	40°42′ N, 099°05′ W
Kenai, Alaska.	60°33′ N, 151°16′ W
Ketchikan, Alaska	55°21′ N, 131°39′ W
Key Largo, Fla.	25°06′ N, 080°27′ W
Key West, Fla.	24°33′ N, 081°49′ W
King City, Calif.	36°13′ N, 121°08′ W
Kingman, Ariz.	35°12′ N, 114°04′ W

Kingsville, Tex.	27°31′ N, 097°52′ W	Midland, Tex.	32°00′ N, 102°05′ W
Kirksville, Mo.	40°12′ N, 092°35′ W	Miles City, Mont.	46°25′ N, 105°51′ W
Klamath Falls, Ore.	42°12′ N, 121°46′ W	Milledgeville, Ga.	33°05′ N, 083°14′ W
Knoxville, Tenn.	35°58′ N, 083°55′ W	Milwaukee, Wis.	43°02′ N, 087°55′ W
Kodiak, Alaska	57°47′ N, 152°24′ W	Minneapolis, Minn.	44°59′ N, 093°16′ W
Kokomo, Ind.	40°30′ N, 086°08′ W	Minot, N.D.	48°14′ N, 101°18′ W
La Crosse, Wis.	43°48′ N, 091°15′ W	Missoula, Mont.	46°52′ N, 114°01′ W
Lafayette, La.	30°14′ N, 092°01′ W	Mitchell, S.D.	43°43′ N, 098°02′ W
La Junta, Colo.	37°59′ N, 103°33′ W	Moab, Utah	38°35′ N, 109°33′ W
Lake Charles, La.	30°14′ N, 093°13′ W	Mobile, Ala.	30°41′ N, 088°03′ W
Lake Havasu City, Ariz.	34°29′ N, 114°19′ W	Moline, Ill.	41°30′ N, 090°31′ W
Lakeland, Fla.	28°03′ N, 081°57′ W	Monterey, Calif.	36°37′ N, 121°55′ W
Lansing, Mich.	42°44′ N, 084°33′ W	Montgomery, Ala.	32°23′ N, 086°19′ W
Laramie, Wyo.	41°19′ N, 105°35′ W	Montpelier, Vt.	44°16′ N, 072°35′ W
Laredo, Tex.	27°30′ N, 099°30′ W	Montrose, Colo.	38°29′ N, 107°53′ W
Las Cruces, N.M.	32°19′ N, 106°47′ W	Morehead City, N.C.	34°43′ N, 076°43′ W
Las Vegas, Nev.	36°01′ N, 115°09′ W	Morgan City, La.	29°42′ N, 091°12′ W
Las Vegas, N.M.	35°36′ N, 105°13′ W	Morgantown, W.Va.	39°38′ N, 079°57′ W
Laurel, Miss.	31°41′ N, 089°08′ W	Moscow, Idaho	46°44′ N, 117°00′ W
Lawton, Okla.	34°37′ N, 098°25′ W	Mount Vernon, Ill.	38°19′ N, 088°55′ W
Lebanon, N.H.	43°39′ N, 072°15′ W	Murfreesboro, Ark.	34°04′ N, 093°41′ W
Lewiston, Idaho	46°25′ N, 117°01′ W	Murfreesboro, Tenn.	35°50′ N, 086°23′ W
Lewiston, Me.	44°06′ N, 070°13′ W	Muskogee, Okla.	35°45′ N, 095°22′ W
Lewiston, Mont.	47°03′ N, 109°25′ W	Myrtle Beach, S.C.	33°42′ N, 078°53′ W
Lexington, Ky.	38°01′ N, 084°30′ W	Naples, Fla.	26°08′ N, 081°48′ W
Liberal, Kan.	37°02′ N, 100°55′ W	Nashville, Tenn.	36°10′ N, 086°47′ W
Lihue, Hawaii	21°59′ N, 159°22′ W	Natchez, Miss.	31°34′ N, 091°24′ W
Lima, Ohio	40°44′ N, 084°06′ W	Needles, Calif.	34°51′ N, 114°37′ W
Lincoln, Me.	45°22′ N, 068°30′ W	Nevada, Mo.	37°51′ N, 094°22′ W
Lincoln, Neb.	40°50′ N, 096°41′ W	New Albany, Ind.	38°18′ N, 085°49′ W
Little Rock, Ark.	34°45′ N, 092°17′ W	Newark, N.J.	40°44′ N, 074°10′ W
Logan, Utah	41°44′ N, 111°50′ W	New Bedford, Mass.	41°38′ N, 070°56′ W
Long Beach, Calif.	33°47′ N, 118°11′ W	New Bern, N.C.	35°07′ N, 077°03′ W
Los Alamos, N.M.	35°53′ N, 106°19′ W	Newcastle, Wyo.	43°50′ N, 104°11′ W
Los Angeles, Calif.	34°04′ N, 118°15′ W	New Haven, Conn.	41°18′ N, 072°55′ W
Louisville, Ky.	38°15′ N, 085°46′ W	New Madrid, Mo.	36°36′ N, 089°32′ W
Lowell, Mass.	42°38′ N, 071°19′ W	New Orleans, La.	29°58′ N, 090°04′ W
Lubbock, Tex.	33°35′ N, 101°51′ W	Newport, Ore.	44°39′ N, 124°03′ W
Lynchburg, Va.	37°25′ N, 079°09′ W	Newport, R.I.	41°29′ N, 071°18′ W
Macomb, Ill.	40°27′ N, 090°40′ W	Newport News, Va.	36°59′ N, 076°25′ W
Macon, Ga.	32°51′ N, 083°38′ W	New York City, N.Y.	40°43′ N, 074°00′ W
Madison, Wis.	43°04′ N, 089°24′ W	Niagara Falls, N.Y.	43°06′ N, 079°03′ W
Manchester, N.H.	43°00′ N, 071°28′ W	Nogales, Ariz.	31°20′ N, 110°56′ W
Mandan, N.D.	46°50′ N, 100°54′ W	Nome, Alaska	64°30′ N, 165°25′ W
Mankato, Minn.	44°10′ N, 094°00′ W	Norfolk, Va.	36°51′ N, 076°17′ W
Marietta, Ohio	39°25′ N, 081°27′ W	Norman, Okla.	35°13′ N, 097°26′ W
Marinette, Wis.	45°06′ N, 087°38′ W	North Augusta, S.C.	33°30′ N, 081°59′ W
Marion, Ind.	40°32′ N, 085°40′ W	North Platte, Neb.	41°08′ N, 100°46′ W
Marquette, Mich.	46°33′ N, 087°24′ W	Oakland, Calif.	37°49′ N, 122°16′ W
Massillon, Ohio	40°48′ N, 081°32′ W	Ocala, Fla.	29°11′ N, 082°08′ W
McAllen, Tex.	26°12′ N, 098°14′ W	Oceanside, Calif.	33°12′ N, 117°23′ W
McCall, Idaho	44°55′ N, 116°06′ W	Odessa, Tex.	31°52′ N, 102°23′ W
McCook, Neb.	40°12′ N, 100°38′ W	Ogallala, Neb.	41°08′ N, 101°43′ W
Medford, Ore.	42°19′ N, 122°52′ W	Ogden, Utah	41°13′ N, 111°58′ W
Meeker, Colo.	40°02′ N, 107°55′ W	Oklahoma City, Okla.	35°30′ N, 097°30′ W
Melbourne, Fla.	28°05′ N, 080°37′ W	Olympia, Wash.	47°03′ N, 122°53′ W
Memphis, Tenn.	35°08′ N, 090°03′ W	Omaha, Neb.	41°17′ N, 096°01′ W
Meridian, Miss.	32°22′ N, 088°42′ W	O'Neill, Neb.	42°27′ N, 098°39′ W
Mesa, Ariz.	33°25′ N, 111°49′ W	Orem, Utah	40°18′ N, 111°42′ W
Miami, Fla.	25°47′ N, 080°11′ W	Orlando, Fla.	28°33′ N, 081°23′ W
Midland, Mich.	43°36′ N, 084°14′ W	Oshkosh, Wis.	44°01′ N, 088°33′ W

Ottawa, Ill.	41°20′ N, 088°50′ W
Ottumwa, Ia.	41°01′ N, 092°25′ W
Overton, Nev.	36°33′ N, 114°27′ W
Owensboro, Ky.	37°46′ N, 087°07′ W
Paducah, Ky.	37°05′ N, 088°37′ W
Pahala, Hawaii.	19°12′ N, 155°29′ W
Palm Springs, Calif.	33°50′ N, 116°33′ W
Palo Alto, Calif.	37°27′ N, 122°10′ W
Panama City, Fla.	30°10′ N, 085°40′ W
Paris, Tex.	33°40′ N, 095°33′ W
Parsons, Kan.	37°20′ N, 095°16′ W
Pasadena, Calif.	34°09′ N, 118°09′ W
Pasadena, Tex.	29°43′ N, 095°13′ W
Pascagoula, Miss.	30°21′ N, 088°33′ W
Paterson, N.J.	40°55′ N, 074°11′ W
Pecos, Tex.	31°26′ N, 103°30′ W
Pendleton, Ore.	45°40′ N, 118°47′ W
Pensacola, Fla.	30°25′ N, 087°13′ W
Peoria, Ill.	40°42′ N, 089°36′ W
Petoskey, Mich.	45°22′ N, 084°57′ W
Philadelphia, Pa.	39°57′ N, 075°10′ W
Phoenix, Ariz.	33°27′ N, 112°04′ W
Pierre, S.D.	44°22′ N, 100°21′ W
Pine Bluff, Ark.	34°13′ N, 092°01′ W
Pittsburgh, Pa.	40°26′ N, 080°01′ W
Plano, Tex.	33°01′ N, 096°41′ W
Plattsburgh, N.Y.	44°42′ N, 073°27′ W
Pocatello, Idaho	42°52′ N, 112°27′ W
Point Hope, Alaska	68°21′ N, 166°41′ W
Port Gibson, Miss.	31°58′ N, 090°59′ W
Port Lavaca, Tex.	28°37′ N, 096°38′ W
Port Royal, S.C.	32°23′ N, 080°42′ W
Portland, Me.	43°39′ N, 070°16′ W
Portland, Ore.	45°32′ N, 122°37′ W
Prescott, Ariz.	34°33′ N, 112°28′ W
Presque Isle, Me.	46°41′ N, 068°01′ W
Providence, R.I.	41°49′ N, 071°24′ W
Provo, Utah	40°14′ N, 111°39′ W
Pueblo, Colo.	38°15′ N, 104°36′ W
Pullman, Wash.	46°44′ N, 117°10′ W
Racine, Wis.	42°44′ N, 087°48′ W
Raleigh, N.C.	35°46′ N, 078°38′ W
Rapid City, S.D.	44°05′ N, 103°14′ W
Red Bluff, Calif.	40°11′ N, 122°15′ W
Redding, Calif.	40°35′ N, 122°24′ W
Redfield, S.D.	44°53′ N, 098°31′ W
Reno, Nev.	39°31′ N, 119°48′ W
Rice Lake, Wis.	45°30′ N, 091°44′ W
Richfield, Utah	38°46′ N, 112°05′ W
Richmond, Ind.	39°50′ N, 084°54′ W
Richmond, Va.	37°33′ N, 077°27′ W
Riverside, Calif.	33°59′ N, 117°22′ W
Riverton, Wyo.	43°02′ N, 108°23′ W
Roanoke, Va.	37°16′ N, 079°56′ W
Rochester, Minn.	44°01′ N, 092°28′ W
Rochester, N.Y.	43°10′ N, 077°37′ W
Rock Hill, S.C.	34°56′ N, 081°01′ W
Rock Island, Ill.	41°30′ N, 090°34′ W
Rock Springs, Wyo.	41°35′ N, 109°12′ W
Rockford, Ill.	42°16′ N, 089°06′ W
Rolla, Mo.	37°57′ N, 091°46′ W
Rome, Ga.	34°15′ N, 085°09′ W
Roseburg, Ore.	43°13′ N, 123°20′ W
Roswell, N.M.	33°24′ N, 104°32′ W
Sacramento, Calif.	38°35′ N, 121°29′ W
Saginaw, Mich.	43°26′ N, 083°56′ W
Salem, Ore.	44°56′ N, 123°02′ W
Salina, Kan.	38°50′ N, 097°37′ W
Salinas, Calif.	36°40′ N, 121°39′ W
Salmon, Idaho	45°11′ N, 113°54′ W
Salt Lake City, Utah	40°45′ N, 111°53′ W
San Angelo, Tex.	31°28′ N, 100°26′ W
San Antonio, Tex.	29°25′ N, 098°30′ W
San Bernardino, Calif.	34°07′ N, 117°19′ W
San Diego, Calif.	32°43′ N, 117°09′ W
San Francisco, Calif.	37°47′ N, 122°25′ W
San Jose, Calif.	37°20′ N, 121°53′ W
San Luis Obispo, Calif.	35°17′ N, 120°40′ W
Sanderson, Tex.	30°09′ N, 102°24′ W
Santa Ana, Calif.	33°46′ N, 117°52′ W
Santa Barbara, Calif.	34°25′ N, 119°42′ W
Santa Fe, N.M.	35°41′ N, 105°57′ W
Santa Maria, Calif.	34°57′ N, 120°26′ W
Sarasota, Fla.	27°20′ N, 082°32′ W
Sault Ste. Marie, Mich.	46°30′ N, 084°21′ W
Savannah, Ga.	32°05′ N, 081°06′ W
Scott City, Kan.	38°29′ N, 100°54′ W
Scottsbluff, Neb.	41°52′ N, 103°40′ W
Scottsdale, Ariz.	33°29′ N, 111°56′ W
Searcy, Ark.	35°15′ N, 091°44′ W
Seattle, Wash.	47°36′ N, 122°20′ W
Sebring, Fla.	27°30′ N, 081°27′ W
Seguin, Tex.	29°34′ N, 097°58′ W
Selawik, Alaska	66°36′ N, 160°00′ W
Seldovia, Alaska	59°26′ N, 151°43′ W
Selma, Ala.	32°25′ N, 087°01′ W
Sharpsburg, Md.	39°28′ N, 077°45′ W
Sheboygan, Wis.	43°45′ N, 087°42′ W
Sheridan, Wyo.	44°48′ N, 106°58′ W
Show Low, Ariz.	34°15′ N, 110°02′ W
Shreveport, La.	32°31′ N, 093°45′ W
Sierra Vista, Ariz.	31°33′ N, 110°18′ W
Silver City, N.M.	32°46′ N, 108°17′ W
Sioux City, Ia.	42°30′ N, 096°24′ W
Sioux Falls, S.D.	43°33′ N, 096°44′ W
Skagway, Alaska	59°28′ N, 135°19′ W
Snyder, Tex.	32°44′ N, 100°55′ W
Socorro, N.M.	34°04′ N, 106°54′ W
Somerset, Ky.	37°05′ N, 084°36′ W
South Bend, Ind.	41°41′ N, 086°15′ W
Sparks, Nev.	39°32′ N, 119°45′ W
Spencer, Ia.	43°09′ N, 095°10′ W
Spokane, Wash.	47°40′ N, 117°24′ W
Springfield, Ill.	39°48′ N, 089°38′ W
Springfield, Mo.	37°13′ N, 093°17′ W
St. Augustine, Fla.	29°54′ N, 081°19′ W
St. Cloud, Minn.	45°34′ N, 094°10′ W
St. George, Utah	37°06′ N, 113°35′ W
St. Joseph, Mo.	39°46′ N, 094°50′ W
St. Louis, Mo.	38°37′ N, 090°11′ W
St. Maries, Idaho	47°19′ N, 116°35′ W
St. Paul, Minn.	44°57′ N, 093°06′ W

St. Petersburg, Fla. . . . . . . 27°46' N, 082°39' W
State College, Pa. . . . . 40°48' N, 077°52' W
Ste. Genevieve, Mo. . . . . . 37°59' N, 090°03' W
Steamboat Springs, Colo. . 40°29' N, 106°50' W
Stillwater, Minn. . . . . 45°03' N, 092°49' W
Sumter, S.C. . . . . 33°55' N, 080°21' W
Sun Valley, Idaho . . . . 43°42' N, 114°21' W
Superior, Wis. . . . . 46°44' N, 092°06' W
Syracuse, N.Y. . . . . 43°03' N, 076°09' W

Tacoma, Wash. . . . . 47°14' N, 122°26' W
Tallahassee, Fla. . . . . 30°27' N, 084°17' W
Tampa, Fla. . . . . 27°57' N, 082°27' W
Tempe, Ariz. . . . . 33°25' N, 111°56' W
Temple, Tex. . . . . 31°06' N, 097°21' W
Terre Haute, Ind. . . . . 39°28' N, 087°25' W
Texarkana, Ark. . . . . 33°26' N, 094°03' W
Thief River Falls, Minn. . . 48°07' N, 096°10' W
Tifton, Ga. . . . . 31°27' N, 083°31' W
Titusville, Fla. . . . . 28°37' N, 080°49' W
Toledo, Ohio . . . . 41°39' N, 083°33' W
Tonopah, Nev. . . . . 38°04' N, 117°14' W
Topeka, Kan. . . . . 39°03' N, 095°40' W
Traverse City, Mich. . . . . . 44°46' N, 085°38' W
Trenton, N.J. . . . . 40°14' N, 074°46' W
Trinidad, Colo. . . . . 37°10' N, 104°31' W
Troy, Ala. . . . . 31°48' N, 085°58' W
Troy, N.Y. . . . . 42°44' N, 073°41' W
Tucson, Ariz. . . . . 32°13' N, 110°58' W
Tulsa, Okla. . . . . 36°10' N, 095°55' W
Tupelo, Miss. . . . . 34°16' N, 088°43' W
Tuscaloosa, Ala. . . . . 33°12' N, 087°34' W
Twin Falls, Idaho. . . . . 42°34' N, 114°28' W
Tyler, Tex. . . . . 32°21' N, 095°18' W

Ukiah, Calif. . . . . 39°09' N, 123°12' W
Utica, N.Y. . . . . 43°06' N, 075°14' W
Uvalde, Tex. . . . . 29°13' N, 099°47' W

Valdez, Alaska. . . . . 61°07' N, 146°16' W
Valdosta, Ga. . . . . 30°50' N, 083°17' W
Valentine, Neb. . . . . 42°52' N, 100°33' W
Vero Beach, Fla. . . . . 27°38' N, 080°24' W
Vicksburg, Miss. . . . . 32°21' N, 090°53' W
Victoria, Tex. . . . . 28°48' N, 097°00' W
Vincennes, Ind. . . . . 38°41' N, 087°32' W
Virginia Beach, Va. . . . . . . 36°51' N, 075°59' W

Waco, Tex. . . . . 31°33' N, 097°09' W
Wahpeton, N.D. . . . . 46°15' N, 096°36' W
Wailuku, Hawaii . . . . 20°53' N, 156°30' W
Walla Walla, Wash. . . . . . . 46°04' N, 118°20' W
Warren, Pa. . . . . 41°51' N, 079°08' W
Washington, D.C. . . . . 38°54' N, 077°02' W
Waterloo, Ia. . . . . 42°30' N, 092°21' W
Watertown, N.Y. . . . . 43°59' N, 075°55' W
Waycross, Ga. . . . . 31°13' N, 082°21' W
Wayne, Neb. . . . . 42°14' N, 097°01' W
Weiser, Idaho . . . . 44°45' N, 116°58' W
West Palm Beach, Fla. . . . . 26°43' N, 080°03' W
Wheeling, W.Va. . . . . 40°04' N, 080°43' W
Wichita, Kan. . . . . 37°42' N, 097°20' W
Wichita Falls, Tex. . . . . . . 33°54' N, 098°30' W
Williamsport, Pa. . . . . 41°15' N, 077°00' W
Wilmington, N.C. . . . . 34°14' N, 077°55' W

Winfield, Kan. . . . . 37°15' N, 096°59' W
Winnemucca, Nev. . . . . . . 40°58' N, 117°44' W
Winslow, Ariz. . . . . 35°02' N, 110°42' W
Winston-Salem, N.C. . . . . 36°06' N, 080°14' W
Worcester, Mass. . . . . 42°16' N, 071°48' W
Worthington, Minn. . . . . . . 43°37' N, 095°36' W
Wrangell, Alaska. . . . . 56°28' N, 132°23' W
Yakima, Wash. . . . . 46°36' N, 120°31' W
Yankton, S.D. . . . . 42°53' N, 097°23' W
Yazoo City, Miss. . . . . 32°51' N, 090°25' W
Youngstown, Ohio . . . . 41°06' N, 080°39' W
Yuba City, Calif. . . . . 39°08' N, 121°37' W
Yuma, Ariz. . . . . 32°43' N, 114°37' W
Zanesville, Ohio . . . . 39°56' N, 082°01' W

URUGUAY . . . . .pg. 184

Aiguá . . . . 34°12' S, 054°45' W
Artigas . . . . 30°24' S, 056°28' W
Belén . . . . 30°47' S, 057°47' W
Bella Unión . . . . 30°15' S, 057°35' W
Carmelo . . . . 34°00' S, 058°17' W
Castillos . . . . 34°12' S, 053°50' W
Casupá . . . . 34°07' S, 055°39' W
Chuy . . . . 33°41' S, 053°27' W
Colonia . . . . 34°28' S, 057°51' W
Constitución . . . . 31°05' S, 057°50' W
Dolores . . . . 33°33' S, 058°13' W
Durazno . . . . 33°22' S, 056°31' W
Florida . . . . 34°06' S, 056°13' W
Lascano . . . . 33°40' S, 054°12'W
Las Piedras . . . . 34°44' S, 056°13' W
Maldonado . . . . 34°54' S, 054°57' W
Melo . . . . 32°22' S, 054°11' W
Mercedes . . . . 33°16' S, 058°01' W
Minas . . . . 34°23' S, 055°14' W
Montevideo . . . . 34°53' S, 056°11' W
Nuevo Berlín . . . . 32°59' S, 058°03' W
Pando . . . . 34°43' S, 055°57' W
Paysandú. . . . . 32°19' S, 058°05' W
Rio Branco . . . . 32°34' S, 053°25' W
Rivera . . . . 30°54' S, 055°31' W
Rocha . . . . 34°29' S, 054°20' W
Salto . . . . 31°23' S, 057°58' W
San Carlos . . . . 34°48' S, 054°55' W
San Gregorio . . . . 32°37' S, 055°40' W
San José . . . . 34°20' S, 056°42' W
Santa Clara . . . . 32°55' S, 054°58' W
Suárez (Tarariras) . . . . 34°17' S, 057°37' W
Tacuarembó
  (San Fructuoso) . . . . 31°44' S, 055°59' W
Tranqueras . . . . 31°12' S, 055°45' W
Treinta y Tres . . . . 33°14' S, 054°23' W
Trinidad . . . . 33°32' S, 056°54' W
Vergara . . . . 32°56' S, 053°57' W
Young . . . . 32°41' S, 057°38' W

UZBEKISTAN . . . .pg. 185

Andijon . . . . 40°45' N, 072°22' E

Angren.................... 41°01' N, 070°12' E
Bekobod.................. 40°13' N, 069°14' E
Beruniy (Biruni)........ 41°42' N, 060°44' E
Bukhara (Bokhoro)... 39°48' N, 064°25' E
Chirchiq.................. 41°29' N, 069°35' E
Denow.................... 38°16' N, 067°54' E
Fergana (Farghona)... 40°23' N, 071°46' E
Guliston.................. 40°29' N, 068°46' E
Jizzakh................... 40°06' N, 067°50' E
Kattaqŭrghon.......... 39°55' N, 066°15' E
Khiva (Khiwa)......... 41°24' N, 060°22' E
Khonqa................... 41°28' N, 060°47' E
Kogon.................... 39°43' N, 064°33' E
Marghilon............... 40°27' N, 071°42' E
Namangan............... 41°00' N, 071°40' E
Nawoiy................... 40°09' N, 065°22' E
Nukus.................... 42°29' N, 059°38' E
Olmaliq.................. 40°50' N, 069°35' E
Qarshi.................... 38°53' N, 065°48' E
Qŭqon.................... 40°30' N, 070°57' E
Samarkand.............. 39°40' N, 066°58' E
Tashkent (Toshkent).. 41°20' N, 069°18' E
Termiz................... 37°14' N, 067°16' E
Urganch.................. 41°33' N, 060°38' E
Zarafshon............... 41°31' N, 064°15' E

VANUATU .... pg. 186

Ipayato.................. 15°38' S, 166°52' E
Isangel................... 19°33' S, 169°16' E
Lakatoro................. 16°07' S, 167°25' E
Lalinda.................. 16°21' S, 168°03' E
Laol...................... 16°41' S, 168°16' E
Loltong.................. 15°33' S, 168°09' E
Luganville.............. 15°32' S, 167°10' E
Lumbukuti.............. 16°55' S, 168°32' E
Natapao................. 17°37' S, 168°13' E
Norsup................... 16°04' S, 167°23' E
Port Olry................ 15°03' S, 167°04' E
Unpongkor.............. 18°49' S, 169°01' E
Veutumboso............ 13°54' S, 167°27' E
Vila (Port-Vila)....... 17°44' S, 168°18' E

VENEZUELA ..... pg. 187

Barcelona............... 10°08' N, 064°42' W
Barinas.................. 08°38' N, 070°12' W
Barquisimeto........... 10°04' N, 069°19' W
Cabimas................. 10°23' N, 071°28' W
Caicara (Caicara de
  Orinoco)............. 07°37' N, 066°10' W
Caicara.................. 09°49' N, 063°36' W
Caracas.................. 10°30' N, 066°55' W
Ciudad Bolívar........ 08°08' N, 063°33' W
Ciudad Guayana
  (San Felix).......... 08°23' N, 062°40' W
Coro..................... 11°25' N, 069°41' W
Cumaná.................. 10°28' N, 064°10' W
Guasdualito............ 07°15' N, 070°44' W
La Asunción........... 11°02' N, 063°53' W

Maracaibo.............. 10°40' N, 071°37' W
Maracay................. 10°15' N, 067°36' W
Maturín................. 09°45' N, 063°11' W
Mérida.................. 08°36' N, 071°08' W
Pariaguán............... 08°51' N, 064°43' W
Petare................... 10°29' N, 066°49' W
Puerto Ayacucho...... 05°40' N, 067°35' W
Punto Fijo.............. 11°42' N, 070°13' W
San Carlos de
  Río Negro........... 01°55' N, 067°04' W
San Cristóbal.......... 07°46' N, 072°14' W
San Fernando de Apure 07°54' N, 067°28' W
San Fernando
  de Atabapo.......... 04°03' N, 067°42' W
Santa Elena............ 04°37' N, 061°08' W
Tucupita................ 09°04' N, 062°03' W
Upata.................... 08°01' N, 062°24' W
Valencia................ 10°11' N, 068°00' W
Valera................... 09°19' N, 070°37' W

VIETNAM .... pg. 188

Bac Can................. 22°08' N, 105°50' E
Bac Giang............... 21°16' N, 106°12' E
Bac Lieu................ 09°17' N, 105°43' E
Bien Hoa................ 10°57' N, 106°49' E
Buon Me Thuot
  (Lac Giao)........... 12°40' N, 108°03' E
Ca Mau.................. 09°11' N, 105°08' E
Cam Pha................ 21°01' N, 107°19' E
Cam Ranh............... 11°54' N, 109°13' E
Can Tho................. 10°02' N, 105°47' E
Chau Doc............... 10°42' N, 105°07' E
Da Lat................... 11°56' N, 108°25' E
Da Nang (Tourane).... 16°04' N, 108°13' E
Dong Ha................. 16°49' N, 107°08' E
Dong Hoi............... 17°29' N, 106°36' E
Go Cong................. 10°22' N, 106°40' E
Ha Giang................ 22°50' N, 104°59' E
Hai Duong.............. 20°56' N, 106°19' E
Haiphong (Hai Phong) 20°52' N, 106°41' E
Hanoi (Ha Noi)........ 21°02' N, 105°51' E
Ha Tinh................. 18°20' N, 105°54' E
Hoa Binh............... 20°50' N, 105°20' E
Ho Chi Minh City
  (Saigon).............. 10°45' N, 106°40' E
Hoi An................... 15°52' N, 108°19' E
Hong Gai (Hon Gai).. 20°57' N, 107°05' E
Hue...................... 16°28' N, 107°36' E
Kon Tum (Cong Tum or
  Kontun).............. 14°21' N, 108°00' E
Lai Chau................ 22°04' N, 103°10' E
Lao Cai.................. 22°30' N, 103°58' E
Long Xuyen............ 10°23' N, 105°25' E
Minh Hoa............... 17°47' N, 106°01' E
My Tho.................. 10°21' N, 106°21' E
Nam Dinh............... 20°25' N, 106°10' E
Nha Trang.............. 12°15' N, 109°11' E
Phan Rang.............. 11°34' N, 108°59' E
Phan Thiet............. 10°56' N, 108°06' E
Pleiku (Play Cu)...... 13°59' N, 108°00' E

Quan Long	09°11′ N,	105°08′ E
Quang Ngai	15°07′ N,	108°48′ E
Qui Nhon	13°46′ N,	109°14′ E
Rach Gia	10°01′ N,	105°05′ E
Sa Dec	10°18′ N,	105°46′ E
Soc Trang	09°36′ N,	105°58′ E
Son La	21°19′ N,	103°54′ E
Tam Ky	15°34′ N,	108°29′ E
Tan An	10°32′ N,	106°25′ E
Thai Binh	20°27′ N,	106°20′ E
Thai Nguyen	21°36′ N,	105°50′ E
Thanh Hoa	19°48′ N,	105°46′ E
Tuy Hoa	13°05′ N,	109°18′ E
Viet Tri	21°18′ N,	105°26′ E
Vinh	18°40′ N,	105°40′ E
Vung Tau	10°21′ N,	107°04′ E
Yen Bai	21°42′ N,	104°52′ E

YEMEN . . . . pg. 189

Aden ('Adan)	12°46′ N,	045°02′ E
Aḥwar	13°31′ N,	046°42′ E
Al-Bayḍā'	13°58′ N,	045°35′ E
Al-Ghaydah	16°13′ N,	052°11′ E
Al-Hudaydah	14°48′ N,	042°57′ E
Al-Luḥayyah	15°43′ N,	042°42′ E
Al-Mukallā	14°32′ N,	049°08′ E
Balḥāf	13°58′ N,	048°11′ E
Dhamār	14°33′ N,	044°24′ E
Ibb	13°58′ N,	044°11′ E
Laḥij	13°04′ N,	044°53′ E
Madīnat ash-Sha'b	12°50′ N,	044°56′ E
Ma'rib	15°25′ N,	045°21′ E
Min'ar	16°43′ N,	051°18′ E
Mocha (al-Mukha)	13°19′ N,	043°15′ E
Niṣāb	14°31′ N,	046°30′ E
Raydah	15°50′ N,	044°03′ E
Sa'dah	16°57′ N,	043°46′ E
Ṣalīf	15°18′ N,	042°41′ E
Ṣan'ā'	15°21′ N,	044°12′ E
Sayḥūt	15°12′ N,	051°14′ E
Saywūn (Say'un)	15°56′ N,	048°47′ E
Shabwah	15°22′ N,	047°01′ E
Shaḥārah	16°11′ N,	043°42′ E
Ta'izz	13°34′ N,	044°02′ E
Tarīm	16°03′ N,	049°00′ E
Zabīd	14°12′ N,	043°19′ E
Zinjibār	13°08′ N,	045°23′ E

YUGOSLAVIA . . . pg. 190

Bar	42°05′ N,	019°06′ E
Belgrade	44°50′ N,	020°30′ E
Bor	44°06′ N,	022°06′ E
Cacak	43°54′ N,	020°21′ E
Gornji Milanovac	44°02′ N,	020°27′ E
Kikinda	45°50′ N,	020°29′ E
Knjaževac	43°34′ N,	022°15′ E
Kosovska Mitrovica (Titova Mitrovica)	42°53′ N,	020°52′ E

Kragujevac	44°01′ N,	020°55′ E
Kraljevo	43°44′ N,	020°43′ E
Kruševac	43°35′ N,	021°20′ E
Leskovac	42°59′ N,	021°57′ E
Majdanpek	44°25′ N,	021°56′ E
Nikšić	42°46′ N,	018°58′ E
Nis	43°19′ N,	021°54′ E
Novi Beograd	44°49′ N,	020°27′ E
Novi Pazar	43°08′ N,	020°31′ E
Novi Sad	45°15′ N,	019°50′ E
Pancevo	44°52′ N,	020°39′ E
Pirot	43°09′ N,	022°36′ E
Podgorica (Titograd)	42°26′ N,	019°16′ E
Priboj	43°35′ N,	019°32′ E
Priština	42°40′ N,	021°10′ E
Prizren	42°13′ N,	020°45′ E
Sabac	44°45′ N,	019°43′ E
Smederevo	44°39′ N,	020°56′ E
Sombor	45°46′ N,	019°07′ E
Sremski Karlovci	45°12′ N,	019°56′ E
Subotica	46°06′ N,	019°40′ E
Titovo Užice (Užice)	43°52′ N,	019°51′ E
Valjevo	44°16′ N,	019°53′ E
Vranje	42°33′ N,	021°54′ E
Zrenjanin	45°23′ N,	020°23′ E

ZAMBIA . . . . pg. 191

Chililabombwe (Bancroft)	12°22′ S,	027°50′ E
Chingola	12°32′ S,	027°52′ E
Chipata (Fort Jameson)	13°39′ S,	032°40′ E
Isoka	10°08′ S,	032°38′ E
Kabwe (Broken Hill)	14°27′ S,	028°27′ E
Kalabo	14°58′ S,	022°41′ E
Kalulushi	12°50′ S,	028°05′ E
Kasama	10°13′ S,	031°12′ E
Kawambwa	09°47′ S,	029°05′ E
Kitwe	12°49′ S,	028°13′ E
Livingstone (Maramba)	17°51′ S,	025°52′ E
Luanshya	13°08′ S,	028°24′ E
Lusaka	15°25′ S,	028°17′ E
Mansa (Fort Rosebery)	11°12′ S,	028°53′ E
Mazabuka	15°51′ S,	027°46′ E
Mongu	15°17′ S,	023°08′ E
Monze	16°16′ S,	027°29′ E
Mpika	11°50′ S,	031°27′ E
Mumbwa	14°59′ S,	027°04′ E
Mwamfuli (Samfya)	11°21′ S,	029°33′ E
Nchelenge	09°21′ S,	029°44′ E
Ndola	12°58′ S,	028°38′ E
Senanga	16°07′ S,	023°16′ E
Serenje	13°14′ S,	030°14′ E
Zambezi	13°33′ S,	023°07′ E

ZIMBABWE . . . . . . pg. 192

Beitbridge	22°13′ S,	030°00′ E
Bulawayo	20°09′ S,	028°35′ E

Chimanimani
  (Mandidzudzure,
  or Melsetter) . . . . 19°48′ S, 032°52′ E
Chinhoyi (Sinola) . . . . 17°22′ S, 030°12′ E
Chipinge . . . . 20°12′ S, 032°37′ E
Chiredzi . . . . 21°03′ S, 031°40′ E
Chitungwiza . . . . 18°47′ S, 032°37′ E
Empress Mine Township . . 18°27′ S, 029°27′ E
Gweru (Gwelo) . . . . 19°27′ S, 029°49′ E
Harare (Salisbury) . . . . . . 17°50′ S, 031°03′ E
Hwange (Wankie) . . . . 18°22′ S, 026°29′ E
Inyanga . . . . 18°13′ S, 032°45′ E
Kadoma (Gatooma) . . . . . . 18°21′ S, 029°55′ E
Kariba . . . . 16°31′ S, 028°48′ E
Karoi . . . . 16°49′ S, 029°41′ E
Kwekwe (Que Que) . . . . . . 18°55′ S, 029°49′ E

Marondera
  (Marandellas) . . . . 18°11′ S, 031°33′ E
Mashava . . . . 20°03′ S, 030°29′ E
Masvingo (Fort Victoria,
  or Nyanda) . . . . 20°05′ S, 030°50′ E
Mhangura . . . . 16°54′ S, 030°09′ E
Mount Darwin . . . . 16°47′ S, 031°35′ E
Mvuma . . . . 19°17′ S, 030°32′ E
Mutare (Umtali) . . . . 18°58′ S, 032°40′ E
Norton . . . . 17°53′ S, 030°42′ E
Redcliff . . . . 19°02′ S, 029°47′ E
Shamva . . . . 17°19′ S, 031°34′ E
Shurugwi (Selukwe) . . . . . 19°40′ S, 030°00′ E
Triangle . . . . 21°02′ S, 031°27′ E
Tuli . . . . 21°55′ S, 029°12′ E
Victoria Falls . . . . 17°56′ S, 025°50′ E

Acronyms for International Organizations

ACP	African, Caribbean, and Pacific Convention
ADB	Asian Development Bank
APEC	Asia-Pacific Economic Cooperation Council
CARICOM	Caribbean Community and Common Market
EEC	European Economic Community
EU	The European Union
FAO	Food and Agriculture Organization
GCC	Gulf Cooperation Council
I-ADB	Inter-American Development Bank
IDB	Islamic Development Bank
ILO	International Labour Organization
IMF	International Monetary Fund
ITU	International Telecommunications Union
OAS	Organization of American States
OAU	Organization of African Unity
OPEC	Organization of Petroleum Exporting Countries
SPC	South Pacific Commission
UNICEF	United Nations Children's Fund
UNESCO	United Nations Educational, Scientific, and Cultural Organization
WHO	World Health Organization
WTO	World Trade Organization (formerly General Agreement on Tariffs and Trade, GATT)

Country	National Capital	Population of National Capital	United Nations (date of admission)	UNICEF	FAO	ILO
Afghanistan	Kābul	700,000	1946	•	•	•
Albania	Tiranë	300,000	1955	•	•	•
Algeria	Algiers	1,507,241	1962	•	•	•
Andorra	Andorra la Vella	22,821	1993			
Angola	Luanda	2,000,000	1976	•	•	•
Antigua and Barbuda	Saint John's	21,514	1981	•	•	
Argentina	Buenos Aires	2,988,006	1945	•	•	•
Armenia	Yerevan	1,226,000	1992	•	•	•
Australia	Canberra	303,700	1945	•	•	•
Austria	Vienna	1,539,848	1955	•	•	•
Azerbaijan	Baku	1,087,000	1992	•	•	•
Bahamas, The	Nassau	172,196	1973	•	•	•
Bahrain	Manama	140,401	1971	•	•	•
Bangladesh	Dhākā (Dacca)	3,839,000	1974	•	•	•
Barbados	Bridgetown	6,070	1966	•	•	•
Belarus	Minsk	1,700,000	1945	•	•	•
Belgium	Brussels	136,424	1945	•	•	•
Belize	Belmopan	3,927	1981	•	•	•
Benin	Cotonou (official)	533,212	1960	•	•	•
	Porto-Novo (de facto)	177,660				
Bhutan	Thimphu	30,340	1971	•	•	
Bolivia	La Paz (administrative)	784,976	1945	•	•	•
	Sucre (judicial)	144,994				
Bosnia and Herzegovina	Sarajevo	250,000	1992	•	•	•
Botswana	Gaborone	156,803	1966	•	•	•
Brazil	Brasília	1,492,542	1945	•	•	•
Brunei	Bandar Seri Begawan	21,484	1984			
Bulgaria	Sofia	1,116,823	1955	•	•	•
Burkina Faso	Ouagadougou	690,000	1960	•	•	•
Burundi	Bujumbura	300,000	1962	•	•	•
Cambodia	Phnom Penh	920,000	1955	•	•	•
Cameroon	Yaoundé	800,000	1960	•	•	•
Canada	Ottawa	313,987	1945	•	•	•
Cape Verde	Praia	61,644	1975	•	•	•
Central African Republic	Bangui	524,000	1960	•	•	•
Chad	N'Djamena	530,965	1960	•	•	•
Chile	Santiago	5,076,808	1945	•	•	•
China	Beijing (Peking)	7,000,000	1945	•	•	•
Colombia	Bogotá	5,237,635	1945	•	•	•
Comoros	Moroni	30,000	1975	•	•	•
Congo, Democratic Republic of the	Kinshasa	4,655,313	1960	•	•	•
Congo, Republic of the	Brazzaville	937,579	1960	•	•	•
Costa Rica	San José	321,193	1945	•	•	•
Croatia	Zagreb	867,717	1992	•	•	•
Cuba	Havana	2,241,000	1945	•	•	•
Cyprus	Nicosia (Lefkosia)	186,400	1960	•	•	•
Czech Republic	Prague	1,213,299	1993	•	•	•
Denmark	Copenhagen	1,353,333	1945	•	•	•
Djibouti	Djibouti	317,000	1977	•	•	•
Dominica	Roseau	15,853	1978	•	•	•

IMF	ITU	UNESCO	WHO	WTO	Commonwealth of Nations	EU	GCC	OAS	OAU	SPC	ACP	ADB	APEC	CARICOM	EEC	I-ADB	IDB	OPEC	Country
•	•	•	•									•					•		Afghanistan
•	•	•	•	•													•		Albania
•	•	•	•						•								•	•	Algeria
	•	•						•			•								Andorra
•	•	•	•						•		•								Angola
•	•	•	•	•	•			•			•			•			•		Antigua and Barbuda
•	•	•	•	•				•				•				•			Argentina
•	•	•	•									•					•		Armenia
•	•	•	•	•	•					•		•	•						Australia
•	•	•	•	•		•						•					•		Austria
•	•	•	•									•					•		Azerbaijan
•	•	•	•		•			•						•			•		Bahamas, The
•	•	•	•	•			•										•		Bahrain
•	•	•	•	•	•							•					•		Bangladesh
•	•	•	•	•	•			•			•			•			•		Barbados
•	•	•	•																Belarus
•	•	•	•	•		•						•					•		Belgium
•	•	•	•	•	•			•			•			•			•		Belize
•	•	•	•	•					•		•						•		Benin
	•	•	•									•							Bhutan
•	•	•	•	•				•									•		Bolivia
•	•	•	•																Bosnia and Herzegovina
•	•	•	•	•	•				•		•						•		Botswana
•	•	•	•	•				•				•					•		Brazil
•	•	•	•	•	•								•						Brunei
•	•	•	•	•															Bulgaria
•	•	•	•	•					•		•						•		Burkina Faso
•	•	•	•						•		•								Burundi
•	•	•	•									•							Cambodia
•	•	•	•	•	•				•		•						•		Cameroon
•	•	•	•	•	•			•				•	•				•		Canada
•	•	•	•						•		•						•		Cape Verde
•	•	•	•	•					•		•						•		Central African Republic
•	•	•	•						•		•						•		Chad
•	•	•	•	•				•					•				•		Chile
•	•	•	•	•								•	•				•		China
•	•	•	•	•				•									•		Colombia
•	•	•	•						•		•						•		Comoros
																			Congo, Democratic Republic of the
•	•	•	•						•		•						•		Congo, Republic of the
•	•	•	•	•				•									•		Costa Rica
•	•	•	•	•													•		Croatia
•	•	•	•					•			•								Cuba
•	•	•	•	•	•												•		Cyprus
•	•	•	•	•															Czech Republic
•	•	•	•	•		•						•					•		Denmark
•	•	•	•						•		•						•		Djibouti
•	•	•	•		•			•			•			•					Dominica

Country	National Capital	Population of National Capital	United Nations (date of admission)	UNICEF	FAO	ILO
Dominican Republic	Santo Domingo	2,138,262	1945	•	•	•
Ecuador	Quito	1,444,363	1945	•	•	•
Egypt	Cairo	6,849,000	1945	•	•	•
El Salvador	San Salvador	422,570	1945	•	•	•
Equatorial Guinea	Malabo	58,040	1968	•	•	•
Eritrea	Asmara	367,300	1993	•	•	•
Estonia	Tallinn	434,763	1991	•	•	•
Ethiopia	Addis Ababa	2,316,400	1945	•	•	•
Fiji	Suva	200,000	1970	•	•	•
Finland	Helsinki	525,031	1955	•	•	•
France	Paris	2,175,200	1945	•	•	•
Gabon	Libreville	362,386	1960	•	•	•
Gambia, The	Banjul	42,407	1965	•	•	
Georgia	Tbilisi	1,279,000	1992	•	•	•
Germany	Berlin	293,072	1973	•	•	•
Ghana	Accra	1,781,100	1957	•	•	•
Greece	Athens	748,110	1945	•	•	•
Grenada	Saint George's	4,621	1974	•	•	•
Guatemala	Guatemala City	823,301	1945	•	•	•
Guinea	Conakry	1,508,000	1958	•	•	•
Guinea-Bissau	Bissau	197,610	1974	•	•	•
Guyana	Georgetown	248,500	1966	•	•	•
Haiti	Port-au-Prince	846,247	1945	•	•	•
Honduras	Tegucigalpa	775,300	1945	•	•	•
Hungary	Budapest	1,909,000	1955	•	•	•
Iceland	Reykjavik	104,276	1946	•	•	•
India	New Delhi	301,297	1945	•	•	•
Indonesia	Jakarta	8,259,266	1950	•	•	•
Iran	Tehrān	11,000,000	1945	•	•	•
Iraq	Baghdad	4,478,000	1945	•	•	•
Ireland	Dublin	478,389	1955	•	•	•
Israel	Jerusalem (Yerushalayim, Al-Quds)	591,400	1949	•	•	•
Italy	Rome (Roma)	2,687,881	1955	•	•	•
Ivory Coast	Yamoussoukro (de jure; administrative)	106,786	1960	•	•	•
Jamaica	Kingston	103,771	1962	•	•	•
Japan	Tokyo	7,966,195	1956	•	•	•
Jordan	Amman	963,490	1955	•	•	•
Kazakstan	Astana	1,150,500	1992	•	•	•
Kenya	Nairobi	2,000,000	1963	•	•	•
Kiribati	Bairki	2,226	1999	•		
Kuwait	Kuwait (Al-Kuwayt)	31,241	1963	•	•	•
Kyrgyzstan	Bishkek (Frunze)	597,000	1992	•	•	•
Laos	Vientiane (Viangchan)	442,000	1955	•	•	•
Latvia	Rīga	839,670	1991	•	•	•
Lebanon	Beirut (Bayrūt)	1,100,000	1945	•	•	•
Lesotho	Maseru	170,000	1966	•	•	•
Liberia	Monrovia	668,000	1945	•	•	•
Libya	Tripoli (Ṭarābulus)	591,062	1955	•	•	•
Liechtenstein	Vaduz	5,067	1990			

IMF	ITU	UNESCO	WHO	WTO	Common-wealth of Nations	EU	GCC	OAS	OAU	SPC	ACP	ADB	APEC	CARICOM	EBC	IADB	IDB	OPEC	Country
•	•	•	•	•				•			•					•			Dominican Republic
•	•	•	•	•				•								•			Ecuador
•	•	•	•	•					•								•		Egypt
•	•	•	•	•				•								•			El Salvador
•	•	•	•						•		•								Equatorial Guinea
•	•	•	•						•										Eritrea
•	•	•	•	•															Estonia
•	•	•	•						•		•								Ethiopia
•	•	•	•	•	•					•	•	•							Fiji
•	•	•	•	•		•						•				•			Finland
•	•	•	•	•		•				•		•				•			France
•	•	•	•	•					•		•							•	Gabon
•	•	•	•	•	•				•		•						•		Gambia, The
•	•	•	•	•															Georgia
•	•	•	•	•		•						•				•			Germany
•	•	•	•	•	•				•		•								Ghana
•	•	•	•	•		•										•			Greece
•	•	•	•	•	•			•			•			•		•			Grenada
•	•	•	•	•				•								•			Guatemala
•	•	•	•	•					•		•						•		Guinea
•	•	•	•	•					•		•						•		Guinea-Bissau
•	•	•	•	•	•			•			•			•		•	•		Guyana
•	•	•	•	•				•			•			•		•			Haiti
•	•	•	•	•				•								•			Honduras
•	•	•	•	•															Hungary
•	•	•	•	•															Iceland
•	•	•	•	•	•							•							India
•	•	•	•	•								•	•				•	•	Indonesia
•	•	•	•														•	•	Iran
•	•	•	•														•	•	Iraq
•	•	•	•	•		•						•				•			Ireland
•	•	•	•	•												•			Israel
•	•	•	•	•		•						•				•			Italy
•	•	•	•	•					•		•						•		Ivory Coast
•	•	•	•	•	•			•			•			•		•			Jamaica
•	•	•	•	•								•	•			•			Japan
•	•	•	•	•													•		Jordan
•	•	•	•														•		Kazakhstan
•	•	•	•	•	•				•		•								Kenya
	•	•	•		•					•	•								Kiribati
•	•	•	•	•			•										•	•	Kuwait
•	•	•	•	•													•		Kyrgyzstan
•	•	•	•									•							Laos
•	•	•	•	•															Latvia
•	•	•	•														•		Lebanon
•	•	•	•	•	•				•		•								Lesotho
•	•	•	•						•		•								Liberia
•	•	•	•						•								•	•	Libya
	•			•															Liechtenstein

Country	National Capital	Population of National Capital	United Nations (date of admission)	UNICEF	FAO	ILO
Lithuania	Vilnius	590,100	1991	•	•	•
Luxembourg	Luxembourg	76,446	1945	•	•	•
Macedonia	Skopje (Skopije)	541,280	1993	•	•	•
Madagascar	Antananarivo	1,052,835	1960	•	•	•
Malawi	Lilongwe	395,500	1964	•	•	•
Malaysia	Kuala Lumpur	1,145,075	1957	•	•	•
Maldives	Male'	62,973	1965	•	•	•
Mali	Bamako	800,000	1960	•	•	•
Malta	Valletta	9,129	1964	•	•	•
Marshall Islands	Majuro	20,000	1991	•	•	
Mauritania	Nouakchott	735,000	1961	•	•	•
Mexico	Mexico City	9,815,795	1945	•	•	•
Micronesia, Federated States of	Palikir	-	1991	•		
Moldova	Chişinău	662,000	1992	•	•	•
Mongolia	Ulaanbaatar (Ulan Bator)	619,000	1961	•	•	•
Morocco	Rabat	1,220,000	1956	•	•	•
Mozambique	Maputo (Lourenço Marques)	931,591	1975	•	•	•
Myanmar	Yangŏn (Rangoon)	3,851,000	1948	•	•	
Namibia	Windhoek	161,000	1990	•	•	
Nepal	Kāthmāndu	535,000	1955	•	•	•
Netherlands, The	Amsterdam (de jure)	722,245	1945	•	•	
New Zealand	Wellington	158,275	1945	•	•	
Nicaragua	Managua	1,195,000	1945	•	•	•
Niger	Niamey	391,876	1960	•	•	•
Nigeria	Abuja	339,100	1960	•	•	•
North Korea	P'yŏngyang	2,355,000	1991	•	•	
Norway	Oslo	487,908	1945	•	•	•
Oman	Muscat	51,869	1971	•	•	•
Pakistan	Islāmābād	204,364	1947	•	•	•
Palau	Koror	10,500	1994	•		
Panama	Panama City	445,902	1945	•	•	•
Papua New Guinea	Port Moresby	193,242	1975	•	•	•
Paraguay	Asunción	502,426	1945	•	•	•
Peru	Lima	421,570	1945	•	•	•
Philippines	Manila	1,894,667	1945	•	•	•
Poland	Warsaw (Warszawa)	1,640,700	1945	•	•	•
Portugal	Lisbon	677,790	1955	•	•	•
Qatar	Doha	313,639	1971	•	•	•
Romania	Bucharest	2,343,824	1958	•	•	•
Russia	Moscow	8,717,000	1991	•	•	
Rwanda	Kigali	232,733	1962	•	•	•
St. Kitts and Nevis	Basseterre	15,000	1983	•	•	
St. Lucia	Castries	13,615	1979	•	•	•
St. Vincent and The Grenadines	Kingstown	15,466	1980	•	•	
Samoa	Apia	32,859	1976	•	•	•
San Marino	San Marino	2,316	1992	•	•	
São Tomé and Príncipe	São Tomé	43,420	1975	•	•	•
Saudi Arabia	Riyadh (Ar-Riyadh)	1,800,000	1945	•	•	•

IMF	ITU	UNESCO	WHO	WTO	Commonwealth of Nations	EU	GCC	OAS	OAU	SPC	ACP	ADB	APEC	CARICOM	EEC	IADB	IDB	OPEC	Country
•	•	•	•			•											•		Lithuania
•	•	•	•			•										•			Luxembourg
•	•	•	•	•															Macedonia
•	•	•	•	•					•								•		Madagascar
•	•	•	•	•	•				•		•								Malawi
•	•	•	•	•	•							•	•				•		Malaysia
•	•	•	•		•							•					•		Maldives
•	•	•	•	•					•								•		Mali
•	•	•	•	•	•											•			Malta
•	•	•	•							•		•							Marshall Islands
•	•	•	•	•					•		•						•		Mauritania
•	•	•	•	•				•					•			•			Mexico
•	•	•	•							•		•							Federated States of Micronesia
•	•	•	•																Moldova
•	•	•	•									•							Mongolia
•	•	•	•	•													•		Morocco
•	•	•	•	•	•				•		•						•		Mozambique
•	•	•	•									•							Myanmar
•	•	•	•	•	•				•		•								Namibia
•	•	•	•	•								•							Nepal
•	•	•	•	•		•										•	•		Netherlands, The
•	•	•	•	•	•					•		•	•						New Zealand
•	•	•	•	•				•								•			Nicaragua
•	•	•	•	•					•		•						•		Niger
•	•	•	•	•	•				•		•						•	•	Nigeria
	•	•	•																North Korea
•	•	•	•	•												•	•		Norway
•	•	•	•	•			•										•		Oman
•	•	•	•	•	•							•					•		Pakistan
•	•	•	•							•		•							Palau
•	•	•	•	•				•								•			Panama
•	•	•	•	•	•					•	•	•	•				•		Papua New Guinea
•	•	•	•	•				•								•			Paraguay
•	•	•	•	•				•					•			•			Peru
•	•	•	•	•								•	•						Phillippines
•	•	•	•	•															Poland
•	•	•	•	•		•										•	•		Portugal
•	•	•	•	•			•										•	•	Qatar
•	•	•	•	•															Romania
•	•	•	•										•						Russia
•	•	•	•	•					•								•		Rwanda
•	•	•	•	•	•			•						•					St. Kitts and Nevis
•	•	•	•	•	•			•						•					St. Lucia
•	•	•	•	•	•			•						•					St. Vincent and the Grenadines
•	•	•	•		•					•	•								Samoa
•	•	•	•																San Marino
•	•	•	•						•		•						•		São Tomé and Principe
•	•	•	•	•			•										•	•	Saudi Arabia

Country	National Capital	Population of National Capital	United Nations (date of admission)	UNICEF	FAO	ILO
Senegal	Dakar	785,071	1960	•	•	•
Seychelles	Victoria	25,000	1976	•	•	•
Sierra Leone	Freetown	669,000	1961	•	•	•
Singapore	Singapore	3,045,000	1965	•	•	•
Slovakia	Bratislava	450,776	1993	•	•	•
Slovenia	Ljubljana	276,119	1992	•	•	•
Solomon Islands	Honiara	43,643	1978	•	•	•
Somalia	Mogadishu	900,000	1960	•	•	•
South Africa	Bloemfontein (judicial)	126,867	1945	•	•	•
	Cape Town (legislative)	854,616				
	Pretoria (executive)	525,583				
South Korea	Seoul (Sŏul)	10,229,262	1991	•	•	•
Spain	Madrid	3,041,101	1955	•	•	•
Sri Lanka	Colombo	615,000	1955	•	•	•
Sudan	Khartoum	924,505	1956	•	•	•
Suriname	Paramaribo	200,970	1975	•	•	•
Swaziland	Mbabane	47,000	1968	•	•	•
Sweden	Stockholm	711,119	1946	•	•	•
Switzerland	Bern (Berne)	128,422	-	•	•	•
Syria	Damascus (Dimashq)	1,549,932	1956	•	•	•
Taiwan	Taipei (T'ai-pei)	2,626,138	-			
Tajikistan	Dushanbe	524,000	1992	•	•	•
Tanzania	Dar es Salaam	1,360,850	1961	•	•	•
Thailand	Bangkok	5,584,288	1946	•	•	•
Togo	Lomé	513,000	1960	•	•	•
Tonga	Nuku'alofa	34,000	1999			
Trinidad and Tobago	Port-of-Spain	52,451	1962	•	•	•
Tunisia	Tunis	674,100	1956	•	•	•
Turkey	Ankara	2,782,200	1945	•	•	•
Turkmenistan	Ashkhabad (Ashgabat)	518,000	1992	•	•	•
Tuvalu	Funafuti	3,839	-			
Uganda	Kampala	773,463	1962	•	•	•
Ukraine	Kiev (Kyyiv)	2,630,000	1945	•	•	•
United Arab Emirates	Abu Dhabi (Abū Ẓaby)	363,432	1971	•	•	•
United Kingdom	London	6,967,500	1945	•	•	•
United States	Washington, D.C.	567,094	1945	•	•	•
Uruguay	Montevideo	1,378,707	1945	•	•	•
Uzbekistan	Tashkent	2,106,000	1992	•	•	•
Vanuatu	Vila	26,100	1981	•	•	
Venezuela	Caracas	1,822,465	1945	•	•	•
Vietnam	Hanoi	2,154,900	1977	•	•	•
Yemen	Ṣanʿāʾ	503,600	1947	•	•	•
Yugoslavia	Belgrade (Beograd)	1,168,454	1945	•	•	•
Zambia	Lusaka	982,362	1964	•	•	•
Zimbabwe	Harare	1,184,169	1980	•	•	•

IMF	ITU	UNESCO	WHO	WTO	Commonwealth of Nations	EU	GCC	OAS	OAU	SPC	ACP	ADB	APEC	CARICOM	EBC	I-ADB	IDB	OPEC	Country
•	•	•	•	•					•		•							•	Senegal
•	•	•	•		•				•		•								Seychelles
•	•	•	•		•				•		•						•		Sierra Leone
•	•	•	•	•									•						Singapore
•	•	•	•	•															Slovakia
•	•	•	•	•													•		Slovenia
•	•	•	•		•					•	•								Solomon Islands
•	•	•	•						•		•						•		Somalia
•	•	•	•	•	•				•										South Africa
•	•	•	•	•								•	•						South Korea
•	•	•	•	•		•										•	•		Spain
•	•	•	•	•	•							•							Sri Lanka
•	•	•	•						•		•						•		Sudan
•	•	•	•		•			•			•			•			•		Suriname
•	•	•	•		•				•		•								Swaziland
•	•	•	•	•		•										•	•		Sweden
•	•	•	•	•													•		Switzerland
•	•	•	•														•		Syria
•	•			•								•	•						Taiwan
•	•	•	•														•		Tajikistan
•	•	•	•		•				•		•								Tanzania
•	•	•	•	•								•	•						Thailand
•	•	•	•						•		•								Togo
•	•	•	•		•					•	•								Tonga
•	•	•	•	•	•			•			•			•			•		Trinidad and Tobago
•	•	•	•						•		•						•		Tunisia
•	•	•	•	•													•		Turkey
•	•	•	•														•		Turkmenistan
•	•	•	•		•					•	•								Tuvalu
•	•	•	•		•				•		•								Uganda
•	•	•	•																Ukraine
•	•	•	•	•			•										•	•	United Arab Emirates
•	•	•	•	•	•	•						•				•	•		United Kingdom
•	•	•	•	•				•				•	•			•			United States
•	•	•	•	•				•									•		Uruguay
•	•	•	•														•		Uzbekistan
•	•	•	•		•					•	•								Vanuatu
•	•	•	•	•				•									•		Venezuela
•	•	•	•									•							Vietnam
•	•	•	•								•						•	•	Yemen
•	•	•	•	•															Yugoslavia
•	•	•	•		•				•		•								Zambia
•	•	•	•	•	•				•		•								Zimbabwe

Country	Airports with scheduled flights (1996)	Persons per Television (1995)	Persons per Telephone (1995)	Mobile Phones per 1000 people (1995)	Computers per 1000 people (1995)
Afghanistan	3	181	770	...	...
Albania	1	11	70	0	...
Algeria	28	14	25	0.2	3
Andorra	0	2.8	2.4	...	...
Angola	17	220	190	0.2	...
Antigua and Barbuda	2	2.3	3.5	...	...
Argentina	43	4.8	8.1	9.9	24.6
Armenia	1	4.7	6.4	0	...
Australia	400	2.3	2.1	127.7	275.8
Austria	6	3	2.2	47.6	124.2
Azerbaijan	1	4.7	11	0.1	...
Bahamas, The	23	5.5	3.3	...	...
Bahrain	1	2.1	4.3	...	...
Bangladesh	8	200	440	0	...
Barbados	1	4.1	3.2	...	...
Belarus	2	3.7	5.7	0.6	...
Belgium	2	2.4	2.3	23.2	138.3
Belize	11	9.4	7.1	...	...
Benin	1	270	260	0.2	...
Bhutan	1	...	400	...	...
Bolivia	14	8.8	33	1	...
Bosnia and Herzegovina	1	3.4	7.3	0	...
Botswana	4	111	32	0	...
Brazil	139	5.2	13	8	13
Brunei	1	3.2	5.1	...	...
Bulgaria	3	2.7	3.8	1	21.4
Burkina Faso	2	244	460	0	0
Burundi	1	1320	390	0.1	...
Cambodia	7	137	1670	1.5	...
Cameroon	5	882	220	0.2	...
Canada	301	1.5	1.7	86.5	192.5
Cape Verde	9	371	26	...	...
Central African Republic	1	419	480	0	...
Chad	4	127	1430	0	0
Chile	18	7.1	9.1	13.8	37.8
China	113	5.3	68	3	2.2
Colombia	63	6.4	8.9	7.1	16.2
Comoros	4	2550	130	...	...
Congo, Democratic Republic of the	12	2000	1110	0.2	...
Congo, Republic of the	5	305	130	0	...
Costa Rica	14	9.8	11	5.5	...
Croatia	5	6	4.5	7.1	20.9
Cuba	14	4.4	31	0.1	...
Cyprus	2	6.3	2	...	...
Czech Republic	2	2.1	5.3	4.7	53.2
Denmark	13	10.2	1.7	157.3	270.5
Djibouti	1	34	78	...	...

Country	Airports with scheduled flights (1996)	Persons per Television (1995)	Persons per Telephone (1995)	Mobile Phones per 1000 people (1995)	Computers per 1000 people (1995)
Dominica	2	14	5.3	...	...
Dominican Republic	4	11	13	...	...
Ecuador	14	13	19	4.6	3.9
Egypt	14	12	24	0.1	3.4
El Salvador	1	12	26	2.5	...
Equatorial Guinea	2	158	290	...	...
Eritrea	2	...	170	0	...
Estonia	3	2.5	4.3	20.5	6.7
Ethiopia	31	367	400	0	...
Fiji	13	59	11	...	...
Finland	24	2.7	1.8	199.2	182.1
France	66	2	1.9	23.8	134.3
Gabon	23	29	41	2.5	4.5
Gambia, The	1	186	63	1.3	...
Georgia	1	...	9.6	0	...
Germany	40	2.7	2.2	42.8	164.9
Ghana	1	66	330	0.4	1.2
Greece	36	4.6	2.2	26.1	33.4
Grenada	2	6.1	4.5	...	...
Guatemala	2	22	43	2.8	2.8
Guinea	2	103	560	0.1	0.2
Guinea-Bissau	2	...	120	0	...
Guyana	1	51	20	...	...
Haiti	2	264	150	0	...
Honduras	8	34	48	0	...
Hungary	1	2.4	6.9	25.9	39.2
Iceland	24	3.5	1.8	...	...
India	66	47	110	0.1	1.3
Indonesia	81	18	110	1.1	3.7
Iran	19	8.8	17	0.1	...
Iraq	...	20	29	0	...
Ireland	9	3.6	3.1	44.1	145
Israel	7	3.6	2.7	153.5	99.8
Italy	31	3.4	2.4	67.4	83.7
Ivory Coast	11	18	140	0	...
Jamaica	5	5.2	9.5	17.9	...
Japan	73	1.3	2.1	81.5	152.5
Jordan	2	17	14	2.6	8
Kazakstan	6	3.5	11	0.3	...
Kenya	13	57	120	0.1	0.7
Kiribati	17	115	43	...	...
Kuwait	1	2.1	4.1	70.7	57.1
Kyrgyzstan	2	5.1	12	0	...
Laos	11	61	530	0.1	...
Latvia	1	2.2	3.7	6	7.9
Lebanon	1	2.7	11	30	12.5
Lesotho	1	8.2	179	0	...

Country	Airports with scheduled flights (1996)	Persons per Television (1995)	Persons per Telephone (1995)	Mobile Phones per 1000 people (1995)	Computers per 1000 people (1995)
Liberia	1	53	590	...	...
Libya	12	9.8	21	0	...
Liechtenstein	0	3	1.6	...	...
Lithuania	3	2.4	4.4	4	6.5
Luxembourg	1	4.1	1.9	0	...
Macedonia	1	5.9	6.8	0	...
Madagascar	19	114	370	0	...
Malawi	4	...	290	0	...
Malaysia	36	6.5	7.9	43.4	39.7
Maldives	5	53	24	0	...
Mali	1	901	670	0	...
Malta	1	2.6	2.3	...	...
Marshall Islands	23	...	23	...	...
Mauritania	10	2070	290	0	...
Mexico	83	6.5	11	7	26.1
Micronesia, Federated States of	4	15	18	...	...
Moldova	1	3.5	8.3	0	2.1
Mongolia	1	17	36	0	0.2
Morocco	12	22	32	1.1	1.7
Mozambique	7	511	270	0	...
Myanmar (Burma)	19	47	560	0	...
Namibia	13	42	22	2.3	...
Nepal	24	80	290	0	...
Netherlands, The	6	2.4	2	33.2	200.5
New Zealand	36	3.2	2.2	108	222.7
Nicaragua	10	21	60	1.1	...
Niger	6	366	830	0	...
Nigeria	12	16	300	0.1	4.1
North Korea	1	12	21	0	...
Norway	50	2.2	1.8	224.4	273
Oman	6	1.4	8.6	3.7	...
Pakistan	34	68	76	0.3	1.2
Palau	1	11	...	...	...
Panama	10	13	9.8	0	...
Papua New Guinea	129	43	100	0	...
Paraguay	5	14	33	3.2	...
Peru	27	12	34	3.1	5.9
Philippines	21	10	76	7.3	11.4
Poland	12	3.9	8.7	1.9	28.5
Portugal	14	5.6	3.2	34.3	60.4
Qatar	1	2.3	4.7	0	...
Romania	12	5.7	8.7	0.4	5.3
Russia	58	2.7	6.3	0.6	17.7
Rwanda	3	...	630	0	...
St. Kitts and Nevis	2	4.2	3.4	...	...
St. Lucia	2	5.7	6.5	...	...
St. Vincent and the Grenadines	4	6.2	6.7	...	...

Country	Airports with scheduled flights (1996)	Persons per Television (1995)	Persons per Telephone (1993)	Mobile Phones per 1000 people (1995)	Computers per 1000 people (1995)
Samoa	2	33	25	...	...
San Marino	0	3	1.6	...	...
São Tomé and Príncipe	2	6.2	52	...	...
Saudi Arabia	25	3.8	11	0.9	25.1
Senegal	7	136	130	0	7.2
Seychelles	2	5.8	6.2	...	...
Sierra Leone	1	180	310	0	...
Singapore	1	4.6	2.3	97.7	172.4
Slovakia	2	4.2	6	2.3	41
Slovenia	1	3.5	3.9	13.6	47.7
Solomon Islands	30	...	65	...	...
Somalia	1	55	560	...	...
South Africa	24	12	11	12.9	26.5
South Korea	14	4.3	2.7	36.6	120.8
Spain	25	2.3	2.7	24.1	81.6
Sri Lanka	1	26	111	2.8	1.1
Sudan	10	112	440	0	...
Suriname	2	10	8.6	...	...
Swaziland	1	73	56	...	...
Sweden	48	2.4	1.5	229.4	192.5
Switzerland	5	2.7	1.6	63.5	348
Syria	5	20	24	0	0.1
Taiwan	13	3	2.6	...	...
Tajikistan	1	6.3	22	0	...
Tanzania	11	351	313	0.1	...
Thailand	25	18	27	18.5	15.3
Togo	1	28	230	0	0
Tonga	6	40	16	...	...
Trinidad and Tobago	2	5.1	6.5	4.3	19.2
Tunisia	5	14	20	0.4	6.7
Turkey	26	5.9	5.4	7	12.5
Turkmenistan	1	5.3	15	0.2	...
Tuvalu	1	...	77	...	...
Uganda	1	162	830	0.1	0.5
Ukraine	20	3	6.7	0.3	5.6
United Arab Emirates	6	13	2.6	54.2	48.4
United Kingdom	50	2.9	2	98	186.2
United States	834	1.2	1.7	128.4	328
Uruguay	1	5.3	5.9	12.6	22
Uzbekistan	9	6.3	15	...	...
Vanuatu	29	80	39	...	...
Venezuela	24	5.9	10	18	16.7
Vietnam	12	30	270	0.2	...
Yemen	11	131	83	0.5	...
Yugoslavia	5	6.4	5.6	0	11.8
Zambia	4	47	110	0.2	...
Zimbabwe	7	82	84	0	3

Name and location	Area (sq mi)
WORLD	
Caspian Sea, *Turkmenistan–Kazakstan–Russia–Azerbaijan-Iran*	149,200
Superior, *Canada–United States*	31,700
Victoria, *Kenya–Tanzania–Uganda*	26,828
Huron, *Canada–United States*	23,000
Michigan, *United States*	22,300
Aral Sea, *Kazakstan–Uzbekistan*	13,000
Tanganyika, *Burundi–Tanzania–Dem. Rep. Congo–Zambia*	12,700
Baikal, *Russia*	12,200
AFRICA	
Victoria, *Kenya-Tanzania–Uganda*	26,828
Tanganyika, *Burundi–Tanzania-Dem. Rep. Congo–Zambia*	12,700
Nyasa (Malawi), *Malawi–Mozambique–Tanzania*	11,430
Chad, *Cameroon–Chad–Niger–Nigeria*	6,875
Bangweulu, *Zambia*	3,800
AMERICA, NORTH	
Superior, *Canada–United States*	31,700
Huron, *Canada–United States*	23,000
Michigan, *United States*	22,300
Great Bear, *Northwest Territories, Canada*	12,028
Great Slave, *Northwest Territories, Canada*	11,031
AMERICA, SOUTH	
Maracaibo, *Venezuela*	5,150
Titicaca, *Peru–Bolivia*	3,200
Poopó, *Bolivia*	1,000
Buenos Aires (General Carrera), *Chile–Argentina*	865
Chiquita, *Argentina*	714
ASIA	
Caspian Sea, *Turkmenistan–Kazakstan–Russia–Azerbaijan-Iran*	149,200
Aral Sea, *Kazakstan–Uzbekistan*	13,000
Baikal, *Russia*	12,200
Balkhash, *Kazakstan*	6,650
Tonle Sap, *Cambodia*	2,525
EUROPE	
Ladoga, *Russia*	6,826
Onega, *Russia*	3,753
Vänern, *Sweden*	2,156
Iso Saimaa, *Finland*	1,690
Peipsi, *Estonia–Russia*	1,373
OCEANIA	
Eyre, *South Australia*	3,600
Torrens, *South Australia*	2,230
Gairdner, *South Australia*	1,845
Frome, *South Australia*	900

Name	Outflow	Length (miles)
WORLD		
Nile	Mediterranean Sea	4,132
Amazon–Ucayali–Apurimac	South Atlantic Ocean	4,000
Chang (Yangtze)	East China Sea	3,915
Mississippi–Missouri–Red Rock	Gulf of Mexico	3,710
Yenisey–Baikal–Selenga	Kara Sea	3,442
Huang (Yellow)	Bo Hai (Gulf of Chihli)	3,395
Ob–Irtysh	Gulf of Ob	3,362
Paraná	Río de la Plata	3,032
AFRICA		
Nile	Mediterranean Sea	4,132
Congo	South Atlantic Ocean	2,900
Niger	Bight of Biafra	2,600
Zambezi	Mozambique Channel	2,200
Kasai	Congo River	1,338
AMERICA, NORTH		
Mississippi–Missouri–Red Rock	Gulf of Mexico	3,710
Mackenzie–Slave–Peace	Beaufort Sea	2,635
Missouri–Red Rock	Mississippi River	2,540
St. Lawrence–Great Lakes	Gulf of St. Lawrence	2,500
Mississippi	Gulf of Mexico	2,340
AMERICA, SOUTH		
Amazon–Ucayali–Apurimac	South Atlantic Ocean	4,000
Paraná	Río de la Plata	3,032
Madeira–Mamoré–Guaporé	Amazon River	2,082
Jurua	Amazon River	2,040
Purus	Amazon River	1,995
ASIA		
Chang (Yangtze)	East China Sea	3,915
Yenisey–Baikal–Selenga	Kara Sea	3,442
Huang (Yellow)	Bo Hai (Gulf of Chihli)	3,395
Ob–Irtysh	Gulf of Ob	3,362
Amur–Argun	Sea of Okhotsk	2,761
EUROPE		
Volga	Caspian Sea	2,193
Danube	Black Sea	1,770
Ural	Caspian Sea	1,509
Dnieper	Black Sea	1,367
Don	Sea of Azov	1,162
OCEANIA		
Darling	Murray River	1,702
Murray	Great Australian Bight	1,609
Murrumbidgee	Murray River	981
Lachlan	Murrumbidgee River	992

Name and location	Height (feet)
AFRICA	
Kilimanjaro (Kibo Peak), *Tanzania*	19,340
Mt. Kenya (Batian Peak), *Kenya*	17,058
Margherita, Ruwenzori Range, *Dem. Rep. Congo–Uganda*	16,795
Ras Dashen, Simyen Mts., *Ethiopia*	15,157
AMERICA, NORTH	
McKinley, Alaska Range, *Alaska, U.S.*	20,320
Logan, St. Elias Mts., *Yukon, Canada*	19,524
Citlaltépetl (Orizaba), Cordillera Neo-Volcánica, *Mexico*	18,406
St. Elias, St Elias Mts., *Alaska, U.S.–Canada*	18,009
AMERICA, SOUTH	
Aconcagua, Andes, *Argentina–Chile*	22,831
Ojos del Salado, Andes, *Argentina–Chile*	22,615
Bonete, Andes, *Argentina*	22,546
Tupungato, Andes, *Argentina–Chile*	22,310
Pissis, Andes, *Argentina*	22,241
ANTARCTICA	
Vinson Massif, Sentinel Range, Ellsworth Mts.	16,066
Tyree, Sentinel Range, Ellsworth Mts.	15,919
Shinn, Sentinel Range, Ellsworth Mts.	15,751
Kirkpatrick, Queen Alexandra Range	14,856
ASIA	
Everest (Chomolungma), Himalayas, *Nepal–Tibet, China*	29,028
K2 (Godwin Austen), Karakoram Range, *Pakistan–Xinjiang, China*	28,251
Kånchenjunga I, Himalayas, *Nepal–India*	28,169
Lhotse I, Himalayas, *Nepal–Tibet, China*	27,940
EUROPE	
Mont Blanc, Alps, *France–Italy*	15,771
Dufourspitze (Monte Rosa), Alps, *Switzerland–Italy*	15,203
Dom (Mischabel), Alps, *Switzerland*	14,911
Weisshorn, Alps, *Switzerland*	14,780
OCEANIA	
Jaya (Sukarno, Carstensz), Sudirman Range, *Indonesia*	16,500
Pilimsit (Idenburg), Sudirman Range, *Indonesia*	15,750
Trikora (Wilhelmina), Jayawijaya Mts., *Indonesia*	15,580
Mandala (Juliana), Jayawijaya Mts., *Indonesia*	15,420
CAUCASUS	
Elbrus, Caucasus, *Russia*	18,510
Dyhk-Tau, Caucasus, *Russia*	17,073
Koshtan-Tau, Caucasus, *Russia*	16,900
Shkhara, Caucasus, *Russia–Georgia*	16,627